Workplace Learning in Context

As policy-makers increase their focus on workplace learning as a way of improving organizational performance, the debate about learning in organizations has grown. *Workplace Learning in Context* is an important contribution to this debate, as it counterbalances the often over-optimistic assumptions made about the future of work and learning. Arguing that without a contextualized analysis of the social relations at work our understanding of the learning environment is limited, this book reconsiders the role and nature of workplace learning.

Grounded in original research, the book features case studies which illuminate how the workplace environment can provide both barriers to and opportunities for learning. It explores learning in different organizational contexts and different countries, sectors, types of public and private sector organization, and by different occupational groups. It employs a multidisciplinary approach to provide a broad perspective on the institutional, organizational and pedagogical contexts of workplace learning.

This groundbreaking text will be welcomed by policy-makers, trainers, trade unionists and educators alike, providing them with the intellectual tools required to understand how learning in the workplace can be improved.

Helen Rainbird is Professor of Industrial Relations at University College Northampton and Associate Fellow at the Industrial Relations Research Unit at the University of Warwick. **Alison Fuller** is a Senior Research Fellow at the Centre for Labour Market Studies at the University of Leicester. **Anne Munro** is Reader in the School of Management at Napier University, Edinburgh.

Workplace Learning in Context

Edited by Helen Rainbird,
Alison Fuller and Anne Munro

Routledge
Taylor & Francis Group

LONDON AND NEW YORK

First published 2004
by Routledge
11 New Fetter Lane, London EC4P 4EE

Simultaneously published in the USA and Canada
by Routledge
29 West 35th Street, New York, NY 10001

Routledge is an imprint of the Taylor & Francis Group

© 2004 Helen Rainbird, Alison Fuller and Anne Munro

Typeset in Garamond by Taylor & Francis Books Ltd

British Library Cataloguing in Publication Data
A catalogue record for this book is available from the British
Library

Library of Congress Cataloging in Publication Data
Workplace learning in context / edited by Helen Rainbird,
Alison Fuller, and Anne Munro.
        p. cm.
Includes bibliographical references and index.
1. Employees–Training of. I. Rainbird, Helen. II. Fuller, Alison.
III. Munro, Anne.
IV. Title.
  HF5549.5.T7W658 2004
  658.3'124–dc22
                                        2003016629
ISBN 0–415–31630–8 (hbk)
ISBN 0–415–31631–6 (pbk)

Contents

Illustrations

Tables

Figures

Boxes

Examples

Contributors

Fiona Anderson-Gough is Senior Lecturer in Critical Accounting and Management at the University of Leicester's Management Centre. She has a number of publications in the area of accountancy education, training and socialization, and professional identity. She is an Associate Director of a research project, funded by the Institute of Chartered Accountants in England and Wales, on the 'wisdom of practice' in workplace and examination-focused learning sites in the accountancy profession in the UK.

David N. Ashton is Emeritus Professor at the Centre for Labour Market Studies, University of Leicester. He has published extensively in the area of employment, labour market analysis, training and workplace learning. His current interests are in national systems of vocational education and training and workplace learning. His latest book, written with Johnny Sung, is *Supporting Learning for High Performance Working*.

Stephen Billett is Associate Professor of Adult and Vocational Education at Griffith University, Brisbane, Australia. He has worked as a vocational practitioner in the clothing industry, a vocational educator, educational administrator, teacher educator, professional development practitioner in Technical and Further Education and in policy development roles. As a university-based researcher, his recent work has focused on the social and cultural construction of vocational practice, learning in workplaces and the development of vocational expertise in workplace settings.

Alan Brown is a Principal Research Fellow at the Institute for Employment Research, University of Warwick. He is also an Associate Director of the Teaching and Learning Research Programme with responsibility for supporting research in workplace learning and continuing professional development.

Ruth Carter is a Staff Tutor for the Faculty of Technology of the Open University. She undertakes research and development through the Open University's Centre for the Analysis of Supply Chain Innovation and Dynamics (CASCAID).

Frank Coffield is Professor of Education at the Institute of Education, London, having previously worked in the Universities of Newcastle,

Durham and Keele. In 1994 he was appointed Director of the ESRC's research programme into The Learning Society which ran until April 2000. Four reports emanating from The Learning Society Programme have been edited by him, as well as two volumes of findings entitled *Differing Visions of a Learning Society*. Since then he has edited *What Progress are we Making with Lifelong Learning? The Evidence from Research*. He is currently working on a systematic and critical review of learning styles for the LSDA.

Yrjö Engeström is Professor of Communication at the University of California, San Diego. He is also Professor of Adult Education and Director of the Center for Activity Theory and Developmental Work Research at the University of Helsinki, Finland. He studies transformations in work and organizations, combining micro-level analysis of discourse and interaction with modelling of organizations as networks of activity systems going through developmental contradictions. His current research is focused on health-care organizations striving toward new forms of collaboration and co-configuration work. Recent books include *Cognition And Communication At Work* (edited with David Middleton), *Perspectives On Activity Theory* (edited with Reijo Miettinen and Raija-Leena Punamäki) and *Collaborative Expertise: Expansive Learning In Medical Work*.

Michael Eraut has been a Professor of Education at the University of Sussex since 1986. His research interests are focused on professional and management knowledge and their acquisition in the workplace. His research projects, funded by ESRC, QCA and the Department of Health, have covered learning before and after qualification in early and mid-career. He edits the new journal *Learning in Health and Social Care*.

Karen Evans is Professor of Education and Head of School, Lifelong Learning and International Development, at the Institute of Education, University of London. Her main fields of research are learning in life and work transitions, and learning at, for and through the workplace. Her publications include: *Working To Learn: Transforming Learning In The Workplace* (with P. Hodkinson, and L. Unwin), and *Learning And Work In The Risk Society* (with M. Behrens and J. Kaluza).

Alison Fuller is a Senior Research Fellow at the Centre for Labour Market Studies at the University of Leicester. She has conducted research and published extensively in the fields of vocational education and training, workplace learning, and trends in adult participation in qualifications. Her most recent publications include papers on workplace learning and apprenticeship in the *Journal of Education and Work*, and on patterns of participation in higher education in the *Journal of Education Policy*. Alison, with colleagues at CLMS, has recently been awarded a major grant by the Economic and Social Research Council to study 'learning as work: teaching and learning processes in the contemporary organisation'.

Paul Hager is Professor of Education at the University of Technology, Sydney. He has published on Bertrand Russell's philosophy and on philosophy of education, with particular focus on workplace learning and vocational education and training. His publications include *Life, Work and Learning: Practice in Postmodernity* (with D. Beckett) and *Continuity and Change in the Development of Russell's Philosophy*, which won the 1996 Bertrand Russell Society Book Award.

Susan Hoddinott has worked as a teacher and researcher in the field of Adult Education in Canada since 1981 and is currently a faculty member at the College of the North Atlantic in St. John's, Newfoundland. She has researched and written about adult literacy policy, public adult education policy and worker basic skills.

Heather Hodkinson has worked as an educational researcher since 1991, following a career teaching in secondary schools in England. She currently works for the Lifelong Learning Institute at the University of Leeds investigating workplace learning. Previous projects have looked at careers guidance, vocational education and training and teacher education. She has published a number of papers and a book, written with Phil Hodkinson and Andrew Sparkes, on the transition from school to work.

Phil Hodkinson is Professor of Lifelong Learning in the Lifelong Learning Institute at the University of Leeds. He is a member of the 'Working to Learn' group of UK researchers, and has written and researched widely on vocational education and training and work-based learning. He is co-author, with Heather Hodkinson and Andrew Sparkes, of *Triumphs and Tears: Young People, Markets and the Transition from School to Work*.

Lesley Holly is a Senior Lecturer in Sociology and Women's Studies at University College Northampton and formerly worked at the Tavistock Institute of Human Relations. Her research interests include barriers to women's careers in management and social exclusion.

Keith Hoskin is Professor of Strategy and Accounting at Warwick Business School. He has published widely in the fields of accounting and management, and is heading a current research project for the Institute of Chartered Accountants in England and Wales, researching into the field of training the chartered accountant as 'Added Value Business Advisor'. He is a member of the ICAEW's Education and Training Board.

Natasha Kersh is Research Officer at the Institute of Education, University of London. Her research interests include aspects of key skills in young people's and adults' learning. She is working on an ESRC research project on the recognition of tacit skills and knowledge in work re-entry, looking at the role of personal skills and competencies in sustaining the learning processes of adult learners with interrupted biographies.

Saul Meghnagi is President of the Istituto Superiore per la Formazione (ISF), Rome. His main research interests concern the relationship between work and education. His publications are on learning processes in different social and occupational contexts.

Anne Munro is Reader in the School of Management at Napier University, Edinburgh. She has been researching and publishing on work and union organization in the health service for over 20 years. Her publications include *Women, Work and Trade Unions* and chapters and journal articles on trade unions and partnerships on workplace learning. Her recent research has focused on workplace learning amongst lower grade workers in the public sector.

Helen Rainbird is Professor of Industrial Relations at University College Northampton and an Associate Fellow at the Industrial Relations Research Unit at the University of Warwick. Her books include *Training Matters: Union Perspectives on Industrial Restructuring and Training* and an edited collection *Training in the Workplace: Critical Perspectives on Learning at Work*. She has researched on the relationship between industrial relations, training and development and has a particular interest in trade unions and training policy.

Ed Rhodes is a Senior Lecturer in the Faculty of Technology of the Open University. He undertakes research and development through the Open University's Centre for the Analysis of Supply Chain Innovation and Dynamics (CASCAID).

Akiko Sakamoto is researcher on training policy at International Labour Office, Geneva and was previously a Research Officer at the Institute of Education, University of London. She has also worked on research projects on different national routes to a high skills economy and the financing of vocational education and training in EU countries. Her main research interests are learning at and for work.

Lorna Unwin is Professor of Vocational Education and head of the Centre for Labour Market Studies, University of Leicester. She has particular research interests in vocational education policy, workplace learning and the professional development of vocational teachers and trainers. Her current research projects are examining the changing nature of apprenticeship and the nature of vocational knowledge.

Michael Young is Emeritus Professor of Education in the School of Lifelong Education and International Development at the Institute of Education, University of London and Research Advisor to the City and Guilds of London Institute. His most recent books are *The Curriculum of The Future*; *Strategies for Achieving Parity of Esteem in European Upper Secondary Education* (with J. Lasonen); and *Education in Retrospect: Education Policy in South Africa: 1990–2001* (with Andre Kraak).

Acknowledgements

The idea for this book followed from an international workshop 'Context, Power and Perspective: Confronting the Challenges to Improving Attainment in Learning at Work', which was organized by Helen Rainbird and Charlotte Spokes at University College Northampton in November 2001. The workshop brought together some of the world's leading experts from a range of disciplinary backgrounds to explore the particular issues relating to learning in the workplace context. We are grateful to the Economic and Social Research Council's (ESRC) Teaching and Learning Research Programme (TLRP) and Research Centre on Skills Knowledge and Organizational Performance (SKOPE) for jointly financing the workshop. This book presents a selection of key contributions developed from that event which benefited from the debates and exchanges at the workshop.

The international workshop was organized in response to some of the key intellectual challenges faced by a Research Network funded under Phase 1 of the ESRC's Teaching and Learning Research Programme. The Network was made up of five linked research projects on the theme of 'Improving incentives to learning in the workplace' (ESRC ref. L139 25 1005). The Network was co-ordinated by Helen Rainbird, from University College Northampton, with administrative support from Charlotte Spokes. Jim Sutherland acted as practitioner advisor to the Network as a whole and we have also benefited from regular interaction with the members of our practitioner advisory group. The research team was made up of Anne Munro (Napier University, Edinburgh), Karen Evans, Akiko Sakamoto and Natasha Kersh (Institute of Education, London), Lorna Unwin and Alison Fuller (University of Leicester), Peter Senker and Dennis Kessler (University College Northampton), Phil Hodkinson and Heather Hodkinson (University of Leeds). Our understanding of workplace learning has benefited enormously from our participation in the Network. Many of the team have written chapters for this book and have contributed to it through their support in organizing the workshop and through ongoing debates throughout the lifetime of the Network.

We are grateful to Francesca Poynter at Routledge for commissioning this book, and to her and Rachel Crookes for their encouragement and assistance in its production.

We would like to thank Charlotte Spokes for her initial work in preparing the papers for publication and Anne Larkan for her thorough and professional preparation of the manuscript. In addition, we have each enjoyed the support of colleagues from our institutions: University College Northampton, Leicester University and Napier University, Edinburgh.

Finally, as work seems to dominate an increasing proportion of life, we would like to acknowledge our appreciation of the continuing support and encouragement of our partners Francisco Salazar, Chris Lines and Stuart Graham.

Helen Rainbird, Alison Fuller and Anne Munro

1 Introduction and overview

Alison Fuller, Anne Munro and Helen Rainbird

Policy-makers preoccupied with finding ways of strengthening the relationship between education systems and the economy are increasingly focusing on workplace learning as a way of improving organizational performance and, at the aggregate level, national economic success. From a human capital perspective, the skills and qualifications of the workforce are believed to be central to productivity. Investing in their (or one's own development) is assumed to result in economic dividends. As Garrick argues, 'The idea of investing in human beings as a form of capital has, since then [the emergence of human capital theory], fuelled a very powerful discourse of workplace learning' (1999: 217).

From the perspective of workplace learning, there are three main problems with the assumptions associated with human capital theory. First, it is incorrect to assume that investment in human capital is the only source of competitive success. An examination of the way companies and, in particular, multinational companies, generate profit suggests that there are a range of strategies they can adopt. As the Industrial Relations Research Unit points out, 'Competitive success based on quality and upskilling is only one of a number of strategies available to organizations. Others include seeking protected or monopoly markets; growth through take-over and joint venture; shifting operations overseas; cost-cutting and new forms of "Fordism"' (1997:7). Second, research evidence suggests that although workforce qualifications have been increasing in recent decades, there have not been corresponding changes in the use of these qualifications in the workplace. Indeed, the 2001 Skills Survey shows that for the UK 'the overall supply of qualifications outstrips demand by a comfortable margin' (Ashton *et al.* 2002: 63). Although increasing educational participation may contribute to the stock of skills and qualifications in the workforce, increasing employer demand and utilization of more highly skilled and qualified employees involves changes in job design and the organization of production. Strategic decisions and decisions relating to the quality of the work environment are normally arenas of management prerogative. Politically it is more difficult for governments to intervene in questions relating to product markets and work organization (though this is not the case in all countries), than it is in educational and training interventions aimed at the supply of qualifications. Third, Human Capital Theory uses qualifications as a proxy for learning and skills and, in so doing, emphasizes the significance of formal qualifications for individuals and the workforce as a whole. However, Senker suggests that a very small proportion of learning in the workplace is recognized by formal qualifications (2000: 240). Eraut *et al.* (1998) have argued that the learning opportunities afforded by the workplace itself are the primary factor affecting the quantity and quality of learning at work. Many of these opportunities are embedded in the structure, organization and practice of work. With this in mind, this edited collection focuses on workplace learning in a variety of forms, rather than limiting the analysis to interventions by trainers and teachers and their impact on individuals.

In the workplace, the nature and focus of strategic decisions, power relations and the employment relationship are central to understanding the opportunities and constraints on learning. Employers' first order decisions concern product market and competitive strategy whilst their second order decisions concern work organization, job design and people management (Keep and Mayhew 1999; Bosworth *et al.* 2001). Such first and second order choices help explain the extent and distribution of opportunities for learning across the workforce. This reminds us that learning is not the primary purpose of the organization but is derived from the needs of fulfilling the organizational goal of providing goods and services (Rainbird 2000).

Several of the chapters in this book focus on learning as an activity embedded within the production and labour processes and the social relations between employees. Their emphasis is on the ways in which the workplace can be conceptualized as what some authors term a learning 'environment' and others a learning 'space', which provides barriers to and opportunities for learning. Some of the opportunities identified consist of participation in off-the-job courses, but most relate to opportunities to participate in activities from and through which employees learn. Participation in formal training programmes has a range of dimensions. It is an important feature of this collection that most of the chapters are research based and provide the reader with plentiful evidence of the forms of participation and types of knowledge available in various settings, as well as revealing the uneven patterns of access to them that employees experience.

The issues raised by different forms of participation, including on- and off-the-job learning and qualifications are a central interest of the book. One concern is that the contemporary emphasis on situated learning tends to assume that all knowledge is situated, and that the knowledge needed to do particular jobs is embedded within the associated tasks, processes and those who are already competent. The related pedagogy aims to enable learners to participate in all relevant workplace activities and to learn from more experienced colleagues. One advantage of this approach is that individuals are not faced with the difficulty of knowledge transfer, as their knowledge and skills have been gained in the context in which they are being applied. However, stressing the situated character of knowledge fails to recognize that there are types of knowledge, such as theoretical ideas not connected to specific contexts, which are not always accessible on-the-job. Denying individuals and groups access to underpinning knowledge is likely to reinforce workforce inequalities and impede employees' progression to positions which benefit from sound theoretical understanding. Failing to provide effective support to facilitate the transfer of learning from one context to another can militate against the integration of theory and practice. One way of broadening employees' access to knowledge is to expand opportunities for boundary-crossing and interaction between people from different specialisms. Research reported in this collection includes examples of networking and boundary-crossing which illustrate the effects on individual and collective learning of these sorts of activities.

The notions of learning through experience and learning by doing have a lengthy association with adult and workplace learning (Boud *et al*. 1993), and tend to foreground individuals and their lived realities. Whilst the accounts of individuals can shed light on how people learn at work and can help make sense of diverse situations, they can also mask the ways in which opportunities and barriers are structured and unevenly distributed across organizations and different groups. It is important to understand the extent to which the organization of work influences workplace learning because benefits in terms, for example, of career progression and self-confidence can accrue to those who have access to a variety of learning opportunities and who have the autonomy necessary for self-direction. Those employees whose knowledge and skills remain tacit are more likely to have their competence underestimated and their contribution to the organization undervalued.

The range of opportunities available to employees across countries, sectors, organizations, employment levels (e.g. manager, specialist, shop-floor operative) and types of employment (permanent, temporary, part time) is patchy, with the most vulnerable groups having access to the fewest chances. Nevertheless, there are pitfalls in adopting an overly deterministic view of the impact of structure on learning. However rich or impoverished the opportunities for learning appear, individuals themselves can make decisions about the extent to which they wish to engage. The evidence presented in this volume indicates that a host of personal, dispositional and motivational factors can influence how people interact with the environments in which they find themselves.

Learning that occurs in specialist educational institutions and which, typically, is associated with the pursuit of qualifications, is often understood in terms of the 'learning as acquisition' metaphor (Sfard 1998). Here, the focus is on the transmission of propositional and codifiable knowledge from expert, or expert source, to learner. It follows that tests (usually written examinations) can be used to measure what the individual has learned. Sfard contrasts 'learning as acquisition' with the metaphor 'learning as participation'. Using the latter metaphor to illuminate the nature of learning at work is gaining popularity, as it enables the difficulties of measuring learning in this context to be acknowledged while drawing attention to the diverse activities and processes which characterize and distinguish workplace learning. Lave and Wenger's (1991) insight that the community of practice (rather than the individual) should form the basis of an analysis of learning, has highlighted the social and collective nature of learning, which is missed in analyses of (individual) attainment. The research included in this volume, signals that identifying changes in the work group, the way work is organized and the way jobs are designed can shed light on how learning occurs.

The role employees can play in improving an organization's effectiveness requires a focus on the types of knowledge and skills learned at work as well as on how they can be supplied, supported and developed. The central argument of this volume is that without a contextualized analysis, the treatment of questions of access to and control of learning opportunities, as well as what is learned and how, is likely to be limited. The chapters show that by locating workplace learning in context, clearer understandings of the factors influencing the learning environment and processes can be gained, and insights about the sorts of changes which may lead to its improvement can emerge. The book adopts a broad approach to the context of learning at work and explores the ways in which factors ranging from national and institutional systems to conditions in particular work groups impinge on the learning process. The range of settings elaborated also provides a broad overview of how learning at work is experienced in different countries, sectors, types of public and private sector organization, and by different occupational groups.

The aim of this edited collection is to contribute to the growing debate about the role and nature of workplace learning. By drawing on theoretically informed empirical research from different disciplines, it aims to explore the institutional, organizational and pedagogical contexts within which it takes place. The analyses presented go beyond the economic rationale for fostering learning at work and challenge the usefulness of traditional theories for explaining how people learn in organizations. Equally, as a research-based collection of papers, it serves as useful counterweight to some of the more optimistic assumptions concerning the future of work and learning which underpin the debate on the 'learning society' and the 'learning organization' (see Coffield 1997; Keep and Rainbird 1999 for critiques).

The book is organized into four sections. The first of these is the context of workplace learning where the institutional factors which structure workplace learning are explored. The second section focuses on the workplace as a learning environment. Here the ways of conceptualizing and theorizing learning in the workplace are examined. The third section groups together chapters examining the nature of skills and knowledge in the workplace. The final section explores how the theoretical and methodological challenges involved in understanding and improving learning at work, examined in the preceding chapters, can be translated into policy and improved practice.

The context of workplace learning

The significance for policy that workplace learning has in any given country and perceptions of its contribution to competitiveness, are dependent on the nature of the vocational education and training system, the relationship between the state, labour and capital, and the production system. To develop an analysis of the political economy of workplace learning, Ashton (Chapter 2) argues that the societal approach of Maurice *et al.* (1986) and the business systems approach of Whitley (2000) need to be brought together. The reason for this is that workplace learning, its recognition and certification only become significant in particular sets of circumstances. These are linked to the process of industrialization and the relative weight of capital, the social partners and the state in driving industrial and training policy.

Ashton identifies three models of workplace learning: the free market model, exemplified by the USA and the UK; the corporatist model of Germany and Denmark; and the developmental state model of South East Asian economies such as Taiwan and Singapore. He argues that in the free market model, employers and individuals are seen as having responsibility for workplace learning and there is only a limited role for the state, primarily in relation to labour market programmes and certification. High-performance work practices based on high levels of skill and employee involvement may be implemented by multinational companies, but have restricted coverage. In contrast, in corporatist models, apprenticeship systems which are co-managed by capital and labour may ensure that inter-mediate level skills are widely available in the labour market. Although institutional structures may support innovation and continuing learning in the workplace, the main focus of certification is on initial rather than continuing training. The certification of the latter, even where it fosters development and innovation, may represent a threat to the status quo. In the developmental state model, there is a strong link between economic devel-opment and training, along with assistance for creating new forms of work organization. The state's involvement in promoting workplace learning and its certification is most proactive where there are no great concentrations of capital, as in Singapore. In contrast, where large companies have emerged, as is the case with the Korean *chaebol*, the establishment of internal labour markets with their own rules of promotion and progression means there is little role for the state in certifying learning.

The way in which the employment relationship is regulated is central to understanding the context of workplace learning. In Chapter 3, Rainbird, Munro and Holly argue that regulation of the employment relationship is relevant on three levels. The first of these is the role the state takes in shaping the education and training system, the framework of employment law and industrial policy, as well as its role as an employer in the public sector and as a customer for goods and services. The second, is the level of the organization, where the way in which the relationship between the employer and employee is conceptualized is fundamental to an understanding of the context of work-place learning. Adopting the Industrial Relations 'frames of reference' approach (see Edwards 1995) they argue that consensus in the workplace has to be constructed, rather than taken as given. Although workplace learning can be the subject of consensual decision-making, this is not automatically the case as the unitarist perspectives of Human Capital Theory and Human Resource Management might suggest (Heyes 2000). The third level concerns the social and power relations of the workplace. It is at this level that issues relating to who controls access to learning, the organization of work, and employee entitlements and voice, are significant.

The authors explore the influence of this three level framework on work-place learning through the case-study analysis of: two teams of women cleaners; a group of male maintenance workers; and a group of care staff in a hospital. Although a range of forms of learning and teaching can be identi-fied even amongst workers who are considered to have a limited range of skills, learning cannot be decontextualized from the social relations of production. To conceive learning solely as a participative activity risks trivi-alizing power relationships and ignoring significant barriers to participation which originate in work organization, the employment relationship and in organizational structures.

The theme of the relationship between institutional systems, work orga-nization and worker competence is developed by Meghnagi in Chapter 4. He discusses an initiative to develop workers' competence in the Italian small firms sector which was based on the involvement of the social partners and researchers. In Italy small firms, or *imprese artigiane*, have a special status which relates to the involvement of the entrepreneur in the production process and which qualifies them for state aid. Despite the fact that many of the workforce have a low level of formal qualification, their level of compe-tence is high, reflecting the way the production process is organized. In developing a framework for assessing future training needs, entrepreneurs' and workers' competences were addressed as well as the organizational capacity of the company. The involvement of experts and the social partners in the process of defining competences and future training brought out differences in their respective definitions of occupational profiles. This finding illustrates the contested nature of competence and knowledge in the workplace and the usefulness of employers' organizations, trade unions and researchers working together to identify future training needs. The companies in Meghnagi's study were classified according to whether they worked on their own account or on a sub-contract basis; their capacity to design projects; their ability to realize the finished product; their ability to sell under their own trademark and to trade beyond local markets. In assessing training needs, it was important not only to assess workers' needs, but those of the organization as well and, in particular, its capacity to expand its design and production capacity and to sell goods beyond local markets. An important concept was that of the 'professional credibility' of the company in relation to banks, its customers and suppliers and the idea that training and competence development are part of the acquired rights of workers.

The need to deal with entrenched interests, in particular those of educational providers and professional bodies, affect the process of reform in relation to workplace learning in many spheres. Hoskin and Anderson-Gough explore changes in the professional work environment of the accountancy profession and the developmental needs of accountants in Chapter 5. They develop the argument that context, power and perspective interplay in ways that frame and limit attempts to develop more effective forms of attainment. They see this as being significant in current attempts to promote transdisciplinarity within accountancy training. The authors uncover a tension within the profession between the wish to be more transdisciplinary and the desire to retain the benefits of being specialist.

A push toward more transdisciplinarity has also been a feature of accountancy education in the USA, Australia and New Zealand, and more recently at a European level. Hoskin and Anderson-Gough present two particular initiatives from the USA during the 1990s to illustrate some of the difficulties of implementing change in this area. One large project failed mainly because of the resistance of academics within the specialist disciplinary fields. This contrasts with a smaller university-based initiative where the management of integrative learning was taken to require more than just the development of the course content. Here the process of managing the change was given greater attention and resulted in a more positive outcome.

In the UK context, there are tensions between the needs of the firm and the needs of the trainees, and between formal and workplace learning. There is a widely held belief that formal or qualification-focused learning (QFL) is 'ritualistic, rote and virtually meaningless' while work-based learning (WBL) is 'real, relevant and meaningful'. Whilst such views are unlikely to be wholly accurate, as accountancy firms offer a wider range of services, some form of transdisciplinarity is increasingly required in both QFL and WBL. Hoskin and Anderson-Gough outline key aspects of their research to assist in the re-engineering of the learning experience into something more integrative. They point to the importance of the support of key organizational and managerial stakeholders (infrastructure) to a successful move towards transdisciplinarity and draw on Bernstein (2000) and Silver (1998) to develop a model of best practice. Whilst the model has been designed in relation to accountancy education, the authors conclude that it may be relevant to other vocational areas that have a grounding in academic disciplines.

An important theme of the book is recognition that employees' and employers' training needs will not always coincide. This issue is addressed directly in Chapter 6 by Hoddinott. In her analysis of concerns about workers' basic skills in the USA, Canada and England, she argues that the workplace is not necessarily the best site for providing learning opportunities for some groups of workers and can be positively harmful to them. She sees the (re)location of basic skills provision in companies as illustrative of a process which is shifting adult education from the public to the private sector. Hoddinott interprets this trend as representing the erosion of what has been an individual right and a public good and its replacement by narrowly defined training, which is properly the responsibility of the employer.

The background for the developments which Hoddinott describes are the claims that schools are failing to teach fundamental skills, and that high levels of illiteracy in the adult population have consequences for economic performance. Yet this gloss on the 'basic skills problem' comes at a time when levels of formal educational qualifications in the workforce are at their highest levels and many workers are overqualified for their jobs (Ashton et al. 2002). In this context, basic skills assessments represent an extension of employer prerogative in relation to the hiring and firing of workers, many of whom have restricted needs for literacy in their jobs. Indeed McIntosh and Steedman's work on basic skills suggests that many jobs are deliberately constructed to reduce literacy content (2001).

The workplace as a learning environment

The workplace is conceptualized as an environment in which people learn because it provides opportunities for them to (co-)participate in activities and practices. In contrast with the behaviourist and cognitive theories which have focused on individual learning, usually in formal educational institutions, the authors in this part of the book conceive learning as a socially situated process where the context, in terms of its structures, activities and relationships, provides the key to theorizing and improving workplace learning. Central to this approach, is the idea that in order to understand how people learn to become what Lave and Wenger (1991) have termed 'knowledgeable practitioners', the analysis should focus on the community of practice in which the activity is occurring and which is the source of knowledge, skills and understandings. This is not to suggest that all workplaces are consensual, or offer equal opportunities for all. The chapters show that the character of the learning environment is not fixed but is an outcome of the changing relationship between organizational factors, social relations and individual agency.

The contributors argue that broad contextual factors, organizational characteristics and approaches to workforce development, underpin the nature of the environment and the forms of participation available to employees. The conception of workplaces as structured and structuring environments for action is evident in the view that the opportunities within workplaces are unevenly distributed across workforces. Whilst acknowledging the workplace as a dynamic environment where opportunities and barriers to learning produce intended and unintended consequences, the analyses also suggest that better quality learning environments can be created.

Although the authors in this part of the book highlight the importance of the workplace as a site for learning, they refer to it in slightly different terms. Billett (Chapter 7) focuses on workplace affordances for learning and the ways in which the structure of work and its control influence the extent and nature of these affordances or 'invitational qualities'. Fuller and Unwin (Chapter 8) focus on organizational and pedagogical features which give the learning environment a more or less expansive or restrictive character. Engeström (Chapter 9) highlights the changing nature of work and its implications for the development and distribution of expertise. He suggests that environments are needed which enable employees to establish transitional communities which facilitate 'knotworking' and the generation of collaborative and transformative expertise. Brown, Rhodes and Carter (Chapter 10), following Nonaka and Konno (1998), introduce the term *ba* to refer to the sorts of learning spaces that are created and which enable people to come together to create knowledge.

Understanding workplace learning in terms of participatory practices is a key concern of Billett's. He argues that the nature of participation (i.e. of workplace learning) depends on two reflexively related factors: the extent to which individuals have the chance to participate in activities and to interact with their co-workers, and the extent to which individuals choose to engage in the opportunities that are available. He challenges the idea that certain forms of participation, such as in educational institutions, are superior to forms of participation in other forms of social practice, such as work. Learning occurs in all social settings, the 'affordances' of the setting influence the forms of participation and therefore the learning that can occur. For Billett the distinction between formal and informal learning is unhelpful as it implies: (1) that the former is more meaningful and substantial and therefore privileged; and (2) that learning at work is conceived as unstructured, random and not amenable to interventions which can facilitate, support and make workplace learning more effective. He draws on research to point out that the goals and activities of the workplace provide a pedagogical framework within which forms of participation can be highly structured.

The imperatives of maintaining the continuity of the workplace and protecting the interests of particular groups often underpin the structuring and patterning of opportunities and barriers to learning: 'Workplace cliques and affiliations (e.g. occupational groupings), the gender, race, language or employment standing and status of workers all influence the distribution of opportunities to participate' (Billett, Chapter 7). This contestation of who participates in what practices goes beyond the displacement of old-timers by newcomers discussed by Lave and Wenger (1991), to recognize the restricted opportunities available to workers whose institutional position is weak, such as part-time workers, those with few if any educational qualifications, and those located at the bottom end of the organizational hierarchy.

The themes of individual and organizational development and how they are more likely to be aligned in workplaces which adopt an 'expansive approach' to workforce development are developed by Fuller and Unwin (Chapter 8). Their research has highlighted the extent to which employees in different organizational and sectoral settings have variable opportunities to learn and leads them to conclude that organizations which offer diverse forms of participation are more likely to foster employee learning. Fuller and Unwin use case study methods to open up the 'black box' of workplace learning and to indicate how this has led to the development of a new framework for analysing approaches to workforce development in terms of their expansive and restrictive characteristics. They draw on Engeström's (2001) concept of expansive learning but also distinguish between their use of the term and his. The authors identify the availability of three types of learning opportunity as central to the creation of expansive learning environments, and which might provide the basis for the integration of personal and organizational development. These are: the chance to engage in multiple and overlapping communities of practice at and beyond the workplace; the organization and design of jobs to foster the opportunity for employees to co-construct knowledge and expertise; and the chance to pursue underpinning and theoretical knowledge through participation in off-the-job courses (leading to knowledge-based qualifications). The participatory practices illustrated in the chapter indicate the relevance and interrelatedness of pedagogical and organizational factors to the expansive – restrictive analytical framework. Fuller and Unwin draw on examples of apprentices and older workers to show how work could be organized to encourage or limit access to diverse forms of participation and, thereby, to create the sort of expansive learning environments likely to foster individual and organizational development.

The themes of expertise and knowledge construction are dealt with in great depth by Engeström. He provides an account of how conceptions of expertise have developed and concludes that new forms of work organization emerging in response to social, economic and technological change require a collaborative and transformative approach to the construction and distribution of expertise. Engeström claims that traditional approaches to expertise are an inadequate response to the challenges confronting many contemporary organizations. He makes two important claims at the start of the chapter: first that expertise based on 'supreme and supposedly stable individual knowledge and ability' is being replaced by 'the capacity of working communities to cross boundaries, negotiate and improvise "knots" of collaboration'. Such new forms of collaboration are better able to solve contemporary organizational problems. Second, reconceptualizing expertise in the way Engeström proposes, draws attention to theories of learning and to what he calls 'the new generation of expertise'. The argument of the chapter is organized around seven theses, which systematically challenge conventional assumptions relating to the acquisition of expertise.

Engeström concludes by acknowledging the provisional nature of his own conception of expertise and the need to identify further working examples to develop and test his ideas. In some respects, Brown, Rhodes and Carter's evaluation of the development project Knowledge and Learning in Advanced Supply Systems (KLASS) resonates strongly with Engeström's claims that new forms of expertise are both emerging and are needed to confront contemporary organizational and technological challenges. The focus of the development project was on improving the performance of small and medium-sized enterprises (SMEs) in the automotive and aerospace industries by supporting the learning and knowledge development of groups of employees. The starting point for the project was the changing context within which such firms are operating and in particular their role and position in the supply chains controlled by large firms.

The design of learning support described by Brown et al. centres on the development of learning networks configured across companies. The network provides a forum where individuals with different levels of experience and specialism could come together to address organizational learning needs. The personal learning needs of individuals are supported via the network, and by the opportunity for individuals to attend bespoke off-the-job training events and to undertake work-related assignments leading to qualifications. The evaluation of the project locates learning through networking activities as facilitating the co-creation of knowledge. Brown et al. draw on the theoretical work of Nonaka and Takeuchi (1995) and Nonaka and Konno (1998) to explain how by making a space available, people can come together to pursue shared goals and to solve common problems. They identify the characteristics of the space which are relevant to creating the conditions under which productive collaboration and creation of knowledge can occur.

In this regard, the discussion resonates strongly with Engeström's focus on new forms of collaborative and formative expertise. The networks created as a result of the KLASS project have many of the features of 'knotworking' described by Engeström, although it should be remembered that the networks referred to by Brown et al. were brought together as a result of a deliberate and funded intervention rather than as a spontaneous response to new organizational or technological challenges.

Skills, knowledge and the workplace

Theoretical debates relating to skills and knowledge in the workplace provide the focus of the third part of this book. The challenge to accepted or dominant approaches to learning, knowledge and knowledge transfer, form the common thread running through these chapters. Young questions the nature of vocational knowledge, whilst Eraut problematizes the notion of the transfer of knowledge between educational and workplace settings. Evans, Kersh and Sakamoto also consider the move between education and work settings, but with a particular focus on tacit knowledge and learning. Hager challenges the traditional notions of learning that ill-fit the work context, a theme developed by Hodkinson and Hodkinson who argue that measuring learning attainment is appropriate to a limited number of work situations.

The nature of vocational knowledge provides the focus for Young (Chapter 11). He argues that in contrast to the centrality of the curriculum in school policy debates, the question as to what knowledge those on vocational education and training (VET) programmes should acquire has been treated superficially. He locates issues concerning the control and content of vocational education within a theoretical framework drawn from the sociology of knowledge. Young distinguishes between three approaches to knowledge that have characterized debates and reforms of VET in the UK up until now – knowledge-based, standards-based and connective.

The knowledge-based approach, which assumes that knowledge can be taken as given and objective, developed from the nineteenth-century industrial need for scientific and mathematical knowledge. This approach proceeded to dominate vocational courses in the further education sector. By the 1970s an alternative standards-based approach was proposed, giving primacy to employer needs. It also produced the National Vocational Qualification (NVQ) system where curriculum outcomes are specified in terms of what employees are expected to do, and not on what they need to know. In the light of limitations associated with the standards-based approach, Young identifies a shift towards the connective approach, which has a greater emphasis on providing opportunities for on- and off-the-job learning.

The three approaches have avoided the issue of how vocational knowledge can be distinguished from academic knowledge, on the one hand, and from the skills and knowledge acquired in the course of work, on the other. In order to address these epistemological concerns Young considers the two main social theories of knowledge, *social constructivism*, which emphasizes knowledge as a product of context, and *social realism*, in which knowledge transcends the conditions of its production. He then turns to the particular (social realist) contributions of Durkheim (1961) and Bernstein (2000). Durkheim's distinction between the sacred and the profane provides a way of analysing the differences between theoretical and everyday (or workplace) knowledge. Bernstein's analysis allows distinctions to be made between types of theoretical knowledge and types of everyday knowledge as well as the problems of bridging the gap between them through the process of recontextualization. Young argues that these distinctions, modified by a social constructivist critique which makes explicit the relations between knowledge and power, provide an important basis for conceptualizing vocational knowledge.

The transfer of knowledge between education and workplace settings is investigated by Eraut (Chapter 12). In the first half of the chapter he analyses the different knowledge cultures of higher education and the workplace, contrasting the kinds of knowledge that are valued and the manner in which they are acquired and used. He suggests that vocational and professional educational programmes claim to provide five types of knowledge: theoretical, methodological, practical, generic skills and general knowledge about the occupation. Eraut argues that there is little chance of theoretical knowledge and practical skills being transferred to the workplace and little evidence of the other three being acquired by students in the first place. Performance in the workplace typically involves the integration of several different forms of knowledge and skill in conditions that allow little time for the analytic/deliberative approach favoured in higher education.

Eraut focuses on transfer, which he defines as 'the learning process involved when a person learns to use previously acquired knowledge/ skills/competence/expertise in a new situation', in the second part of the chapter. The emphasis is on transfer as a learning process, which requires both understanding and positive commitment from individual learners, formal education, employers and local workplace managers. He identifies five stages of transfer spanning from the extraction of potentially relevant knowledge from the context of its acquisition, to its integration with existing workplace skills and knowledge. Eraut argues that the past neglect of transfer results from the cultural gap between formal education and the workplace and profound ignorance of the nature and amount of the learning involved. Although professional preparation programmes include both theory and practice, few of them give serious attention to the process of transfer. He calls for more integrated vocational programmes and the introduction of a practice development role that incorporates responsibility for both students and new staff, and the facilitation of continuing learning in the workplace by experienced staff. Without such developments, he argues that the impact of education on the workplace will continue to be lower than expected and the quality of work will suffer from the limited use of relevant knowledge.

The significance of tacit forms of personal competences for adults reentering work, education or training is considered by Evans, Kersh and Sakamoto (Chapter 13). This research is unusual in so far as it focuses on the way in which adults draw on tacit abilities when moving between learning and work settings over time. A key feature of the research is that a number of adult learners have been tracked as they move into work or further study.

The chapter addresses first, the acquisition of tacit skills, second, the utilization of tacit skills in a learning environment, and third, the influence of tacit skills in the process of work re-entry.

Significant differences between men and women in the identification of tacit skills are noted by the authors. Women tend to recognize the skills they have developed in the family or domestic context, but are aware that such skills are difficult to present to prospective employers and that employers give little recognition to such skills. In contrast men see little value in domestic skills and tend to ignore them. They concentrate on skills gained in other work contexts. Interestingly, men are more likely to identify the potential for the transfer of skills from the economic to the domestic sphere. Those returning to learning reported the use of tacit skills relating to time management, organizing and multitasking. The utilization of such skills is particularly facilitated by certain forms of learning, such as group working. Furthermore, the recognition of these tacit skills by others raises the confidence of the returner and encourages them to further develop their skills. Indeed, the development of self-confidence may be as important as formal learning outcomes such as results or certificates.

In the process of work re-entry the importance of expansive or restricted work environments to the further development and deployment of skills is identified by Evans *et al.* who draw on the work of Fuller and Unwin (see Chapter 8). The research is important for highlighting the way in which competences are ascribed to people along gender or other lines of social cleavage such as class and race, reflecting the tacit requirements of jobs and reinforcing inequalities in employment. An expansive work environment, which enables hidden abilities to become visible, may enable such inequalities to be challenged.

Two conceptions of learning and their implications for understanding learning at work are contrasted by Hager in Chapter 14. He argues that the most influential conceptualization of learning, one that has decisively shaped formal education systems, is very problematic when it comes to understanding learning and measuring learning at work. The first conception, the 'standard paradigm of learning' is based on three assumptions: that learning is a process of mental accumulation of ideas; that the most valuable form of learning is based on thinking rather than action (interiority); and that learning must be readily retrievable (transparency) as opposed to tacit knowledge or informal learning.

The second conception is the 'emerging paradigm of learning', which Beckett and Hager (2002) have developed in response to the limitations of the 'standard' model. In essence, the emerging paradigm conceives learning as action in the world where learning changes both learners and their environment. According to this alternative paradigm, learning is conceived as inherently contextual, since what it does is to continually alter the context in which it occurs. Its principles include: knowledge resides in individuals,

teams and organizations; knowledge embraces not just propositional understanding but cognitive, conative and affective capacities as well as other
abilities and learned capacities such as bodily know-how, and skills of all
kinds; and acquisition of knowledge alters both the learner and the world
(since the learner is part of the world).

Learning identified through the standard paradigm represents only a
small part of the kind of learning that takes place in the work context, and
Hager further suggests that the emerging paradigm, with its focus on
holism, judgement, action and context, better represents the kinds of
learning that occur in workplaces. He argues that the learning as acquisition
metaphor which rests on notions of the individual, stability and reliability
also fails to fit the context of the workplace and that much learning at work
belongs to a type of human practice that evades the standard paradigm.
Hager uses a case history of learning at work to illustrate why the emerging
paradigm offers a better way of understanding how learning is embedded
within the context in which it occurs.

The limitations of the acquisition metaphor are also a central concern of
Hodkinson and Hodkinson (Chapter 15). They argue that attempts to
measure attainment in workplace learning results in a narrow definition of
learning. Through their research, based on the continuing development of
qualified secondary-school teachers, the authors develop a typology of six
types of learning. This typology uses two intersecting dimensions: the degree
of intentionality of the learning (whether it is planned or unplanned); and the
extent to which what is learnt is already known (that which is known to
others, the development of existing capacity and learning which is new in the
workplace). They demonstrate that research which starts by measuring identifiable learning attainments is workable for only some types of learning.

Through illustrations from the experience of school teachers, Hodkinson
and Hodkinson suggest that it is difficult to specify and measure clear
learning attainments for all types of unplanned learning. This is significant
given the importance of these forms of learning in the workplace. It is only
the category of planned learning of what is already known to others which
comfortably fits the acquisition model of learning, yet this type of learning
accounts for only a small proportion of the learning identified. In both the
planned development of existing capacity and the planned new learning it
may theoretically be possible to identify attainment, although in practice it
is extremely difficult to separate out the planned from the unplanned. The
potential limitations of their typology are acknowledged by the authors. The
six types are not mutually exclusive or discrete. There may be further
dimensions, such as: whether the learning is voluntary or imposed, for
example, through government policy; the extent to which access to learning
may be influenced by the power relations within the workplace; the relevance of individual learners' dispositions to learning. Nonetheless, the value
of the typology lies in its ability to demonstrate the small proportion of

workplace learning that fits the acquisition model. Hodkinson and Hodkinson conclude by emphasizing the importance of not giving primacy to any one type of learning, but rather the need to see the relationships between different learning practices.

Research and policy

This collection locates workplace learning in its institutional, organizational and pedagogical context. It is not a prescriptive training text, but combines a critical analysis of learning in a variety of settings with an understanding of theories of learning, and the insights gained from leading edge research. The contents will be of interest to students, researchers, practitioners and policy-makers at a time when workplace learning is assuming increasing significance.

The final chapters (16 and 17) address the ways in which research findings can improve incentives to learning at work. There are two critical issues: how the findings and insights from research can inform policy, on the one hand, and practice, on the other. In Chapter 16, Coffield addresses the relationship between researchers and policy-makers, their different priorities, timescales and scope for considering alternative policy scenarios. Using his own experience of participating in the academic advisory group of the UK government's Performance and Innovation Unit, he explores the scope the initiative had for accepting the findings of academic researchers and following through their implications for policies, which were realistic politically. The territories of influence of different government departments and the interests of ministers with relatively short-term allegiances to education and training responsibilities, contributed to inertia, despite promising early signs of progress. In the UK context, the civil servants' understanding and acceptance of the problem of employer demand for skills (as opposed to increasing the supply of qualifications through increasing participation in the education system) was a major breakthrough. Whether this will be followed through by reforms to institutional arrangements and structures, has yet to be seen.

In contrast, some very practical conclusions can be drawn on the ways in which learning can be supported, encouraged and nurtured in the workplace. In Chapter 17, Fuller, Munro and Rainbird argue that there are many positive points that emerge from bringing together theories of workplace learning and vocational knowledge with an understanding of the context in which learning takes place. Institutions are important: they can contribute to the quality of the work and learning environment through the systematic structures of incentives that they put in place. They are significant in the extent to which they allow both employers' and workers' needs to be expressed and addressed. This is not to argue that 'islands of excellence' are absent in deregulated training systems and labour markets. The problem is, as Streeck (1989) argues, that they are not more widely disseminated. This book will have achieved its objectives if it provides policy-makers, practitioners, trainers, trade unionists and educators with intellectual tools to think about how learning in the workplace can be improved.

References

Ashton, D., Davies, B., Felstead, A. and Green, F. (2002) *Work Skills in Britain*, Oxford: Oxford University and University of Warwick, Centre for Skills, Knowledge and Organisational Performance.

Beckett, D. and Hager, P. (2002) *Life, Work and Learning: Practice in Postmodernity*, Routledge International Studies in the Philosophy of Education 14, London and New York: Routledge.

Bernstein, B. (2000) *Pedagogy, Symbolic Control and Identity*, revised edn, Lanham, MD: Rowman and Littlefield Publishers.

Bosworth, D., Davies, R. and Wilson, R.A. (2001) *Skills and Performance: An Econometric Analysis of the Employer Skill Survey 1999*, London: Department for Education and Skills.

Boud, D., Cohen, R. and Walker, D. (1993) 'Understanding Learning from Experience', in D. Boud, R. Cohen and D. Walker (eds), *Using Experience for Learning*, Buckingham: SRHE and the Open University Press.

Coffield, F. (1997) 'Introduction and Overview: Attempts to Reclaim the Concept of the Learning Society', *Journal of Educational Policy*, 12, 6: 449–55.

Durkheim, E. (1961) *The Elementary Forms of Religious Life*, New York: Free Press.

Edwards, P.K.E. (ed.) (1995) *Industrial Relations: Theory and Practice in Britain*, Oxford: Blackwell.

Engeström, Y. (2001) 'Expansive Learning at Work: Toward an Activity Theoretical Reconceptualization', *Journal of Education and Work*, 14, 1: 133–55.

Eraut, M., Anderton, J., Cole, G. and Senker, P. (1998) 'Learning from Other People at Work', in F. Coffield (ed.), *Learning at Work*, Bristol: Policy Press.

Garrick, J. (1999) 'The Dominant Discourses of Learning at Work', in D. Boud and J. Garrick (eds), *Understanding Learning at Work*, London: Routledge.

Heyes, J. (2000) 'Workplace Industrial Relations and Training', in H. Rainbird (ed.), *Training in the Workplace: Critical Perspectives on Learning at Work*, Basingstoke: Macmillan.

Industrial Relations Research Unit (1997) *Comments on the European Commission's Green Paper 'Partnership for a New Organization of Work'*, mimeo, Coventry: University of Warwick, November.

Keep, E. and Mayhew, K. (1999) 'The Assessment: Knowledge, Skills and Competitiveness', *Oxford Review of Economic Policy*, 15, 1: 1–15.

Keep, E. and Rainbird, H. (1999) 'Towards the Learning Organization?', in S. Bach and K. Sisson (eds), *Personnel Management in Britain: A Comprehensive Guide to Theory and Practice*, 3rd edn, Oxford: Blackwell.

Lave, J. and Wenger, E. (1991) *Situated Learning – Legitimate Peripheral Participation*, Cambridge: Cambridge University Press.

McIntosh, S. and Steedman, H. (2001) 'Learning in the Workplace: Some International Comparisons', in F. Coffield (ed.), *What Progress are we Making on Lifelong Learning?*, Newcastle: University of Newcastle, Department of Education.

Maurice, M., Sellier, F. and Silvestre, J.J. (1986) *The Social Foundations of Industrial Power*, Cambridge, MA: MIT Press.

Nonaka, I. and Konno, N. (1998) 'The Concept of "Ba": Building a Foundation for Knowledge Creation', *California Management Review*, 40 (3): 40–54.

Nonaka, I. and Takeuchi, H. (1995) *The Knowledge Creating Company: How Japanese Companies Create the Dynamics of Innovation*, Oxford: Oxford University Press.

Rainbird, H. (2000) 'Training in the Workplace and Workplace Learning: Introduction', in H. Rainbird (ed.), *Training in the Workplace: Critical Perspectives on Learning at Work*, Basingstoke: Macmillan.

Senker, P. (2000) 'What Engineers Learn in the Workplace and How they Learn It', in H. Rainbird (ed.), *Training in the Workplace: Critical Perspectives on Learning at Work*, Basingstoke: Macmillan.

Sfard, A. (1998) 'On Two Metaphors for Learning and the Dangers of Choosing Just One', *Educational Researcher*, 27, 2: 4–13.

Silver, H. (1998) *The Languages of Innovation: Listening to the Higher Education Literature*. Working Paper no. 1 ESRC Learning Society Programme, Plymouth: University of Plymouth.

Streeck, W. (1989) 'Skills and the Limits to Neo-liberalism: The Enterprise of the Future as a Place of Learning', *Work, Employment and Society*, 3, 1: 89–104.

Whitley, R. (2000) *Divergent Capitalisms: The Social Structuring and Change of Business Systems*, Oxford: Oxford University Press.

Part I

The context of workplace learning

2 The political economy of workplace learning[1]

David N. Ashton

Chapter summary

In this chapter it is argued that the certification of workplace learning only becomes problematic as an issue for public policy under certain specified social conditions. One of the most important of these has been the emergence of new forms of work organization which place a premium on workplace learning. However, just whether or not this translates into issues of public policy will depend on the underlying relations between capital, labour and state and in particular on how these are shaped by the institutional framework of the system of vocational education and training. The chapter uses examples from a range of different types of vocational education and training (VET) framework to illustrate the argument.

Introduction

The central argument in this chapter is that any attempt to develop our understanding of workplace learning and its certification, must start by locating it in the context of two components of the productive system. The first is the national system of vocational education and training (VET), including the administrative capabilities of the state and the second is the way in which production is organized.

National VET systems take their determining characteristics from the underlying relationship between the state, capital and labour. In a sense this is building on the lessons we learnt form the French 'societal' school (Maurice et al. 1986) and which are being further developed by Whitley (2000) and others through the 'business systems' approach. However, VET cannot be reduced to the power relations and institutions surrounding the organization of business. This is largely because VET policy is also conditioned by the state structures and the ability of the state to administer a central policy initiative. For this reason we start the analysis by locating the significance of workplace learning in a typology of national VET systems. This enables us to identify whether the certification of workplace learning is an issue and, if it is, the form it takes.

The second factor responsible for the emergence of workplace learning as a policy issue, is the way in which we organize production. Workplace learning only becomes important under certain conditions. First, when those occupations that deal with the application of knowledge grow in numerical and political significance as is currently the case (International Labour Organization (ILO) 1998). Second, with the emergence of new ways of organizing industrial production which rely on the exploitation of the skills of employees for creating added-value. It is the latter which forms the focus of this chapter.

Countries outside the Anglo-Saxon world, such as Germany and Japan, have already made substantial use of highly skilled workers in the manufacturing industry to create added-value. In recent years, some multinational corporations (MNCs)[2] operating in Anglo-Saxon and developing countries have responded through the development of high-performance work organizations or high-involvement work organizations.[3] In older forms of organization which utilize Fordist techniques of production and Tayloristic forms of management, workplace learning for the mass of employees is minimized. As Braverman (1974) and others have demonstrated, in those organizations work is designed to minimise the involvement of workers in the determination of production, as work tasks are reduced to their basic elements to facilitate the use of cheap, unskilled labour. At the other extreme, high-performance work organizations are designed to maximize the involvement of workers and make full use of their skills.[4] Between these two extremes jobs within organizations vary considerably in the extent to which they facilitate workplace learning. For the sake of clarity of presentation we concentrate on the two extremes in this chapter.

When it comes to workplace learning, the contrast between these two extreme forms of organization is dramatic. In the Fordist organizations we find an extreme form of the division of labour, in which production workers have narrow job descriptions, repetitive tasks and very restricted autonomy. They are often subjected to close supervision and exercise little or no discretion in their jobs, whether those jobs are in a factory, fast-food outlet or a call centre. Here the organizations provide little opportunity for learning or personal development, jobs can be learnt within hours and the organization of work provides no possibility of further promotion or learning. In these jobs there is little point for either the company or the individual to push for, or achieve, the certification of attainment, as there is little learning worth certifying. The qualities employers are concerned with are those of obedience, loyalty, reliability and compliance.

The situation is very different in high-performance work organizations, where work is designed to increase the opportunities for learning and skill acquisition. Workers are rotated between jobs, multiskilling is practised to ensure that workers are competent in a range of tasks, workers are encouraged through the use of self-managed work teams to take control over aspects of the production process, requiring them to become proficient in decision making and problem solving. In addition to technical skills, team-working and communication and problem-solving skills become essential. Here learning is continuous over the course of the person's employment within the organization. It is the spread of these organizational forms that is also pushing the issue of workplace learning into the policy arena and to which national VET systems are having to respond.

The first part of the chapter outlines a typology of national systems of vocational education and training which locates workplace learning and its certification in the context of the broader relations between the state, capital and labour.[5] The second part examines the impact of these national systems on the manifestation of workplace learning and certification in selected countries. This is used to illustrate the ways in which the interaction of these two sets of factors creates different policy issues and tensions in each of these societies.

National systems

For the purpose of this chapter we distinguish three different types of VET system, the free market (e.g. US, UK, Canada), the corporatist (Germany, Denmark, Austria) and the developmental state (Singapore, Taiwan, South Korea) models. The labels themselves are not that important; what is important is that they point to very different relations that have been created between the state, capital and labour through the process of industrialization.

The free market model

In societies characterized by the free market model, industrialization has been led by a strong manufacturing and business elite, supported by a strong state with the unions playing a subordinate role. The fact that the business elite succeeded in leading the process of industrialization, means that the free market remains virtually unchallenged as the main mechanism through which economic growth is achieved. The state plays a subordinate role, providing the legal framework which guarantees the free play of market forces and hence the dominance of capital over labour.

These underlying relationships have been reflected in the emergence of similar institutional structures for the delivery of training in all the societies characterized by this model. Within the context of a culture of individu-alism, training and workplace learning is seen as the province of the individual and employer, leaving a limited role for the state. The government accepts responsibility for basic education, both for citizenship and certification. However, beyond basic education, the socialization of young and older people for work is seen as the responsibility of the individual or employer. Here reliance is placed on the market to provide training and skills, which in reality means the employer and the individual, sometimes through the intermediary of a private training provider. This has led to a preponderance of in-company training or company financed training (outside the professions). In the area of certification it has recently led to experiments with competence-based systems aimed at providing employers with ownership of the certification process.

The corporatist model

The corporatist model is characterized by the state playing a more active role in the process of industrialization and in mediating the relationship between capital and labour. These are countries where the state either played a central part in initiating the process of industrialization and/or where the process utilized the traditional apprenticeship as the main mechanism for skill formation. One consequence was that labour retained an interest in training and skill formation, another was that political leaders sought to pursue economic growth through a more co-operative relationship between capital and labour. Here, labour's interest is not just confined to the employment relationship but encompasses training and welfare provision. This means that the operation of the market is contained within a broader framework determined by the three partners.

With regard to the VET system, the state has a stronger involvement in the education and training system, providing both general education and technical training through the apprenticeship system or vocational education. The achievement of a consensus with the social partners means that this model creates a more institutionally dense environment surrounding training, usually focused on the apprenticeship system. This has also produced a more regulated system of industrial relations. In this model, the control of workplace learning is no longer the sole province of the employer but is part of the more general consensus between the state, unions and employers. This consensus can also extend to the area of certification, as this is an integral part of the apprenticeship system.

The developmental state model

This is the model found in the new industrial economies of South East Asia. These were countries which, as late industrializers, had to break into world markets after the Second World War. The state initially led the process of industrialization, playing an important role in either generating or attracting capital, while at the same time regulating labour. Following Japan, these countries developed strong industrial policies that helped shape the structure of industrial production. Traditionally this has provided the state with a high degree of autonomy in relation to both capital and labour. This has led authors such as Lauder (2001) to refer to their labour markets as state shaped.

State control over education is much stronger than in the case of the free market countries. This is because it was important both for the process of nation building (Green 1999) and the delivery of technical skills for the new industries. In the absence of a strong apprenticeship tradition or initially a strong business elite, the state became more involved in the delivery of training and its certification, using knowledge from the experience of the older industrial countries. Where state policy was to develop powerful concentrations of capital, as in the Japanese *zaibatsu* or the Korean *chaebol*, then the state tended to withdraw from an active engagement in training and certification, leaving that to the internal markets. However, where capital remained fragmented, as in Singapore, then the state continues with a high level of involvement in training, learning for work and certification.

The free market model

Workplace learning in the USA

There is little involvement of the Federal state in workplace learning.[6] There are two main reasons for this. The first is the adherence to the free market ideology that limits the involvement of the state in the delivery of training in instances of market failure. The second is the inability of the Federal state to deliver national programmes because of the decentralized nature of political authority in the US, and the tensions between the Federal government and the individual states.

Traditionally the Federal government has provided a variety of programmes for those at risk in the labour market and those groups exposed to market failures. Mainstream training has remained firmly in the hands of the employers. The Federal programmes aimed at the 'marginal' groups have recently been rationalized through the Workforce Investment Act (WIA) 1998, which aimed at improving the delivery of publicly financed programmes of employee development in a market environment. However, the new system is very much in the spirit of enhancing the effectiveness of the market rather than introducing direct government intervention in the process of workplace learning (Pantazis 1999: 50). In the mainstream labour market, the only other area of government intervention is the attempt to introduce a system of national standards and certification which links certification to workplace learning.

Skill standards are not new in the USA. Before the turn of the twentieth century, many of the skilled trades, medicine, law, social work, and real estate had established collective, but self-imposed, 'standards' for their professional practitioners. By 1990, approximately 400 professional societies and industry-based associations were involved in the promotion of skills-based certification. It is this 'system' that the Federal government sought to rationalize.

Following experimental schemes by the Departments of Education and Labour to identify skill standards, the Clinton administration set up a National Skill Standards Board (NSSB) in 1994 under the National Skill Standards Act (1994). Its task was to formulate a voluntary national system of skill standards, assessment and certification for 15 industrial sectors. However, progress has been very slow, by the late 1990s three Voluntary Partnerships – the Manufacturing Skill Standards Council (MSSC), the Sales and Service Voluntary Partnership, Inc. (S&SVP) and the Education and Training Voluntary Partnership (E&TVP) were established, but only one had delivered any standards (Wills 1998).

The reason for the slow progress is that the process is voluntary, necessitating the building of coalitions of business, education and professional bodies. The sheer size of the task is daunting as between them the MSSC and S&SVP cover 40 million workers.

The initiative faces other problems. Because the national skills recognition system is a Federal initiative it often faces opposition at the level of the individual states. Politicians and employers resent what is perceived as the 'interference' of the Federal government. Thus, although the Federal government has attempted to help provide some support for developing workplace learning, the decentralized character of the political system has so far prevented it from introducing a national competence-based scheme. In view of this, the field is left to the employers and to a lesser extent the trade unions.

The main push for the development of workplace learning in the US has therefore come from some larger employers, especially multinational corporations (Doeringer et al. 2002) and professional associations such as the American Society for Training and Development (ASTD) through the introduction of high-performance working practices. Individual trade unions have also been indirectly involved through partnership arrangements with employers that have helped introduce these high-performance working practices (HPWPs).

Workplace learning in the United Kingdom

The UK framework for workplace learning is similar to that of the USA, in part because the UK government also accepts that workforce development is the province of employers and individual workers and therefore best delivered through the market. However, the UK government has been more active in developing programmes than the USA.[7] Unions, although involved in the previous tri-partite system, have been largely excluded from having any input into the national framework. The only remnants of the old tri-partite system are the construction and engineering sectors where a form of the old levy system remains in place, subject to continuing support from the majority of employers. With these exceptions, the UK government only intervenes directly in the market in the case of market failures and initial youth training.

In the field of youth training, the major government programme is the Modern Apprenticeship scheme, but this has only reached 4 per cent of employers and, where it has been taken up, it does not necessarily provide the same level of skill formation, or indeed the same integration of theoretical and workplace learning that characterizes the national variants of the dual system. The Modern Apprenticeship, government designed and initiated, is a loose arrangement which provides employers with greater freedom to determine the content and duration of any training that takes place (Unwin and Fuller 2001).

The New Deal provides training and advice for those at risk in the labour market and is geared toward facilitating their movement back into the labour market. The Learning and Skill Councils administer government programmes at the local level, although with a remit extended to cover all post-16 vocational education and training.

Compared to the US government, the UK Labour administration has been more active in exploring other ways of making the market work better. Toward this end it has instituted sector-based Sector Skills Councils. These are largely funded by the government and have the task of identifying sector skill needs and advising on workplace learning. In addition, the Regional Development Agencies are funding some experiments in workplace learning. However, these agencies are primarily involved in the delivery of formal training programmes, leaving employers to determine the agenda with regard to workplace learning.

The main official policy mechanism for supporting workforce development is the Investors in People award (IiP). This provides a template for best practice in the field of human resource development and for the certification of those organizations which meet the national standard. IiP has only reached a small percentage of employers, although it has now been achieved by a substantial proportion of larger employers. However, this is a blanket initiative to encourage good human resource development (HRD) practice, there is nothing in the IiP standards which explicitly encourages employers to use the workplace per se as a source of learning.

In recent years the Labour administration has attempted to strengthen the operation of the market through the provision of information and training facilities for individuals. One example is the Union Learning Fund and the new statutory role for the union learning representatives, designed to reach those employees in the lower levels of the labour market who have been excluded from training. Another example is the University for Industry (now Learn Direct) to provide more accessible courses for individuals to purchase. However, none of this is explicitly geared to enhancing the use of the workplace as a source of learning.

In the field of certification the UK government has been more successful than the US Federal government in linking certification to workplace learning. Part of this success is due to the fact that the UK is characterized by a greater degree of centralization of power enabling the state to implement polices without the fear that subordinate agencies, such as local authorities, will challenge them. This makes it easier for the UK central government to launch national programmes such as the National Vocational Qualifications (NVQs). However, even here there have been limits to the success of the NVQs. Despite having created a comprehensive set of national standards and competence-based qualifications, employers have generally been reluctant to make much use of them. Where the traditional qualifications were weak, in the fields of retail, office administration, hospitality and care skills, the new competence-based qualifications have filled a major gap, aided by the UK system of output related funding.[8]

The fact that employers were not keen to take up what were ostensibly employer-led and employment-based qualifications, suggests that workplace learning per se is not high on their agenda. This reticence is largely a result of the fact that only a small proportion of employers are engaged in high value-added forms of production, the areas normally associated with the use of high-performance working practices.[9]

Where high-performance working systems have been introduced then companies have been able to achieve high levels of workplace learning (Felstead and Ashton 2000). However, the employers still remain in control of the agenda and learning is focused primarily on performance improvement. The unions have traditionally shown little interest in workplace learning but this is starting to change as the Trades Union Congress now has its own unit dedicated to developing workplace learning.

The corporatist model

Workplace learning in Denmark

The Danish economy is small and dominated by small and medium-sized enterprises (SMEs). Labour is well organized with high levels of unionization and a history of collaboration between capital and labour. The state acts as a facilitator for this collaboration, which extends to the fields of apprenticeship training and certification. The state also provides for market failures, delivering extensive welfare and unemployment provision.

All forms of continual training in Denmark have been heavily influenced by the country's employers and trade unions. At ministerial and institutional level, employers and trade unions play an influential role in determining the content, structure and delivery of programmes (Down 1997). The VET system is heavily subsidized with the state compensating employers for costs associated with employees attending training courses, including those costs associated with travel, accommodation and loss of wages.

The system is highly decentralized. At the enterprise level, training agreements are formulated between the employers and trade unions at the beginning of each year. Normally, this involves the employers and trade unions designing an individual training or development plan for each company employee. Although no statistics are available on how many training agreements are made each year, it is estimated that in the late 1990s between 80 per cent and 90 per cent of large enterprises had development plans for their employees, although among small enterprises only 50 per cent had such plans (Danish Ministry of Labour 1999).

Qualifications at the skilled worker and semi-skilled worker level are determined and 'owned' by Trade Committees. These are appointed by the employer and the employee organizations in the relevant occupational area, with equal representation of the two sides. They decide on the duration and structure of courses. These qualifications may or may not correspond very precisely to the specific competences required for the job although in general they will come fairly close. However, they also reflect the vested interests of the respective parties, thus the skilled craft workers have an interest in enhancing the qualification level required for skilled work (Nielsen 1998).

One of the main reasons for this strong commitment of employers and trade unions to training is the unique characteristics of Danish enterprises. In Denmark, an enterprise consists of a number of mini-enterprises and within each of these mini-enterprises 'a skilled worker, with the support of semi-skilled workers, integrates, plans, programmes, sets operations, engages in maintenance and introduces innovations into the workplace' (CEDEFOP (European Centre of the Development of Vocational Training) 1996). These skilled workers have considerable power and autonomy over their workplace. This results in the skilled workers' unions seeking to continually improve and update worker skills.

The unions therefore have a strong stake in the existing system. With 80 per cent of the country's employees in a union, one of the ways in which individual unions can attempt to retain their members is by ensuring that they receive access to continual training (Nielsen 1998). This strong co-operation between employers and trade unions ensures that change can be implemented quickly and effectively without the use of government legislation.

Like employers in the Anglo-Saxon countries, the Danish employers are also facing pressures to introduce new technology and new ways of organizing production, demanding greater flexibility, more theoretical knowledge, creativity, collaboration and better communication skills among the workforce. This has led to a concern in all circles to understand better the process of non-formal learning and to explore ways in which this learning of the new skills of communication, team-working and problem-solving can be certified, especially for the mature worker who may have no previous professional qualifications.

One such attempt is through the SUM system (Strategic Development of Employees) which provides a method for assessing the qualification needs of the enterprise as well as the employees. It is based on agreement between the social partners that every employee should attend two weeks vocational training per year. This leads to the identification of the skills before and after the training, but rarely to their certification. The reasons for this is the reluctance of employers to certify skills in case they lose the employee, while the employees, because they expect to stay with the employer, also have no interest in certification. Hence there are no serious pressures from companies or employees to certify non-formal learning (Nielson 1998).

Another, perhaps more serious reason why non-formal learning has not been certified is that it threatens to undermine the existing relationship between the employers and the skilled unions. As Nielsen (1998) argues, the crux of the problem facing the Danish system in recognizing non-formal learning lies in the form taken by the existing system of accreditation. Attempts to introduce certification of non-formal learning are likely to be supported by the semi-skilled unions as it would help their members achieve the highly respected 'skilled' status. However, the skilled unions see such a move as a threat to their membership and therefore resist it. In this way these new developments not only threaten the existing hierarchies within the workplace but also undermine the well-established and institu-tionalized 'ownership' of vocational qualifications by the Trade Committees.

Workplace learning in Germany

Like Denmark the German system is moulded around inputs from the social partners. However, Germany is a much larger country with a Federal polit-ical system. Nevertheless there is a history of collaboration between capital and labour over the regulation of the labour market. This includes extensive welfare provision and a system of help for groups at risk from the labour market which aims to sustain their skills rather than merely push them back into the lower levels of the labour market. For those in employment it provides for limited worker input into employers' decision making with respect to employment conditions through the Works Councils. The organi-zation of training is a joint enterprise between the Federal government, the states, chambers of commerce, the enterprise and the unions. However, this is primarily concerned with initial apprenticeship training (Crouch *et al.* 1999; Culpepper 1999; Culpepper and Finegold 1999; Shackleton 1995).

This system of initial vocational training is highly regulated, but there-after, when it comes to continuing training, the State maintains a 'minor role' and there is little sense of a particular framework, incentive scheme, or a standardization of provision. Indeed, there is no particular emphasis on workplace learning and training as a separate system.

On the regional level, ten of Germany's states, or *Länder*, have their own training leave laws (*Bildungsurlaubsgesetze*), which ensure that each year, employees have the right to up to five days of paid leave for general training courses. Attempts by trade unions to encourage joint regulation of all worker training, have, in the main, been unsuccessful. Further work-based and workplace training is, therefore, primarily subject to a range of informal agreements and patterns of financing, between employers and employees (Gatter 1999: 245).

Precisely because the German apprenticeship has delivered such high levels of skill and worker productivity, the impact of the new forms of organizing production (HPWP) has been later in coming to Germany. Nevertheless they have still been felt through the use of 'lean' production techniques, delayering and teamwork to name but a few (OECD 1999; Arnal et al. 2001). This has created two problems for the German system. The first is how to modernize the apprenticeship to incorporate the soft skills required for the new system of production, for example problem-solving, teamworking and communication into the curriculum. The second is how to accommodate the demand for continuous, lifelong learning.

In response to the first, the Federal Institute of Vocational Training and Education (BIBB), responsible for the apprentice curriculum, has been working with several large enterprises such as VW and Mercedes Benz AG to modify the curriculum. One way this is being done is through the use of 'Learning Islands'. These provide the opportunity for training trainees within the real work environment, while the trainees continued to work and learn as a team on 'real job orders' (Dybowski 1998: 129). This enables the trainees to integrate the acquisition of the new key skills such as team-working with the acquisition of technical skills.

Dehnbostel and Molzberger (2001) report that there are currently more than 50 industrial middle-sized and large companies operating learning islands. These were introduced in an attempt to tackle two main problems. First, there was the need to create skills such as teamworking and multi-skilling and break down the traditional 'vertical and horizontal division of tasks' (Dybowski 1998). Second there was also a concern that training and learning, which was generally provided in workplace simulations, or 'learning laboratories', had become detached from the real experience of the workplace.

While the apprenticeship system shows signs of successfully adapting to these forces of change, there is less evidence of such success when it comes to the continuous training required to constantly upgrade workers' skills. There are a number of reasons for this. The very success of the dual system in creating a high level of skill formation may have militated against many employers becoming proactive in developing new ways of working which function to upgrade skills later in the worker's career (Gatter 1999; Scott and Cockrill 1997). There is also some evidence that this reactive stance may be linked, in part, to the rejection by many workers of moves towards the generalization of skills (Finegold and Wagner 1998). Many of the existing institutions have a vested interest in maintaining the occupational special-ization which has characterized the German labour market. The dual system is still seen by many as providing all the practical and theoretical foundation required for a lifetime's work.

Where the demand for continual learning is acute, as in the high-tech region of Baden-Wurrtemburg, Crouch *et al.* (1999: 146) report that in recent years in-service training has become increasingly important. They suggest that companies are trying to solve the problem of further training by using in-company schemes to retrain relatively small parts of their labour force. However, outside the apprenticeship, the certification of workplace learning remains highly problematic.

The developmental state model

Workplace learning in Singapore

In Singapore, the state still retains a high degree of autonomy from both capital and labour. Although there are many multinational corporations, the power of capital is fragmented and does not form a coherent block that can exert continuous pressure on the government. Labour has been co-opted by the government into supporting the government's agenda. That agenda is to continue to develop the economy in the direction of higher value-added forms of production, for example by developing industries such as life-sciences and electronics where it perceives Singapore to have a competitive advantage in world markets and by encouraging the introduction of new ways of organizing production (Ashton *et al.* 1999). There the government is proactive in anticipating and fostering the demand for higher levels of work-place learning.

It has done this in two ways. The first is to encourage employers to adopt best practices in business management which are detailed in the Business Excellence Award. This encourages the introduction of high-performance working practices by encouraging employers to enhance employee produc-tivity through new forms of work organization. Help is therefore provided to achieve higher levels of productivity through the Job Re-design Programme. This builds on earlier work pioneered by the Productivity and Standards Board aimed at encouraging employers to continuously search out new ways of enhancing productivity through restructuring the work process. Specifically it provides for government subsidized advice from consultants on how to improve productivity through the redesign of work. This comple-ments other advice available for companies seeking the People Developer Award, which provides certification for companies achieving national stan-dards of HRD.

The second way is by increasing the supply of the new skills. This is done in two different ways. One is through helping employers enhance their on-the-job training by providing guidance on how to structure informal, on-the-job training (OJT) for key workers. This is done through the provision of OJT blueprints for selected industries and the establishment of Approved OJT Centres, both of which are subsidized through the Skills Development Fund. The other way in which the supply of new skills is increased is through the Critical Enabling Skills Programme (CREST), which delivers modules in a range of 'new skills' from communication to leadership and problem solving. This second prong of the overall strategy ensures that when the new working practices are in place the workers will have the appropriate skills.

In the field of certification, the government has sought to accommodate the demands from labour for some form of recognition of workplace competences by introducing a National Skills Recognition System. This is a national competence-based system but it only operates at the middle and lower levels of the labour market where existing qualifications were seen to be lacking. It provides a framework for workers to learn and relearn throughout their working life.

Workplace learning in South Korea

In Korea the issue of workplace learning has taken on a different form. There the success of the initial government strategy to develop indigenous companies, following the model of the Japanese *zaibatsu*, led to the emergence of giant Korean conglomerates known as the *chaebol*. The power of these organizations is such that the government can no longer influence them in the same way that the Singaporean government can influence employers in their economy. In addition, labour organizations which were initially repressed by the state are now legitimate and able to exert considerable independent pressure on the government. As a result the state has lost a lot of its relative autonomy. This has had important implications for the ability of the state to determine the skills agenda.

In the earlier stage of economic development the Korean government was able to influence the development of workers' skills through a series of measures, including the use of public training centres as well as a training levy system introduced in the 1970s (Ashton *et al.* 1999). As the *chaebols* grew in size, skill formation became centred in their internal labour markets. The government has responded by encouraging companies to train through the introduction of an employee development component in the social security tax which is levied on all companies.

The fact that skill formation in Korea came to be delivered through the internal labour markets of large corporations with their near lifetime employment meant that there was little demand for a system of skills certification. The large companies would train internally and remained firmly in control of the agenda as workplace learning became more important. Outside the large corporations the situation in the SMEs is very different as they provide relatively little training. However, this also means that there is little demand from them for a system of workplace skills certification. As a result there is little interest from the Koreans for either a competence-based system of certification or for an apprenticeship system. This is very similar to Japan where the large companies have developed their own internal systems of skill formation (Koike 1995) and where there has been little interest in developing forms of certification.

Conclusions

Each of these different types of national system has encountered different problems in dealing with the challenges posed by the new ways of organizing the productive system. In the free market model, the insistence by the agencies of the state that training and workplace learning is not their area of responsibility has led to the workforce learning agenda remaining largely in the hands of employers. In view of this it is not difficult to see why this agenda in the Anglo-Saxon countries is dominated by the performance model. The focus is almost exclusively on addressing learning that improves the performance of the organization. This makes it very difficult to develop public forms of assessment that can certify such learning.

In the corporatist model the problem is one of adjusting the existing apprenticeship system to the demands of the new system, and in particular the interests of the skilled workers. In this instance skilled workers are threatened by the certification of workplace learning, especially non-formal learning, because of the threat this poses to the existing system of industrial relations. Moreover, the establishment of highly successful systems of initial training does itself create institutional conditions which militate against the development of continuous learning.

It is in societies with the developmental state model that we find the most proactive endorsement by the state of workplace learning, as in Singapore. There the state not only helps certify it, but also encourages employers to adopt the new methods of organizing production while at the same time providing support for workers to learn the appropriate skills. The problem here is for the state to obtain support from both employers and workers. In Singapore the state is actively working with the major employers on this issue. Moreover, such a policy requires that the state sustains its autonomy relative to both capital and labour. Where this has not been the case, and the state has lost out to capital in terms of its autonomy, as in South Korea, then the employers once again assert their control over the agenda.

Notes

1   Acknowledgement: this chapter is a further development of earlier work with Johnny Sung, Arwen Raddon and Marcus Powell, commissioned by the CIPD and published in 2001 under the title 'National Frameworks for Workplace

Learning', in J. Stevens (ed.), *Workplace Learning in Europe*, pp. 35–60. For reasons of space, much of the empirical data on which this analysis is based has been cut but is available in that publication.

2   There is no single measure for identifying high-performance work organizations. Ashton and Sung (2002), pp. 101–16 provide a summary of recent evidence. This shows a fairly extensive take up of the individual practices which comprise high-performance working systems, but the take up varies between countries. For example in Sweden, 29 per cent of establishments used team-based work, 60 per cent employee involvement and 46 per cent the use of flat hierarchies, although not all will use all three practices and thereby qualify as high-performance work organizations. In Germany 20 per cent used team-based work, 19 per cent employee involvement and 30 per cent had introduced flat hierarchies. In Portugal 22 per cent used team-based work, 9 per cent employee involvement and 3 per cent had a flat hierarchy. In the UK, Ashton and Sung (2002: 103–4) using data from the CIPD annual HRD survey, report that approximately 20 per cent of UK establishments can be meaningfully labelled as high-performance work organizations, a similar estimate to that made by Wood from the UK Workplace Employee Relations Survey data. For specific work on MNCs see OECD (2001), for a more general discussion of the OECD evidence see Arnal *et al.* (2001), pp 9–10.

3   This debate revolves around the question of whether the link between this type of organizational design and enhanced performance has been established. Those who use the term 'high-involvement working practices' argue that this link has yet to be established, whereas those who use the term 'high-performance working practices' argue that the link to performance has been established.

4   See Ashton and Sung (2002) for a discussion of the evidence.

5   This framework is detailed in Ashton *et al.* (2000). For a similar approach to the analysis of national VET systems see Keating *et al.* (2002).

6   We concentrate on the Federal government as this is the only agency with responsibility for the national labour market.

7   The Performance and Innovation Unit's Review of workforce development 'In Demand' (2001) suggests that the Labour administration is starting to take a more proactive approach.

8   This system provides funding to training providers who successfully deliver the new qualifications.

9   For a discussion of the evidence see Ashton and Sung (2002).

Bibliography

Arnal, E., Ok, W. and Torres, R. (2001) *Knowledge. Work Organization and Economic Growth*, Labour market and social policy – Occasional Paper No. 50. Paris: OECD.

Ashton, D. and Felstead, F. (2000) 'From Training to Lifelong Learning: The Birth of the Knowledge Society?', in J. Storey (ed.), *Human Resource Management: A Critical Text*, 2nd edn, London: Routledge.

Ashton, D. and Sung, J. (2002) *Supporting Workplace Learning for High Performance Working*, Geneva: ILO.

Ashton, D., Green, F., James, D. and Sung, J. (1999) *Education and Training for Development in East Asia: The Political Economy of Skill Formation in East Asian Newly Industrialized Economies*, London: Routledge.

Ashton, D., Sung, J. and Turbin, J. (2000) 'Towards a Framework for the Comparative Analysis of National Systems of Skill Formation', *International Journal of Training and Development*, 4, 1: 8–25.

Ashton, D., Sung, J., Raddon, A. and Powell, M. (2001) 'National Frameworks for Workplace Learning', in J. Stevens (ed.), *Workplace Learning in Europe*, London: Chartered Institute of Personnel and Development (CIPD)/Skills, Knowledge and Organisational Performance (SKOPE), pp. 35–60.

Braverman, H. (1974) *Labor and Monopoly Capitalism*, New York: Monthly Review Press.

CEDEFOP (1996) *The Role of the Company in Generating Skills – The Learning Effects of Work Organization. Denmark Country Study*, Luxembourg: CEDEFOP.

Crouch, C., Finegold, D. and Sako, M. (1999) *Are Skills the Answer?*, Oxford: Oxford University Press.

Culpepper, P.D. (1999) 'The Future of the High-Skill Equilibrium in Germany', *Oxford Review of Economic Policy*, 15, 1, Spring: 43–59.

Culpepper, P.D. and Finegold, D. (eds) (1999) *The German Skills Machine: Sustaining Comparative Advantage in a Global Economy*, New York: Berghahn Books.

Danish Ministry of Labour (1999) National Webpage http://www.am.dk/english.htm.

Dehnbostel, P. and Molzberger, G. (2001) 'Combination of Formal Learning and Learning by Experience in Industrial Enterprises', in Jan. N. Streumer (ed.), *Perspectives on Learning at the Workplace*, Proceedings of the Second Conference on HRD Research and Practice Across Europe, University of Twente Enschede, The Netherlands, 26–27 January, UFHRD (Universities' Forum for Human Resource Management), pp. 77–88.

Doeringer, P.B., Evans-Klock, C. and Terkla, D. (2002) *Start-Up Factories: High-Performance Management. Job Quality, and Regional Advantage*, New York: Oxford University Press and W.E. Upjohn Institute.

Down, T. (1997) 'Developing Skills Policies in Six Countries', draft report for DfEE.

Dybowski, G. (1998) 'New Technologies and Work Organization – Impact on Vocational Education and Training', in CEDEFOP, *Vocational Education and Training – the European Research Field. Background Report 1998*, vol. 1, Thessaloniki: CEDEFOP.

Felstead, A. and Ashton, D. (2000) 'Tracing the Link: Organizational Structures and Skill Demands', *Human Resource Management Journal*, 10, 3, Nov.: 3–21.

Finegold, D. and Wagner, K. (1998) 'The Search for Flexibility: Skills and Workplace Innovation in the German Pump Industry', *British Journal of Industrial Relations*, 36, 3: 469–87.

Gatter, J. (1999) 'Continuing Occupational Training in An Ageing German Economy', in P.D. Culpepper and D. Finegold (eds), *The German Skills Machine: Sustaining Comparative Advantage in a Global Economy*, Oxford: Berghahn Books.

Green, A. (1999) 'East Asia Skill Formation Systems and the Challenge of Globalisation', *Journal of Education and Work*, 12 (3): 253–80.

International Labour Organization (ILO) (1998) *World Employment Report 1998–99. Employability in the Global Economy. How Training Matters*, Geneva: ILO.

Keating, J., Medrich, E., Vollkoff, V. and Perry, J. (2002) *Comparative Study of Vocational Education and Training Systems*, Leabrook SA: NCVER.

Koike, K. (1995) *The Economics of Work in Japan*, Tokyo LTCB International Library Foundation.

Lauder, H. (2001) 'Innovation, Skill Diffusion and Exclusion', in P. Brown, A. Green and H. Lauder (eds), *High Skills: Globalization, Competitiveness and Skill Formation*, Oxford: Blackwell.

Maurice, M., Sellier, F. and Silvestre, J.J. (1986) *The Social Foundations of Industrial Power*, Cambridge, MA: MIT Press.

Nielsen, S.P. (1998) *Identification, Assessment and Recognition of Non-Formal Learning. The Case of Denmark*, Luxembourg: CEDEFOP.

OECD (1999) *Employment Outlook June*, Paris: OECD.

—— (2001) *Measuring Globalisation: The Role of Multinationals in OECD Economies. Vol 1: Manufacturing Sector*, Paris: OECD.

Pantazis, C. (1999) 'The New Workforce Investment Act', *Training and Development*, ASTD, August: 48–50.

Performance and Innovation Unit (2001) 'In Demand: Adult Skills in the 21st Century', London: UK Cabinet Office, December.

Scott, P. and Cockrill, A. (1997) 'Multi-skilling in Small- and Medium-sized Engineering Firms: Evidence from Wales and Germany', *The International Journal of Human Resource Management*, 8, 6, December: 807–24.

Shackleton, J.R. (1995) *Training for Employment in Western Europe and the United States*, Cheltenham: Edward Elgar.

Unwin, L. and Fuller, A. (2001) 'Modern Apprenticeships', University of Leicester, Centre for Labour Market Studies.

Whitley, R. (2000) *Divergent Capitalisms: The Social Structuring and Change of Business Systems*, Oxford: Oxford University Press.

Wills, J. (1998) 'Standards: Making them Useful and Workable for the Education Enterprise', Center for Workforce Development, Institute for Educational Leadership. A report for the US Department of Education.

Wood, S. with de Menezes, Lilian and Lasaosa, Ana (2001) 'High Involvement Management and Performance', paper delivered at CLMS, University of Leicester, May.

3 The employment relationship and workplace learning

Helen Rainbird, Anne Munro and Lesley Holly

Chapter summary

The workplace is an important site of learning, but it needs to be understood in the context of the power relations which characterize the employment relationship. These influences, some of them beyond the immediate workplace, may encourage or discourage employers' investment in formal learning and the adoption of forms of work organization conducive to the promotion of informal learning. Theories of situated learning tend to stress the consensual and participative nature of learning at work rather than the constraints on individual and collective capacity for action. The authors analyse workplace learning in three small workgroups in the broader organizational and regulatory context in which they are located. Although training can be the subject of consensual decision-making, the authors argue that consensus and participation have to be constructed as a means for facilitating learning in the workplace, rather than taken as given.

Introduction

The employment relationship is fundamental to studying workplace learning. In societies where the majority of the population do not own their own means of production, paid employment and the relationship between the employer and the employee are central to 'the ways in which employees are rewarded, motivated, trained and disciplined' (Edwards 1995: 3). These processes are influenced by the institutions governing the employment relationship, namely the state, management and the trade unions. The system of industrial relations and the institutions of vocational training in each country have been shaped through the process of industrialization and the ways in which the rules governing the employment relationship have been established. Comparative international studies suggest that societal factors and social institutions contribute to the supply of skills in the workforce and have qualitative implications for patterns of labour deployment in the workplace (Maurice *et al.* 1986; Ashton in this volume). These influences beyond the workplace, including the broader regulatory structures of the

employment relationship, may encourage or discourage employers' investment in formal learning and the adoption of forms of work organization
conducive to the promotion of informal learning.

Whether workers are employed in unionized or non-unionized workplaces the employment relationship is governed by rules. Edwards argues
that rules cover all forms of paid employment. A rule is 'a social institution
involving two or more parties which may have a basis in law, a written
collective agreement, an unwritten agreement, a unilateral decree or merely
an understanding which has the force of custom' (1995: 5). In this chapter,
we focus on the influence of the employment relationship on workers' access
to workplace learning. We understand this as operating at a number of
different levels. The first of these involves the role of the state in structuring
the education and training system. It provides general education, oversees
the initial training of employees, sets standards and identifies the rights and
responsibilities of the different parties to the employment relationship with
respect to continuing training and lifelong learning. The influences on
workplace learning do not derive solely from the institutions of vocational
training. The state also contributes to the regulation of the employment
relationship by setting the framework of labour law, within which employers
and trade unions bargain, and acts as an employer itself in the public sector.
It can also exercise considerable influence in areas where it is the purchaser
of goods and services and through its industrial policy, it can promote the
adoption of particular forms of work organization and technology.

A second level at which the employment relationship is regulated is at
the level of the organization. Some of the dominant theories concerning the
way in which skills and qualifications are mobilized in the workplace
operate within a unitarist framework. Human Capital Theory and Human
Resource Management assume employers and employees have mutual interests in relation to investment in training and in the deployment of labour
(Heyes 2000). In contrast, we argue that training strategies must be located
in the context of the tensions between different management objectives and
functions and the extent to which training and development is seen as
central or peripheral to market strategy. Moreover, three 'frames of reference'
have been identified to the study of the employment relationship. Fox
(1966) distinguished between unitary and pluralist approaches. The
unitarist view of the employment relationship assumes that management
and employees have similar interests. In contrast, the pluralist view sees
conflict as inevitable because management and employees have different
interests and the parties to the employment relationship have different bases
of authority. The third approach, the radical or Marxist approach, exemplified by Hyman (1978) identifies the unequal nature of the power resources
of management and labour. This is not to argue that there are no areas in
which managers and employees have shared interests (indeed, training and
development has often been identified as one of these more consensual

arenas). Rather than representing a normal state of relations, as suggested by the unitarist approach, the way in which employee consent is constructed in the context of deep-seated antagonistic relations between capital and labour is fundamental to understanding the employment relationship. According to Edwards management is therefore 'a continuous, active and uncertain process' (1995: 14). This is due to the fact that firms pursue the contradictory objectives of control and consent of the labour force in the context of an uncertain external environment.

Training strategies and the developments which they support and underpin need to be located in the social relations of the workplace and this constitutes the third level of analysis. They are implemented in the context of workplace industrial relations and questions concerning the control and reward of effort. The way in which jobs are designed and linked to career progression routes in internal labour markets do not only determine access to formal training. The organization of workgroups and their relationship to other occupational groups are also significant in determining access to learning environments linked to different kinds of job tasks and levels of job discretion. Patterns of inclusion and exclusion in workgroups, and the ability to move into related areas of work affect the capacity of individual workers to access informal learning. At the same time, entitlement to formal training and the capacity to access informal learning are also factors constitutive of the balance of power in the workplace. We adopt a perspective from the labour process debate which has its origins in the recognition that the wage buys only the worker's capacity to work and not a specific level of effort (Braverman 1974). Therefore two central concerns of labour process theory are managerial strategies of labour control, on the one hand, and workers' strategies of resistance, on the other (see Thompson 1983, for an introduction to debates on the labour process).

Situated learning is one of the dominant theories applied to learning in the workplace, developed by Lave and Wenger (1991). We acknowledge the importance of recognizing the social nature of learning at work and in particular the contribution of the metaphor of learning as participation to debates in educational theory. However, as a theory for understanding learning in contemporary workplaces, its conceptualization of power relations and the structural constraints on learning is weak.

We believe there are three key problems with Lave and Wenger's formulation. First, the theory was developed, in their own words, to examine craft or 'craft-like' forms of production (1991: 62), exemplified in the case studies of learning amongst Guatemalan midwives and Liberian tailors. Even in these examples, where the paradigm of craft production is most applicable, the social relations of production are not theorized. Second, two of the case studies that are used to develop their theoretical framework do refer to workers in wage labour relationships: the quartermasters and the butchers. Here, Lave and Wenger recognize that novices may not gain access to the learning potential of given situations and that the presence of overlapping communities of practice may prevent them from becoming experienced practitioners. They maintain that '[t]he social structure of this practice (the cultural practice in which any knowledge exists), its power relations and its conditions for legitimacy define the possibilities of learning' (1991: 98). Whilst their theoretical framework does not preclude this possibility, in practice their analysis remains within a pluralist framework. A consequence of this is that they emphasize the consensual and the participative at the expense of an analysis of the power relationships which underpin workplace practices. Finally, although the recognition of the significance of ongoing social practice as a source of learning has been of enormous significance, Lave and Wenger tend to downplay the importance of formal learning and its certification. Formal education and training provide workers with resources and positional goods which are of value individually and collectively.

So far we have focused on the ways in which the employment relationship creates structural constraints on workplace learning as well as affordances for learning. In this chapter we focus on the internal dynamics of workgroups as a means of examining workplace learning. The work of Eraut and his colleagues shows that there are a range of ways in which the highly qualified learn about their jobs outside structured learning (1998) and our own research demonstrates that workers in routine jobs also actively seek learning opportunities for themselves (Rainbird et al. 1999). Our analysis concerns the ways in which individual employees and work groups create formal and informal learning opportunities within the constraints of the workplace.

This chapter aims to bring a perspective on the labour process and the employment relationship to the analysis of workplace learning. A focus on the workplace, inevitably involves a focus on the social relations of the work-group and ongoing social practice. Writers in the labour process tradition tend to view skill as a power resource to be exercised, rather than as the means by which work-related knowledge is acquired. We draw on two major research projects examining workplace learning and workers' access to training in the public sector. They both focus on workers on the lowest salary grades who often have limited access to employer-provided training and, in some cases, little scope to access informal learning as well.[1] Like Eraut and his colleagues (1998) we have focused on workers' own accounts of their formal qualifications, access to training and how they learned to do their jobs. We start by outlining the general context of local government and National Health Service (NHS) reform before examining case studies of three small workplaces, located in larger public sector organizations. These have been chosen as a mechanism for exploring the impact of different levels of regulation of the employment relationship on learning at work. We contrast a group of female cleaners, performing work that is constructed as low skilled with a group of apprentice-trained male maintenance workers. A third case study explores the impact of work reorganization on healthcare assistants' jobs and learning in an NHS Trust. We argue that in each case, although workers exercise some control over workplace learning, this has to be analysed in the context of power relations within the workgroup, organizational structures and broader regulatory frameworks. This is followed by a conclusion.

The public sector context

There are substantial changes taking place in the public sector in the United Kingdom, with central government reforms driving a number of significant developments. These include the Labour government's introduction of a bench-marking process known as 'Best Value' in the letting of contracts for local government services. This replaced the regime of compulsory competitive tendering, introduced by the Conservatives (1979–97), which required contracts to be awarded to the lowest bidder. In the National Health Service, the Private Finance Initiative is increasing private sector involvement in the funding of new buildings, which has consequences for the employment of ancillary staff. Government requirements on mental health and care in the community are leading to major reconfigurations of NHS trusts, while initiatives such as 'Working Together' are forcing trusts to consider how they involve staff from all levels in their decision-making processes. At the same time there are a range of pressures towards professionalization: this is particularly the case in personal social services where the distinction between nursing and social care has shifted. Change has been facilitated to some extent through the developments in industrial relations: the single status agreement in local government and the introduction of elements of local bargaining in the health sector. The public sector's support for the government's National Education and Training Targets is evident in many organizations' commitment to achieving the Investors in People (IiP) standard and in adopting competence-based assessment in the form of National Vocational Qualifications (NVQs). They have contributed to Human Resource strategies which emphasize the extension of development reviewing and managers' consideration of the training and development needs of staff in a wide range of occupations within organizations. In addition, the unions organizing workers in the lowest grades, the public sector union (UNISON), The Transport and General Workers Union (TGWU) and the General Municipal and Boilermakers (GMB), have taken initiatives on training and development, both as an item on the collective bargaining agenda and as a potential arena for developing approaches based on social partnership with the employer.

Learning to clean and the role of the supervisor

Cleaning work is one of the areas which has been subject to compulsory competitive tendering (CCT) and this has resulted in downward pressure on wages. This occurred even where contracts were being retained in-house.

Women's employment was particularly prone to CCT (Escott and Whitfield 1995) and to work intensification. The workgroup studied was made up of two teams of cleaners: one working in a museum and art gallery, the other in a town-hall. Other parts of the cleaning department have been subject to the pressures outlined above and to work intensification, but these two groups have managed to retain a degree of control because of the prestigious public buildings they clean.

Although cleaning has been socially constructed as unskilled work, cleaners have to learn many things about their work and develop skills which are not always acknowledged. It is important to emphasize that formal qualifications play a relatively small role in recruitment and in moving into supervisory roles. The senior supervisor explained 'Qualifications? I had none. They didn't bother in those days, they just handed out the chemicals.' Her decision to go into supervision had been partly to counteract the monotony of cleaning work and to obtain some job autonomy.

> I went into supervision because no one else wanted to do it...I don't like standing still. I used to work at a unit...and I was sick of it. Supervising gets you off the section, you move around, go from floor to floor instead of being brain dead on the section. I used to empty the bins a different way round to vary the work.

What she valued about supervision was the autonomy it brought her and the role it gave her in planning workloads. She emphasized the need to organize the work in a logical way especially in public buildings where sections are open to the public and the fact that they are used for prestigious functions. She had found the units that cleaners were assigned were not organized in the most logical way. She had developed her own system and a series of routines for organizing the work.

Supervision also involved a formal role in teaching the correct cleaning methods and ensuring that the work is performed to standard. This teaching role was recognized by her own staff. Members of her team commented 'she's taught me everything, it's what I know today'. Another cleaner said 'The best way to learn is to have someone like her who's been there and done it. I couldn't change my system now.' Another commented 'I would hate to be reported to her because my work was not done properly. She'd say "that's not how I taught you to do it". I couldn't face that.'

Although it is often assumed that commercial cleaning is similar to domestic cleaning, there are many things that cleaners have to learn about the work. There is an assumption that anyone can do it but in practice cleaners may have to *unlearn* what they learned to do in a domestic context. The supervisor reported that when she was recruited 14 years previously she had been asked 'can you clean?' and if you were a housewife it was assumed that you could. Now they have to use coloured-coded cloths, buckets and mops for different areas (e.g. toilets, public spaces, eating areas). A range of formal courses and certificates is now required. She explained, 'there is a correct way for cleaning everything – it is easy to do it the way it's taught – it saves time and energy and makes it cleaner and makes the job easier'.

Social skills are important too both in buildings which are open to the public and in areas where cleaners come into contact with other workers. These skills are not essential but can help make the job easier. One cleaner explained,

> I feel I'm a better cleaner now. A housewife cleans a house, but there are different little things you've learnt. This is a big building, it's open to the public and the customers say things like 'it's nice to see clean toilets'. There's lots of contact with the public – they ask where things are – it's a security job really…you mix a lot with the public and they expect friendliness and sociability.

Another cleaner reported,

> I loved the floor I was on. I communicated well with the staff. I knew what I could do for them and they knew what they could do for me. They used to treat me as one of the staff…they would have a collection for the cleaners at Christmas…people here are really considerate.

Nevertheless, supervision also involves enforcement of work routines. A recently recruited supervisor encountered difficulties in getting experienced staff on her section to stick to the colour coding (she had come from a cleaning job in a different department of the City Council) because they did not accept her authority. She had to call a meeting with them in her second week to make sure they did the work correctly. She had to reinforce the hygiene and health and safety standards that were required on the staff. Here, the link between formal training programmes and the acceptance, reinforcement and legitimation of sources of expertise can be seen. Significantly, she finds the staff are more confident in what they do and pay more attention to what she says when they have been on courses. There are also tensions in the supervisory role: this is partly as an experienced practitioner and partly in ensuring that work is done to standard, with a disciplinary role if necessary. Other experienced workers can challenge this role and it is this challenge to authority that results in other workers' perceptions that supervision involves dealing with conflict.

Cleaning is a relatively low status job, with few prospects for job promotion. As with other low status jobs, it is the quality of the work environment and tasks which 'rubs off' on the staff who perform them (cf. Munro 1999). This aspect of status has little to do with formal knowledge and knowledgeable practice, but the status of the public buildings in which the cleaners work. This provides them with a public profile and pride in their work, in contrast to many cleaning jobs which involve isolation, little social contact with the public or co-workers, and infrequent control by a supervisor. In this instance, the public profile of the buildings the cleaners worked in also affected the resources and specialist cleaning equipment that were available to them and, thus, to their pride in their 'patch'.

Learning a skilled job: male maintenance workers in the cleansing department

This workgroup was made up of five men who were skilled in the traditional sense of having served an apprenticeship or undergone a formal training programme. They were maintenance workers in the cleansing department, responsible for rubbish collection, road sweeping, clearing fly-tipping, road-clearing and gritting. They had a wide range of mechanical and electrical skills. They often needed to undertake delicate work inside an electrical system then use brute force to lift the lifting gear. They had all been apprenticed or trained by their employer and they also learned by trying things out, using the manual, watching each other as well as drawing on their past knowledge. They worked in shifts in small teams and were highly interdependent. The work is often dangerous so reliance on team members is essential. As maintenance workers, they are the most skilled of all the workers in the cleansing department. Although they all had certain specialisms, they were a small group and learned from each other. The work itself was varied and they had to maintain a range of engines, the lifting equipment on dustcarts, the sweeping mechanisms on sweepers, working on both the inside and outside of vehicles.

The way in which they acquired their skills depended on their age. Three of the men had been apprenticed at garages. 'I am 50 years old. My dad started me when I was 13. I been doing it all my life.' In contrast, two younger men had come into the section as trainees. The department had paid their wages and for them to attend college on a day-release basis. The older men did not find it easy to accept the credentials of the younger men and this was manifested in a form of bullying. In this workgroup a pecking order had been established between younger and older workers which was reinforced through banter and intimidation. The source of conflict was the formal knowledge of the younger workers which is contrasted to the knowledge learned through experience of the older workers. One younger fitter explained:

> I've learned a lot from working here on the technical side. But they (the older fitters) think I should be the same as them, able to do what they do. It's impossible. I've only been doing it four years and they've been doing it over 20 years. They joke that because I've passed my exams I should know everything. That's not on really.

Problems arise when the younger men make mistakes which the older fitters do not let them easily forget.

Many of the men had taken advantage of training courses offered by the council before the stringent redrawing of financial boundaries. Two fitters had a certificate of professional competency which means they could run a fleet of trucks if such a thing was on offer with the council. However the ongoing formal training fell short of what will be needed for the job. Twelve new dust-carts with specialized lifts had been purchased and none of the fitters really understood how to repair them.

Despite all the limitations outlined above, the fitters are empowered by their skills, even the younger men. They have to be trained up to a certain standard to be able to accomplish their work. They celebrate their own skills and admit to enjoying their work. Despite fears of redundancy among all workers in this local authority, these workers are optimistic about finding other jobs if necessary because whoever runs the department they will still need fitters.

Refuse collection, like cleaning, has been subject to compulsory competitive tendering, but fewer contracts have been let to private contractors in these male areas of employment than in the female-dominated areas such as cleaning and catering work (Escott and Whitfield 1995). Because of the financial problems of the council only one fitter had a permanent contract. The others were on endless short-term contracts with all the accompanying fears about redundancy. There were also rumours of privatization and the contracting out of services. This made for a highly insecure work environment, though until then local political conditions and union opposition had prevented sub-contracting and redundancies.

Loss of skill: redefining qualifications in the secure care home

This group of female, state-enrolled nurses had had their job roles redefined as healthcare assistants involving a more narrow range of activities. They had been excluded from participation in tasks they had formerly performed which had become the remit of a different occupational group, the registered nurses. The healthcare assistants experienced this as both disempowering and demoralizing. It illustrates the process of reconstitution of workgroups at the local level as a consequence of organizational restructuring and closures.

This workgroup was based in a secure care home for the elderly mentally ill within an NHS trust. It was run by a general manager, supported by a clinical manager and one administrator. There were six primary or registered nurses, each responsible for a total of 30 healthcare assistants plus two catering assistants. An activities co-ordinator also worked there, with responsibilities for a number of residential homes in the trust. The client base has changed over the years. Patients without major problems go into social services residential homes ('the little old ladies who just get confused'), while the more aggressive and mobile clients are placed in here. There were three wings to the building, each with ten clients, staffed during the day by one primary nurse and two healthcare assistants. At night one healthcare assistant was allocated to each wing and there was one 'floater' for back-up. The healthcare assistants were allocated a number of clients each day and were responsible for all aspects of their care (observation for pressure sores, booking the hairdresser, skin care, nails, toiletries, washing and feeding) as well as general duties such as hoovering the wing.

Most of the healthcare assistants were older Afro-Caribbean women, who had been working in healthcare for well over ten years. Many had been previously employed at the old psychiatric hospital which had been closed down. As a part of the reorganization the old enrolled nurse grade had been removed and employees were offered the new post of healthcare assistant. Since older women from ethnic minority groups had been over-represented in the enrolled nurse grade, reorganization had a disproportional impact on them. The new role involved fewer nursing tasks (such as taking blood and dealing with dressings) and was on locally agreed and lower pay scales. At the psychiatric hospital there had been a notion of the ward as a community of workers, with enrolled nurses acting as the experienced practitioner working alongside auxiliaries recruited with no formal qualifications. When the reorganization took place, healthcare assistants who had been enrolled nurses were offered the chance to undertake a conversion course to become registered nurses. This was not regarded as a viable possibility by most of the staff (because of their age, lack of time or lack of resources), although a small number had taken this route. The result was that many felt abandoned by the trust, left to do a job, alongside the old auxiliaries, in which a considerable amount of time is spent cleaning, cooking and feeding.

In the secure care home, the primary nurses had a formal responsibility for working out personal development plans with the healthcare assistants in their teams. As new demands were placed on primary nurses to take a mentoring role some felt unable or unwilling to take responsibility for coaching healthcare assistants. Development at the home could take the form of observing, shadowing, visiting other parts of the trust as well as attending formal courses which might include short one-day sessions (such as handling aggression and dealing with diabetics), the Return to Learn programme or NVQ assessment. In this context many of the healthcare assistants spoke of the empowering nature of taking part in formal learning opportunities, especially the NVQ level 3 in care. This was because it gave them confidence, status and legitimized their role in relation to clients, relatives and the qualified nurses. They had learnt how to do the job through informal learning, but it was the formal certification process that established their right to practice. It was the process of assessment of competence combined with attendance at formal courses as a part of the NVQ programme that resulted in them feeling empowered and raised their status in the eyes of the primary nurses.

While the primary nurses were the formal, if sometimes reluctant, mentors to the staff, the activities co-ordinator, who set up social and cultural events for clients (for example bingo, arts and crafts, music, visits by animals etc.), had taken on an informal role as practice adviser. She acted as mentor to the healthcare assistants, involving them in designing and running various sessions for the clients. In this way practice was shifting towards general care from nursing care, which had been the focus at the psychiatric hospital. There had been other attempts to expand the healthcare assistant role, by involving them in developing care plans for clients, but because the main part of the job is structured as cleaning, little time is left for participation in other activities.

The removal of the enrolled nurse post and creation of the lower status, lower paid healthcare assistant post, created a formal barrier to inclusion in one occupational group and made existing expertise 'invisible'. We can see the healthcare assistants as forming a new, occupational group with a more limited range of skills and tasks to perform, yet inclusion even in this lower grade occupational group still requires the formal acknowledgement of competence through the NVQ programme.

Discussion: the organizational and regulatory context of workplace learning

These three workgroups have to be located in the context of recent organizational and financial changes in local government services and NHS provision and the power relations within workgroups, which have consequences for the context in which workers practice and develop their skills. Even in workplaces where work tasks were most fragmented and routine, forms of 'knowledgeable practice' were in evidence. In other words, the social nature of learning in the workplace is evident, along with tacit skills which are not formally acknowledged but allow workers to do their work with the minimum of effort and provide them with elements of job control.

In exploring the workplace as a site of learning for workers on the lowest salary grades, we have found that structural factors such as job design, organizational change, financial constraints and staffing levels are more significant in determining patterns of access to formal and informal learning than membership of workgroups. This is not to argue that workgroups are not a source of 'knowledgeable practice' within 'elements of control', as Thompson suggests (1983: 92). The way in which work tasks have been defined means that in many (but not all) cases, conception and execution have been separated and workers exercise limited control over the content and pace of their work. Cockburn's recognition of the multifaceted nature of skill is central here. She argues that it refers first, to the workers' accumulated experience;

second, to the skill demanded by a particular job; and third, to a political dimension whereby a group of workers or a union defends its skills against the challenge of the employer or another group of workers (1983: 113). This tension between skills which reside in the worker and the demands of the job is missing from the concept of communities of practice and learning as participation. Moreover, as our examples of the cleaners and the fitters demonstrate, different groups of workers have a differential capacity to defend themselves and their skills. This derives from the extent to which their labour can be substituted by other workers; their ability to mount effective action and cause disruption; and their visibility.

Knowledgeable practice is a resource for workers, but it is not the primary power resource in the workplace. The workgroups examined are not independent producers controlling their own means of production. Rather, they are employees working for large organizations, whose financial resources are determined by the state as an outcome of local and national political processes. We have located our analysis in the context of recent reforms to public sector finance where workers in manual and routine jobs have borne the brunt of changing practices in service delivery. Their jobs have been subject to compulsory competitive tendering in local government and to market testing and outsourcing in the NHS. This has resulted in reductions in public sector employment and cost reductions achieved at the expense of the wages and conditions of the workforce. Even where contracts have been retained in-house, managers have been required to control expenditure, monitor performance and introduce private sector management techniques. As a consequence, workload and staffing levels have become a particular source of grievance (Waddington and Whitston 1996: 173).

Nowhere has this process of work intensification been more evident than in cleaning work, where the increasing use of part-time and temporary staff, and increases in productivity without a corresponding reward have been the pattern (Escott and Whitfield 1995). The overall context in which cleaning teams operate in local government is one in which resources for the service have been cut to the minimum. The fact that our cleaning teams work in prestigious public buildings has sheltered them, to some extent, from the worst excesses of sub-contracting. At the same time, the impact of sub-contracting has had a highly gendered impact on jobs (Escott and Whitfield 1995; Munro 1999). Fewer contracts were let to private contractors in refuse collection – a predominantly male area of employment – compared to areas of predominantly female employment. The relative invisibility of cuts in women's part-time hours has been a factor in these developments (Munro 1999), while workers in refuse collection have greater capacity to organize to resist the threat of sub-contracting, given the public health hazards and high visibility of their strike activity (McBride 2001). Even so, the future of our refuse collectors was in question. Temporary contracts and the possibility of future redundancies lay outside the control of this workgroup and emphasized the fragility of its continuity, even though in the past, trade union resistance has acted as a brake on redundancies.

State-initiated reforms have also impacted on the secure care home, where the impact of the devaluation of a formal qualification, that of State Enrolled Nurse, was examined. The origin of this change was central NHS policy on nursing qualifications. Changes in the national regulatory framework for the nursing profession were implemented at local level by trust managers. The formal devaluation of the qualification was reinforced by moving staff on to lower pay scales and by restricting the range of work tasks they could perform. These dynamics had an impact on the motivation and willingness of staff to undertake conversion training and also on the extent to which primary nurses were prepared to take on the role of mentor. The NVQ programme certified staff competence in a way that was recognized by significant others in the community of practice and beyond, raising their status and giving them a sense of empowerment.[2] The devaluation of informal learning on the job and its replacement by a formal training programme was also in evidence among the fitters. Here, the formal qualifications of the younger workers had the effect of undermining the authority of older workers who had acquired their skills through a traditional form of apprenticeship training. Their bullying, joking and drawing attention to mistakes therefore served to undermine the confidence of younger workers.

Workgroups also need to be located in broader social and class divisions. Feminist writers have argued that both jobs and workers are gendered (e.g. Cockburn 1983; 1988) and this is true of other ascriptive attributes such as ethnicity and age. When workers enter the workplace they bring with them their status in society and in turn, the workplace is a significant site of socialization (Purcell 1989), providing workers with expectations about their access to learning and job mobility. In contrast to the relatively low status of the women cleaners, the fitters in the cleansing department represent a group of male skilled manual workers.

Supervisors and their subordinates may articulate their role in terms of teaching or training, but this instructional role is not the only source of the supervisor's status and power. Cleaning supervisors enjoy a degree of job autonomy, responsibility for organizing the work of others as well as a formal role in teaching the correct procedures and enforcing them. This gives them status in the workforce which is reinforced by wage differentials. However, supervisors have sources authority invested in them by the organization which do not relate to their role as experienced practitioners, but to their position as intermediaries, responsible to the employer for enforcing work discipline. Formal training programmes allow them to ensure that work practices are performed correctly but also have the role of reinforcing their own authority. Equally, there are sources of status which derive not from knowledgeable practice, but the ability of individuals and groups to create a position for themselves within a hierarchy. This may relate to the ability to control the more interesting work tasks and additional resources, and to work in locations or in relation to other communities of practice which attract status (cf. Munro 1999). The relative status of the cleaning teams derives from the prestigious public buildings they clean.

While learning through practice is important, it would be erroneous to dismiss the potential of formal learning to contribute to workers' own sense of empowerment and to their ability to improve their material conditions of work. Formal qualifications, whether acquired through the education system or through employer-sponsored training are significant in acting as filters to internal organizational labour markets. The absence of formal qualifications can be a criterion of exclusion from particular types of job, access to training and development opportunities and to opportunities for job progression. They can affect both managers' perceptions of employees' needs and employees' own expectations and aspirations (see Rainbird *et al.* 1999). In contrast, external recognition of skills, achieved informally or formally, provides workers with resources. Despite job uncertainty, the skills of the fitters were recognized in the external labour market and they did not anticipate problems In finding alternative employment. Equally, learning in formal learning environments can be experienced as personal growth and empowerment.

Conclusion

In this chapter we have tried to demonstrate that the social relations of production are significant for understanding workplace learning. Although the immediate workgroup is an important source of learning, the workgroup needs to be located in an understanding of power relations at work. The small workgroups analysed here have their own internal dynamics which affect individuals' access to learning and the ways in which formal learning is used to enforce discipline, to serve as a reward and, in some cases, to act as a motivator and build confidence. Nevertheless, these workers are not independent producers but are employed by large organizations. As public sector bodies, they are affected by the resources allocated to the provision of public services and the value that is placed on different kinds of skills and formal qualifications in the wage structure. These in turn affect the possibilities for, and constraints on, workplace learning and the extent to which different groups of workers can deploy their own resources to resist attacks on their jobs and on their skills.

In arguing that workplace learning needs to be located in an understanding of the employment relationship, we are not denying that training and development can be the subject of consensual decision-making. Indeed, training has been a classic arena for the development of corporatist arrangements, as Ashton demonstrates in his discussion of Germany in Chapter 2. In contrast to the German context, the UK is not characterized by consensus and social partnership on institutional training arrangements, nor is the employee voice on training present in the workplace, let alone in other aspects of the employment relationship. Rather, consensus and participation have to be constructed as a means for facilitating learning on the basis of recognizing the different and opposing interests of workers and employers, rather than taken as given.

Notes

1 'The Future of Unskilled Work: Learning and Workplace Inequality' was funded through the Economic and Social Research Council's 'Future of Work' programme during 1998/99 (ref. L212 25 2017). There were two major elements to the research: case studies of three local authorities and three hospital trusts, involving more than 330 face-to-face interviews and a survey of employees' learning experiences which produced a similar number of responses. In each case study interviews were conducted at a corporate level; with trade union representatives; with managers and trainers in particular departments; and with workers, their managers and supervisors in individual, often quite small, workplaces, which were part of these organizational structures. Officers of the trade union UNISON facilitated access to all six organizations which were chosen because they had established partnership agreements with the union on the provision of learning and development opportunities for low-paid workers (for example, Communications Skills and Return to Learn). The face-to-face interviews with workers and supervisors in the same workplace allowed the different sources of informal and formal learning to be examined. See Rainbird et al. (1999) 'The Future of Work in the Public Sector: Learning and Workplace Inequality', ESRC Future of Work Programme discussion paper No. 2, University of Leeds. These issues are being explored further in our current project on the influence of the regulatory framework of the employment relationship on workplace learning, which is one of five related research projects on the theme of 'Improving Incentives to Learning at Work'. This is funded under the ESRC's Teaching and Learning Research Programme (ref. L139 25 1005).

2 However, this is not always the case with NVQ assessment. We also encountered examples of staff who believed it was degrading and a waste of time (see Rainbird et al. 1999).

Bibliography

Ashton, D. (1998) 'Skill Formation: Redirecting the Research Agenda', in F. Coffield (ed.), *Learning at Work*, Bristol: Policy Press.

Braverman, H. (1974) *Labor and Monopoly Capital*, New York: Monthly Review Press.

Cockburn, C. (1983) *Brothers: Male Dominance and Technological Change*, London: Pluto Press.

—— (1988) 'The Gendering of Jobs: Workplace Relations and the Reproduction of Sex Segregation', in S. Walby (ed.), *Gender Segregation at Work*, Milton Keynes: Open University Press.

Edwards, P.K.E. (ed.) (1995) *Industrial Relations: Theory and Practice in Britain*, Oxford: Blackwell.

Eraut, M., Alderton, J., Cole, G. and Senker, P. (1998) 'Learning from Other People at Work', in F. Coffield (ed.), *Learning at Work*, Bristol: Policy Press.

Escott, K. and Whitfield, D. (1995) *The Gender Impact of CCT in Local Government*, Manchester: Equal Opportunities Commission.

Fox, A. (1966) *Industrial Sociology and Industrial Relations*, London: HMSO.

Heyes, J. (2000) 'Workplace Industrial Relations and Training', in H. Rainbird (ed.), *Training in the Workplace. Critical Perspectives on Learning at Work*, Basingstoke: Macmillan.

Hyman, R. (1978) 'Pluralism, Procedural Consensus and Conflictive Bargaining', *British Journal of Industrial Relations*, 16, 1: 16–40.

Lave, J. and Wenger, E. (1991) *Situated Learning: Legitimate Peripheral Participation*, Cambridge: Cambridge University Press.

Maurice, M., Sellier, F. and Silvestre, J.-J. (1986) *The Social Foundations of Industrial Power: A Comparison of France and Germany*, trans. of *Politiques d'Education et Organization Industrielle en France et en Allemagne*, Cambridge, MA and London: MIT Press.

McBride, A. (2001) *Making a Difference? Gender Democracy in Trade Unions*, Aldershot: Ashgate.

Munro, A. (1999) *Women. Work and Trade Unions*, London and New York: Mansell.

Purcell, K. (1989) 'Gender and the Experience of Employment', in D. Gallie (ed.), *Employment in Britain*, Oxford: Blackwell.

Rainbird, H., Munro, A., Holly, L. and Leisten, R. (1999) 'The Future of Work in the Public Sector: Learning and Workplace Inequality', Future of Work Programme discussion paper no. 2: University of Leeds.

Thompson, P. (1983) *The Nature of Work: An Introduction to Debates on the Labour Process*, Basingstoke: Macmillan.

Waddington, J. and Whitston, C. (1996) 'Empowerment versus Intensification: Union Perspectives of Change at the Workplace', in P. Ackers, C. Smith and P. Smith (eds), *The New Workplace and Trade Unionism: Critical Perspectives on Work and Organization*, London and New York: Routledge.

4 Work organization, 'fields of activities' and workers' competence

The case of Italian small firms

Saul Meghnagi

Chapter summary

The significance of workers' skills and knowledge to the competitiveness of Italian firms has been recognized. The Italian small firm sector is an interesting site to explore workers' competence because, despite the low level of formal qualifications held by the workforce, these organizations have a high level of production capacity and many operate in national and international markets. This chapter reports on a research project conducted for the Ente Bilaterale Nazionale dell'Artigianato (EBNA) the joint body of the small firms sector which examined the firms' organizational capacity and workers' competences, with a view to identifying training needs and occupational enhancement pathways. The author argues that training should aim to enhance the organizational capacity of firms and that workers' competence is made up of cognitive resources of different kinds. Competence is integral to workers' rights and the quality of the work environment. Its development can be fostered through participation in training and through experiences in the work environment which already have cognitive qualities and may be formative in themselves. The social partners have a role in collective bargaining and in joint bodies at different levels. These involve agreeing the conditions for defining and certifying knowledge and also for improving the quality of work, not only as a means of contributing to production but also as a condition for learning.

Introduction

In Italy, the knowledge, skills and competences of citizens and workers have been recognized as competitive factors for firms, local and national economies. This, in turn, has spurred processes aimed at reforming training systems, creating entirely new forms of collaboration between the social partners. The forms of this collaboration were laid down in collective agreements that, in the last decade, have increasingly focused on educational issues.[1] Without fail the core issue in both the analysis of these issues and in collective bargaining has been the mismatch between the production levels achieved and the educational level of the population and the workforce.

The low level of formal qualification of sections of the population is evident in data provided by the National Institute of Statistics (ISTAT). In 2000, 12.5 per cent of the workforce aged between 15 and 69 years – slightly under 3 million people – had only completed primary schooling. Whilst 36 per cent had achieved the certificate for completing eight years of compulsory education (Scuola Media Inferiore), only 8 per cent had a recognized vocational qualification. Moreover, these low levels of achievement are not restricted to older age groups. In the same year, just over 3 per cent of 20 to 24 year olds in the workforce had only completed primary schooling, 38 per cent the Scuola Media and under 10 per cent had a recognized vocational qualification. In other words approximately 48 per cent of the workforce had only obtained a Scuola Media diploma and had no recognized vocational qualification. The schooling level outlined above is a reflection of semi-illiteracy, understood as the capacity to write one's signature or a brief text but not to write a letter addressed to an office or to read a newspaper article and understand it. The lack of access, from the start, to a satisfactory level of language and mathematical skills is an index of socio-economic vulnerability. Early school leavers make less use of knowledge-acquisition opportunities that are available elsewhere. They do not watch highly cultured television programmes, they do not tune in on cultural programmes on the radio, they do not go to libraries or to the theatre, they do not participate in political or social debates. They also have difficulty in helping their children with their schoolwork, enabling them to improve on their parents' achievements.

The impact of educational disadvantage on life chances has been well researched (see Schwartz 1997; Gelpi 1997). The greatest risk factors derive from four specific forms of disadvantage. These are: going to a vocational school rather than a high school; restricted occupational and geographical mobility arising from poor qualifications; the difficulty of facing up to cut-throat competition with other people in the labour market; and the material and cultural disadvantage suffered from being confined to a degraded social environment. Sections of the population with a low level of formal education suffer different forms of disadvantage and they are also culturally ill equipped to improve their status. Generally speaking, there is a strong correlation between the amount and the quality of education received and occupational achievement. This does not only affect the skills that they can make use of in an occupational context but also has an increasing impact on their capacity to improve their level of training. This capacity is in turn associated with acquired knowledge that, among other things, would enable them to access information, use it for their own purposes and interact with the surrounding environment.

The Italian small firm sector is an interesting site in which to explore workers' competence because, despite employees' low level of formal schooling, there is a high level of production capacity. The firms operate in national and international markets and a high level of worker competence is found throughout the system of firms in this sector. This makes it particularly interesting to understand the characteristics and the nature of the knowledge that is largely acquired through practice, on the job and developed into high levels of occupational ability. The term 'small firm' is used to indicate the enterprises called in Italian *imprese artigiane*, since the literal translation 'art and craft firms' would be incorrect. In Italy, *imprese artigiane* are regulated by Law 445 of the 8 August 1995, which describes them as those enterprises in which the entrepreneur participates manually as well as otherwise in the production process or in providing the service. The Commissione Provinciale dell'Artigianato (Provincial Commission for Arts and Crafts – literally) performs a public check to verify the existence of this condition which, once ascertained, allows the firm to be enrolled in the registry of *imprese artigiane*. This registration amounts to an incorporation giving rise to constraints and access to subsidies. The number of employees working for an *impresa artigiana* can vary from sector to sector but, in general, does not exceed 20 although in some firms (for example in those with a more art-oriented production) this number is often higher.

The nature of skills and knowledge acquired through practice was the focus of a research project carried out as part of a nationwide survey of training by the national joint representation agency for the craft sector (EBNA).[2] This was a longitudinal study divided into three different phases: a first phase in which the research project was prepared, the literature was reviewed and the project was defined in terms of the fieldwork to be carried out. The second phase of fieldwork involved multidisciplinary scenarios based on interviews with decision-makers and experts and a research approach based on the analysis of occupational profiles. The third phase involved the development of joint work by the social partners.

This chapter is divided into four sections. The first discusses the theoretical framework and methodology adopted. The second discusses the significance of organizational context to the development of skills and knowledge. The third examines how competences were identified and occupational enhancement pathways developed and discusses how the concept of 'fields of activities' contributed to competence development. This is followed by a conclusion.

The theoretical framework and the concept of competence adopted

The concept of competence which informed the research depends on a multitude of factors connected to the actions performed in the training system, on the job, within the social context and that are related to the duration and the location of one or more activities. Competence can also be defined in terms of the degree of autonomy and innovation that these activities allow, the range of ways of performing a given task, the model of authority and the assignment of duties, whether formally established or assumed. It can also be described by referring to a single performance, the skill in performing a given task, the abilities recognized by others or the knowledge acquired and certified by a diploma. It can further be clarified by referring to the larger or smaller amount of resources relied upon to produce results in terms of either material or immaterial goods.

Research on knowledge acquisition processes shows how different information processing approaches develop and make it possible to specify diverse but interrelated phases of knowledge transformation, reduction, storage and recovery (see Meghnagi 1992; Ajello and Meghnagi 1998). It also outlines the means of implementing complex cognitive activities such as understanding, remembering, reasoning and problem-solving. It describes forms and operational options aimed at enhancing and fine-tuning these activities.

Individual cognitive processes are the outcome of mental activities in which individuals reconstruct and re-elaborate their particular relationship with the context in which they live (Engeström et al. 1995). This involves certain values, ways of being and reasoning that arise from economic and social realities, the characteristics of gender and class as well as linguistic, ethnic, demographic and generational differences. A culture-sensitive transmission issuing from individual transformation and elaboration processes contributes to differentiating, on an individual basis, the form in which subjects or issues are perceived in relation to individual past experience. This leads to heterogeneity in the forms of accessing knowledge and developing abilities. The acquisition of knowledge occurs in any social situation in which one acquires more or less formalized knowledge, competence and abilities according to a pre-established learning process (Resnick and Wirth 1996). In essence, knowledge is not the outcome of a mechanical accumulation process in which contents are deliberately transmitted to and received by an individual who has decided to learn something new. It is more the outcome of a complex crossing of pathways that, for it to be understood, life and work contexts must be taken as the unstructured source of acquired and processed knowledge and experience. This gives rise to the complexity of the relationship that exists between structured knowledge and life experiences. It is difficult to explain how a given knowledge content can be appropriately acquired without first understanding how other externally provided contents have been organized into a perceptive and cognitive pattern, affecting behaviour, knowledge and values.

Knowledge and cognitive development interact on the basis of the experience drawn from different contexts that facilitates the association between what is new and what one already knows. This occurs through cognitive processing techniques that depend, among other things, on the frame of reference used by the individual who attributes significance to the contents of the experience. Following this reasoning through, competence may be defined as the outcome of a cognitive pathway based on the processing of the experience accumulated in a given work context, in a specific market or organization and in a given society, with all the cultural characterizations that typify it.

In actual fact, competence is always contextualized, being therefore 'situated knowledge', a form of expertise in which assertive knowledge is highly procedural and automatic and in which heuristic efforts pool together to solve very specific problems. This formal definition allows us to examine the details of a wide range of levels of competence and also to consider their relative implications in order to understand how it is acquired and how it functions, differentiating between individual levels of knowledge and the effectiveness of any action referred to. Non-experts and experts have a different way of organizing knowledge: for the former, problem-solving is organized mainly through trial and error. For the latter, it entails an assertive knowledge based on concepts and contents as well as a procedural knowledge that prevents them from resorting to more general norms in problem-solving exercises. This enables experts to control their solution-finding process, by turning back and stopping to reconsider and perhaps change what was previously done if it is no longer consistent with what is done subsequently. On extending this view even further, we could say that the difference does not only lie in the presence or absence of concepts that are necessary for the problem-solving exercise but rather in the different way in which these are organized or put into a procedure.

People reprocess the information that they receive from the environment and reorganize it into broader assumptions and into an orderly transmission-acquisition process by relying on strategies that are not always identifiable or predictable (Leinhardt et al. 1995). This makes work context situations particularly relevant in cognitive growth and the development of knowledge demand.

Moreover, individuals observe, remember, act and react to the surrounding reality by filtering and screening incoming information through their sense organs, thus constructing notions and images. This process, that is unquestionably highly personalized, does not depart from definitions and representations that are significantly shared by a fair proportion of community members and that direct the processing of information and the construction of ideas. The cognitive process is a way of continuously addressing empirical data that are acquired from a variety of sources in the course of a complex knowledge acquisition process.

The representations used to introduce new perceptions, images and information in an organized framework of ideas and judgements about reality, make it possible to convert them from unknown to partially known. In any case, they are controllable in terms of how they are integrated in a comprehensive framework of knowledge and understanding (see Gherardi 1998). In this process, a significant role is played by memory and past experiences.

The representations are constructed in a way as to make customary what is not in order to be able to master it and integrate it in a mental universe that is thus enriched and transformed. Human activity involves attributing meaning to the moment of contact with reality. The crucial point of these meaning-attribution processes is that they are expected to condition what we do, what we think and what we feel. This applies to every single individual, to those who study them and to every meaning-attribution activity. We all act on the basis of what is meaningful for us and what we deem to be important. It is possible to claim that certain meaning-attribution procedures are better or more reliable than others and, within a given range, they are. But there are no universal standards on the basis of which to attribute valid meanings in every context. In summary, every cognitive act should be seen as a specific response to a set of specific circumstances. Learning should be considered as a socially situated activity within the context of a particular practical situation (Brown *et al.* 1989; Lave and Wenger 1991; Pontecorvo *et al.* 1995).

This theoretical framework informed the survey of training needs in the small firm sector. The preparatory phase involved an analysis of studies on the small firm sector, including policy documents produced by the social partners and the definition of all the issues in collective agreements that might in some way be associated with knowledge and training. It also included a review of the literature on competence, with special focus on what might be directly or indirectly related to the reality of small firms.[3] In the second phase, the survey aimed to map the small enterprises in the sectors identified and create the conditions for a permanent monitoring system. It also aimed to identify the organizational context in and between sectors by means of a description of corporate activities and individual tasks in different situations and to validate the analytical models. These were referred to as the 'structural analysis' and the 'organizational context analysis'. Finally the research aimed to define the tasks relative to specific competences and to study the pathways through which these were achieved by identifying minimum constituent units, possible sources of acquisition, mandatory learning pathways, and the possibility of formalizing results and processes. This was referred to as the 'analysis of competences and occupational enhancement pathways'.

The significance of organizational contexts

The structural analysis

The structural analysis analysed competences in small firms on the basis of their socio-economic conditions, their products and production processes, and the nature of their markets and regional locations. Consequently, the analysis had the dual target of giving an indepth and detailed description of the characteristics of the small firm sector which are often omitted in statistical surveys. It identified a typology of small firms, based on their production system and the knowledge that was specific to it. This was the approach taken to make an initial outline of competences by analysing the 'capacity' of the system rather than of the workers. This analysis contributed to overcoming the shortcomings of national statistics as far as small firms are concerned.

To conduct the structural analysis, 11,000 enterprises were contacted. Of these, 10,240 agreed to participate in a telephone interview. The enterprises were located in 19 regions and were engaged in 11 sectors of activity. The variables examined included the economic and market trends affecting the enterprise, problems encountered and the employment structure of the enterprise as well as the occupational profile of the entrepreneur. The results provided a panoramic overview of the small firm sector in Italy.

A classification system was developed based on organization characteristics, whereby companies were separated into two principle categories. These were enterprises that work on their own account and those that work on a sub-contract basis. Within each category, four variables were identified: the capacity to design projects autonomously; the capacity to realize the finished product; the capacity to sell under its own trademark; the capacity to sell in markets larger than local markets.

The identification of this typology makes it possible to plan for training activities in relation to the companies' local needs, development strategies and the amount of investment allocated. In the light of this information, the training needs can be defined in terms of skills found in the firms, whether they are used or not, and those which are lacking and can result in the enhancement of the firm's organizational capacity. For example in the textile industry in Puglia, enterprises work on a sub-contract basis at a high level specification, but not under their own trademark. Therefore training needs to be related to the enterprises' ability to sell under its own trademark and to sell beyond the local labour market. These needs do not necessarily reflect on the skills of the workers' employed in the firm.

The 'organizational context analysis'

The second stage of the study focused on case studies of firms in six sectors: in mechanical engineering; textiles, clothing and footwear; food; carpentry and furniture; construction and ceramics. The analysis of organizational contexts took the study of competences further by establishing a connection between the socio-economic system of the sector in different fields of activity and the characteristics of the production process. This made it possible to identify a set of correlations between the production system and the workers operating in it, taking into account aggregate data relative to the firm and its workforce.

The case study analysis made it possible to further develop the typology resulting from the survey research. The analysis of organizational contexts was carried out on the basis of 64 company case studies. The methodology involved a questionnaire, semi-structured interviews, direct observation and indirect data and information collection as well as different analytical techniques. This included the reconstruction of the company history, the analysis of critical incidents and the direct observation of work activities. The occupational competence of operators and workers in a small firm could be effectively described by taking into consideration three separate types of knowledge (conventionally defined as exclusive, contextual and connotative) that could in turn be subdivided into job-related competence and organizational competence.

'Exclusive knowledge' refers to knowledge that belongs to the heritage individuals and is associated with their personal history. 'Contextual knowledge' refers to knowledge that belongs to the heritage of the individual, incorporated in a given context (and therefore context-bound). It is pervasive although entirely or partly 'silent'. 'Connotative knowledge' refers to knowledge that can be identified, deciphered and socialized. This exclusively applies to, and is typical of, a given trade or profession and is defined as such in terms of its essential knowledge requirements. 'Job-related competence' refers to a competence associated with the production process, with sector-specific technologies and with the product (and the relative product mix). 'Corporate competence' refers to a competence that is closely associated with corporate implementation activities. It is of a management and organizational nature. It therefore refers to variables associated with the presence in the market, management and administrative capacities, the organizational and inter-organizational composition of labour in the firm. These variables are interrelated and cross-referenced in the definition of the characteristics of competence.

A fourth area of knowledge to be specified by the study concerns the sets of knowledge associated with one's nature, value systems, personal and professional behaviour that determine the *credibilità professionale* (professional credibility) of the firm in respect of the social system to which it belongs. This refers to the organization's reputation in relation to banks, customers, suppliers and insurance companies.

There is no hierarchical relationship between knowledge and competence, which are interlinked to a varying degree in any work activity. Furthermore, despite the fact that it is a component part of any given occupational profile, there are areas of competence that can apply to a range of different profiles. The analysis of organizational contexts makes it possible to identify the characteristics of competence in this sector. In this case, they prove to be associated with the firms and not with the individuals and they serve as the basis on which to plan training which is better targeted to objectives and priorities.

Identifying competences and occupational enhancement pathways

The analysis of competences and of occupational enhancement pathways was developed by establishing a connection between the socio-economic context of small firms in different sectors, the characteristics of their organization, management and workforce. Attention was focused on the knowledge described by the representatives of the social partners, and the employees and entrepreneurs themselves.

The analysis of competences and of occupational enhancement pathways was carried out by reconstructing the occupational histories of 461 entrepreneurs and/or workers in small firms belonging to the six sectors in which the case studies were conducted. Profiles were analysed through an exchange of ideas between the representatives of the social partners in a workshop situation. This was fine-tuned by asking participants to describe, out of a list of items, the characteristics of each sector in relation to their structural, production, organizational and occupational characteristics. The information acquired allowed us to link the quantitative and the qualitative phases of the research. This work also produced hypotheses for the subsequent survey and served to describe the way in which the occupational competence of small firm workers is expressed and developed. This phase of the research aimed at establishing the distinctive features of competences and at identifying occupational enhancement pathways in the small firm sector.

The analysis was based on the diagnosis of competences and the reconstruction of the occupational pathways followed by individuals through a review of their careers, a detailed account of their work and by stimulating their occupational self-assessment. The researchers identified a unit of analysis which served as a grid for individual workers and entrepreneurs in the small firms sector. We formulated a model for the analysis of findings, which allowed us to diagnose competence areas relating to different types of activity for each of the sectors under scrutiny. In the light of our findings we were able to redefine the concept of competence and to confirm the definition given when the research was set up: an undivided complex of knowledge, abilities, ideas and ways of doing things that make it possible to carry out an occupation. As a result of our study we also found that connotative competence (i.e. knowledge that can be identified, deciphered and socialized) does not form an exceptional part of competence, nor is it specifically linked to a specific geographical area or company. In essence, this phase of the research allowed us to experimentally test a model for the diagnosis of occupational competence and occupational enhancement pathways.

The data analysis consisted of the observations made by small firm workers during interviews in response to the issues raised by researchers. Therefore, we dealt with information, ideas, remarks collected in a relational situation. The interview methodology allowed researchers to survey both the specific features of each situation and all the elements necessary for the subsequent systematization of the material collected. The activity of the interviewers was monitored to correct possible distortions.

The study of interview reports allowed the data to be classified into four categories of information. Personal experiences were treated analytically with reference to the individual person and synthetically with reference to the common features of a group of people. Both levels were essential to the aims of this phase of the investigation. Analysing the detail makes it possible to compare both the situation of people who work at the same level within a certain sector and people who operate within the same organizational environment. In our analysis, and for workers at both levels, we were able to consider the influence exercised by individual biography (gender, age, level of education) and those determined by the company where they work (size of the company and its position in the production process). In turn the synthesis allowed us to move from the particular to the general and to devise typologies for ways of working and competences.

A model for the diagnosis of competences was devised to systematize and interpret the data. The categories were: actions performed by individuals; activities consisting of a series of actions; identification of fields of activity; identification of areas of connotative competence within each field of activity. The reconstruction of the social, cultural and cognitive context of small firm workers represents the scenario in which to introduce further information. This reconstruction fundamentally used two techniques for the analysis of qualitative data which are not mutually exclusive: the analysis of the content of interview reports and the identification of 'key words' and the definition given to them by different actors. Given the interdisciplinary nature of the approach, in this phase of the research, the application of the analytical techniques called for further methodological consideration and produced specific interpretation procedures.

On the basis of the results of these analyses a number of cross-sectional issues were identified, which seem pivotal in ascertaining the vision of the world shared by both the workers and the entrepreneurs of the small firms sector. As is customary for any investigation using qualitative methods, particular significance was attached to the identification of basic units (actions, activities, fields of activity, areas of competence) as a starting point to develop the analysis in all its parts. Overall, the investigation model developed utilizing the following categories of analysis and fine-tuning their conceptual formalization. The categories of analysis are shown in Box 4.1.

The research showed that those activities carried out with the contribution of several workers cannot be encompassed by a single occupational profile and that the ability to act in different phases of production cannot be explained by technical abilities alone. If operators work with different types of machine, besides their normal work and, when necessary, carry out the tasks usually performed by others, this is explained by the fact that in small firms work is carried out according to 'fields of activity'. This is shared out socially, so that several workers contribute to the creation of a common product.

The concept of a 'field of activity' is therefore better at explaining reality than other concepts such as that of occupational profile, task or role. This is because it conveys the greater versatility of specializations in the work carried out in small firms. It also allows the complexity of the work of the

Box 4.1 Model of investigation

Reference occupational profiles
These are the profiles identified by social partners in the workshop phase. They reflect their perception of the organization of labour and of the breakdown of activities.

Company occupational profiles
These are the profiles that are actually present in companies. They reflect the interviewees' perceptions of their own positions and tasks.

Actions
These represent the conscious and intentional way in which a task, explicitly or implicitly given to an individual, is interpreted.

Activities
These are aggregations of actions built around the segment of the production cycle in question.

Fields of activities
These are aggregations, which group together activities aimed at reaching the same production goal regardless of the possible break-down of the connected activities among several people. They have a mobile boundary since this is not defined once and for all and cannot be linked exclusively to a segment of the production cycle.

Connotative competences
These are the competences that characterize the action of individuals within a certain field of activity regardless of their position in the hierarchy. The concept of connotative competence is not based on a distinction between basic and specialized competences, since it assumes that within the same context it is possible to catalogue experiences linked to differing levels of experience, to differing levels of formalized knowledge and which are given different hierarchical status.

workforce in small firms to be interpreted. This almost always covers several fields of activity and underlines how difficult it is to encompass the representation of the work and occupational knowledge of small firm operators in a single dimension. It allows researchers to diagnose the critical features and the possibilities for evolution of competences in small firm sectors and suggests pathways for the enhancement of occupational competences through intentional and targeted training actions aimed at modernizing the sector.

In order to do this, a 'field of activity' can aggregate different types of activities and actions. It can group together activities of different natures and the actions of people who operate at different levels and contribute in different ways through their different responsibilities and specializations to the pursuit of the same objective. It can be limited in its boundaries in relation to the targets established for a series of actions – rarely in a formalized way but always in actual practice – by company organizational strategy. It can take on a 'moving' boundary because the field is not established once and for all and cannot be connected exclusively to a segment of the production cycle. Indeed, it has different confines depending on the specific features of the sector and of the activities and actions linked together.

In the light of the subdivision into actions, activities and fields of activity the model suggests a diagnosis of 'connotative competences' which, as underlined in the definition given above, characterize the actions of an individual within a certain field of activity. These are the premises for the analysis of the specific elements that feature in the competences of small firms, as studied in specific sectors and expressed in a different way in the various realities, sectoral or regional, under examination.

The investigation allowed researchers to make a clear distinction between reference occupational profiles, defined by the social partners, and company profiles. Job content and the skills required to do a job are contested. Indeed, in describing their job, interviewees defined it in a way which, at times, did not match the definitions worked out by the experts of the social partners. The research has taken this difference – derived from different perceptions of the same reality – as a benchmark. The gap points to both the specific characteristics of work in the small firms sector and to possible generalizations. Interviewees were then classified on the basis of their self-definition (company occupational profile) and, whenever possible, this definition was juxtaposed to the one expressed by social partners (reference occupational profile). This comparison represents a first result of the research.

The problem of what to put under scrutiny was resolved by deciding to devote specific attention to the detailed description made by workers of their job, to identify the individual actions performed and to place them within fields of activity. The concept of 'action' includes the operations carried out by individuals, the procedures used, the objectives pursued and presupposes that the actions themselves represent conscious and intentional ways of interpreting the task given, explicitly or implicitly, by the individual worker. The concept of 'activity' refers to the production cycle segments under examination.

The result of this methodological approach to the analysis of data was the creation of a grid showing the reference occupational profiles and the company occupational profiles used during the interviews on the basis of which actions and activities were indicated. This first grid produced a second that defined fields of activity and their relative competences and followed the form outlined above.

The definition and description of company occupational profiles was followed by a redefinition of the reference occupational profiles worked out by social partners. These were adopted with the aim of applying them in different contexts at a later stage (from training to labour market interventions) according to a constant feedback mechanism. In the small firm sector each occupational profile consists of areas of competence that include knowledge and abilities of different kinds, so that each worker is different from the other although they may be placed within the same occupational category. As members of the same category this includes areas of competence which overlap only partially. The area of competence shared by different profiles is the connotative part of the profile which is built by integrating areas that differ from individual to individual. Consequently, the profile cannot be decoded and described in its entirety because it consists of a theoretically infinite variety of combinations of different items of knowledge and experiences, with a minimal common foundation for the same category. This involves practitioners in co-determination practices and on to research activities and then back to research and then co-determination, as is necessary to achieve joint operational objectives.

Conclusion

Knowledge of a theoretical and practical nature which is inherent in any competence can be validated by the social partners through the process of social dialogue, as we have shown through this discussion of our research on the small firms sector. This applies to formal education and to job-related training and experience.

The definition of competences must lead to different forms of validation (De Mauro 2000). If certification is not founded on the assumption of a hierarchy between the different parts of the system, it should envisage the possibility of recognizing acquired credits in one part of the system as useful in another. This is not because they may have equal weight in terms of content but because of the equal standing attributed to different competences. The validation of acquired knowledge cannot be based exclusively on objectively determinable skills since a competence expressed in one context may not be exploitable in another. This is because not all performances are measurable and because skills can be recognized and evaluated on the basis of an experience of a certain duration and not over a short time-span.

In addition, the validation of work experiences necessarily entails that these are defined with a view to formal certification. Competence is linked to the carrying out of activities aimed at reaching an objective. It can be described by identifying interconnected skills which do not necessarily coincide with the content of knowledge, nor with knowledge acquired through education. In fact, competence is the demonstration of cognitive resources of different kinds which govern the processes of performing actions and making decisions.

Workers' rights (*tutela* in Italian) are not just defined by their formal legal entitlements and as a result of trade union action, but also by the quality of the work environment. Indeed, Trentin (2001) argues that training is a fundamental condition for workers' protection. If competence is the outcome of the knowledge possessed and the application of this knowledge to activities aimed at reaching an objective, we need to define the characteristics of experiences. Consequently the problem is to be able to appreciate a competence which is made up of knowledge acquired through education and informal learning processes undertaken at different times and in different places. It is also linked to a code of practice which may direct the workers' attention towards innovation, membership of a work community and to knowledge achieved in the field. For this reason, the quality of experiences appears decisive and a clear distinction can be made between work experiences that are useful as experiences, placement experiences aimed at getting to know and testing out practical aspects of a job or occupation, and apprenticeship experiences which lead to a qualification. Furthermore, the whole range of training opportunities is also important in non-standard forms of work which are not covered by collective bargaining (Braga 2000). Here, experiences can vary and take place at different moments in time.

Concerning these issues, research is ongoing on the need to operate on the basis of social partnership (Guarriello 2000; Rainbird 2000; Ranieri 2001; Jobert 2001). Where the social partners are engaged in the definition of occupational qualifications and in their formal recognition in collective agreements, they have to confront the problem of competences acquired outside work and outside the educational system. In this overall context, validation must be considered in relation to the objectives it pursues, to the possible use of this certification, to the adjudicating body and to the validity of the knowledge acquired. This is why it is essential not to consider occupational competence in isolation from social competence and from work-related knowledge which is closely connected to the organizational context where it is expressed and developed (Cevoli 2001). These are the issues social partners are called upon to tackle at different levels and, in particular, the rules for certification.

In order to ensure the social and occupational integration of workers as well as their future job mobility a number of conditions are necessary. First, there must be formal possibilities for the recognition of competences on the basis of shared definitions. This is the main aim of the investigations on training needs suggested by collective agreements and partly undertaken by joint-representation agencies (such as EBNA). These investigations should identify the characteristics of occupational profiles, fields of activities and competences in relation to the different sectors and production contexts. Second, the research demonstrates that it is not possible to describe, foresee, order and plan all the elements contributing to competence, which are acquired in different ways. This is why certification will take place only if agreements are reached between social partners and between them and other institutions. In this way certification will be based on elements that can be verified objectively and which will have been acquired following study and work experiences. Third, all this allows us to affirm that processes of labour mobility can be fostered by training not only because the workers attend training courses but also because their work experiences already had cognitive qualities and were formative in themselves. This is the foundation for planning of job mobility that can be supported by training, in agreement with the social partners who will have contributed to the creation of the process itself.

Because of these reasons, the role of social partners is extremely significant and complex. There are many co-determination and bargaining levels and not all of them belong to the main ones highlighted here. These include the establishment of common conditions for the definition and certification of knowledge, wherever acquired, through rigorous co-determination practices. They also extend to the improvement of the quality of work as useful not only for production, but as a condition to learn.

This is the ground for both dialogue and confrontation, both of which are necessary for a positive evolution of the overall framework. Social representations and notions, in addition to reflecting different opinions and sensitivities, characterize the constant dialectics between continuity and innovation, linked to the history and memory of individuals and groups. These are the supporting elements of our culture, our way of life and our way of accessing knowledge. We can describe relations between social partners at the present moment by using a metaphor drawn, not by accident, from studies on expertise. In order to describe competence these studies utilize a seldom-used distinction between routine expertise, characterized by speed, accuracy and automatism, but which is only relatively adjustable to new situations. In contrast, adaptive expertise is more flexible and, above all, based on a greater understanding of the context and situation in which the action is performed. This distinction is relevant because it introduces a cultural dimension to the discourse, and considers not only efficiency but also the ability to understand and interpret the meaning of the processes underway. This does not mean ignoring efficiency and specialization, but rather to make them relative vis-à-vis the definition of objectives, the representation of reality in the present and in the future and the consequent hypotheses aimed at changing it.

It appears essential that training experiences connected to work should not be defined in relation to a particular job or trivialized by affirming that the growth of general knowledge, per se, will help workers consolidate their occupational abilities. On the contrary, this experience should be developed by investigating, through negotiation, possible forms of promoting workers' cognitive and professional abilities beyond the specific context in which they are applied, and in relation to the civil and democratic growth of the individual and of the organizations in which they work.

Notes

1   A number of collective agreements in the 1990s were aimed at orienting reform of the Italian educational system. These included the Agreement on Incomes Policies in 1993; the Agreement on Labour in 1996; and the Social Pact for Development and Employment in 1998. Reform of the educational system was implicit in the first two agreements, which privileged macro-economic aspects of the labour market, and explicit in the third, where reference to training is ample and detailed. These agreements set the guidelines for a number of legal provisions and agreements aimed at regulating the labour market and training.

2   The National Survey on the Training Needs of the Small Firms Sector was promoted by the Ente Bilaterale Nazionale dell'Artigianato (EBNA – the Joint Agency of the Crafts Sector) and was supported by the Ministry of Health and of Social Security. It was conducted under the guidance of a management team, made up of Dario Bianconi and Marida Cevoli; with three co-ordinators: Sebastiano Brusco for the structural analysis; Michele Rosa for the analysis of the organizational contexts; and Anna Maria Ajello for the analysis of the competences and professional enhancement pathways. Giovanna de Lucia was the organization leader and Saul Meghnagi was the scientific manager. The outcomes of the first three years of research have been published by EBNA and the Ministry of Labour and Social Security as *Indagine Nazionale sui Fabbisogni Formativi nell'Artigianato* (2000). This is a boxed collection containing the volumes of the preliminary national and regional results.

3   The preliminary phase is outlined in two research reports: EBNA a and b (1998) *Indagine Nazionale sui Fabbisogni Formativi nell'Artigianato. Indagine di Sfondo. Le Caratteristiche del Comparto*, Volume 1, Rome, and EBNA (1998) *Indagine Nazionale sui Fabbisogni Formativi nell'Artigianato. Indagine di Sfondo. Gli Studi Sulla Competenza*, Volume, 2, Rome.

Bibliography

Ajello, A. and Meghnagi, S. (eds) (1998) *La Competenza tra Flessibilità e Specializzazione*, Bologna: Il Mulino.

Braga, A. (2000) 'Domande individuali e identità collettiva nel lavoro atipico', *Quaderni di Rassegna Sindacale*, 3: 161–84.

Brown, J.S., Collins, A. and Duguld, P. (1989) 'Situated cognition and the culture of learning', *Educational Researcher*, 18: 32–42.

Cevoli, M. (2001) 'Organizzazione e diagnosi delle competenze', *Quaderni di Rassegna Sindacale*, 2: 65–75.

Chi, M.T.H., Glaser, R. and Farr, M.J. (eds) (1988) *The Nature of Expertise*, Hillsdale, NJ: Lawrence Erlbaum.

Cole, M., Engeström, Y. and Vasquez, O. (1997) *Mind, Culture, and Activity*, Cambridge: Cambridge University Press.

De Mauro, T. (2000) 'Un nuovo percorso di studi da realizzare con il contributo di tutti', *Annali della Pubblica Istruzione*, 3–4: 3–8.

Engeström, Y., Engeström, R. and Karkkainen, M. (1995) 'Polycontextuality and Boundary Crossing in Expert Cognition in Complex Work Activities', *Learning and Instruction*, 5: 319–36.

Gelpi, E. (1997) *Éducation des Adultes. Inclusion et Exclusion*, Rennes: Atopies.

Gherardi, S. (1998) 'Competence – the Symbolic Passe-partout to Change in a Learning Organization', *Scandinavian Journal of Management*, 4: 373–93.

Guarriello, F. (2000) *Trasformazioni Organizzative e Contratto di Lavoro*, Naples: Jovene Editore.

Jobert, A. (2001) 'Negoziare la formazione professionale: la posta in gioco per i sindacati francesi', *Quaderni di Rassegna Sindacale*, 2: 101–14.

Lave, J. and Wenger, E. (1991) *Situated Learning: Legitimate Peripheral Participation*, Cambridge: Cambridge University Press.

Leinhardt, G., McCarthy Young, K. and Merriman, J. (1995) 'Integrating Professional Knowledge: The Theory of Practice and the Practice of Theory', *Learning and Instruction*, 5: 401–8.

Meghnagi, S. (1992) *Conoscenza e Competenza*, Turin: Loescher.

Pontecorvo, C., Ajello, A.M. and Zucchermaglio, C. (eds) (1995) *I Contesti Sociali dell'Apprendimento*, Milan: LED.

Rainbird, H. (ed.) (2000) *Training in the Workplace*, Basingstoke: Macmillan.

Ranieri, A. (2001) 'L'obbligo formativo come politica del lavoro', *Quaderni di Rassegna Sindacale*, 2: 77–84.

Resnick, L.B. and Wirth, J.G. (1996) *Linking School and Work*, San Francisco, CA: Jossey-Bass.

Schwartz, B. (1997) *Modernizzare Senza Escludere*, Rome: Anicia (original edition 1995).

Trentin, B. (2001) 'Ripartire dal-lavoro che pensa', Mimeo, DS Party, Rome.

5 The context of learning in professional work environments

Insights from the accountancy profession

Keith Hoskin and Fiona Anderson-Gough

Chapter summary

Any understanding of the learning that takes place in a professional work environment demands a focus on aspects of learning that are often dichotomized: formal and informal, theory and practice. Indeed one of the central challenges facing all those involved in developing understandings of workplace learning is that of conceptualizing how these aspects of learning actually come together within the experience of the learners. This chapter outlines key aspects of our research into the accountancy profession which aims, amongst other things, to assist in the re-engineering of the learning experience within accountancy, into something more 'integrative'. We believe a focus on context, power and perspective, within an understanding of the 'disciplinary ways of being' at the heart of modern learning, is fundamental to understandings of learning and also to the process of change management within education and training. We offer an analysis of our template for change within education and training in the accountancy profession framed within a discussion of those aspects of context, power and perspective salient in this case.

Introduction – the professional work environment

The three key terms, 'context, power and perspective', can, we suggest here, be seen as a potential trinity of terms for enabling and enacting change in attainment. We see them functioning as a set of relational terms, together raising important questions that need to be asked together, if we are to begin dealing more adequately with the issue of attainment and how it may potentially be improved, whether in general or in the workplace in particular. Context, power and perspective interplay in ways that frame and limit attempts to develop more effective forms of attainment. In our view some such reflection is helpful at this more general level, if we are to understand the potential for learning change, even in professional fields such as accountancy where considerable resources are devoted to providing training, both to pass the professional examinations and to develop skills in the workplace.

Here we wish to propose that the interplay of context, power and perspective is historically grounded, in the sense that there is a historically given frame within which such interplays work themselves out in contemporary learning contexts. The specific nature of the interplays will vary, and not everything that we will find occurring in the elite professional context of accountancy will play out in similar ways elsewhere. Nevertheless, we consider it helpful to reflect upon the extent to which the past is embedded in the present, in looking to develop ways of enabling attainment that will be effective over the medium to long term. Ignoring the influence of the past too easily allows its influence to continue undisturbed.

We see this as having a significance for the changes being currently attempted in the accountancy field. There is a real sense in which a 'transdisciplinary' imperative has been adopted in developing attempts to re-think and re-configure attainment. There have been projects to develop less rote and technically focused approaches to teaching accounting knowledge, both in academic and professional contexts (though with the more experimental or adventurous attempts generally being small-scale and in the academic arena). There have also been a number of larger-scale initiatives launched by professional institutes, which are designed to implement more integrative forms of professional training, and promote a more contextually and critically aware understanding of accounting in its business and professional contexts.

As one sign of these changing times we would draw attention to a significant change in nomenclature that has been adopted by the Institute of Chartered Accountants in England and Wales (hereafter ICAEW) in talking about training. The object (or subject) of that training is no longer defined as 'the Accountant' but instead as 'the Added-Value Business Advisor'. This name change perhaps brings home how far perspectives have begun to shift at the professional level towards a view that sees accountancy as requiring more than just the possession of requisite skills in the technical discipline. Even if these remain a necessary condition for being a successful professional, they are far short of sufficient. Instead, the new professional must be 'transdisciplinary' in the sense of grafting other business disciplines and skills onto an accountancy base. Arguably this kind of shift is taking place in other 'knowledge professions' as well, in law and consultancy for instance.

To address these issues this chapter is divided into five main sections. In the first two sections we review how learning in the accountancy field is changing in some general ways and outline the experiences of two initiatives in the USA. In the third section we reflect on context, power and perspective in relation to integrative learning. In the fourth we discuss how we are attempting, via an action research approach, to contribute to enabling more effective attainment across the trainee learning experience, both in the workplace and in undergoing the professional qualification process. In the final section we conclude by outlining some implications for workplace learning.

On becoming a professional: from disciplinarity to transdisciplinarity?

In all that follows we take it as a given that the professions, of which accountancy is one, are explicitly structured and focused to produce 'experts'. This follows from their history, wherein expert knowledge has been at the heart of their practice since the first emergence of professions beginning in the medieval university world. It is apparent that the so-called 'old professions' – teaching, law, medicine and the church – were initially developed by the graduates of the first universities (Parsons 1968; Hoskin 1986). Furthermore the key practices that define and constitute a field as a profession are themselves derived from that university world. As sociologists such as Goldstein (1984) have pointed out, these boil down to three or perhaps four: (1) defining a distinct field of expert knowledge; (2) developing a system of examinations to test for attainment and regulate entry; (3) obtaining a licence from an external authority, usually the state, sanctioning the right to practise as a profession; and (4) some form of ethics or service ideal.

Historically the conjunction between the development of the university and the emergence of the professions is striking. The medieval universities were the first educational institutions to develop a system of formal examining leading to the award of some externally sanctioned qualification (Cobban 1975).[1] Their graduates then translated the practices involved in that new educational regime to the purpose of forming themselves into 'professional bodies'. In so doing, they ensured an inevitable engagement with what we may define as 'disciplinary' practices in the process of becoming a professional.

These practices are disciplinary in two related but distinct senses. First they involve a close study of some form of specialist expertise, grounded in some kind of academic 'discipline'. Second, that disciplinary expertise has to be proven through submitting to the pedagogic 'discipline' of studying for and passing through the examining and credentialing processes. Professional attainment, like schooled learning, therefore requires an immersion in a doubly disciplinary world, where disciplinary expertise is required, but where its acquisition also requires passing through a disciplined and disciplining learning under examination and credentialing.

This doubly disciplinary process has both intensified and extended to new fields with the emergence of the modern 'ecosystem' of academic disciplines, from early in the nineteenth century (Hoskin 1993). If before there was a fairly small and stable set of academic 'knowledges', as in the 'seven liberal arts', today new knowledges are constantly being generated and old ones fading away across the potential field of knowledge, from hard sciences, through the new social sciences and across into the arts.

In this changed knowledge ecosystem, professionalization has expanded, with new professions and would-be professions proliferating, but always by claiming some new form of disciplinary expertise as their knowledge base (Bledstein 1976; Goldstein 1984). Nonetheless, there is continuity within this change, in that all would-be professions make their claim by adopting the older set of disciplinary practices, i.e. laying claim to the disciplinary knowledge base and then erecting the disciplines of examination and credentialing upon it. Even the service ideal ends up having the same double disciplinary base, since it involves a mix of 'knowing that' expertise (knowing what ethical behaviour is in the expert disciplinary context of the particular profession) combined with 'knowing how' expertise (attained through internalizing the self-discipline of 'good' professional work practice).

We would therefore argue that 'disciplinarity', understood in this double sense, is the historically embedded frame within which becoming a professional has been and still is located. Disciplinarity, therefore, forms the historically grounded context of professionalization. This applies both at the level of the profession as such, which must conform to double disciplinary imperatives if it is to become and remain a profession, and at the level of the individual, who can only succeed in the professional quest through following the selfsame route.

In order to understand the professional learning environment, researchers must appreciate the central and continuing significance to the professionalization project of (a) attaining expert disciplinary *knowledge*, and (b) engaging in disciplinary *conduct*, focused on examination passing, arguably supplemented by (c) a commitment to *self*-discipline in order to become a 'real professional' (cf. Messer-Davidow *et al.* 1993).

The continuing commitment to this whole set of practices reinforces the socially understood links between elite knowledge, learning and attainment, and the notion that the 'real' knowledge of the profession is in large part disciplinary. At the same time, one can see that there are huge areas for conflict, in terms of how participants define the local context of learning within the disciplinary frame, how their particular takes on disciplinarity shape their learning perspectives, and how disciplinarity enacts power relations.

If looking to be 'transdisciplinary' is one rational variation on the disciplinary theme, fields such as accountancy must confront the equally rational option of looking to be sub-disciplinary. In a sense knowledge-dependent fields need both. In addition, they must confront the way in which disciplinarity never stands still. Particularly within the modern knowledge ecosystem, a 'blurring, cracking and crossing' of existing knowledge boundaries has become endemic (Klein 1993). Unsurprisingly this blurring and transgression extends into the professional field, as is evidenced by the constant battles that have to be fought over disciplinary boundaries between adjacent professions and, increasingly, in recent decades the felt need for a constantly changing disciplinary knowledge base within a given field (Abbott 1988; Anderson-Gough 2002).

If we apply this disciplinary frame of analysis to accountancy specifically, we may see all these contrary trends at work. First accountancy had to become a profession, a project initiated before the end of the nineteenth century in Britain by the establishment and chartering of such bodies as the ICAEW and ICAS (Institute of Chartered Accountants of Scotland) (Anderson-Gough 2002). These bodies came to occupy (and defend) the elite end of an expanding profession where other bodies established a right to practise, and ultimately to become chartered in turn.[2] In recent decades these elite bodies have recruited predominantly graduate intakes (around 95 per cent currently for the ICAEW).

Given that those who have qualified via these institutes have traditionally provided the top ranks of the leading firms and the professional bodies, it is understandable that both firms and institutes have an increasingly 'graduate' outlook. In that context, both specialist disciplinarity and transdisciplinarity increasingly make sense as responses to the knowledge demands of the market for accountancy. They are responses that 'make sense' to the profession's leading members, however they understand these terms at the level of detail. They also make sense to graduate professionals, who will typically in the UK context have entered professional training with some form of specialist training (not necessarily in accounting and finance for ICAEW entrants, where a relevant degree has never been a condition of entry into training). However, as individuals they have increasingly been looking, for personal competitive advantage, to add transdisciplinary strings to their knowledge bows, e.g. by getting a professional qualification on top of a first degree and then adding further qualifications, e.g. a generalist Master's degree such as the Master in Business Administration (MBA).

We see a historically grounded frame of disciplinarity within which there are a limited but variable number of ways in which attainment may be understood and pursued in the accountancy field. In particular, we see a significant move towards wishing to be more transdisciplinary, but with a desire to retain all the benefits of being specialist at the same time. This is, therefore, a particularly interesting moment in which to be proposing new approaches to attainment. There is, in our view, a considerable openness to radical forms of change. At the same time, to achieve such change is likely to need particular attention being paid to the issues of context, power and perspective, given the new way that disciplinarity is potentially to be enacted.

In our next section, we therefore propose to reflect on recent initiatives that in one way or another have attempted to develop, from within some form of commitment to a more 'transdisciplinary' path, what is claimed to be a more relevant, reflective or integrative approach to learning accounting. It seems to us (with the benefit of hindsight) that issues of context, power and perspective have in one key way or another been insufficiently addressed in such initiatives. At the same time, such initiatives are significant pointers of how far change is desired, and how change might, with more attention to those issues, be effectively set in motion.

Learning accounting: towards a more transdisciplinary path?

The UK is not alone in the felt need to address the state of its accounting education provision. Since the late 1980s there have been similar calls and blueprints for change, some, as noted above, small-scale and radical in terms of pedagogy (usually in higher education contexts) and others more large-scale and supported by professional institutes. We propose to review the latter first, in terms of their transdisciplinary aspirations and achievements.

Blueprints for professional education change have been proliferating over this recent period, at first in the English-speaking world, e.g. in the USA, Australia and New Zealand, and latterly at a European level. So for instance, the ICAEW and ICAS are currently working with institutes in mainland Europe, on a 'Common Content' project, which is looking to define a common set of transdisciplinary technical and business knowledges required by all accountants. If this initiative proves successful, it will embed transdisciplinarity at the core of a new transnational qualification. We will examine the most extensive (and expensive) attempt to date to remake professional training in a more transdisciplinary guise, that undertaken in the 1990s by the Accounting Education Change Commission (AECC) in the USA.

Accounting educational change in the USA

The AECC was established by the American Accounting Association with the support of the major accountancy firms and its objective was to move beyond what was perceived as an over-narrow technical curriculum in undergraduate degrees with an accounting major (having such a major is prerequisite to sitting the state-run Certified Practising Accountant (CPA) examinations required for professional practice). There were three key innovations, each of which implicitly carries the discipline of learning or the disciplines learned in a more integrative direction:

- the focus was on 'learning', in particular 'learning to learn' and 'developing in students the capacity to continue to learn outside the formal educational environment' (AECC 1990: 310);
- accounting education became just one out of four parts of the necessary education of the accountant (the four parts being: general education, general business education, general accounting education and specialized accounting education);

- the overall curriculum was broadened to include a range of interpersonal skills and personal capacities such as empathy, persistence and integrity.

Not only did the AECC project start with fine words and high hopes, it is clear that at both content and delivery levels an integrative transdisciplinary agenda could hardly have been more clearly laid out. At the same time, the number of credit hours available for study of accounting and business-related topics was expanded. Yet the overall outcome has been recently summarized, in the official review of the project, as one of almost unmitigated failure (Albrecht and Sack 2000). This review concluded that what had undermined the integrative intent was the continued power of disciplinary specialization in terms of content offered, plus a self-interested focus across accounting faculties on retaining teaching within the accounting field rather than allowing students to take more transdisciplinary options. The report speculates whether this failure may sound the death knell for academic accounting in the US in its current form, asserting that 'more of the same' is no longer an option. Yet from within a disciplinary frame of analysis, it is arguable that the AECC diagnosis is doubly wrong. First, it was its own worst enemy, in not sufficiently recognizing the possible levels and forms of resistance that a transdisciplinary approach would face. Second, academics continue to inhabit a professional world where *they* live or die on their sub-disciplinary research expertise.

Project Discovery, University of Illinois

We may compare this general outcome with that of a specific much smaller scale, US university-based new learning initiative, Project Discovery, begun in 1995, which again had support from leading accountancy firms. This time the transdisciplinary and integrative orientation operates at the level of a new programme for accounting majors initially running alongside the traditional programme. In this case the management of integrative learning is seen to require more than just the development of a relevant and meaningful course content, which perhaps is a material factor in its apparent success. The key developments in this initiative were:

- an 'integrated experience' through (a) integrating knowledge of accountancy with organizational and business knowledge and (b) organizing accounting knowledge into process (measurement, disclosure and attestation) and functional uses (decision making, control and institutional regulation) (University of Illinois 1999);
- the use of more active and interactive learning approaches;
- the introduction of a wider range of teaching staff, appropriate teaching facilities and use of new technology teaching aids.

Here one of the striking features is the way in which transdisciplinarity is rendered more palatable in terms of the management of change, e.g. by parallel running of the new and old programmes and in the provision of staffing and resources. That is not to say that all faculty and students immediately and necessarily accepted the new model (but they did not need to at first, since the old one still had to be staffed and supported). The 1999 review reports that students studying under the two approaches did not differ in their technical accounting skills during the course, however, by the end of the course the Project Discovery students were better at problem structuring and writing, identifying accounting information resources and ethical issues. In addition, their 'cognitive complexity' was measured as operating at a higher level than that of students on the old scheme. Meanwhile the report notes that the 'Accountancy faculty voted unanimously in December 1995 to replace the existing undergraduate accountancy curriculum' (University of Illinois 1999: 8). Furthermore, the programme was still running successfully, with continued support from accountancy firms, at the time of writing.

Now these are only two brief samples of ways in which transdisciplinary aspirations have begun to be worked out on the ground. At the same time, they indicate how context, power and perspective need to be borne in mind, and how easily noble aspirations, even with high resourcing levels, can end up in unanticipated consequences.

Re-thinking attainment under disciplinarity: context, power and perspective and the paths to integrative learning

The research projects we have been involved with, both to date and currently, have focused mainly on the education, training and socialization of trainee accountants who have three-year training contracts with the Institute of Chartered Accountants in England and Wales (ICAEW). As stated above, these recruits are now predominantly graduates, although only a minority have a 'relevant degree' in accounting. Trainees contract to be paid employees of a particular accountancy firm and to study for the ICAEW examinations. The firm contracts to provide enough appropriate working experience to satisfy what was until recently an 'hours' requirement that is part of the qualification process and to provide paid study leave and tuition at independent tutorial firms as exam preparation.

The firms training and employing the would-be professionals have a particularly intense concern that trainees should acquire both formal *and* work-based skills. Certain aspects of professional expertise are seen as being acquired most economically and efficiently (though questions will be raised over whether most effectively) through formal learning. In the accountancy context, both technical skills (e.g. in bookkeeping and cost accounting), and specialist 'book knowledge' (e.g. on accounting standards, law and tax), have traditionally fallen into this category. Furthermore, the dependence on formal learning and certification expands with the constant flow of new knowledge required in professional work. At the same time, workplace learning has also been seen as essential. This has increasingly led to a strongly felt need for both formal and workplace learning environments that are fit for the purpose, and which will provide sustainable competitive advantage for the profession and for the professional firms.

In the accountancy context, it is fair to say that competitive pressures have ensured that a number of issues are never off the training agenda, one of which is the cost of training (estimated as at least £100,000 per trainee in some of the large firms). At the same time, in the battle between firms to attract and retain good recruits, perceived quality and effectiveness of training are also strategically crucial. Good recruits are seen as key to the future success of the firms, including a continuation of the high fees, profits and salaries that are a hallmark of accountancy work today. They also have to be retained beyond qualification (an increasing problem as graduates see the accountancy qualification as a step to success in general business), so the training has to be not only effective but also enjoyable.

Consequently the scope for mixed messages, conflicting perspectives, differently perceived contexts and unresolvable power struggles is considerable. The firms want effectiveness at minimal cost (in financial and time terms). Line managers want trainees 'on task'. Those involved in training and in the tutor firms want to ensure they pass the professional exams, which are widely perceived as tough, demanding and stressful. There are consequently 'turf wars' of all kinds all the time. There is also widespread consensus that the current forms of both formal and workplace learning are insufficiently effective in attainment terms (even though how and why this is so continues to occasion disagreement).

One conclusion that we draw from earlier research in which we have been involved (e.g. Anderson-Gough et al. 1998; Hoskin and Geddes 1997) is that this learning environment leads to various important issues over identity that affect attainment, some affecting firms more and others trainees, but all in important ways that need addressing. For instance at the firm level, our research indicates a strongly felt need to maintain a strong professional identity for the firm and among employees, for reasons of management, regulation and commercial survival and success. At the level of the trainee, the strongly felt need is to succeed in their learning in the two key ways: passing the examinations via 'qualification-focused learning' (QFL) and becoming a successful (professional) employee via 'work-based learning' (WBL). So being both a successful 'worker' and a successful 'student' (simultaneously yet separately) becomes key to completion of the three years in the firm and qualification as a Chartered Accountant.

At the same time, there is a particular issue that arises from the disciplinary frame of reference and shapes learner perceptions of what 'really' matters (and not just learner perceptions since this particular 'perspective' is more widely disseminated). This is the widely held perspective that QFL work is ritualistic, rote and virtually meaningless while WBL work is real, relevant and meaningful. This dichotomy is not only widely disseminated in professional practitioner fields but is reflected in the research literature on professionalization (Anderson-Gough 2002), where there is a strong tradition of seeing WBL as 'learning the ropes' while QFL is purely instrumental and forgettable.

However, there are strong grounds (empirical as well as reflective) for arguing that not all QFL is forgettable or forgotten, since many technical and more critical skills are most easily transmitted and learned here. Similarly, not all WBL is relevant and meaningful, with poor mentors and work environments often outnumbering good ones. Nevertheless, this perceived opposition dies hard and is clearly still operative among accountancy trainees. There is both a strongly felt split between QFL and WBL activities and an explicit devaluing of the formal qualification part of the learning experience, where examination learning is perceived as studying useless 'theory' and experienced as isolated cramming.

While this perspective is influential, it has to operate in a climate where the transdisciplinary imperative is increasingly high profile. Firms become more transdisciplinary as they increasingly commit to being 'professional service' firms and hire a mix of specialists from areas beyond accountancy, to meet client demands for multiskilled and multitasking project teams. Trainees experience this within the firms, in WBL contexts, as well as internalizing it in the multiple qualification career path. Transdisciplinarity is increasingly getting embedded in the QFL context too, for professional institutes are setting an increasing number of transdisciplinary examinations, alongside the traditional technical exams. Most UK bodies now have some form of integrative case-study exam at or near the end of the exam process. The ICAEW has also introduced a more systematically transdisciplinary examining strategy, wherein all the examinations to be sat beyond the first (professional) stage are set up to forestall single-discipline focused answers. Subject-specific competence is still tested at the professional stage but the new advanced stage has two parts. In the first examinees have to sit a Test of Advanced Technical Competence (TATC) in which a range of short questions are set, none of which can be answered drawing on one technical area only. In the second, a final Advanced Case Study poses one three-hour case-type question. This can be answered from within any of the specializations that trainees follow (typically audit or tax) but examinees must answer the question by using their particular analytical skills in a synthetic and contextually aware way, to have a realistic prospect of passing.

Our research process has itself been affected by this change. Our latest project has taken advantage of the changes already underway in order to propose a research agenda which looks not only to promote or enable more integrative or transdisciplinary learning within each of the WBL and QFL arenas, but also between them. One of the other contextual changes that we have therefore encountered is a willingness on the part of firms and tutorial organizations to participate in the research project, since they already have their own forms of commitment (for whatever mix of reasons) to a transdisciplinary agenda. There remains the issue of how to *translate* this research opportunity into an effective way of enabling attainment in this emergent transdisciplinary frame. The next section offers our reflection on how we have attempted to set up a viable action research approach, in the light of all the above considerations. We begin by reflecting on how we have drawn upon earlier theories of teaching and learning, which have already approached the problem of creating a more integrative kind of learning experience.

Re-thinking perspectives: re-appropriating existing theorizing in the new context

At one level there is nothing new about promoting integrative ideas about knowledge. Such an ideal is arguably as old as Plato's Republic and the learning there proposed to render philosophers competent as kings. But such understandings have, within the modern world of disciplinarity, been honoured more in the breach than the observance, not least as the learning practices developed in universities from around 1800 on have become endemic in mass education generally. We are thinking here of the historically unprecedented joint emphasis on making students write, examining them and then numerically grading their performance, a set of practices which have proven to have great success in the construction of well-disciplined (and increasingly self-disciplining) experts with single-discipline expertise (Hoskin 1993).

In this particular world of disciplined and disciplinary learning, where integrative theories were advanced, they typically fell at the unyielding bar of being 'unrealistic'. Ironically, however, they now have a new potential currency in the 'real world', as that world, as indicated, becomes increasingly wedded for reasons of enlightened self-interest to transdisciplinarity. So what previously failed because of the dominance of disciplinarity could now succeed precisely because of disciplinarity's own transdisciplinary move.

We see a new currency for the theorizing of one of the more radical educational thinkers of the recent past, Basil Bernstein, and in particular his 'integrated code' model (Bernstein 1971). Here Bernstein drew a distinction between traditional silo-based curricula, which he saw as exemplifying a 'collection code' model of knowledge and a different kind of 'integrated code' model. These were for him two different kinds of knowledge classification. Collection code practices essentially aim to transmit received blocks of knowledge in distinct subject packages, which might be specialized or non-specialized (1971: 51). Integrated code practices promote and enable the integration of disciplinary knowledges, through breaking the old classification and enabling learners to see knowledge in what we may now call a more transdisciplinary way, through having a transdisciplinary *structure*. The predicted outcome of integrated code learning would be to produce both a better understanding of the particular issues at hand while enabling learners to think outside or across subject-specific boundaries. Bernstein then also drew a distinction in terms of 'framing', between modes of pedagogic delivery. One kind of framing remained focused on one teacher or pedagogic voice, i.e. a univocal one-source framing of the delivery of learning. This he opposed to a multivocal, more multiple source approach, which would operate for him as a further destabilization of the traditional silo model of knowledge.

Both of Bernstein's conceptual categories we now find useful in trying to promote changes in the conditions of learning that will enable more integrative learning and competence acquisition across the QFL and WBL arenas. At an immediate level, what we take from Bernstein is a sense that generating a new approach through focusing on the conditions of learning involves a systematically distinctive mode of engaging with issues both of *content* and *delivery*. At the same time, in part because the contextual frame within which Bernstein devised this model was that of schooling, we have found it insufficient to draw on Bernstein alone. In pursuing this issue, one key additional insight has come from an analytical approach developed by Silver (1998), in reviewing innovations in teaching and learning in UK higher education since 1980. Silver distinguishes between innovations in (1) curriculum, (2) teaching and learning, and (3) organization and management (Silver 1998: 8).

In other words, he adds an extra dimension to the Bernstein analysis which has particular resonance in researching a professional training context, and one that we consider of particular importance at this current juncture, when there is such willingness to entertain integrative solutions that will advance a transdisciplinary agenda. One way in which context, power and perspective can line up to undermine radically different approaches to attainment is at the peripheral or penumbral level, beyond the areas of immediate focus and concern. This is arguably what happened in the case of the AECC initiative. By way of contrast, if the key organizational and managerial players who are interested in but not directly involved in the attainment issue can be brought on side with specific integrative initiatives, there is potentially a far greater opportunity for bringing them to successful fruition.

That, in a very real sense, has been how we have attempted to set up our current action learning initiative, via a form, so to speak, of 'indirection'. In other words, rather than trying, as our first step, to get 'active' with those most immediately interested in the initiative, we have looked to enable action through aligning more penumbral, but significant, actors with the initiative's objectives. In that process, we have found the ideas of Bernstein and Silver, together, of particular value. However, we have also subjected them to a certain level of translation to fit the particular circumstances of the accountancy field.

The first level of translation has been linguistic and has involved us in selecting a range of terms that would, we felt, best express both for us and for key others (central and penumbral) the requisite breadth of transdisciplinary vision. While we found Silver's tripartite division helpful, we readdressed his terminology, largely because in each case we felt it would promote too narrow a frame of reference, particularly when the conditions of learning stretch across QFL and WBL arenas. Where Silver uses the term 'curriculum' we have preferred 'content', as curriculum has such strong QFL connotations. For similar reasons, where Silver refers to 'teaching and learning', we substitute 'delivery'. This is in part to ensure that focus does not revert to direct pedagogic solutions as the primary way forward, either in the QFL or indeed the WBL context, and also to reduce any tendency to see those two contexts as seamlessly complementary rather than 'problem twins'.

Additionally, if the use of teaching is problematic in this context, so arguably is 'learning', for in managing change in both QFL and WBL arenas we can already see that there is considerable 'unlearning' to be engaged in. On the QFL side within the ICAEW examination system at least, both trainees and trainers are already having to face *some* level of unlearning well-established beliefs about what learning techniques count, cramming, question-spotting, and satisficing at the level of exam performance via narrow fact and technique competence. On the WBL side, there is perhaps more unlearning still to be initiated, e.g. over the widespread belief that all the 'real' learning happens on the job. The term 'delivery', we therefore feel, better signals the need to think in tandem and across both arenas about modes of teaching, learning and assessment and the various interrelations between them. If anything, this redefinition is all the more important when a system is looking to promote a greater commitment to informal teaching and learning, e.g. in the workplace, as an integral part of the education and training process. Here the question of how we manage the change given that not only the trainees but everyone involved in the change process has 'learned to learn' under the traditional formal approach to exam passing just outlined is an important sub-issue.

Finally, for 'organization and management' we have preferred the term 'infrastructure'. In the context of developing a new professional qualification as the ICAEW are looking to do, a diverse range of relevant bodies (which now includes accountancy firms, tutorial organizations, and increasingly the universities too) has to be brought in and kept 'on side'. Within those bodies, 'organization' and 'management' are terms that have highly specific direct meanings and rather over-directive secondary connotations. So direct organization and management issues remain of key importance to the ICAEW in implementing the new vision, not least because the complexity and cost involved in changing systems for managing learning and assessment are themselves key areas of risk. But we need also to bring a specific analytic focus to bear on the penumbral issue, concerning the extensive indirect or less direct ways in which the key institutional players interrelate, not least because certain of these indirect connections have in the past proved to be particularly directive and determinative.

If our first translation move has been linguistic, it has been complemented by a second more visual one, in the sense of formulating a model to capture the frame within which action research needs to proceed in order to enable a more integrative kind of attainment within a transdisciplinary frame of reference. Our current visualization takes the form of a 3 × 2 matrix (Figure 5.1), which tries to summarize what is entailed in moving away from an educational regime dominated by collection code practices and ways of seeing to an integrated code one, while also giving appropriate names to the individual boxes making up the matrix.

The current result retains on the vertical axis Bernstein's original terms, signalling what we see as the continuing conceptual objective, to move away from a collection code 'world', in which both practices and ways of seeing conspire to maintain a silo-based discipline-specific content, purveyed through a range of discrete disciplinary delivery practices. If we succeed in moving to an 'integrated code' world, we will be engaging in teaching and learning of transdisciplinary contents in integrative ways, through delivery modes which will still involve disciplinary practices (with a continuing major role for writing, examining and grading) but no longer constructed as discrete QFL and WBL packages.

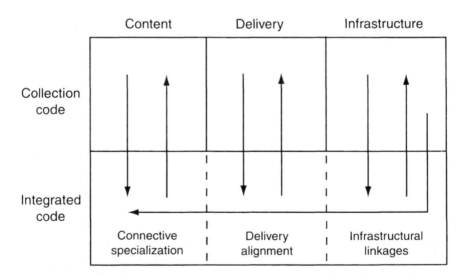

Figure 5.1 Integrating best practice

However, to succeed in moving to such a world, we have to engineer series or relays of linkages that begin from the right-hand side of our matrix, i.e. at the *infrastructural* level, ensuring that we promote alignment first among the penumbral but key actors as well as among those with direct interests in the new approach. The dynamic of the action research we are thereby attempting to set up proceeds in a contrary direction to that adopted in many attempts to engineer changes in learning, teaching and attainment. Classically such attempts have begun at the level of content, redefining what needs to be learned (in this instance in more transdisciplinary terms), and have then proceeded to re-think issues of delivery in order to enable these new contents to be effectively internalized. Infrastructural concerns have then surfaced third, if at all, and often too late (another way, arguably, of interpreting the AECC project failure).

Beginning from the right-hand side of the matrix and then attempting to generate change in a leftwards direction poses its own challenges. There is no simple progression (as we attempt to mark by the inclusion of opposed vertical arrows running across each pair of boxes), instead there is a contrarian motion playing across the whole change process. Nevertheless that does not necessarily mean that all is stasis or that in the long run every forward step is cancelled out by a step back. Instead, we believe that with appropriately strong infrastructural linkages we may then develop an effective form of delivery alignment, in this case across QFL and WBL contexts, and enable the development of the new kind of 'transdisciplinary self' that is now clearly a professional aspiration.

There remains one last qualification or clarification we need to add, concerning the term in our bottom left-hand box. There is one particular issue left unaddressed as yet, concerning the precise *way of knowing* that needs to be developed by the elite professional in the transdisciplinary age. There are various ways that have been developed for trying to capture this, e.g. Gibbons *et al*.'s (1994) formulation of a distinction between traditional or mode 1 and integrative mode 2 knowledge. However, the term that in our view best expresses the approach needed is 'connective specialisation' (Young 1998). To us the term has a specificity that 'mode 2' does not, but also, as Young himself argues (1998: esp. 77–9), it captures better than alternatives such as 'flexible specialization' the shift involved in both the extensiveness and intensiveness of knowledge internalization. The new professional must be competent not just across a range of disciplinary specializations but at the level of making connections across them. This is an objective that seems to us to need specifying beyond a general reference to being 'transdisciplinary', and it is what Young's term sums up so well.

Conclusion: new beginnings or another false start?

The use of the interrogative here is essential. We have not had the time to fail yet, by discovering how far our model may be deficient, whether at the level of conceptualization or of realization, or both. The model is also very much conditional at this stage in terms of its potential generalizability. We have devised it very much with the specific circumstances of elite professional training in mind, and of this particular form of professional training. It is possible that, if it proves applicable at all, it may only be so at this level. Or it may only be so in the foreseeable future, since this is a knowledge area that is peculiarly conducive to the successful development of a transdisciplinary and integrative kind of learning.

There are a couple of more general possibilities that we do see flowing from this research. The first is a hope that the 'disciplinary' form of analysis may help counter the easy opposition so widely perceived as existing between WBL and QFL experiences. Insofar as both kinds of attainment involve a disciplinary grounding, which both involve immersion in relevant expert knowledge and commitment to the self-disciplining of the good professional, they are in important respects versions of the same learning. This approach may in principle not appear as relevant in fields which are less grounded in academic disciplines. But insofar as training there involves some form of disciplinary delivery, whether in terms of pedagogy or examination and accreditation, then transdisciplinarity may well be of increasing significance. Indeed, insofar as all work fields require or demand some form of transdisciplinarity, perceived differences between them may be narrowing across the board, as all move in a more generally 'disciplinary' direction.

The other possibility is that the approach to managing change towards better attainment sketched out in our model may have some more general applicability, whether one is doing action research or not. In other words, in setting out to render workplace learning more integrative, the move from infrastructure to delivery and content may be a more generally useful tactic, regardless of how 'disciplinary' the content is.

Acknowledgement

We gratefully acknowledge the financial support of the PD Leake Trust and the Centre for Business Performance of the Institute of Chartered Accountants in England and Wales (ICAEW) who have generously supplied the funding for the projects on which this chapter is based.

Notes

1   The examinations were typically oral, as in the defence before the body of masters of some thesis, and only shifted to being written in the late eighteenth century (Hoskin 1993). The right to issue a 'licence to teach' (*licentia docendi*) had previously been a geographical right vested in the senior local clergy. In 1215 Pope Innocent III (himself a university man) gave a new right to issue licences to the university faculties at Paris and then Bologna, thereby setting up the structure that would be adopted by the bodies that would then become the first professions (Hoskin 1986).

2 The other major bodies established in the UK out of a much larger pool of
   initially competing bodies include CIMA (the Chartered Institute of Management
   Accountants), CIPFA (the Chartered Institute of Public Finance Accountants) and
   the ACCA (the Association of Chartered Certified Accountants).

References

Abbott, A. (1988) *The System of Professions: An Essay on the Division of Expert Labor*,
    Chicago, IL: Chicago University Press.
Accounting Education Change Commission (AECC) (1990) 'Objectives of Educa-
    tion for Accountants: Position Statement Number One', *Issues in Accounting
    Education*, 5 (2): 307–12.
Albrecht, W.S. and Sack, R.J. (2000) *Accounting Education. Charting the Course
    Through a Perilous Future*, Sarasota, FL: American Accounting Association.
Anderson-Gough, F. (2002) 'On Becoming the New Accounting Expert: Between
    Formal and Informal Learning', Ph.D. Thesis: The University of Leeds.
Anderson-Gough, F., Grey, C. and Robson, K. (1998) *Making Up Accountants: The
    Organisational and Professional Socialization of Trainee Chartered Accountants*,
    London: Ashgate.
Bernstein, B. (1971) 'On the Classification and Framing of Educational Knowl-
    edge', in M.F.D. Young (ed.), *Knowledge and Control: New Directions for the Sociology
    of Education*. London: Collier-Macmillan.
Bledstein, B.J. (1976) *The Culture of Professionalism: the Middle Class and the Develop-
    ment of Higher Education in America*, New York: W.W. Norton & Co.
Cobban, A.B. (1975) *The Medieval Universities: Their Development and Organization*,
    London: Methuen.
Gibbons, M., Limoges, C., Nowotny, H., Schwartzman, S., Scott, P. and Trow, M.
    (1994) *The New Production of Knowledge*, London: Sage.
Goldstein, J. (1984) 'Foucault Among the Sociologists: The 'Disciplines' and the
    history of the Professions', *History and Theory*, 23 (2): 170–92.
Hoskin, K. (1986) 'The Professional in Educational History', in J. Wilkes (ed.), *The
    Professional Teacher: Proceedings of the 1985 Annual Conference of the History of Educa-
    tion Society of Great Britain*, London: History of Education Society.
——— (1993) 'Education and the Genesis of Disciplinarity: The Unexpected
    Reversal', in E. Messer-Davidow *et al.* (eds), *Knowledges: Historical and Critical
    Studies in Disciplinarity*, Charlottesville, VA: University of Virginia Press, pp.
    271–304.
Hoskin, K. and Geddes, B. (1997) 'ICAEW Pass Rates Research: Final Report',
    Report to the ICAEW Education and Training Directorate.
Klein, J. (1993) 'Blurring, Cracking and Crossing: Permeation and the Fracturing
    of Discipline', in E. Messer-Davidow *et al.* (eds), *Knowledges: Historical and Critical
    Studies in Disciplinarity*, Charlottesville, VA: University of Virginia Press, pp.
    185–211.
Messer-Davidow, E., Shumway, D.R. and Sylvan, D.J. (eds) (1993) *Knowledges:
    Historical and Critical Studies in Disciplinarity*, Charlottesville, VA: The University
    of Virginia Press.
Parsons, T. (1968) 'Professions', in D.L. Sills (ed.), *International Encyclopedia of the
    Social Sciences*, New York: The Macmillan Company and Free Press.

Silver, H. (1998) 'The Languages of Innovation: Listening to the Higher Education Literature', Working Paper No. 1 ESRC Learning Society Programme.

University of Illinois (1999) 'Documentation for the Implementation of Project Discovery Curriculum', http://www.cba.uiuc.edu/accountancy/projdisc/ (Accessed 10 August 2000).

Young, M. (1998) *The Curriculum of the Future*, London: Falmer Press.

6 The assessment of workers' 'basic skills'

A critique based on evidence from the United States, Canada and England[1]

Susan Hoddinott

Chapter summary

This chapter critically examines the heightened scrutiny of low-wage workers, both employed and unemployed, effected through the widespread use of basic skills' assessments. Employers are increasingly using literacy, numeracy and language skills assessments as the basis of hiring decisions as well as a range of other employment decisions, including promotion, assignment or reassignment, and firing. Assessment is used in 'workplace basic skills' programmes, both in the 'needs assessment' phase prior to the establishment of programmes and in the post-programmes 'learning assessment' phase. In the workplace, the unequal nature of the employment relationship and the requirement for programmes of education or training to have a measurable impact on profitability tend to conflict with the need for the dispassionate and unthreatening assessment required in programmes of fundamental education. This tendency has been magnified in the recent past as performance on literacy, numeracy and language proficiency assessments has been interpreted as a consummate indicator of 'fitness' for work. The chapter concludes that the use of 'basic skills' assessments represents an area of fundamental conflict between capital and labour and that, in cases where training programmes are designed to remediate basic skills 'deficiencies', the quality of the training itself is frequently as problematic as the assessment.

Introduction

In both North America and England over the last two decades, the state has largely withdrawn from active labour market planning in favour of market-driven (and employer mediated) approaches to the production and reproduction of skill. National training agendas, such as those developed through federal legislation in both Canada and the United States in the 1960s, began to be radically revised from the early 1980s. Systems of vocational education, planned and funded by the state, were significantly reduced as more and more public training allocations were directed to the private sector. Similarly in England, the late 1980s saw the established tripartite control of training shift entirely to a system controlled by business interests.[2] What has remained of the public training sector in all three countries has been required to become increasingly responsive to the self-defined needs of business and industry.

At the same time as training policy and spending have moved away from the public and towards the private sector, the definition of training has become increasingly broad and amorphous and the distinction between education and training has blurred. One particularly clear example of this has been the trend towards the conflation of programmes of adult education, historically viewed as an individual right and a public good, with training – if not the actual responsibility of the employers of labour, then appropriately within their jurisdiction. It is this aspect of the new training agenda – the sanctioning of an educational assessment role for employers and the re-working of programmes of adult fundamental education as 'basic skills training', both subject to the input of employers in terms of content and organization and able to be assessed by the employer – that provides the context for the discussion in this chapter.

From the mid-1980s, the assessment of workers' literacy, numeracy and language skills by (or for) employers became commonplace. The context for this development was three-fold. First, a conservative 'school reform' movement claimed that schools were failing to teach the most fundamental skills and produced 'evidence' of widespread adult (and worker) illiteracy both to support those claims and to underline the dire consequences of schooling's failure. Second, new approaches to training significantly extended employers' jurisdiction and prerogative in respect of the definition and assessment of 'skill'. Third, a combination of high unemployment and unprecedented numbers of relatively well-educated job applicants enabled employers to raise hiring criteria and to be much more selective in their hiring processes without increasing their labour costs. In this context, 'literacy', though variously defined and measured, became a proxy for 'employability', and literacy or 'basic skills' assessments gained credibility and wide support as objective instruments for the selection of workers for primarily low-skill, low-pay work. Basic skills assessments have also been used over the past two decades among employed workers, by employers as the basis for the ranking and 'de-selection' of workers when layoffs are planned. They have also been used by educationalists, or other would-be programmes deliverers, as a means of assessing the need for 'workplace basic skills' programmes.

This chapter provides a critical examination of the trend towards the use of 'basic skills' assessment. It begins with a brief discussion of the construction of a workforce 'basic skills crisis' in the late twentieth century. In the context of the putative crisis, there was a sharp increase in the use of generic language and mathematics testing as a screening tool for the selection and de-selection of workers. In the second section of the chapter, the misuse of such testing and the potential for both negative and unfair impacts on workers is examined through the example of the United States. The third and final section discusses the emergence of remedial 'basic skills' programmes for workers and the use of assessments both as a means of establishing the need for such programmes and of measuring attainment.

The basic skills 'crisis' and the expansion of workforce testing

The idea that 'illiteracy' or 'basic skills deficits' may be widespread among workers, including millions of school graduates, was first promulgated in the early 1980s by business advocacy groups in the United States. It would later be quite literally exported to Canada and, after nearly a decade, to England as well. Its most direct links were to the recurrent American campaigning around the issue of adult illiteracy, an issue which, by the late 1970s, had become thoroughly intertwined with conservative school reform. One main objective of conservative school reform on both sides of the Atlantic has been the pursuit of a closer fit between schooling and work and much of the debate about 'illiteracy' in the employed workforce – in North America, in particular – has been couched in terms of the 'dysfunctionality' of school-based learning.

In the context of the Reagan-era agenda of right wing reform, 'worker illiteracy' served double-duty as a public issue around which the country could rally. On the one hand, it provided 'proof' that American schools were failing in the most fundamental sense. On the other hand, it provided a 'natural' explanation for the worsening situation of American workers. For, although the American workforce possessed higher levels of education than at any time in the country's history, the majority of workers experienced dramatic declines in wages and living standards over the last quarter of the twentieth century (Rumberger 1981, 1984; Gordon 1996). Indeed, from the early 1980s an unprecedentedly high proportion of the population of both Canada and the United States was pursuing post-secondary education and training, and high school graduation had become substantially devalued. By the mid-1990s, a report on the displacement of blue-collar workers in Canada, for example, was able to characterize a displaced worker 'with only a Grade 12 education' as having 'little more to offer an employer than his brute strength' (Schachter 1995: 32). This devaluation has been reflected in a precipitous decline in wages for high school graduates in particular (Rumberger 1981, 1984; Gordon 1996).

The school reform movement and the adult literacy campaigns which, from the early 1980s, began to focus sharply on workers explicitly challenged the validity of school credentials and promoted the use of a range of direct assessments, including standardized reading and numeracy testing and so-called 'intelligence' tests. The idea was generally embraced. A survey of basic skills testing by the American Management Association reported that in 1989, two years after the launch of a national campaign to 'raise awareness' about worker illiteracy, testing of the basic skills of employees had doubled; one year later, it had doubled again and it rose a further 35 per cent in 1991 (Greenberg 1992). Whereas, in 1989, 5 per cent of surveyed companies utilized literacy testing and mathematics testing, in 1992 the percentage had risen to 22.3 per cent utilizing literacy testing and 27.3 per cent using mathematics testing. Indeed, in 1989 even the US Employment Service in the majority of states was tying its job placement service (for the unemployed) to the administration of a strictly timed general aptitude test. Those who did not do well on the test simply did not get jobs through the Employment Service. In Canada, a 1992 study reported that '40 per cent of the surveyed employers carry out pre-employment testing to screen applicants for basic skills. Those companies report screening out an average of 15 per cent of job applicants because of inadequate literacy and numeracy levels' (Conference Board of Canada 1992: 8). Similarly, in England, nearly half of all respondents in a 1990 employer survey commissioned by the Adult Literacy and Basic Skills Unit indicated that they assessed reading skills of blue-collar applicants; 63 per cent tested writing skills (which, of course, assume reading competency) and 79 per cent tested oral communication skills (Kempa 1993: 25).

Employers were not simply using the tests to screen job applicants; they were also using basic skills testing as a basis for employment decisions. In the United States, for example, 6 per cent of companies surveyed by the American Management Association reported that in 1990, at the peak of workforce literacy campaigning, they were dismissing employees deemed to be 'skills deficient'. A further 11.5 per cent responded by reassigning workers and 10 per cent made training mandatory for those who exhibited basic skills deficiencies (Greenberg 1992).

It should be noted that the increased use of testing has not been confined to individual assessments by firms; nor has it been confined to the private sector. There were many highly publicized industry-wide and institution-wide 'basic skills assessments' of employed workers in both the United States and Canada at the peak of workforce literacy campaigning. The US Postal Service, for example, announced in 1991 that it was beginning to examine the basic skills and language 'needs' of its 760,000 strong workforce (Business Council for Effective Literacy (BCEL) No. 26, January 1991: 5). At the same time in Canada, sawmill workers in the province of British Columbia became the subjects of a literacy assessment endorsed by their union – an assessment which was greeted with suspicion and resistance by the majority of the workers (Goetz et al. 1991: 3).

> ## Box 6.1 Commercial drivers and literacy assessment
>
> In what may represent the most significant industry-wide assessment, the US federal government in the late 1980s announced that all commercial drivers would have to pass a 'comprehensive written and oral knowledge exam and related driving test (by April 1992) or risk losing their licenses and their jobs'. No less than four million workers were affected by the ruling. Even the Business Council for Effective Literacy, a leading advocate of 'basic skills assessments' balked at this. Their report on the federally mandated driver's test observed that the official manual for the test was a '120-page document...with technical terminology and diagrams'.
>
> > Even drivers with average reading skills and a 'hands-on' knowledge of their trade may have lost their test-taking skills over the years, or may have difficulty with the technical nature of the materials and exam questions. For those with low literacy or ESL skill, the challenge is even more formidable.
> >
> > (BCEL, No. 29, October 1991: 7)

Basic skills testing and the 'contested terrain' of employer prerogative: the US example

The experience of workers in the United States demonstrates most clearly the problematic nature of employers' use of testing and, indeed, workplace 'basic skills' training for targeted workers. For it has been in the US that the campaigns around worker illiteracy and the institution of testing, as well as 'basic skills' training programmes, have been directly linked to the extension of employer prerogative and the concomitant diminution of workers' protection from discrimination. In the face of widespread racial and ethnic discrimination, minority American workers have long recognized the potential for testing and qualification requirements to be used as a means of legitimizing discrimination, both in the hiring process and in internal labour markets. The Civil Rights Act of 1964 explicitly addressed the problem. Title VII of the Act prohibits the use of testing to influence any employment decision if it results in discrimination (Philippi 1993). The Act requires that, before a test can be used to influence an employment decision, it must be 'validated' for job-relatedness. This means that the employer must be able to demonstrate a high correlation between successful test performance and successful job performance. Further, unless job progression is likely within a 'reasonable period of time', employees can only be tested at or near the entry level for the position (BCEL, No. 17, 1988: 6).

The Civil Rights legislation provides a basis for challenging employers' use of testing in a way which is not possible in either Canada or England. Not surprisingly, however, it is legislation which has been the subject of struggle since its enactment, as employers have tried to extend the definition of 'job-relatedness' and, thus, their control over the use of testing, and workers have been obliged to seek protection from the unfair use of testing through litigation. That the sides in the struggle are not balanced goes without saying, and the evidence of excessive use of testing by American employers during the 1980s and 1990s points to a fairly blatant disregard for the legislation. A 1990 article in the newsletter of the Business Council for Effective Literacy noted that 'as standardized tests have come into sweeping use throughout...employment, so have complaints about them and challenges to their validity. They have been the subject of lawsuits in state and federal courts' (BCEL, January 1990: 1). Though no such official or legal controversy has accompanied the use of workplace testing in either Canada or England, this is probably attributable to a range of factors other than workers' perceptions and reactions to such assessments including, for example, the Civil Rights legislation itself and the prominence of litigation as an institutional mechanism for effecting change in the American system (Martin 1990). Notwithstanding the legal challenges, there is little to indicate that American employers are more restrained in their use of tests than their counterparts in Canada or England. On the contrary, in spite of the legal protection theoretically provided by Title VII, the screening of applicants in the United States has frequently been extreme.

The workforce literacy campaign literature from the US also provides examples of company-wide and plant-wide 'basic skills' testing of employed workers where the consequences for the workers tested are, at the very least, questionable. The Business Council for Effective Literacy reported the results of a company-wide assessment at Eastman Kodak, for example, where some 10,000 employees had been found to lack 'the basic skills needed to implement the organizational and technological changes required to make the company more competitive' (BCEL, No. 15, April 1988: 4). Similarly a General Motors official was quoted in a report by a policy board of the southern US states as saying, 'It was an awful shock when we assessed the workforce in one of our plants and found that 87 per cent of our employees are incapable of doing work beyond the fifth grade' (Rosenfeld 1987: 1).

In fact, literacy testing of groups – which appears to have peaked in the late 1980s – has been challenged by equal opportunities and affirmative action authorities as unfair and discriminatory. However, as a 1989 article in *Management World* observed, 'it [basic skills testing] is perfectly legitimate if administered to individuals who have exhibited literacy deficiencies that affect performance and it is used to determine the degree of deficiency and the type of training needed' (Goddard 1989: 9). The article recommended that department managers be charged with determining 'job-related literacy problems' in their work units and with highlighting these deficiencies in performance appraisals and management reports. Having documented a deficiency, of course, they could then proceed with legally defensible testing. They could also require the worker(s) to participate in basic skills training. Thanks to another gain which employers made during the period of campaigning around the worker illiteracy 'crisis', the basic skills training would now cost them less than it would have previously. US federal legislation, contained in the Fair Labor Standards Act, mandated that where workers are required by employers to participate in training programmes outside of working hours, they must not only be paid for the training, but they must also be paid overtime wages. The legislation was changed, however, following calls for a review in light of the worker illiteracy 'crisis'. A December 1991 ruling on the Wage and Hour provisions made an exception to the provisions for less formally educated workers. As a report by the Business Council for Effective Literacy noted, 'employers can require workers who lack a high school diploma or who read below 8th grade level [presumably, even if they have a high school diploma] to participate in basic skills training outside of work hours without paying them at the usual overtime rate' (BCEL, No. 32, July 1992: 4). Under the provisions of the rule, workers could be required to spend as much as 10 hours a week over their regular 40-hour week in reading or other basic skills instruction with no entitlement to overtime pay.

Methods of assessing need and attainment

In both Canada and the United States, the putative problem of 'worker illiteracy' became a public issue through the purposeful construction of a broad-based campaign, funded in part by business advocacy groups and business philanthropy and, in part, by the state. The use of workforce-wide 'basic skills' testing and the publication of the 'dramatic' results of some of those assessments in the business as well as the popular press were both responses to, and elements of, the campaigns. Another key campaign element was the production (again by business organizations and state-funded groups or agencies) of national, state-wide/province-wide, and local studies and reports which claimed to demonstrate that workers' literacy and numeracy competencies were woefully inadequate for the demands of their jobs and, more broadly, for the success of their workplaces (See, for example, Johnston and Packer 1987; US Departments of Education and Labor 1988; Creative Research Group 1987; DesLauriers 1990). Similar reports were also produced in England. They followed, and were directly derivative of, the North American reports (see, for example, Kempa 1993).

A central message of the majority of those reports was the need for prevention of worker illiteracy through the reform of schooling. Many also advocated more immediate responses to the supposed problem of workforce literacy deficits, including the use by all employers of 'basic skills' assessments of their workforces and where such assessments established a need, the introduction of programmes of fundamental education into workplaces. Indeed, for those representing adult education institutions, volunteer literacy tutoring agencies and labour, the promotion of such programmes had always been the primary motivation for becoming involved with the campaigns. The studies and reports which they produced, purporting to demonstrate the extent and the seriousness of the problem, were directly intended to persuade employers of the need to sanction and/or provide remedial programmes for their workers. In many cases, the would-be deliverers of workplace literacy programmes themselves conducted 'needs assessments' of workforces, or sections of workforces, as a first step in persuading individual employers to purchase their services or, more frequently, to accept their voluntary or publicly funded service (see, for example, McIntyre 1991).

Although the workplace basic skills 'revolution' never happened to the extent that its advocates might have hoped, there was real growth from the late 1980s in work-related or workplace-based programmes purporting to teach fundamental education. In the United States, the federal government initiated a National Workplace Literacy Programme (NWLP) in 1988. A programme of the US Department of Education, the NWLP awarded grants totalling $41 million in its first three years of operation, 1988/89 to 1990/91. The grants had funded programmes serving approximately 67,000 workers in 360 different businesses (BCEL, No. 33, October 1992: 12). In Canada, a 1991 national survey of workplace literacy programmes documented 71 distinct programmes or programme models (Johnston 1991). In some cases, a programme model might be operating in a number of worksites. The Ontario Federation of Labour, for example, was reportedly offering its own version of 'workplace basic skills' in 100 work sites in that province in 1991 (ibid.). In England, although there was a marked shift in adult literacy education towards work-based and work-related tuition, the total number of workplace literacy programmes in operation at any one time from the commencement of such programmes in the mid-1980s through the mid-1990s might be counted in the tens. A 1991 estimate, for example, put the number of such programmes at 30, with fewer than 300 workers involved (Hoddinott 1997). A 1994 report on the state-funded basic skills at Work initiative observed that only 40 programmes had been conducted in companies through the initiative in the three years since its establishment in 1991.

A wide variety of work-related and workplace-based programmes were instituted under the 'literacy' or 'basic skills' banner, particularly in the early 1990s when state-funded promotion of the idea was at its peak. Workers typically targeted for recruitment to programmes have been those in manual and low-wage jobs, those with few or no formal qualifications, and those with limited English (and, in Canada, French) proficiency.[4]

There are two ways in which workers have been subjected to assessment in relation to workplace basic skills: the general 'basic skills needs assessment'; and the assessment of 'learning' in workplace basic skills programmes, either during the course of the programme or at the end. Both assessments may be conducted by the employer, though it has been more common for outside agencies (the deliverers or would-be deliverers of workplace basic skills programmes) to conduct assessments, usually with the involvement of the employer.

Workplace basic skills 'needs assessments' may be conducted on a group or an individual basis, and they may or may not result in the establishment of a workplace basic skills programme. An employer may, for example, agree to a needs assessment being carried out whether or not there is an intention to follow through with support for a basic skills programme in the event a need is demonstrated. More frequently, however, those who provide the needs assessment service are also seeking funding support from public sources to deliver programmes. The needs assessment in such a scenario is basically one element of a funding proposal, so whether or not a needs assessment is followed by a programme depends on the proponents' success in securing funding. In any event, the information gained from the needs assessment phase may be used by the employer as the basis of employment decisions.

In practice, virtually all workplace basic skills needs assessments result in the establishment of a 'need', irrespective of whether or not a programme is established. In cases where standardized reading, mathematics and language tests are the basis of assessment, the targeting of particular classes of worker for assessment virtually guarantees that 'basic skills deficiencies' will be exhibited and, thus, the need for remediation established. Whether there are actual deficiencies in relation to the *literacy, numeracy or language requirements of the job* is an entirely different matter. There are many documented cases in the literature on workplace basic skills which suggest that there may be little or no relation between the literacy or language 'needs' alleged by programme deliverers or employers and the actual requirements of the job or the workplace. A report by an educator engaged in developing educational programmes for private industry in Los Angeles, for example, quoted a workplace programme participant who said:

> Look at my hands! See them? These hands have contributed to the wealth of this company, and not once in twenty years have I had to read English, nor have I had to speak it in order to do my work. Now they're telling me that I need to read English in order to do the same work and compete with another worker?

(Anorve 1989: 40)

Indeed, although workplace literacy programmes are typically instituted on the assumption that participants' jobs require greater literacy competencies than workers themselves possess, there is considerable anecdotal evidence that many such programmes are themselves the only 'literacy content' in participants' working lives. As one participant in a workplace literacy programme in England, for example, commented on a student evaluation form: 'It [the time spent in the programme] is the only time in the week that I use my intellect' (quoted in Nieduszynska 1992: 2). A study of a workplace literacy programme in a southern US hospital found that written instructions for work processes were actually developed expressly to inject a literacy component into work after the establishment of a workplace literacy programme (Gowen 1992).

In many (and perhaps most) cases, workplace basic skills needs assessments do not use standardized tests or any other kind of formal testing; rather, what is used is a miscellany of workplace 'standards' or expectations against which groups of workers or individuals are informally assessed. Almost without exception, this type of 'basic skills assessment' demonstrates significant 'need', as the assessors link virtually every conceivable workplace problem to the likelihood of worker ('basic skills') deficiency. In both North America and England, the state has funded or produced guides to this latter type of needs assessments for employers to use in the assessment of the basic skills needs of their own workforces. An 'employer's guide' to planning adult basic skills programmes produced by the state of Massachusetts, for example, advised employers to look for 'typical indicators of need for a basic skills programme'. Among these indicators were listed: reluctance of workers to participate fully in new management strategies and employee involvement programmes; the failure of workers to apply for job upgrades or to sign up for computer courses and other subjects; errors in forms, checklists and a range of workplace written documents; more accidents than expected; and conflicts between ethnic groups that impact(ed) on production. Other 'hidden costs' which the guide linked to basic skills deficits included less efficient use of supplies and increased volume of scrap, more accidents and workers' compensation claims, and more sick time and staff turnover (Sperazi 1991). In England, a 1990 survey commissioned by the Adult Literacy and Basic Skills Unit asked employers to identify the effects of basic skills difficulties on their companies from a list which included lack of flexibility among workers; lack of efficiency/professionalism; loss of customers/business; lower quality of customer service; loss of profits/financial loss; and time wasting/not able to get on with the job (Kempa 1993). Similarly, a practitioner's guide to setting up workplace basic skills programmes in that country identified a number of 'shopfloor problems' purportedly stemming from basic skills difficulties (Rees 1990). These included: 'time-consuming mistakes...; high level of supervisor intervention to compensate for lack of staff self-reliance; insufficient flexibility in work arrangements; inaccurate completion of records; and failure to take up promotion opportunities' (Rees 1990: 9). The linking of such a broad range of workplace problems and issues to worker 'basic skills deficiency' – or, indeed, any kind of worker deficiency – is quite blatantly one-sided and very revealing of the underlying politics of much of the workplace basic skills 'project'. Its potential for prejudicing workers' employment conditions and prospects, even at the 'needs assessment' stage, is obvious.

Constructing fundamental education programmes as necessary 'training' has involved persuading employers to support workplace basic skills programmes and convincing workers to attend such programmes. This has entailed problematizing workers' literacy and language proficiencies. However, when programmes are established to address supposed workplace basic skills deficiencies, they generally promise to deliver much more than individual gains in literacy or numeracy skills or language facility. For, whether the basic skills needs assessment utilizes standardized tests or the more wide-ranging assessment of workplace problems allegedly linked to basic skills 'deficiencies', the deliverers of workplace basic skills programmes typically make highly exaggerated claims for the benefits of their programmes to the employer. Generally, it is these claims rather than the programme content which form the basis of the assessment of workers. Indeed, even when the post-programme assessment is limited to the evaluation of literacy, numeracy and language gains, it is frequently based on quite unrealistic expectations, bearing little relation to either the content or the quality and duration of the programme. It is, thus, no less problematic for the worker participants. Also at issue is the fact that it is likely that any standard assessment of reading, numeracy or language skills would fail to indicate the adequacy of workers' skills for the particular demands of their jobs. Even direct measures of particular jobs (such as constitute the 'literacy task analyses' of much workplace literacy practice) fail to account for the variable ways in which written material may be read or the relative importance of the printed material relating to a job. Many researchers undoubtedly make the mistake of treating all reading material as they might a narrative or expository text and, thus, overstate both the time and skill required to complete work-related reading (see, for example, Evetts and Flanagan 1991).

One key objective of the majority of workplace basic skills programme deliverers, on both sides of the Atlantic, has been to demonstrate the benefits of workplace literacy/basic skills programmes, in the hope that employers will assume the costs of longer term provision. This has meant that most, if not all, such programmes are, in effect, 'demonstration', 'pilot', or 'experimental' programmes and that the worker/participants are, ultimately, experimental subjects. It has also meant that programme deliverers have tended to view the employers, rather than the workers who participate in the workplace basic skills programmes, as their clients. The result of this has, in many instances, been less than positive for workers. For, while the scope of programmes may be narrowed and the duration of programmes limited to suit the employer's priorities, deliverers' claims for their programmes' benefits to the employer are rarely tempered.

The gap between workplace basic skills providers' claims and their capacity to deliver

The duration of workplace literacy programmes is generally far too short for participants to achieve meaningful change in their literacy competencies. Yet, even if courses were extended significantly, there are a number of other issues which would render many programmes unable to prepare workers adequately for the assessments they are likely to be subjected to following the programmes. In both Canada and the United States, for example, much workplace literacy programming is provided by minimally trained volunteers. In their zeal to carve out new territory, many workplace literacy providers have evidently abandoned the standards they might otherwise apply to the delivery of education. Reports on workplace literacy programmes reveal that, in many cases, providers agree to organize programmes even where the employer is clearly not sufficiently committed to create the conditions for the programmes to be conducted properly. In one instance, for example, college staff began classes at midnight to accommodate workers' changing shift schedules (BCEL, No. 24, July 1990). Workplace literacy reports also provide numerous examples of the use of inappropriate facilities for programme delivery (see, for example, Hikes 1989; Collins *et al.* 1989). In many cases, no space is assigned at all; teachers carry their flip-charts, markers and other supplies and have to locate an available space each time a class is scheduled. Such was the case, for example, with a programme offered at a Canadian general hospital (Garlick-Griffin 1993).

If we take the standards for the public provision of education and training as our guide, it is clear that many workplace literacy programmes are patently sub-standard. They are also frequently below the standards normally observed for employer or union provided training. Yet workers who participate in such programmes are commonly evaluated as if they had participated in either well-established and well-supported education programmes or in quality workplace training.

Those who market their workplace literacy programmes typically promise a wide range of measurable results. Even the most general (and, therefore, least threatening) types of programme evaluation ask supervisors to monitor workers' performance for evidence of improvement (see, for example, Schultz 1992; Evaluation Research 1992). Although programmes may be provided by minimally trained volunteers who do not require 'specific knowledge', such programmes may, nevertheless, be evaluated through asking 'superiors or co-workers (whether they have) noticed differences in the learner's job-related literacy skills or performance' (Ioannou *et al.* 1991: 146). A US federal government report on workplace literacy programmes noted that in one workplace education programme (Polaroid's much celebrated in-house basic skill programme), instructors 'check in' with the employee/student's supervisor 'after every 10 hours of tutoring to determine whether there is any skills transfer back to the job' (US Departments of Education and Labor 1988: 21).

In many cases, workplace literacy providers have promoted the use of productivity studies as a means of assessing the benefits of their programmes to the firm. A review of the Massachusetts state workplace programmes, for example, noted that one company was looking into the possibility of tracking the difference in hourly output pre- and post-ESL (English as a Second Language) classes (Hikes 1991: 326). Indeed, the statute creating the US National Workplace Literacy Programmes required a demonstrated impact on productivity in return for investment of federal funds (Evaluation Research 1992). A report from a conference of project directors of the US national programmes included, among a number of methods for assessing workers' performance in the NWLP programmes, establishing productivity ratings, measuring employees' safety records, assessing employees' attitudes and ('where the workers' abilities have a direct impact on company sales') measuring sales volumes (ibid.: 37–8).

In fact, many workers enrolled in NWLP programmes would seem to have been subjected to doubly unrealistic (and, thus, unfair) assessment as Schultz's (1992) study found that most of the NWLP programmes which taught ESL used standardized ESL testing before and after the programme to assess gains. In spite of the fact that the NWLP itself prohibited the use of standard adult education curricula and mandated a strictly job-related programme content established through the 'literacy task analysis' process. Indeed participants were expected to make significant gains in reading levels as measured on standardized tests notwithstanding the fact that most programmes were limited to 120 hours or less of instruction.

It is clear from such examples that assessment, as it has tended to be practised in respect of workplace literacy/basic skills programmes, has the potential to put worker participants under considerable pressure and, in many cases, in some degree of jeopardy. That 120 hours (or less) of language instruction, for example, can result in an employer 'expectation' of increases in individual productivity or improvements in individual safety records is good reason to ask whether such programmes are supported by employers because they provide a legitimized opportunity both to evaluate workers and to exert pressures on individuals as well as targeted groups. Indeed, even if workplace basic skills programmes were of a much higher standard, the use of such measures to assess 'learning' would be questionable. For what is being measured in most cases (productivity, product quality, workplace safety) is not only outside the scope of fundamental education programmes, it is also largely outside the control of individual workers, irrespective of their learning gains in such programmes.

Conclusion

This chapter has provided a critical examination of the use of 'basic skills assessments' by (and for) employers and the institution of literacy/basic skills programmes in the workplace in response to supposed basic skills 'deficits' among workers. It has argued that the use of basic skills assessments has involved increased, and in all likelihood, unwarranted scrutiny of workers in low-skill, low-pay work. The potential for this increased scrutiny to further marginalize already disadvantaged workers is enormous. It is in the United States where this potential has been most clearly and most generally realized in regressive changes to employment legislation which have specifically taken protections away from less formally educated workers. However, such negative impacts have not been confined to the United States; and, though they may be less recognized where they are not entrenched in law, the consequences are no less real for the affected workers. For, wherever workers are subjected to assessment in the context of employment (or job seeking), that assessment is potentially of 'make or break' significance for the individual assessed. Where assessments bear little relationship to the actual skills (or attributes) required by the job, they must necessarily function to screen out many individuals who might be well capable of doing the job but whose educational attainment or linguistic background limits their ability to successfully complete the tasks assessed. Those who promote the use of basic skills assessment in the workplace (including government agencies, educationalists and trade unionists) need to recognize that such assessments may well place workers at increased risk of a number of negative consequences including loss of promotion opportunities or pay increases, enforced participation in basic skills programmes over and above their normal working hours – and even job loss.

Where basic skills assessments are commonly assumed to have a positive outcome for workers, that is, when the response to the assessment is the establishment of a workplace literacy/basic skills programme, this chapter has argued that targeted workers are frequently subjected to further scrutiny which may be even more problematic than the initial assessment. For, though workers may be singled out and required to participate in such programmes, they are rarely provided with opportunities to gain significant new (or transferable) skills. The gap between employer expectations and the capacity of the programme to prepare workers to meet those expectations means that they are frequently subjected to unfair assessments and, most probably, suffer consequences in their employment. Again, those who promote the establishment of programmes of fundamental education in the workplace need to recognize that the objectives of such education may not coincide and indeed, may even conflict, with the objectives of employers or the demands of many jobs. The conditions under which such programmes must frequently (perhaps inevitably) be conducted are in many respects inimical to the pursuit of genuine educational endeavour. Unrealistic time limitations, narrow curricular objectives of questionable educational value, assessments which may influence employment or pay prospects, all of these must necessarily affect the quality of the experience for participants. Any programme which claims to provide general or fundamental education, including literacy, numeracy, second language acquisition, educational upgrading, needs to be conducted in a setting where participants are free to question and to develop skills and abilities to their potential without the threat that failure to meet prescribed criteria could jeopardize their livelihood. Programmes which conflate specific organizational objectives (increased productivity, enhanced loyalty, improved industrial relations) with educational objectives are unlikely to be of real educational benefit to the participants and, it must be acknowledged, may actually be of negative worth to the individual.

The principal focus of this chapter has been on the ways in which both the use of tests or assessments unrelated to job content and the institution of programmes of general education in workplaces are likely to be problematic for targeted workers, and unlikely to be of benefit to them. It may be argued that many of the problems discussed in the chapter are attributable to the fact that both the assessments and the programmes under discussion have been undertaken in the context of a supposed 'crisis' of worker literacy. Undoubtedly, the social campaigning which has provided the justification for the hugely expanded use of testing has also provided opportunities for misuse, whether deliberate or otherwise. However, it should also be recognized that there are fundamental tensions between employers' goals (which will necessarily relate to productivity/profitability/efficiency) and the objectives of programmes of general education or the self-defined educational goals of individual workers. Any attempt to establish workers' entitlement to general educational upgrading must acknowledge these tensions and ensure that the development of programmes does not unfairly jeopardize job security and that it does present genuine opportunities for workers' educational goals to be realized. Although employer/workplace training needs will sometimes coincide with the general educational or training needs of individual workers, very often they will not. It is important, therefore, not to conflate the two. Above all, any assessment needs to be meaningfully related to programme content. If workers are to participate willingly and to benefit from programmes, they will need assurance that the assessment of their attainment is objective and fair and is not a means to an unstated end.

Notes

1   The chapter draws on research conducted in the United States, Canada and England over the 1990s decade. The principal focus of the discussion is North America, with particular reference to the United States where the widespread use of 'basic skills' testing and the promotion and institution of workplace-based fundamental education programmes have been purposely used to effect an extension of employer prerogative and the reversal of legislative protection for less formally educated workers. Where applicable, reference is also made to England which has been influenced, albeit relatively moderately, by the North American developments.
2   Since Labour came to power in the United Kingdom in 1997, there has been a shift to a stronger role for the State.
3   In the United States, workplace literacy programming peaked in the early 1990s, and had significantly declined by 1997 when the National Workplace Literacy Programme was terminated. In Canada, the peak in activity similarly occurred in the early 1990s; however, a 1997 increase of $7 million to the National Literacy Secretariat was largely earmarked for workplace literacy. Since the publication of the Moser Report (1998) in the UK there has been a resurgence of interest in basic skills provision in the workplace.
4   Schultz (1992) has estimated that possibly as many as half of all programmes developed under the NWLP initiative in the US were language programmes for workers with limited English proficiency.

Bibliography

Anorve, R.L. (1989) 'Community-Based Literacy Educators: Experts and Catalysts for Change', in A. Fingeret and P. Jurmo (eds), *Participatory Literacy Education*, San Francisco, CA: Jossey-Bass.

Business Council for Effective Literacy (BCEL), *Newsletter*, various issues (September 1984–July 1993).

Collins, S.D., Balmuth, M. and Jean, P. (1989) 'So We Can Use Our Own Names and Write the Laws by Which We Live: Educating the New US Labor Force', *Harvard Educational Review*, 59, 4: 454–69.

Conference Board of Canada (1992) *Basic Skills – Basic Business*, Report to the National Literacy Secretariat, Government of Canada, Toronto: The Conference Board of Canada.

The Creative Research Group (1987) *Literacy in Canada: A Research Report*, prepared for Southam News, Ottawa, Toronto: Southam Newspaper Group.

DesLauriers, R.C. (1990) *The Impact of Employee Illiteracy on Canadian Business*, Toronto: The Conference Board of Canada.

Evaluation Research (1992) *Workplace Education: Voices from the Field*, Washington, DC: Department of Education.

Evetts, J. and Flanagan, P. (1991) 'Basic Skills Upgrading: A Trades Training Perspective', in M.C. Taylor, G.R. Lewe and J.A. Draper (eds), *Basic Skills for the Workplace*, Toronto: Culture Concepts.

Garlick-Griffin, C. (1993) 'Evaluation of the Workplace Education Programmes, Victoria General Hospital, Halifax, Nova Scotia', unpublished report.

Goddard, R.W. (1989) 'Combating Illiteracy in the Workplace', *Management World*, 18, 2: 8–11.

Goetz, E., Bent, B. and Sharpe, S. (1991) 'A Preliminary Study of Job-related Communications in British Columbia Sawmills', report prepared for the Council of Forest Industries, British Columbia and International Woodworkers' Association Canada, Vancouver: Job Communication Project (JCP) Research.

Gordon, D.M. (1996) 'Underpaid Workers, Bloated Corporations: Two Pieces in the Puzzle of US Economic Decline', *Dissent*, Spring: 23–4.

Gowen, S.G. (1992) *The Politics of Workplace Literacy: A Case Study*, New York: Teachers College Press.

Greenberg, E.R. (ed.) (1992) *1992 AMA Survey of Basic Skills Testing and Training*, New York: American Management Association.

Hikes, J. (1989) 'The Massachusetts Workplace Education Programmes', *Connections: A Journal of Adult Literacy*, 3: 12–17.

—— (1991) 'The Massachusetts Workplace Education Programmes', in M.C. Taylor, G.R. Lewe and J.A. Draper (eds), *Basic Skills for the Workplace*, Toronto: Culture Concepts.

Hoddinott, S. (1997) 'The Abuses of Literacy: The Making of a Worker "Basic Skills" Crisis in England and North America', Ph.D. Dissertation, Coventry: University of Warwick.

Ioannou, M., Nore, G., Poulton, B. and Thompson, S. (1991) 'How to Assess Learners and Build Workplace Literacy Programmes', in M.C. Taylor, G.R Lewe and J.A. Draper (eds), *Basic Skills for the Workplace*, Toronto: Culture Concepts.

Johnston, W. (1991) *1991 Inventory of Workplace Literacy Programmes*, Toronto: ABC Canada.

Johnston, W.B. and Packer, A.H. (1987) *Workforce 2000: Work and Workers for the Twenty-first Century*, Indianapolis, IN: Hudson Institute.

Kempa, S. (1995) *The Cost to Industry: Basic Skills and the UK Workforce*, London: The Adult Literacy and Basic Skills Unit.

McIntyre, M. (1991) *Promoting Workplace Literacy in Kingston: A Process Report*, Kingston, Ont.: Kingston Literacy.

Martin, J. (1990) 'Workplace Testing: Why Can't We Get It Right?', *Across the Board*, xxvii, 12, December: 32–9.

Moser, K. (1998) *A Fresh Start. Improving Literacy and Numeracy*, Sudbury, DfEE.

Nieduszynska, S. (1992) 'Work-Place Basic Education', *RaPAL Bulletin*, 17: 1–5.

Philippi, J.W. (1993) *Legal Considerations Concerning Literacy Testing in the Workplace*, Springfield, VA: Performance Plus Learning Consultants.

Rees, L. (1990) *Setting up Workplace Basic Skills Training: Guidelines for Practitioners*, London: The Adult Literacy and Basic Skills Unit and Workbase Training.

Rosenfeld, S.A. (1987) 'Learning While Earning: Worksite Literacy Programmes', *Foresight: Model Programmes for Economic Development*, Research Triangle Park, NC: Southern Growth Policies Board.

Rumberger, R.W. (1981) *Overeducation in the US Labor Market*, New York: Praeger.

—— (1984) 'The Growing Imbalance Between Education and Work', *Phi Delta Kappan*, 65, 5: 342–6.

Schachter, H. (1995) 'The Dispossessed', *Canadian Business*, May: 30–40.

Schultz, K. (1992) *Training for Basic Skills or Educating Workers?: Changing Conceptions of Workplace Education Programmes*, Berkeley, CA: National Center for Research in Vocational Education, University of California at Berkeley.

Sperazi, L. (1991) *Education in the Workplace: An Employer's Guide to Planning Adult Basic Skills Programmes in Small Business and Industry in Massachusetts*, Newton, MA: The Commonwealth Literacy Campaign.

United States Department of Education (USDOE) and United States Department of Labor (USDOL) (1988) *The Bottom Line: Basic Skills in the Workplace*, Washington, DC: US Government Printing Office.

Part 2

The workplace as a learning environment

7 Learning through work

Workplace participatory practices

Stephen Billett

Chapter summary

This chapter proposes workplace learning in terms of participatory practices. Learning through work is interdependent between the individuals' participation and workplace affordances. Rather than being informal, workplace activities, opportunities and support for learning are directed towards its continuity and in ways often inherently pedagogical. Individuals, likewise, engage and learn in workplaces as directed by their personal goals and directions. Core tensions in this relationship are between these two sets of continuities. A critique of the current discourse on workplace learning is used as a basis to propose an alternative view of workplace learning environments as participatory practices.

Introduction

This chapter proposes fresh ways of considering workplaces as learning spaces where individuals learn through experiences that are mediated by both the contributions of workplaces and individuals' agency. An elaboration of the duality of these contributions is used to: (1) advance a fresh conception of workplaces as learning environments; (2) promote their legitimacy as sites for learning; and (3) provide bases by which workplace learning experiences can be understood, evaluated and made more effective. These purposes are realized through advancing the processes and outcomes of workplace learning as participatory practices. Such practices are held to be both dually and reciprocally constituted. Their duality is located, on the one hand, in how the workplace affords opportunities for individuals to participate in activities and interactions, and on the other, on how individuals elect to engage with what the workplace affords. Their reciprocity is found in the interdependence between the key elements of participatory practices, the affordance of workplaces and individuals' agencies. Underpinning the significance of these reciprocal processes to learning, are the propositions that the knowledge to be learnt has social sources and is constructed by individuals through inter-psychological processes (Vygotsky 1978) – between social sources and individuals – and that these processes are ongoing in everyday conscious thinking and acting, such as that exercised when participating in workplace tasks. Therefore, as individuals engage in social practices, such as work, they engage in an ongoing process of knowledge construction and refinement.

In proposing and elaborating these views, learning through working life is not seen as distinct from individuals' participation and learning in other kinds of social practices, such as family life, or in educational settings. The knowledge learnt through participation in these settings will be more or less applicable to the setting where it is learnt and across other settings. No category of social practice (e.g. educational institutions) has a monopoly in promoting robust learning. Instead, the kinds of activities and interactions individuals engage in are central to the type and quality of learning that occurs in social practices. The combination of and reciprocity between the contribution of the particular setting and the individual's interest and capacity shapes the qualities of what is learnt. Therefore, workplaces, homes or community settings can be as rich learning environments as any other setting. Nonetheless, different kinds of settings provide experiences (e.g. practice in workplaces; instruction in classrooms) that can make particular contributions. These settings are all learning spaces with intents, activities, and interactions focused on sustaining their practices through participant learning (Billett 2002). As with family and educational activities, participation in workplace practices is focused on maintaining the: (1) continuity of the social practice; (2) the interests of those within the social practice; and (3) the developmental trajectory of those individuals who exercise their agency through their participation in the social practice that comprises the workplace.

In elaborating this case, the chapter is structured as follows. In the first section, it proposes that individuals' participation in work activities is richly associated with their learning. Moreover, different kinds of participation have different developmental consequences for individuals. Therefore, how individuals participate and interact in workplaces is central to their learning. The second section advances the rationale for and bases of considering workplace learning as participatory practices. This participation includes the kinds of activities individuals are permitted to engage in and the kinds of support and guidance afforded by the workplace. It follows that the invitational qualities of the workplace (i.e. the degree by which and in what ways individuals are invited to participate) shape opportunities for learning through work. However, participation and learning are not situationally determined, as individuals elect how they engage in workplaces. In the third section, these bases are elaborated in terms of continuities. Intersecting workplaces' need for continuity are the individuals' aspirations, subjectivities and identities, reflected in how they exercise their engagement and learning in workplaces. In the fourth section, a critique of the current discourse of workplace learning is used to press for consideration of different concepts to understand workplaces as learning environments in their own right. It questions the appropriateness of referring to workplace learning experiences as being 'informal' when they are structured by historical and cultural practices and micro-social processes. Instead, it proposes viewing workplace learning in terms of participation, continuity of practices and individuals' engagement underpinned by their agency. Finally, in conclusion, it is proposed that such a reconceptualization of workplaces as learning environments assists how they are discussed, evaluated and exercised as learning spaces.

Learning as participation

Workplaces, like homes, community settings and educational institutions are generative of social practices in which learning occurs through participation in those practices. Learning can be understood as permanent or semi-permanent changes in how individuals think and act. When individuals engage in thinking and acting, more than merely executing a process or task, their knowledge is changed in some way, however minutely, by that process. When cognitive processes are engaged, the experience is always new in some way (Valsiner 2000). Accordingly, the processes of thinking and acting become indistinguishable from learning. Therefore, learning when considered as changes in existing knowledge and ways of knowing, is inherent in everyday thinking and acting. It is not reserved for particular settings or interludes, although some experiences may provide richer learning outcomes than others. The most likely change arising through everyday thinking and acting, will be to reinforce or hone what is already known. A likely outcome from engaging in a task that is new to the individual is to extend what they already know: the development of new knowledge. Moreover, the sources of the knowledge to be learnt are mostly social, which require interactions with social partners (e.g. other workers, experts), who possess that knowledge or with artefacts (e.g. tools, text, workplaces), which embody the knowledge to be learnt. Through the need to engage with others, and in activities that have social genesis and because of associations between change and this engagement, the process of learning can be understood through the concept of participatory practices.

These propositions find support across a range of learning theories. Cognitive learning theories hold that in overcoming perturbations or problems, new learning arises. However, the routineness of the activities determine whether they provide opportunities for new learning or the refining of what has already been learnt as cognitive processes become increasingly automated (Anderson 1982). Piaget's (1976) notion of overcoming disequilibrium, the unknown in what is encountered, through the processes of assimilation (i.e. reconciling what is experienced with what individuals already know) and accommodation (i.e. inciting new categories of knowledge from experiences) position thinking and learning as one process. Similarly, Meade (1934) proposed learning as an ongoing stream of conscious thought that constitutes and contributes to individuals' cognitive processes over a lifespan. Lave (1993), an anthropologist, also recognized associations between engagement in tasks and learning when she concluded that whenever you examine individuals engaging in practice you identify learning. The sociocultural constructivist psychological perspective (e.g. Rogoff 1995) explicitly links participation in activities with learning, emphasizing the inter-psychological processes that occur through engagement in goal-directed activities that have social geneses. Lave and Wenger (1991) and Rogoff (1995) refer directly to participation in social practice as being analogous to learning. Rogoff (1990, 1995) draws on ideas about micro-genesis, the accrual of knowledge through encounters with the social world, when she refers to micro-genetic development, the moment-by-moment learning that occurs through engagement with the social world. Collectively, these theoretical perspectives, albeit with different emphases, hold that more than an end in itself, participation in activities, such as those in workplaces, incites change in individuals' understandings and capacities (i.e. learning). While some cognitive theorists only associate encountering novel problems with learning, this fails to account for the person-dependent nature of what constitutes a novel task and the different ways of engagement with the same 'new' task. In keeping with ideas of the ongoing processes of knowledge construction advocated above, it is proposed that learning and participation in work are inseparable.

The activities that individuals engage in and from which they learn are not aberrant, they are sourced in historical and cultural practice and manifested in particular ways in social practices, which are then construed in particular ways by individuals. Therefore, the change or learning that occurs is shaped by social sources, inter-psychologically. Most of the knowledge humans learn is not innovative, although it may be new to the individuals involved. Instead, it has developed over time and has particular purposes that are applicable to the circumstances where it needs to be enacted. Vocational practices have historical, cultural and situational origins that include their distribution (Billett 1998). The same goes for domestic tasks in the home (Goodnow and Warton 1991) or parenting (Rogoff 1990) and those practices privileged in educational institutions. They are all practices that have evolved over time to meet the requirements of particular cultural needs (Scribner 1985) and are constituted in particular ways in each setting (Billett 2001b). The manifestation of the particular social practice is shaped by a complex of cultural needs and situational factors such as local requirements, the individuals involved, and locally negotiated goals for the activities, including bases for judgements about performance (see Engeström and Middleton 1996; Suchman 1996). So when individuals engage in activities in workplaces, they access knowledge that is socially sourced and situationally constituted. The goals to which these efforts are directed and from which learning occurs are likewise socially generated.

Nonetheless, when considering learning as participation in social practice, it is important to stress that engagement in and what is learnt from socially determined practices is not wholly determined by the social practice. Instead, individuals determine how they participate in and what they construe and learn from their experience. Rather than being uni-directional, the knowledge is co-constructed (Valsiner 1994) through interactions between the social practice and the individuals who participate in learning.

Workplace participatory practices

A consideration of learning in workplaces as participation is important for two key reasons. First, if learning is seen as a consequence of participation in social practices generally (such as those involved in the production of goods or services), rather than as something privileged by practices within educational institutions, this may broaden the understanding of learning generally and learning through work, in particular. Clearly, learning occurs in circumstances other than educational institutions. Neither Piaget's processes of overcoming disequilibrium, nor micro-genesis, are reserved for particular settings. They are responses to everyday encounters and experiences. When learning is conceptualized as being the process and product of participation in social practice (e.g. Rogoff 1995) this prompts a broader consideration of learning and what this means for the promotion of intentional learning. An appraisal of individuals' engagement in workplace activities and access to its affordances may inform a broader view of learning experiences in workplaces and their enhancement. Certainly, the widening acceptance of learning as an inter-psychological process (i.e. between individuals and social sources of knowledge) prompts a consideration of learning as engagement with the social world generally, and not only through close personal interactions as Vygotsky (1978) emphasizes, but through engagement in the physical and social environment that constitutes the workplace.

Second, there are important procedural reasons for making participation and participatory practices a central concern for a workplace pedagogy. For most workers, the workplace represents the only or most viable location to learn and/or develop their vocational practice. Therefore, understanding workplaces as sites for learning is important in attempting to foster ongoing learning at work. This goal has become urgent given that in current lifelong learning policies and practices (OECD 1998) the responsibility for maintaining the currency of vocational practice is being increasingly transferred to workers. In this context, a more finely grained analysis of how the opportunities to engage in work, the kinds of tasks individuals are permitted to participate in, and the guidance provided becomes key to understanding and evaluating how and what individuals learn through work.

As work sites are the prime source of the knowledge required for work, how opportunities to participate are distributed across workers or cohorts of workers in often-contested workplaces becomes central to understanding learning through working life. Workplace affordances or invitational qualities are also likely to shape how individuals elect to engage in goal-directed activities and to secure direct guidance through close or proximal interpersonal interactions between experts and novices or more indirect (distal) kinds of guidance, for example, through opportunities to observe and listen (Billett and Boud 2001). Both of these kinds of guidance have consequences for the knowledge individuals construct. Close guidance is salient to learning knowledge that would be difficult to learn without the assistance of a more knowledgeable partner. Learning the concepts underpinning vocational practice (e.g. service requirements, force factors, hygiene) or processes and concepts that are hidden (e.g. electronic processes, the structure of hair, past practices that shape current approaches) are likely to require close interactions with more experienced co-workers who can make these concepts and practices accessible. Indirect guidance contributes to how tasks are undertaken and completed. However, as with participation in activities, the contribution of guidance is dependent on learners' engagement (Billett 2001a). What directs individuals to engage in the demanding tasks of learning new knowledge and refining what they already know is premised on their agency. Put simply, participation and learning need to be seen as dual and reciprocal processes in which individuals exercise their agency.

It would be remiss to conclude this brief discussion on learning as participation without referring to the quality of learning outcomes. It is often assumed that learning in social settings other than those specializing in teaching will lead to highly specific and concrete outcomes (Resnick 1987; Marsick and Watkins 1990; Prawat 1993; Evans 1993). That is, the scope of the application of what has been learnt will be limited to the circumstances of its construction. However, the learning arising from activities in workplaces is not necessarily concrete. Adaptable learning can be incited in places other than educational institutions. Rogoff (1982) and Rogoff and Gauvain (1984) found that the potential for transfer from non-schooling kinds of activities was as great as that from school-based activities. The development of what Vygotsky (1978) refers to as scientific concepts, which are held to be more robust than everyday concepts, is not dependent on where they were learnt but whether the concepts and procedures were made accessible in ways that incite their adaptation to other circumstances (Glassman 2001). Moreover, assumptions about widespread transfer need to be challenged given the paucity of transfer of learning from educational institutions (e.g. Raizen 1994).

In all, the idea that there are inherently transferable capacities that can be learnt and applied universally seems fanciful. The requirements for what constitutes a problem and the bases for judging performance, such as elegance of solution, are highly situational (Billett 2001b). Given the need to account for diverse situational factors, it is unlikely that capacities that have universal applicability can ever be realized. Put straightforwardly, expectations of high levels of transfer from learning in any social practice and, particularly between different practices, are unrealistic. The exceptions are specific procedures, for example, key boarding and wiring a power point, whose enactment can be transferred directly (although the goals to which they are directed will vary), and top-level heuristics, such as look before you leap and think before you act (Evans 1993). Conceptualizing adaptability and expectations for transfer should shift from a focus on capacities to perform across broad domains of activities (i.e. an occupation) to a focus on situational performance requirements (i.e. in a particular workplace).

Having advanced the case for learning as participation, the next section elaborates the bases for participation in workplace settings.

Bases for participation in workplaces

As proposed above, the invitational qualities of a workplace are consrituted by factors associated with its norms and practices and directed to assist its continuity. These include those associated with the continuity of the work practice itself and the maintenance of particular interests within the workplace.

Continuity of the practice and interests within the practice

Evidence is available of the deliberate structuring of learning experiences within social practices to maintain their continuity. This evidence refers to both the overall structuring of learning experiences and the intentional development of specific procedures and concepts. The Guarenos of the Orinoco Delta of Venezuela teach children cultivation, animal husbandry, hunting and fishing through providing an initial understanding of each task and its goals and then by engaging in learning by doing (Ruddle and Chesterfield 1979, cited in Rogoff and Gardiner 1984). Yucatan birth attendants learn their profession through the structured observation of more experienced practitioners (Jordan 1989). This approach to learning midwifery proceeds with little or no separation between participation in working life and learning midwifery. Hutchins (1983) identified a deliberately structured approach that was used in assisting fishermen to learn to navigate. Substitute objects (shells and other beach debris) were used to represent star and constellations patterns that cannot be seen during the day. So where the learning required to sustain the practice (fishing) could not proceed through normal work activities, a substitute activity is provided. The structuring of these kinds of learning experiences is essential to the continuity of social practices and communities. Moreover, they are structured and 'formalized' by their community's norms and practices. Although concerned with the continuity of that practice or community, rather than individual learning, the structuring of these experiences is often inherently pedagogic. This is the same for accessing workplace activities. Their pedagogic qualities are shaped by participatory practices: that is how individuals engage in the inter-psychological process of thinking-acting-learning through (workplace) activities.

The deliberate structuring of learning experiences often serves the needs of particular interests. Workplace cliques and affiliations (e.g. occupational groupings), the gender, race, language or employment standing and status of workers all influence the distribution of opportunities to participate (Bernhardt 1999; Billett 2001c; Hull 1997). What is afforded and to whom, can be directed towards maintaining the standing of these interests. To preserve their standing, full-time workers deliberately constrained what activities part-time workers can engage in and the degree of support that is afforded (Bernhardt 1999), coal workers provide access to support to workers on the basis of their industrial affiliations and seniority (Billett 2001c), and Korean workers in US workplaces were scape-goated and labelled as incompetents and marginalized by other workers because of their poor English language skills (Hull 1997). Hence, workplace participatory practices are often contested. This contestation arises between 'newcomers' who are seeking to participate more fully and 'old-timers' who fear displacement (Lave and Wenger 1991); full- or part-time workers (Hughes and Bernhardt 1999); and workers with different roles and status (Darrah 1996; Hull 1997). Seniority in workplaces (Dore and Sako 1989) and work demarcations (Danford 1998) influence the bases of access to work-tasks and guidance, particularly for opportunities prized for their potential to promote individual advancement. There is also contestation between institutionalized interests, such as those of workers and management (Danford 1998).

Work practices can deliberately constrain individuals' participation in the workplace (Billett 2001a) in order to best suit the enterprises' goals and continuity. This constraint might be used to maintain the work practice's viability, in terms of its required level of skill utilization, or quality of service. Alternatively, the distribution of opportunities may also reflect employers' attempts to maintain control of the workplace's activities and thereby limit the range of tasks and decision-making in which workers engage (Danford 1998). Overall, this contestation serves to distribute opportunities for engaging in new or prized work activities (from which new learning might be derived) and access to guidance and support. Consequently, individuals or cohorts of individuals will experience different kinds of affordances, depending on their affiliation, associations, gender, language skills, employment status and standing in the workplace.

The bases for maintaining continuity of practice are multifaceted, complex, negotiated and contested. Given the salience of access to the kinds of activities individuals engage in and the guidance and support required to secure what cannot be learnt alone, how the work practice and interests within it distributes these opportunities is central to the quality of individuals' learning. In all these, the exercise of power and control is evident in the distribution of opportunities. It is not ad hoc, workplace learning experiences are structured by power and interests (Bierema 2001; Solomon 1999). In these ways, workplaces represent a socially contested and physically constituted learning space in which participatory practices are key pedagogical devices.

Individual engagement

Despite the complex bases of contributions to learning provided by workplaces, decisions about engagement in and learning from work are not situationally determined. Individuals' agency mediates and shapes their engagement in work practice and what is learnt through that engagement. Individuals are not passive in their participatory practices and learning (Billett et al. in press) or construction of occupational identities (Somerville 2002). Instead, their agency determines how what workplaces afford is construed and judged worthy of participation. As foreshadowed, individuals' agency determines how they engage in the process of learning, with rich learning being particularly effortful. Individuals' socially constituted personal histories or ontogenies (Cole 1998; Scribner 1985) engender identities and subjectivities that incite particular ways of knowing, understanding and engaging with the social world. Ontogenies are uniquely socially shaped through participation in different social practices throughout life histories (Billett 1998). Consequently, individuals' engagement in and learning through work will always be unique in some ways (Valsiner 2000), made so by the inevitable negotiation between the workplace's norms and practices and individuals' subjectivities and identities. Therefore, not surprisingly, individuals can elect to dis-identify with social practices in which they engage (Hodges 1998); workers resist engaging in team work when it clashes with their cultural mores (e.g. Darrah 1996); workers avoid participating in training that compromises their employment; and new recruits ignore and deny affordances intended to assist their participation (Billett 2001a). To illustrate this last point, Billett's study revealed how one new worker treated with belligerence his assigned workplace mentor and scoffed at the affordances of the workplace, as he believed he was more competent than his mentor and his vocational practice more sophisticated than that being enacted in his new workplace. The tension here is between the goals of the social practice and those of the individual.

Much of the above has argued against the unquestioned privileging of educational institutions as sites for learning. However, a key distinction between workplaces and educational institutions may be the identity of the learners. Individuals participating in educational institutions may hold different kinds of identities and subjectivities, whose purposes are to engage deliberately in knowledge acquisition, than those who are positioned as workers in workplaces. Hence, there may be different bases from which individuals exercise their agency. For instance, Somerville (2002) reported cathartic incidents had to occur in workers' lives (e.g. work accidents or serious health problems) before they embraced an identity associated with deliberate learning (e.g. to work more safely, to live healthier). Therefore, learners' personal experiences are likely to incite them to take actions that are central to learning through work.

In sum, workplace learning experiences represent an interaction between the enactment of the social practice of the workplace and individuals' agency as they engage in the workplace. Whether considering workplace learning through participation in everyday work or through intentionally organized learning activities, these reciprocal participatory practices are likely to shape both the learning process and outcomes.

Re-conceptualizing workplace learning

In order to re-conceptualize workplaces as legitimate learning spaces in their own right, it is necessary to transform the current discourse on learning through work. Even when well intentioned (e.g. Marsick and Watkins 1990), describing workplaces as informal, non-formal or unstructured learning environments is negative, imprecise and ill-focused. These descriptions do little to assist the understanding or standing of workplaces as learning spaces. From what has been argued above, three propositions critique the use of these kinds of terms to describe and discuss learning experiences and outcomes in workplaces.

First, describing something by what it is not (e.g. informal, not formalized or unstructured, not structured) does little to illuminate its qualities or characteristics. The use of concepts and assumptions associated with educational institutions are often advanced as premises for what constitutes the formalisms and structure of legitimate learning experiences. As teaching and learning are commonly, albeit erroneously, held to be synonymous, the absence of qualified teachers and classroom-like interactions in workplaces leads to assumptions that the learning will be inferior to that in educational institutions (Collins *et al.* 1989; Prawat 1993; Ericsson and Lehmann 1996). From a perspective that privileges the practices of educational institutions, the absence of a written curriculum document used to plan teachers' actions and learners' experiences and qualified teachers and didactic practices, raises the concern that learning through work will be ad hoc, weak, concrete and incidental (Marsick and Watkins 1990; Resnick 1987). Workplace learning experiences may be seen as ad hoc because they are not consistent with practices adopted in educational institutions. Yet, as discussed above and elaborated below, it is imprecise and misleading to describe engagement in work activities as being unplanned or unstructured, as they are intentional. Moreover, rather than being incidental these experiences are often central to the continuity of the work practice. While concerns about the development of transferable knowledge through experience outside of educational institutions are legitimate (Evans 1993; Prawat 1993), they are also relevant to schooling (e.g. Scribner 1984; Raizen 1994). There is evidence of both adaptable learning occurring away from educational institutions and concrete learning arising from experiences inside educational institutions. This evidence challenges the easy assumptions about workplace learning experiences being ad hoc, weak and concrete. Instead, it seems the kinds of contributions furnished by social practices will shape the potential richness of the learning experience.

Second, rather than being without structure and intent workplace activities are actually highly structured. Just as the goals, norms and practices of educational institutions frame the activities students participate in, similarly workplace goals and practices determine the tasks and activities in which workers engage (Billett 2001a; Lave 1990; Scribner 1997/1998). As argued, rather than being unintentional, participants' engagement in different kinds of social practices are often central to the continuity of that practice. Whether participating in navigation tasks (Hutchins 1983), weaving (Childs and Greenfield 1980), coal mining (Billett 2001a), the calculation of dairy products (Scribner 1984), midwifery (Jordan 1989) and tailoring (Lave 1990), this activity is intentionally organized to structure workers' access to the knowledge needed to sustain those practices. Some components of this structuring have been referred to by Lave (1990) as the 'learning curriculum', a pathway of experiences that leads to full participation. The key point is that participation and learning are central to the ongoing existence of these practices.

Although not stated in the form of a syllabus, pathways of activities exist in workplaces that are often inherently pedagogical. For instance, Lave (1990) found that tailors' apprentices learnt by participating in work activities that were sequenced to provide engagement in tasks of increasing accountability and complexity. This pathway of participation incrementally provided greater access to the capacities required for work. Pathways of learning activities have also been identified in other work settings. In hairdressing salons, the tasks apprentices engage in and their progress through these tasks are determined by the particular salon's approach to hairdressing (Billett 2001a). In one salon, where clients are attended to by a number of hairdressers, the apprentices first engage in 'tea and tidy' activities, such as keeping the salon neat and providing beverages for clients. Through these activities, apprentices learn about hygiene, cleanliness and procedures for determining client needs and develop confidence in interacting with clients. Next, the apprentices wash and then later rinse out of clients' hair the chemicals used to shape and/or colour. Engagement in these tasks advances the apprentices' capacities to communicate and negotiate with clients in more intimate ways. The apprentices learn inter-psychologically through direct interpersonal interactions and more indirect kinds of participation (observation and listening) to understand and practise important elements of each task (e.g. the importance of removing all the chemicals), and each task's place and significance in the hairdressing process (Billett 2001a). Later, the apprentices work alongside experienced hairdressers, helping to place rods and curlers in clients' hair. Before being permitted to cut women's hair, they commence cutting men's hair, which is held to be less difficult and of lower accountability than cutting women's hair. The apprentices continue on this pathway of activities until they can style hair independently.

However, in another salon, where each hairdresser undertakes the entire hairdressing task, the apprentice is required to learn to cut and colour far earlier than in the first salon. The structured pathway of activities in the second salon includes gaining competence with procedures that permit early independent practice. Consequently, in the same occupation, the particular workplace's goals and practices determined much of the structuring of activities and the kinds of tasks to be undertaken and to what standard. The two salons have quite distinct hairdressing goals and practices, and different bases for learning to ensure their continuity (Billett 2001a). As illustrated, the two pathways for participation directed at learning are structured quite differently, thereby reinforcing the localized factors that constitute a particular work practice. Darrah (1996) has also shown how access to work in a computer manufacturing company is sequenced to structure learning through a pathway of activities. In commercial aviation, a pathway exists comprising movement from the role of flight engineer, to first officer through to captain (Hutchins and Palen 1997). These examples indicate that there are intentions and formalisms that structure the processes of participation in and learning from work.

Third, to describe a learning environment as being either 'informal' or 'formal' suggests an irreducible relationship between the circumstances in which the learning occurs and changes in individuals. This view promotes situational (social) determinism and ignores the role of human agency in the construction and further development of their knowledge. Even the most structured learning experiences can only shape individuals' learning. Wertsch (1998) notes how unwelcome 'social press' may lead to a kind of learning, which he refers to as mastery, that is a superficial learnt response to that press. He distinguishes this kind of learning from appropriation (Luria 1976) where individuals embrace as their own the knowledge to be learnt. Knowledge constructed through mastery is less likely to be exercised voluntarily, than what is appropriated (Wertsch 1998). Nevertheless, much of the learning that arises may be unintentional and different from what is intended by the exercise of the workplace's norms and practices. Unintended learning still occurs as a product of these experiences, but may not reflect the kinds of values and practices that were intended to be secured through practice. For instance, what Hodges (1998) learnt from participation in a teacher education course was quite contrary to what was intended.

If learning is adopted as a process and outcome of thinking and acting that occurs through engagement in goal-directed activities, structured by workplace experiences and mediated by individuals, then this provides richer bases to discuss and conceptualize workplace learning experiences. It is imprecise to claim that the process of learning occurs wholly in terms of the circumstances in which it occurs (i.e. informal or formal). Such descriptions deny the inter-psychological processes between what is afforded by the work practice and how individuals, as agents, construe learning. All this suggests the need for terms other than 'informal' or 'formal' to describe the relations between the circumstances in which individuals engage in activities and the consequences for their thinking, acting and learning.

Conclusion

This chapter has advanced that participation in social practice is synonymous with learning and that participatory practices offer a fresh way of considering workplaces as learning spaces that are reciprocally constituted. These practices are complex, contested and negotiated. More than being constituted by the contributions of the physical and social environment of the workplace and cultural practices and historical legacies, they are captive to how individuals elect to engage according to their capacities and needs, subjectivities and identities. Much of the current workplace learning discourse fails to present workplaces as legitimate learning environments or to reflect the complexity of the interrelations that constitute these environments. I have proposed participation and participatory practices as explanatory principles for learning in workplaces. The quality of learning experiences can be seen in terms of workplace affordances, in particular the kinds of activities and guidance that individuals are able to access and the sequencing of experiences which can improve their workplace performance. Moreover, it is useful to consider the invitational qualities of the workplace, the bases by which opportunities in the oft-contested workplace are distributed and how power relations are exercised in shaping learning. Accounting for individuals' agency and their actions rightly emphasizes the dual and reciprocal nature of learning and the role of ontogeny or personal histories in learning.

The chapter raises procedural concerns about enhancing workplaces as environments for individuals to learn throughout their working lives. The provision of opportunities to engage in activities and be in receipt of support to access hard-to-learn knowledge should be brought centre stage. This seems more urgent at a time when individuals are being expected to organize their learning throughout their working lives. The structuring of a learning curriculum (Lave 1990) should be premised on these provisions as well as a sequencing of experiences that move learners towards full participation and in ways which provide access to new activities, including the practices required to refine and hone new learning.

Engaging workers as participants and learners is salient. However, more than expecting their compliant participation, there will always be issues of the alignment between individuals' interests and goals, and their access to tasks and progress in ways consistent with those of the workplace. Reconciling workplace contestation among affiliates and cliques and between the interests of the work practice and individuals' practice will remain a complex goal. There will always be conflict in workplaces as power and personal politics are played out, and there will always be tensions between the goals of the enterprise and the individual. In my view, there may never be enough support, opportunities or advancements for these to be entirely overcome, within the level of resource necessary to ensure the continuity of the workplace. Such areas of tension are likely to remain as key elements in the negotiated and contested participatory practices of the workplace and what constitutes its curriculum.

Bibliography

Anderson, J.R. (1982) 'Acquisition of Cognitive Skill', *Psychological Review*, 89 (4): 369–406.

Bernhardt, A. (1999) 'The Future of Low-Wage Jobs: Case Studies in the Retail Industry', Institute on Education and the Economy, Working paper No. 10, March.

Bierema, L.L. (2001) 'Women, Work, and Learning', in T. Fenwick (ed.), *Sociocultural Perspectives on Learning Through Work*, San Francisco, CA: Jossey Bass/Wiley.

Billett, S. (1998) 'Situation, Social Systems and Learning', *Journal of Education and Work*, 11 (3): 255–74.

—— (2001a) *Learning in the Workplace: Strategies for Effective Practice*, Sydney: Allen and Unwin.

—— (2001b) 'Knowing in Practice: Re-conceptualising Vocational Expertise', *Learning and Instruction*, 11 (6): 431–52.

—— (2001c) 'Learning Throughout Working Life: Activities and Interdependencies', *Studies in Continuing Education*, 23 (1): 19–35.

—— (2002) 'Critiquing Workplace Learning Discourses: Participation and Continuity at Work', *Studies in the Education of Adults*, 34 (1): 56–67.

Billett, S. and Boud, D. (2001) 'Participation In and Guided Engagement at Work: Workplace Pedagogic Practices', Research Work and Learning, Second International Conference, pp. 321–8, Faculty of Continuing Education, University of Calgary, Alberta, 26–28 July.

Billett, S., Barker, M. and Hernon-Tinning, B. (in press) 'Participatory Practices at Work', *Pedagogy. Culture and Society*, 11 (3).

Childs, C.P. and Greenfield, P.M. (1980) 'Informal Modes of Learning and Teaching: The Case of Zinacanteco Weaving', in N. Warren (ed.), *Advances in Cross-cultural Psychology*, vol. 2, London: Academic Press.

Cole, M. (1998) 'Can Cultural Psychology Help us Think about Diversity?', *Mind. Culture and Activity*, 5 (4): 291–304.

Collins, A., Brown, J.S. and Newman, S.E. (1989) 'Cognitive Apprenticeship: Teaching the Crafts of Reading, Writing and Mathematics', in L.B. Resnick (ed.), *Knowledge, Learning and Instruction. Essays in Honour of Robert Glaser*, Hillsdale: NJ: Erlbaum & Associates.

Danford, A. (1998) 'Teamworking and Labour Regulation in the Autocomponents Industry', *Work, Employment & Society*, 12 (3): 409–31.

Darrah, C.N. (1996) *Learning and Work: An Exploration in Industrial Ethnography*, New York: Garland Publishing.

Dore, R.P. and Sako, M. (1989) *How the Japanese Learn to Work*, London: Routledge.

Engeström, Y. and Middleton, D. (1996) 'Introduction: Studying Work as Mindful Practice', in Y. Engeström and D. Middleton (eds), *Cognition and Communication at Work*, Cambridge: Cambridge University Press.

Ericsson, K.A. and Lehmann, A.C. (1996) 'Expert and Exceptional Performance: Evidence of Maximal Adaptation to Task Constraints', *Annual Review of Psychology*, 47: 273–305.

Evans, G. (1993) 'Institutions: Formal or Informal Learning?', keynote address presented at the international conference, After Competence: The Future of Post-compulsory Education and Training, Brisbane, 1–3 December.

Glassman, M. (2001) 'Dewey and Vygotsky: Society, Experience, and Inquiry in Educational Practice', *Educational Researcher*, 30 (4): 3–14.

Goodnow, J.J. and Warton, P.M. (1991) 'The Social Bases of Social Cognition: Interactions about Work and their Implications', *Merrill-Palmer Quarterly*, 37 (1): 27–58.

Hodges, D.C. (1998) 'Participation as Dis identification with/in a Community of Practice', *Mind, Culture and Activity*, 5 (4): 272–90.

Hughes, K. and Bernhardt, A. (1999) *Market Segmentation and the Restructuring of Banking Jobs*, IEE Brief number 24 February, New York: Institute on Education and the Economy.

Hull, G. (1997) 'Preface and Introduction', in G. Hull (ed.), *Changing Work. Changing Workers: Critical Perspectives on Language, Literacy and Skills*, New York: State University of New York, New York Press.

Hutchins, E. (1983) 'Understanding Micronesian navigation', in D. Genter and A. Stevens (eds), *Mental Models*, Hillsdale, NJ: Lawrence Erlbaum.

Hutchins, E. and Palen, L. (1997) 'Constructing Meaning from Spaces, Gesture, and Speech', in L.B. Resnick, C. Pontecorvo and R. Saljo (eds), *Discourse. Tools and Reasoning: Essays on Situated Cognition*, Berlin: Springer.

Jordan, B. (1989) 'Cosmopolitan Obstetrics: Some Insights from the Training of Traditional Midwives', *Social Science and Medicine*, 289: 925–44.

Lave, J. (1990) 'The Culture of Acquisition and the Practice of Understanding', in J.W. Stigler, R.A. Shweder and G. Herdt (eds), *Cultural Psychology*, Cambridge: Cambridge University Press.

—— (1993) 'The Practice of Learning', in S. Chaiklin and J. Lave (eds), *Understanding Practice: Perspectives on Activity and Context*, Cambridge: Cambridge University Press.

Lave, J. and Wenger, E. (1991) *Situated Learning – Legitimate Peripheral Participation*, Cambridge: Cambridge University Press.

Luria, A.R. (1976) *Cognitive Development: Its Cultural and Social Foundations*, Cambridge, MA: Harvard University Press.

Marsick, V.J. and Watkins, K. (1990) *Informal and Incidental Learning in the Workplace*, London: Routledge.

Meade, G.H. (1934) *Mind. Self & Society: Works of George Herbert Meade*, vol. 1, Chicago, IL: University of Chicago Press.

Organisation for Economic Co-operation and Development (OECD) (1998) 'Lifelong Learning: A Monitoring Framework and Trends in Participation', *Educational Policy Analysis*, Paris: OECD.

Piaget, J. (1976) *Behaviour and Evolution*, trans. D. Nicholson Smith, New York: Pantheon Books.

Prawat, R.S. (1993) 'The Value of Ideas: Problems versus Possibilities in Learning', *Educational Researcher*, 22 (6): 5–16.

Raizen, S. (1994) 'Learning and Work: The Research Base', in *Vocational Education and Training for Youth: Towards Coherent Policy and Practice*, Paris: OECD.

Resnick, L. (1987) 'Learning in School and Out', *Educational Researcher*, 16 (9): 13–20.

Rogoff, B. (1982) 'Integrating Context and Cognitive Development', in M.E. Lamb and A.L. Brown (eds), *Advances in Developmental Psychology*, vol. 2, Hillsdale, NJ: Erlbaum.

—— (1990) *Apprenticeship in Thinking – Cognitive Development in Social Context*, New York: Oxford University Press.

—— (1995) 'Observing Sociocultural Activities on Three Planes: Participatory Appropriation, Guided Appropriation and Apprenticeship', in J.V. Wertsch, P. Del Rio and A. Alverez (eds), *Sociocultural Studies of the Mind*, Cambridge: Cambridge University Press.

Rogoff, B. and Gardiner, W. (1984) 'Adult Guidance of Cognitive Development', in B. Rogoff and J. Lave (eds), *Everyday Cognition – Its Development in Social Context*, Cambridge, MA: Harvard University Press.

Rogoff, B. and Gauvain, M. (1984) 'The Cognitive Consequences of Specific Experiences – Weaving versus Schooling among the Navajo', *Journal of Cross-Cultural Psychology*, 15 (4): 453–75.

Scribner, S. (1984) 'Studying Working Intelligence', in B. Rogoff and J. Lave (eds), *Everyday Cognition: Its Development in Social Context*, Cambridge, MA: Harvard University Press.

—— (1985) 'Vygostky's Use of History', in J.V. Wertsch (ed.), *Culture, Communication and Cognition: Vygotskian Perspectives*, Cambridge: Cambridge University Press.

—— (1997/1998) 'Mental and Manual Work: An Activity Theory Orientation', in E. Tobah, R.J. Falmagne, M.B. Parlee, L.M. Martin and A.S. Kapelman (eds), *Mind and Social Practice: Selected Writings of Sylvia Scribner*, Cambridge: Cambridge University Press.

Solomon, N. (1999) 'Culture and Difference in Workplace Learning', in D. Boud and D.J. Garrick (eds), *Understanding Learning at Work*, London: Routledge.

Somerville, M. (2002) 'Changing Masculine Work Cultures', 10th Annual International conference on post-compulsory education and training, *Envisioning Practice – Implementing Change*, 3: 149–55. Surfers Paradise Park Royal, Gold Coast, Queensland, Australia, 2–4 December.

Suchman, L. (1996) 'Constituting Shared Workspaces', in Y. Engeström and D. Middleton (eds), *Cognition and Communication at Work*, Cambridge: Cambridge University Press.

Valsiner, J. (1994) 'Bi-directional Cultural Transmission and Constructive Sociogenesis', in W. de Graaf and R. Maier (eds), *Sociogenesis Re-examined*, New York: Springer.

—— (2000) *Culture and Human Development*, London: Sage Publications.

Vygotsky, L.S. (1978) *Mind in Society – The Development of Higher Psychological Processes*, Cambridge, MA: Harvard University Press.

Wertsch, J.W. (1998) *Mind as Action*, New York: Oxford University Press.

8 Expansive learning environments

Integrating organizational and personal development

Alison Fuller and Lorna Unwin

Chapter summary

This chapter argues that learning environments that offer employees diverse forms of participation foster learning at work. Case-study evidence is used to illuminate the relationship between work and learning in relation to three participatory dimensions: (1) opportunities for engaging in multiple (and overlapping) communities of practice at and beyond the workplace; (2) access to a multidimensional approach to the acquisition of expertise through the organization of work and job design; and (3) the opportunity to pursue knowledge-based courses and qualifications relating to work. Our research indicates that where organizations have created 'expansive learning environments' and practise an expansive approach to learning, they also provide the basis for the integration of personal and organizational development.

Introduction

The primary goal of the workplace is to produce goods and services but our research[1] has confirmed that it is also an important site for learning. Not surprisingly, however, the extent to which employees in different organizational and sectoral settings have the opportunity and are encouraged to learn is variable. Furthermore, the relationship between individual and organization learning is complex and poorly understood. All too often it is assumed that there is a causal relationship from individual learning to improvements in organizational performance. However, there is strong evidence to suggest that management decisions about competitiveness and product market strategies provide a framework within which choices about how work is organized and people are managed are taken (Metcalf *et al.* 1994; Bosworth *et al.* 2001). According to this argument, the distribution of opportunities for informal and formal learning across the workforce flows from the resolution of these prior issues (Coleman and Keep 2001). We acknowledge the relevance of economic drivers and commercial decisions to setting the broad parameters within which opportunities and barriers to workplace learning exist. The purpose of this chapter, though, is to concentrate on opening up the 'black box' of learning at work to illuminate the character of different learning environments and approaches to workforce development.

Our study of learning at work in four private sector companies in the steel industry in England and Wales provides an opportunity to explore the relationship between differing organizations, the approach taken to workforce development and employees' experience of workplace learning. We have used a range of data collection methods (including interviews, observations and weekly learning logs) to investigate learning in diverse organizational and cultural contexts. The chapter outlines how this investigation has informed the development of a conceptual framework which identifies a range of pedagogical and organizational factors, and highlights their relevance to the quality and extent of workplace learning for different groups of employees. We conclude that *expansive* rather than *restrictive* environments foster learning at work and the integration of personal and organizational development. Individuals can, of course, exercise choice over the extent to which they engage in learning and their response is shaped, at least to some extent, by their personal backgrounds, prior educational experiences, and aspirations, which we refer to as their *learning territory*. We acknowledge too that organizations may adopt restrictive approaches to workforce development as a deliberate strategy for supporting models of work organization which are based on limiting the learning of at least some groups of employees.

The chapter is organized in three main sections. In the first section, we introduce a new conceptual framework, which we call the 'expansive – restrictive continuum', for analysing workplace learning. We explain how it originated in our attempt to understand and distinguish between the approaches to apprenticeship found in three of our case studies and their implications for the learning opportunities experienced by apprentices. The section also differentiates our use of the term expansive (and restrictive) from the notion of 'expansive learning' advanced by Engeström (1994, 2001). At the end of the section we clarify our view of the relationship between the individual and the learning environment.

Section two makes connections between some of the characteristics of the expansive and restrictive framework and the theoretical perspectives which underpin them. Using contrasting evidence from our case studies, we argue that the relationship between organizational context and the approach taken to workforce development is dynamic, creating learning environments that to a greater or lesser extent foster employee learning. The findings show that organizations, departments, or targeted groups within organizations, can be analysed in terms of their expansive and restrictive features.

In section three, we propose the idea that an expansive approach to workforce development is more likely to facilitate the integration of personal and organizational development. This has important implications for managers, trainers and personnel charged with human resource development for it requires them to perceive workplace learning as something which both shapes and is shaped by the organization itself rather than as a separately existing activity. Such an understanding might enable closer integration and transfer between training sessions provided for specific purposes (e.g. to instruct employees in new procedures or to enable them to gain qualifications) and the learning which occurs as part of everyday life in the workplace.

Expansive – restrictive continuum

In our research into apprenticeship in the United Kingdom (Fuller & Unwin 1998, 1999, 2001, 2003), we have drawn on Lave and Wenger's (1991) situated learning theory to explain the process by which new entrants to an occupation or workplace gain the knowledge and skills that enable them to become 'old-timers'. Based on ethnographic studies of newcomers in a variety of traditional crafts and activities, Lave and Wenger have developed the interrelated concepts of legitimate peripheral participation and communities of practice to explain how novices (legitimate peripheral participants) progress to full participant status (in a community of practice). They conceive learning as a collective and relational process involving the co-participation of newcomers with more experienced others. In essence, learning for Lave and Wenger is an integral part of (all) social activity:

> In our view, learning is not merely situated in practice – as if it were some independently reifiable process that just happened to be located somewhere; learning is an integral part of generative social practice in the lived-in world.
>
> (Lave and Wenger 1991: 35)

In this regard, Lave and Wenger can be seen as part of a wider attempt, often by anthropologists, to focus on learning in settings outside formal educational institutions and to locate school or specialist learning simply as a variant of a broader social theory of learning (see inter alia Brown et al. 1989; Collins et al. 1989). Lave and Wenger envisage situated learning theory as relevant to all areas of social practice and that it contributes to attempts to overcome what Engeström (1991) has called 'the encapsulation of school learning'. Nevertheless, the foregrounding of apprenticeship and learning in non-formal educational settings has, as this volume also testifies, fostered research into workplace learning (see inter alia Boud and Garrick 1999; Ainley and Rainbird 1999; Evans et al. 2002).

While recognizing the relevance of Lave and Wenger's perspective to understanding what is involved in apprenticeship learning and, generically, when a 'newcomer' becomes an 'old timer', much of our work has focused more specifically on its application to the sort of contemporary workplace settings offered in advanced industrial societies such as in the UK. Rainbird et al. (2001: 3) point out the difference between Lave and Wenger's 'focus on craft or "craft-like" forms of production in communities of practice which are relatively undifferentiated', and 'situations where wage labour is generalised and the craft origins of labour have not only been undermined but in some cases destroyed'. Although Lave and Wenger recognize that a community of practice is defined as a set of relations or, to put it another way, as a social structure involving relations of power, they acknowledge that their empirical examples are 'on the whole silent' on the relevance to learning of structural constraints and inequalities (1991: 36). In addition, situated learning theory tends to dismiss the role formal education institutions can play in employees' learning. The case-study material we discuss later in the chapter illustrates why it is important to address these two shortcomings in the situated perspective, in order to gain a better understanding of the learning chances of employees in contemporary workplaces.

To help understand the barriers and opportunities to learning being experienced by workers in our case studies, we have developed a framework for categorizing approaches to workforce development according to their expansive and restrictive features, as shown in Figure 8.1. The list is not intended to be exhaustive but represents an initial attempt to try and bring the factors (pedagogical, organizational and cultural) that contribute to approaches to workforce development and the creation of learning environments, into a single conceptual framework. We argue that an approach to workforce development characterized by the features listed as expansive will create a stronger and richer learning environment than one consisting of features associated with the restrictive end of the continuum. The frame work addresses the shortcomings we have identified in Lave and Wenger's perspective by recognizing the importance of (1) the way work is organized, jobs are designed and skills are treated, and their relevance for both opportunities and barriers to learning, and (2) the configuration of informal and formal learning, and qualification options for understanding the uneven quality of the learning environments we have encountered.

Differentiating expansive learning

Before focusing directly on the expansive – restrictive continuum, it is necessary to indicate briefly how our use of the term 'expansive' can be distinguished from Engeström's concept of 'expansive learning' (see e.g. 1994, 2001). The purpose of Engeström's theory of expansive learning is to achieve substantial changes at the organizational level: 'The object of expansive learning activity is the entire activity system in which the learners are engaged. Expansive learning activity produces culturally new patterns of activity. Expansive learning at work produces new forms of work activity' (Engeström 2001: 139).

Engeström has designed an intervention strategy, based on expansive learning, to help achieve organizational change. He has written in detail

Approaches to Workforce Development

EXPANSIVE	RESTRICTIVE
Participation in multiple communities of practice inside and outside the workplace	Restricted participation in multiple communities of practice
Primary community of practice has shared 'participative memory': cultural inheritance of workforce development	Primary community of practice has little or no 'participative memory': no or little tradition of apprenticeship
Breadth: access to learning fostered by cross-company experiences	Narrow: access to learning restricted in terms of tasks/knowledge/location
Access to range of qualifications including knowledge-based VQ	Little or no access to qualifications
Planned time off-the-job including for knowledge-based courses and for reflection	Virtually all-on-job: limited opportunities for reflection
Gradual transition to full, rounded participation	Fast – transition as quick as possible
Vision of workplace learning: progression for career	Vision of workplace learning: static for job
Organizational recognition of, and support for employees as learners	Lack of organizational recognition of, and support for employees as learners
Workforce development is used as a vehicle for aligning the goals of developing the individual and organizational capability	Workforce development is used to tailor individual capability to organizational need
Workforce development fosters opportunities to extend identity through boundary crossing	Workforce development limits opportunities to extend identity: little boundary crossing experienced
Reification of 'workplace curriculum' highly developed (e.g. through documents, symbols, language, tools) and accessible to apprentices	Limited reification of 'workplace curriculum' patchy access to reificatory aspects of practice
Widely distributed skills	Polarized distribution of skills
Technical skills valued	Technical skills taken for granted
Knowledge and skills of whole workforce developed and valued	Knowledge and skills of key workers/groups developed and valued
Team work valued	Rigid specialist roles
Cross-boundary communication encouraged	Bounded communication
Managers as facilitators of workforce and individual development	Managers as controllers of workforce and individual development
Chances to learn new skills/jobs	Barriers to learning new skills/jobs
Innovation important	Innovation not important
Multidimensional view of expertise	Uni-dimentional top-down view of expertise

Figure 8.1 Expansive – restrictive continuum

about the nature of the intervention (see e.g. 1996, 2001), which is conceived as a method (known as 'the Change Laboratory') to be followed by work teams, initially with the help of a facilitator (Engeström 1996). Although, for Engeström, the purpose of expansive learning is organizational transformation, he has little directly to say about aspects of organizational context (e.g. top-down strategic decisions on product markets, competitiveness and people management) which influence organizational learning. Although he is extremely interested in how people learn, drawing on the tradition of cultural-historical activity theory (see e.g. Vygotsky 1978; Leont'ev 1981), situated learning theory, and Bateson's (1972) concept of levels of learning, Engeström tends to jump quickly from this concern to a preoccupation with organizational transformation. In this latter regard, he tends to read across from the type of (organizational) learning taking place to forms of work organization and activity.

In contrast to Engeström's concentration on organizational learning, the focus of our conceptualization of expansive – restrictive approaches to apprenticeship, and to creating and analysing the nature of learning environments, is on *people* and *learning* (workforce development). The purpose here is to identify features of the environment or work situation which influence the extent to which the workplace as a whole creates opportunities for, or barriers to, learning. By identifying such features and analysing them in terms of their expansive and restrictive characteristics, we provide a conceptual and analytical tool for evaluating the quality of learning environments and for analysing an organization's approach to workforce development. We do not assume that identification of a restrictive approach will automatically lead organizations to reform along expansive lines. There may be a host of strategic and practical reasons, as Keep and others have suggested, for why organizations might (rightly in some cases) resist making such changes. Nor, moreover, do we assume that creating more expansive learning environments will automatically produce new forms of work activity or culturally new patterns of activity. However, evidence from empirical research suggests that an expansive approach to workforce development is likely to increase the quantity and range of opportunities for participation and, therefore, for employee learning (Wenger 1998; Fuller and Unwin 2003; Billett this volume). Our evidence also allows us to explore the idea that an expansive approach is more likely, than its restrictive counterpart, to promote synergies between personal and organizational development.

In relation to our use of the term 'expansive', we would argue that from a definitional perspective, and particularly when it is deployed in juxtaposition with the term 'restrictive', it helps capture and illuminate a dimension of empirical reality found in the data. The ability to contrast expansive with restrictive has helped us to focus attention on issues, such as access to forms of participation and work organization within communities of practice, that are underdeveloped by Lave and Wenger (1991) but which have significant influence on the quality of the learning environment. Moreover, as the research has progressed we have been increasingly concerned to understand the relationship between organizational context, workplace learning environment and individual learning and how differentiating between approaches to workforce development may shed light on the relationship between them. We have hypothesized elsewhere (Fuller and Unwin 2003) that an expansive approach to apprenticeship is more likely to contribute to, or even be in reflexive relationship with, the sort of organizational learning and transformation which Engeström has termed 'expansive learning'. In this regard, we suggest that more research is needed to explore whether approaches to workforce development which allow employees more opportunities to engage in learning can be aligned with the more progressive and transformational forms of organizational learning highlighted by Engeström (1994, 2001, this volume).

The relationship between the individual and the learning environment

The expansive – restrictive framework enables us to expose the features of different learning environments and so make them available for inspection and critique. We suggest that there are two broad categories of expansive and restrictive features: those which arise from understandings about the organizational context and culture (e.g. work organization, job design, control and distribution of knowledge and skills) and those relating to understandings of how employees learn (through engaging in different forms of participation).

In focusing on the creation of learning environments, it is important to clarify the relationship between individuals and the opportunities and barriers to learning they may encounter at work. We agree with Billett (this volume) that there is a distinction between the extent to which the organizational and pedagogical context affords access to diverse forms of participation and the extent to which individuals 'elect to engage' in those opportunities, through the exercise of individual agency. The reasons why individuals engage and respond differently to the (same) workplace learning environment are explained by writers such as Hodkinson and Hodkinson (2002) in terms of individual biographies and dispositions for learning. Eraut et al. (2000), on the other hand, have a 'pragmatic focus on knowledge use'. They describe 'personal knowledge' as 'what people bring to practical situations that enables them to think and perform. Such personal knowledge is acquired not only through the use of public knowledge but is also constructed from personal experience and reflection' (Eraut et al. 2000: 233).

While being in broad sympathy with Billett, Eraut, and Hodkinson and Hodkinson in valuing the individual perspective, we are wary of the dangers of excessive individualism or voluntarism. In this regard, we are guided by

Marx's insight that: 'Men make their own history, but they do not make it just as they please; they do not make it under circumstances chosen by themselves, but under circumstances directly encountered, given and transmitted from the past' (Marx cited in Armstrong 1987: 21).

Hence, in our view, an overemphasis on the structural character and environmental features of organizational context can underplay the role of individuals' backgrounds, prior attainments, attitudes, wider experiences and agency, whereas an overemphasis on the individual can divert attention from the influence of the organizational and wider institutional context in which learning at work occurs. In order to clarify our position on this issue, we are developing the metaphor of 'learning territory'. By this, we mean that every individual has, and has had, access to a (unique) range of learning opportunities which make up their learning territory. The territory is divided into regions. For example, one region would cover classroom-based learning and qualifications, while another would cover learning at home. A key region for employees is the workplace. We argue that the character and scope of the individual's learning territory (as well as how they respond to it) influences how he or she perceives and engages with opportunities and barriers to learning at work. In terms of the focus of this chapter, we are interested in understanding the extent to which the creation of expansive learning environments can act as a mechanism for 'smoothing' out individual differences and fostering more even take up of opportunities and, by so doing, facilitate the integration of personal and organizational development.

Forms of participation

In this section of the chapter, we have selected some of the dimensions of the expansive – restrictive continuum to illustrate, with evidence from our case-study research, how the framework can be used to analyse workplace learning environments. We also make connections between the features addressed and the theoretical perspectives which underpin them. This involves reference to situated learning theory, types of knowledge and theories of expertise. At the heart of the situated learning perspective is the metaphor 'learning as participation', which suggests that learning equates to the extent and richness of the available opportunities to participate.

Participation in communities of practice

The notion of participation is central to the expansive – restrictive continuum and to understanding the opportunities and barriers to learning employees encounter at work. As new entrants to their companies, apprentices in our research all embark on journeys from peripheral to mainstream participation. Learning takes place as they engage (increasingly) in the practices of the community and interact with more experienced colleagues. In this respect, the apprentices have common experiences defined, following Lave and Wenger (1991), by their legitimate peripheral partici- pation in a community of practice. However, the nature of the apprenticeship journey varies from company to company and this variation seems germane to the quality of learning which the apprentices experience (Fuller and Unwin 2003). Importantly, it indicates that Lave and Wenger's account of learning does not highlight the relevance of other forms of participation, such as boundary crossing between multiple communities of practice and off-the-job learning and qualifications, which can expand the forms of participation (learning) available to contemporary apprentices and other employees. With this issue in mind, Wenger's more recent book (1998) is helpful. In his detailed conceptual analysis of the processes involved in learning through belonging to communities of practice, Wenger argues that communities which provide participants with the 'ability to disengage' (as well as to engage), are more likely to become effec- tive learning communities. Building on this point, we suggest that the theme of opening up opportunities for learning through moving beyond a tightly situated and context bound approach to participation, runs through many of the attributes we have associated with an expansive approach to workforce development. The research in our case-study companies has provided evidence in support of this view, such that we would categorize the chance for employees to operate in only one community of practice (e.g. a department) as restrictive. As the Examples 8.1 and 8.2 illustrate, this finding is particularly applicable in relation to the learning experiences of apprentices where we can contrast the expansive opportunities to partici- pate in one company with the restrictive nature of another.

The learning as participation perspective conceives learning as flowing from the forms of participation available. Expansive features of participation (as shown in Example 8.1) were clearly available to the apprentices in Company A and included:

• Participation in multiple communities of practice inside and outside the workplace;
• Primary community of practice has shared 'participative memory': cultural inheritance of workforce development (and apprenticeship);
• Breadth: access to learning fostered by cross-company experiences;
• Planned time off-the-job includes formal education and time for reflection;
• Access to a range of qualifications including knowledge-based awards.

In contrast, participation for apprentices in Company B was much more restrictive.

Example 8.1   Expansive participation in (multiple) communities of practice

Company A manufactures bathroom showers and employs some 700 people. It has a well-established apprenticeship programme which has been used to develop successive generations of skilled and qualified engineers and technicians. Many of the company's ex-apprentices have progressed to senior management positions. Currently, the company employs five apprentices in engineering, one in steel production and processing, and one in accountancy. Participation takes place over time and in many internal communities of practice (through rotation around different departments). Apprentices attend college on a day-release basis where they pursue knowledge-based vocational qualifications that can also qualify them for entrance to higher education. Outward boundary crossing also happens when apprentices take part in residential courses to develop team-working skills and, through the company's apprentice association, they get involved in charity activities in the local community.

Example 8.2   Restricted participation in communities of practice

Company B is a small, family-run company (around 40 employees), which provides steel polishing services to other businesses. The vast majority of employees work on the shop floor as semi-skilled machine operators. The company offered its first apprenticeships two years ago, as a response to difficulties it was having in recruiting adults with relevant experience. The company currently employs two apprentices in (steel) production processes. The apprentices are primarily members of one community of practice which centres on the operation of steel polishing machines in a shop-floor environ-ment. They have learned from more experienced employees and have become full participants in under one year. Access to participation in communities of practice beyond the workplace is limited to atten-dance at a series (about 10) of off-the-job, half-day sessions on 'steel industry awareness'. The apprentices pursue standards-based National Vocational Qualifications (NVQs) at work with the help of their supervisor and a training provider who makes occasional visits to monitor their progress.

Linking the acquisition of expertise to work organization and job design

An important dimension of participation, and, therefore of unpacking expansive and restrictive approaches to workforce development, relates to the opportunity employees have to acquire expertise. We would argue that an expansive view of expertise entails the creation of environments which allow for substantial horizontal, cross-boundary activity, dialogue and problem-solving. This fits with Engeström et al.'s (1995) review of expertise where they characterize the conventional vertical view of expertise as top-down: here knowledge resides in the experts who can (elect) to transfer it to 'novices'. Engeström and his colleagues acknowledge that this vertical dimension is important but argue that a 'broader, multi-dimensional view of expertise' with an emphasis on the 'horizontal dimension is rapidly becoming increasingly relevant for the understanding and acquisition of expertise' (ibid.: 319).

In terms of the expansive – restrictive framework, it follows that there is overlap and interrelation between the view of expertise adopted and existing organizational factors, such as the way work is organized and jobs are designed. In Figure 8.1, we located a 'multidimensional' view of expertise at the expansive pole and a 'uni-dimensional top-down' view of expertise at the restrictive pole. We would argue that in order to be consistent an approach to workforce development which incorporates a multidimensional view of expertise 'should' also adopt an expansive approach to work organization and job design. The following examples (8.3 and 8.4) from our research are illustrative of how changes in job design and work organization can facilitate an expansive approach to the acquisition of expertise and, hence, foster workforce learning.

Several writers have stressed that the way in which work and jobs are designed directly affects the amount and type of knowledge available to, and created and needed by, employees (see, inter alia, Appelbaum and Batt 1994, and Nonaka and Takeuchi 1995). The conceptualization of knowledge and work has been advanced by the work of the German researcher Kruse (1986) who conceived the term *Arbeitsprozeßwissen* (translated in English as 'work-process knowledge'). Boreham builds on this work and explains:

> The new idea which the concept of work process knowledge introduced is that workers need to understand not just the technical system they are operating, but the work process in which they themselves are participating – and creating – by way of operating that system. And this involves reconceptualising the worker as a member of a much broader system, where knowledge is partly owned by the individual workers and partly by the organization.
>
> (Boreham 2002: 10)

Example 8.3 Work organization, job design and the acquisition of expertise

Company C is a steel 'stockholder' with some 80 employees. It is part of a large Swedish corporation but operates as a stand-alone business buying and selling steel. In order to compete, Company C must successfully market and sell its steel products by assuring their quality, value for money and the efficiency of the company's services. To meet these business goals, the company is investing in management development and customer service training.

To address the concern that sales staff had developed specialist knowledge of a limited number of products, the company decided to rearrange the way their work was organized, jobs were designed and the way desks were arranged. Under the new system, sales staff were required to sell *all* the company's product lines, hence, they needed to learn about different products and get to know new customers. To support the change and to encourage the sharing of knowledge and information, desks were reconfigured in a circular seating arrangement which facilitated knowledge exchange, and problem-solving. Interviews indicated that while some of the sales staff had initially felt that their specialist (expert) status would be undermined by the changes, in practice they perceived that they had added to their knowledge and had gained from seeing how other people worked and the greater opportunities available for collaborative problem-solving.

This emphasis on knowledge as being shared and mutually created across all parts of a workplace is particularly helpful to our understanding of where knowledge fits in terms of the expansive – restrictive continuum. Boreham (2002) acknowledges that many workplaces still operate along Fordist and Taylorist lines with strict boundaries between workers so that knowledge is seen as the preserve of those on higher grades. Huys and Hootegem (2002) stress that this conservatism is very powerful because traditional ways of working are particularly resilient despite many exhortations from external bodies, including governments, for change. In our case-study Examples 8.3 and 8.4, a shift towards the expansive end of the continuum occurred when knowledge was seen to be a central component of all jobs and that employees needed to cross workplace boundaries in order to both demonstrate their existing knowledge and acquire new knowledge.

Example 8.4 Job design and the acquisition of expertise

Company D employs some 300 people and manufactures large steel rods and bars mainly for use in the construction industry. Management and unions have negotiated a substantial package of changes in employees' pay, terms and conditions, involving a reorganization of shifts and shift patterns and the guarantee of pay rises for those workers signed off as competent in 60 per cent or more of their shift's tasks. A simplified and less highly stratified division of labour was introduced to encourage flexible working and reduce what were seen as restrictive practices. An important component of the new system related to the creation of a new post of team leader to replace the traditional job of foreman. Several of the team leaders had previously been foremen and were able to contrast the roles. There were two major extensions to the original job and both of these were direct consequences of the reorganization of work, pay and conditions. First, team leaders were responsible for helping all members of their teams to achieve the 60 per cent 'competency threshold'. In some cases, this meant that much of their time was spent training others and recording their achievements. Second, tasks relating to the organization of work and the attainment of targets (e.g. on production and health and safety) was delegated from shift managers to team leaders, so team leaders were now responsible for motivating their teams as well as monitoring progress. The extended job design together with support from off-the-job workshops created opportunities for new learning and a multidimensional approach to the acquisition of expertise.

Access to knowledge (knowledge-based qualifications) and off-the-job learning

We have suggested that an important shortcoming of Lave and Wenger's (1991) situated learning perspective was that it does not include a role for formal education institutions in the workplace entrant's learning process. Indeed, they see the off-the-job educational components in their case studies of naval quartermasters and butchers as adding little or having a detrimental effect. Young (this volume) argues that the situated learning perspective is linked to a 'process based' view of knowledge. He suggests that a weakness in this approach is that it conceives *all* knowledge as situated or context specific, and fails to recognize that there are different types of knowledge, some of which are more situated than others.

In some of the cases we have been investigating, work-based learning includes off-the-job provision leading to qualifications. We would argue that the opportunity to study away from the workplace and gain knowledge-based qualifications provides an expansive dimension to workforce development in that it: (1) gives employees the opportunity to extend their membership to other communities of practice and to cross boundaries between communities of practice; (2) provides for employees to 'stand back' from, and reflect on, workplace practice; and (3) provides the chance to pursue knowledge-based courses and qualifications. These three points recall the contrasting forms of participation available to apprentices in companies A and B. In terms of courses and qualifications, Company A's apprentices have access to a range of qualifications, including knowledge-based awards pursued at college. This gives the participant access to theoretical and conceptual knowledge and understanding that is unlikely to be made available solely through experience on-the-job. It also offers the option of gaining the sort of general vocational and educational credential which qualifies recipients to enter higher level education and which can support career progression.

Examples 8.5 and 8.6 draw attention to the different types of knowledge and qualifications available in our case-study companies and to the implications for the learning experiences of employees.

Example 8.5 Work-based qualifications

Company C, the steel stockholder, employs one business administration apprentice. The apprenticeship is entirely work-based and the apprentice is expected to learn his skills on-the-job and from more experienced colleagues. In Lave and Wenger's terms, he is clearly a legitimate peripheral participant engaged in a process of learning to become a full participant. He has access to the situated, context-specific knowledge available in the workplace necessary to becoming a 'knowledgeable practitioner' in the community of practice. As part of his apprenticeship he is working towards the competence-based NVQ in Business Administration which assumes that all vocational knowledge is embedded within workplace performance. The apprentice is, therefore, denied the opportunity to acquire conceptual and theoretical knowledge, and knowledge-based qualifications.

Example 8.6 Non job-related, knowledge-based qualifications

Company D has a tradition of supporting employees who want to take up educational opportunities outside work in their own time on the basis that it creates goodwill, helps the individual and may promote employee loyalty. Individuals are invited to make requests to the personnel manager for financial help in paying course fees. Examples include four men, aged between 39 and 44 years old, who are studying as follows: to teach basic skills; for a humanities degree; for a Higher National Certificate in Business and Information Systems; and for a Computing and IT degree. Although they recognize that there is no direct relationship between their work for the company and the topics they are studying, the men believe that the courses are helping them to maintain a positive attitude at work despite there being negligible possibilities for any career progression. They had all chosen knowledge-based courses to be stretched intellectually and because they led to well-respected qualifications which might be useful should they need to seek alternative employment.

Conclusions

This chapter has focused on the question of whether expansive learning environments were likely to facilitate personal and organizational development. Notwithstanding the important point that individuals can 'choose' the extent to which they actively participate in the available opportunities, the theoretical perspectives and empirical evidence we have presented suggest that this may be the case. We conclude by drawing attention to three ways in which the quality of learning environments affect both individual and organizational learning.

First, the limited forms of participation available to the apprentices in Companies B and C, including their lack of access to multiple communities of practice and knowledge-based qualifications, have consequences for their personal development. The relatively restrictive approach taken to their apprenticeships (in comparison with the approach taken in Company A) is indicative that it has not been embedded within a more expansive approach to overall workforce development. In this regard, the apprentices in Company B were particularly disadvantaged in that their learning environment restricted them to acquiring a relatively narrow range of activities and skills on-the-job. The apprentices rapidly became full participants in the community of practice and were considered to have acquired the expertise to enable them to train subsequent new entrants. However, there was no provision in the way work was organized for them to gain further skills and knowledge, or to progress in their 'careers'. In this sense, the (restricted) horizon for employees' personal development through work could be viewed as being in close alignment with the organizational horizon of the company.

Second, the expansive approach evident in Company A with its emphasis on participation in multiple communities of practice, including off-the-job learning and knowledge-based vocational qualifications, appears to provide an environment in which personal and organizational development can be aligned. In terms of organizational culture, employee learning is central to the way work (and apprenticeships) are organized and the opportunities for the acquisition of knowledge and skills are distributed and valued. Interestingly, the company has recently made competence-based NVQs available to workers on the shop floor. NVQs are usually used as a mechanism for validating what employees already know and can do. However, in this company their introduction is underpinned by the principles that they must have a developmental function and fit into the overall company philosophy. The training officer in charge of the implementation commented:

> I asked our director why we were doing it [introducing NVQs], what was the aim?...He said 'enhanced capability'.... If someone is more capable and more employable then the business benefits anyway because they can do more and they are better at it.

Third, the example supplied by Company D of employees being funded to pursue non-job related, knowledge-based qualifications provides an interesting contrast. Here the employees perceived their participation in courses outside work as extremely positive in terms of personal development but the experience was not seen as relevant to, or connected with, their jobs or organizational development more broadly.

There is a link to be made between the conceptual framework of expansive and restrictive, and the concept of learning territory. We suggest that an expansive approach to workforce development, by definition, enriches and extends an individual's learning territory. It does this by providing access to new learning regions (for example, structured on-the-job training and attendance at college), which become part of and enlarge each person's overall learning territory. Extending the metaphor, the larger and more fertile the territory, the more opportunity the individual has for personal development and identity formation. In this sense, the workplace can be conceived as a more or less bounded and expansive region within his or her learning territory. The contrasting examples of the apprentices in companies B and C are relevant here. The apprentices in the former company came with limited educational attainment, and from relatively poor socio-economic backgrounds. Although their apprenticeships provided them with the opportunity to learn a job and earn money, there were insufficient expansive dimensions to their experience to facilitate career or educational progression and to really overcome their other disadvantages. Put another way, the workplace as a learning region was making only a limited contribution to extending their existing learning territory. In contrast, Company C's apprentice already had a broader learning territory containing good academic qualifications and social skills. He was fully aware that these could be utilized elsewhere should the opportunities provided by his employer prove too restricted.

In this chapter we have used examples from our research to illustrate the relationship between the expansive – restrictive continuum and approaches to workforce development. The case studies have confirmed that access to diverse forms of participation represents a fundamental yardstick for evaluating the expansive and restrictive characteristics of the workplace learning environment. Moreover, the selection of features illustrated in the paper indicates the relevance and interrelatedness of pedagogical and organizational factors to our analytical framework. Finally, we have proposed the idea that an expansive approach to workforce development is more likely to facilitate the integration of personal and organizational development.

Note

1   The project 'The Workplace as a Site for Learning', is one of five projects funded under the Improving Incentives to Learning in the Workplace Network, funded by the Economic and Social Research Council's Teaching and Learning Research Programme, Phase I, award number L139 25 1005.

Bibliography

Ainley, P. and Rainbird, H. (eds) (1999) *Apprenticeship: Towards a New Paradigm of Learning*, London: Kogan Page.

Appelbaum, E. and Batt, R. (1994) *The New American Workplace: Transforming Work Systems in the United States*, New York: Cornell University Press.

Armstrong, P.F. (1987) 'Qualitative Strategies in Social and Educational Research: The Life History Method', Newland Papers 14, University of Hull.

Bateson, G. (1972) *Steps to an Ecology of Mind*, New York: Ballantine Books.

Boreham, N. (2002) 'Work Process Knowledge in Technological and Organizational Development', in N. Boreham, R. Samurcay and M. Fischer (eds), *Work Process Knowledge*, London: Kogan Page.

Bosworth, D., Davies, R. and Wilson, R.A. (2001) *Skills and Performance: An Econometric Analysis of the Employer Skill Survey 1999*, London: Department for Education and Skills.

Boud, D. and Garrick, J. (eds) (1999) *Understanding Learning at Work*, London: Routledge.

Brown, J.S., Collins, A. and Duguid, P. (1989) 'Situated Cognition and the Culture of Learning', *Educational Researcher*, 18: 32–42.

Coleman, S. and Keep, E. (2001) Background Literature Review for PIU project on Workforce Development, Cabinet Office website: www.cabinet-office.gov.uk/innovation/2001/workforce.

Collins, A., Brown, J.S. and Newman, S.E. (1989) 'Cognitive Apprenticeship: Teaching the Crafts of Reading, Writing and Mathematics', in L.B. Resnick (ed.), *Knowing, Learning and Instruction, Essays in Honor of Robert Glaser*, Hilldale, NJ: Erlbaum.

Engeström, Y. (1991) '*Non Scolae Sed Vitae Discimus*: Toward Overcoming the Encapsulation of School Learning', *Learning and Instruction*, 1: 243–59.

—— (1994) *Training for Change: New Approach to Instruction and Learning in Working Life*, Geneva: International Labour Office.

—— (1996) 'The Change Laboratory as a Tool for Transforming Work', *Lifelong Learning in Europe*, 2: 10–17.

—— (2001) 'Expansive Learning at Work: Toward an Activity Theoretical Reconceptualization', *Journal of Education and Work*, 14, 1: 133–55.

Engeström, Y., Engeström, R. and Karkkainen, M. (1995) 'Polycontextuality and Boundary Crossing in Expert Cognition: Learning and Problem Solving in Complex Work Activities', *Learning and Instruction*, 5: 319–36.

Eraut, M., Alderton, J., Cole, G. and Senker, P. (2000) 'Development of Knowledge and Skills at Work', in F. Coffield (ed.), *Differing Visions of a Learning Society*, vol. 1, Bristol: The Policy Press.

Evans, K., Hodkinson, P. and Unwin, L. (eds) (2002) *Working to Learn: Transforming Learning in the Workplace*, London: Kogan Page.

Fuller, A. and Unwin, L. (1998) 'Reconceptualizing Apprenticeship: Exploring the Relationship Between Work and Learning' *Journal of Vocational Education and Training*, 50, 2: 153–72.

—— (1999) 'A Sense of Belonging: The Relationship Between Community and Apprenticeship', in P. Ainley and H. Rainbird (eds), *Apprenticeship: Towards a New Paradigm of Learning*, London: Kogan Page.

—— (2001) 'From Cordswainers to Customer Service: The Changing Relationship Between Apprentices, Employers and Communities in England', Monograph 3, SKOPE: Oxford and Warwick Universities.

—— (2003) 'Learning as Apprentices in the Contemporary UK Workplace: Creating and Managing Expansive and Restrictive Participation', *Journal of Education and Work*, 16, 4.

Hodkinson, P. and Hodkinson, H. (2002) 'Biography, Context and Communities of Practice: A Study of Teachers' Learning in the Workplace', Leeds: University of Leeds.

Huys, R. and Hootegem, G.V. (2002) 'A Delayed Transformation? Changes in the Division of Labour and Their Implications for Learning Opportunities', in N. Boreham, R. Samurcay and M. Fischer (eds), *Work Process Knowledge*, London: Kogan Page.

Kruse, W. (1986) 'On the Necessity of Labour Process Knowledge', in J. Schweitzer (ed.), *Training for a Human Future*, Basle: Weinheim.

Lave, J. and Wenger, E. (1991) *Situated Learning: Legitimate Peripheral Participation*, Cambridge: Cambridge University Press.

Leont'ev, A.N. (1981) *Problems of the Development of the Mind*, Moscow: Progress.

Metcalf, H., Walling, A. and Fogarty, M. (1994) 'Individual Commitment to Learning: Employers' Attitudes', *DfEE Research Series*, No 40, Sheffield: Department for Education and Employment.

Nonaka, I. and Takeuchi, H. (1995) *The Knowledge-Creating Company*, Oxford: Oxford University Press.

Rainbird, H., Munro, A. and Holly, L. (2001) 'Between Communities of Practice and the Employment Relationship: A Perspective from the Labour Process', paper presented at the joint SKOPE/Teaching and Learning Research Programme Phase 1 Network, International Workshop, University College Northampton, November.

Vygotsky, L.S. (1978) *Mind in Society*, Cambridge: Cambridge University Press.

Wenger, E. (1998) *Communities of Practice: Learning. Meaning and Identity*, New York: Cambridge University Press.

9 The new generation of expertise

Seven theses

Yrjö Engeström

Chapter summary

The title of this chapter is to be understood in two ways. First, there is a new generation of expertise around, not based on supreme and supposedly stable individual knowledge and ability but on the capacity of working communities to cross boundaries, negotiate and improvise 'knots' of collaboration in meeting constantly changing challenges and reshaping their own activities. Second, this new type of collaborative and transformative expertise needs to be generated in a new way; it requires serious rethinking of what we mean by learning. The chapter lays out the argument for these two claims in the form of seven theses and a conclusion.

Introduction

The title of this chapter is to be understood in two ways. First, there is a new generation of expertise around, not based on supreme and supposedly stable individual knowledge and ability but on the capacity of working communities to cross boundaries, negotiate and improvise 'knots' of collaboration in meeting constantly changing challenges and reshaping their own activities. Second, this new type of collaborative and transformative expertise needs to be generated in a new way; it requires serious rethinking of what we mean by learning. In the following, I will lay out the argument for these two claims in the form of seven theses and a conclusion. The theses are based on research reported in detail in a forthcoming book (Engeström, in press).

Thesis 1: the dominant cognitivist approach is based on assumptions of individualism and stability

Two classes of mundane events are becoming increasingly pervasive and 'normal', yet also increasingly difficult to deal with for traditional studies of expertise. These events are disturbances or breakdowns on the one hand, and rapid overall transformations in technologies and organizational patterns on the other hand. The two are interconnected. The introduction of novel technologies and organizational patterns often increases the likelihood of disturbances and breakdowns – and recurring disturbances often force the practitioners and their management to seek new technological and organizational solutions (e.g. Hirschhorn 1984; Zuboff 1988). These events make it difficult if not impossible to build expertise on huge amounts of repetitive practice in relatively stable conditions. Experts must face, diagnose and resolve novel situations for which they have little or no directly applicable practice.

Such factors create situations where employees at all levels of the hierarchy face tasks that they find impossible to solve. There is something curious about this impossibility. Each individual, including highly educated professionals and managers, may testify that the situation was clearly beyond his or her control. Yet, most of those situations are somehow resolved and the work goes on. Moreover, often none of the persons involved can quite reconstruct or fully understand what actually happened and how the solution was found. In other words, people at work somehow go beyond their own limitations all the time. What makes this possible?

Ericsson and Smith define the 'original expertise approach' of cognitive science as seeking to 'understand and account for what distinguishes outstanding individuals in a domain from less outstanding individuals in that domain' (1991: 3). They point out that the approach focuses on those cases where the outstanding behaviour can be attributed to 'relatively stable characteristics of the corresponding individuals' (ibid.). The study of expertise is basically identification of superior and stable individual performances reproducible under standardized laboratory conditions. Given these requirements, it is no surprise that the most frequently studied form of expert performance is memory for meaningful stimuli from a well-constrained task domain. There are three basic assumptions behind the dominant information processing approach to expertise. First, expertise consists of superior and stable individual mastery of discrete tasks and skills. The understanding of expertise does not require that a more encompassing collective form of practice is taken as a unit of analysis. Second, within a given domain of knowledge and practice, expertise is universal and homogeneous. The aim is to identify 'the expert' in a given field. There is no need to differentiate between substantively different types of expertise within the given domain. Third, expertise is acquired through internalization of experience, gained gradually by massive amounts of practice in the stable skills exhibited by the established masters of the given specialty (the famous novice–master continuum). Expertise does not include questioning or reconceptualizing the skills and knowledge of established masters, nor the generation of culturally novel models of practice.

Serious problems in mainstream cognitivist models of expertise began to surface in the 1990s. A number of studies on expert decision making found a pervasive tendency toward overconfidence and compartmentalization in the judgements of experts in various domains. Massive amounts of experience in no way guarantee an improved ability to deal with uncertainty and probabilistic reasoning tasks. Experts often 'appear to be mainly interested in how consistent the evidence is with the hypothesis they are testing and fail to consider its consistency with alternative hypotheses' (Ayton 1992: 95). Argyris (1992) coined 'skilled incompetence' as the dilemma of professionals, and Shchedrovitskii and Kotel'nikov (1988) highlighted the growing need for multidisciplinary teams to solve complex problems.

Thesis 2: there is a new wave of research that goes beyond individualism and stability in analyses of expert work and cognition

Some ten years ago, Lave and Wenger (1991) opened what was to become a multifaceted discussion on situated learning. They suggested that the proper unit of analysis of skilled human activity is a community of practice rather than an isolated individual. Skill, knowledge and competence reside in local working communities, not in transportable packages. They also suggested that the foundational mechanism of becoming competent in a domain is legitimate peripheral participation in a relevant community of practice rather than transmission of knowledge in school-like forms. Legitimate peripheral participation may best be observed in various settings of apprenticeship.

Bereiter and Scardamalia (1993) criticized strictly individualist notions of expertise and suggested that teamwork should be taken seriously as a priority of expertise. More importantly, they suggested that expertise should be reconceptualized as a process of going beyond the normal course of learning, or progressive problem solving. Accordingly, experts 'tackle problems that increase their expertise, whereas nonexperts tend to tackle problems for which they do not have to extend themselves' (Bereiter and Scardamalia 1993: 78). Instead of trying to reduce novel problems to simple components that can be handled with familiar routine procedures, experts construct new concepts and methods for unfamiliar cases.

Hutchins (1995) maintained that cognition in real world settings is typically not a solitary achievement of an individual but a distributed achievement of a 'functional system' consisting of human practitioners, their artifacts and their representations. Cognitive performance, such as expert problem solving, is best analysed as propagation of representational states across humans and artifacts in a functional system, for example in a unit responsible for the navigation of a large ship or in the cockpit of a passenger jet. The acquisition of expertise takes place as members of such distributed functional systems gradually acquire a broader and more flexible mastery of the task domain for which the system is responsible, and as the system itself adapts to changing circumstances.

The contributions of Lave and Wenger, Bereiter and Scardamalia, and Hutchins may be assessed with the help of a two-dimensional conceptual space depicted in Figure 9.1. The vertical dimension represents the locus of expertise, ascending from an isolated individual to a team or functional system, to a community of practice and up to a field of multiple interacting communities dealing with partially shared objects and tasks.

Along this vertical dimension, Bereiter and Scardamalia stay closest to the traditional emphasis on the individual expert. Hutchins focuses on relatively well-bounded functional systems or teams, while Lave and Wenger discuss at least potentially larger and more diverse communities of practice. None of the three seriously addresses the possibility that expertise may be located and distributed in fields of multiple interacting communities of practice.

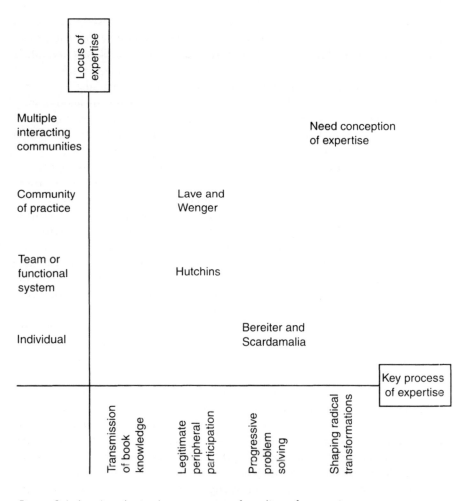

Figure 9.1 Landmarks in the new wave of studies of expertise

The need for multi-sited and mobile research has been emphatically acknowledged (if not practised) in ethnography (e.g. Marcus 1998; Burawoy 2000), not to speak of organizational and management literature which has radically shifted its emphasis onto multi-organizational partnerships and alliances (e.g. Alter and Hage 1993; Spekman *et al* 2000). It is time this step is taken in studies of expertise.

The horizontal dimension in Figure 9.1 represents key processes in the formation and performance of expertise. Lave and Wenger as well as Hutchins take apprenticeship-like learning or legitimate peripheral participation in fairly stable settings as the foundational process, leaving largely aside issues of radical change, creation and expansion in expert work and cognition. Bereiter and Scardamalia focus on progressive problem solving which takes the expert beyond the given task and procedures. However, progressive problem solving is conceptualized as continual improvement of performance in a given world rather than as questioning and changing the world itself. Again, a curious lag may be observed. Organizational and management literature is increasingly preoccupied with the pervasive challenge of radical, discontinuous change (e.g., Beer and Nohria 2000; Brown and Eisenhardt 1998; Kanter 1989). It is time that expertise is redefined within the context of facing and shaping such radical transformations at work.

Thesis 3: cultural-historical activity theory is a serious candidate for a new framework for theorizing expertise

In its current shape, cultural-historical activity theory may be summarized with the help of five principles (Engeström 1987, 1993, 1996, 1999a). The first principle is that a collective, artifact-mediated and object-oriented activity system, seen in its network relations to other activity systems, is taken as the prime unit of analysis. Goal-directed individual and group actions, as well as automatic operations, are relatively independent but subordinate units of analysis, eventually understandable only when interpreted against the background of entire activity systems. Activity systems realize and reproduce themselves by generating actions and operations.

The second principle is the multi-voicedness of activity systems. An activity system is always a community of multiple points of view, traditions and interests. The division of labour in an activity creates different positions for the participants, who carry their own diverse histories. The activity system itself carries multiple layers of history engraved in its artifacts, rules and conventions. The multi-voicedness is multiplied in networks of interacting activity systems. It is a source of trouble and innovation, demanding actions of translation and negotiation.

The third principle is historicity. Activity systems take shape and get transformed over lengthy periods of time. Their problems and potentials can only be understood against their own past. The local history of the activity and its objects, and the theoretical ideas and tools that have shaped the activity need to be studied.

The fourth principle is the central role of contradictions as sources of change and development. Contradictions are not the same as problems or conflicts. Contradictions are historically accumulating structural tensions within and between activity systems. The activity system is constantly working through tensions and contradictions within and between its elements. Contradictions manifest themselves in disturbances and innovative solutions. In this sense, an activity system is a virtual disturbance- and innovation-producing machine.

Contradictions are not just inevitable features of activity. They are 'the principle of its self-movement and [...] the form in which the development is cast' (Il'enkov 1977: 330). This means that new qualitative stages and forms of activity emerge as solutions to the contradictions of the preceding stage and form. This in turn takes place in the form of 'invisible breakthroughs', or innovations from below (Il'enkov 1982).

The fifth principle of activity theory proclaims the possibility of expansive transformations. Activity systems move through relatively long cycles of qualitative transformations. As the contradictions of an activity system are aggravated, some individual participants begin to question and deviate from its established norms. In some cases, this escalates into collaborative envisioning and a deliberate collective change effort. An expansive transformation is accomplished when the object and motive of the activity are reconceptualized to embrace a radically wider horizon of possibilities than in the previous mode of the activity. A full cycle of expansive transformation may be understood as a collective journey through the 'zone of proximal development' of the activity.

This fifth principle leads me directly to the need to redefine learning for the new generation of expertise.

Thesis 4: expansive learning is a core process in the new generation of expertise

Standard theories of learning are focused on processes where a subject (traditionally an individual, more recently possibly also an organization) acquires some identifiable knowledge or skills in such a way that a corresponding, relatively lasting change in the behaviour of the subject may be observed. It is a self-evident presupposition that the knowledge or skill to be acquired is itself stable and reasonably well defined. There is a competent 'teacher' who knows what is to be learned.

The problem is that much of the most intriguing kinds of learning in work organizations violates this presupposition. People and organizations are all the time learning something that is not stable, not even defined or understood ahead of time. In important transformations of our personal lives and organizational practices, we must learn new forms of activity which are not yet there. They are literally learned as they are being created. There is no competent teacher. Standard learning theories have little to offer if one wants to understand these processes.

Bateson's (1972) theory of learning is one of the few approaches helpful for tackling this challenge. He distinguished between three levels of learning. Learning I refers to conditioning, acquisition of the responses deemed correct in the given context – for instance, the learning of correct answers in a classroom. Wherever we observe Learning I, Learning II is also going on: people acquire the deep-seated rules and patterns of behaviour characteristic to the context itself. Thus, in classrooms, students learn the 'hidden curriculum' of what it means to be a student: how to please the teachers, how to pass exams, how to belong to groups, etc. Sometimes the context bombards participants with contradictory demands. Such pressures can lead to Learning III, where a person or a group begins to radically question the sense and meaning of the context and to construct an alternative context. Learning III is essentially a collective endeavour.

Bateson's conceptualization of Learning III was a provocative proposal, not an elaborated theory. The theory of expansive learning develops Bateson's idea into a systematic framework. Learning III is seen as learning activity which has its own typical actions and tools. The object of expansive learning activity is the entire activity system in which the learners are engaged. Expansive learning activity produces culturally new patterns of activity. Expansive learning at work produces new forms of work activity.

The theory of expansive learning (Engeström 1987) is based on the dialectics of ascending from the abstract to the concrete. This is a method of grasping the essence of an object by tracing and reproducing theoretically the logic of its development, of its historical formation through the emergence and resolution of its inner contradictions. A new theoretical idea or concept is initially produced in the form of an abstract, simple explanatory relationship, a 'germ cell'. This initial abstraction is step-by-step enriched and transformed into a concrete system of multiple, constantly developing manifestations. In an expansive learning cycle, the initial simple idea is transformed into a complex object, into a new form of practice. At the same time, the cycle produces new theoretical concepts – theoretically grasped practice – concrete in systemic richness and multiplicity of manifestations.

In this framework, abstract is partial and separated from the concrete whole. In empirical thinking based on comparisons and classifications, abstractions capture arbitrary, only formally interconnected properties. In dialectical-theoretical thinking, based on ascending from the abstract to the concrete, an abstraction captures the smallest and simplest, genetically primary unit of the whole functionally interconnected system (e.g. Davydov 1990).

The expansive cycle begins with individual subjects questioning the accepted practice, and it gradually expands into a collective movement or institution. The theory of expansive learning is related to Latour's actor-network theory in that both regard innovations as stepwise construction of new forms of collaborative practice, or technoeconomic networks (Latour 1987, 1993).

Ascending from the abstract to the concrete is achieved through specific epistemic or learning actions. Together these actions form an expansive cycle or spiral. An ideal-typical sequence of epistemic actions in an expansive cycle may be described as follows (Engeström 1999c).

1 *Questioning*, criticizing or rejecting some aspects of the accepted practice and existing wisdom.
2 *Analysing* the situation. Analysis involves mental, discursive or practical transformation of the situation in order to find out causes or explanatory mechanisms.
3 *Modelling* the newly found explanatory relationship in some publicly observable and transmittable medium.
4 *Examining* the model, running, operating and experimenting on it in order to fully grasp its dynamics, potentials and limitations.
5 *Implementing* the model, concretizing it by means of practical applications, enrichments, and conceptual extensions.
6 *Reflecting* on and evaluating the process.
7 *Consolidating* its outcomes into a new stable form of practice.

The expansive formation of new ideas and models does not take place merely as vertical interaction between given scientific concepts and experienced everyday concepts. Horizontal moves emerge in which a new idea or concept is formulated by some participants as an alternative to those previously debated. This horizontal or sideways aspect of expansive learning requires further conceptualization. The theory of 'cognitive trails' (Cussins 1992) is a useful resource for this purpose. One might say that if trajectories are the appropriate units for bounding the new object of expertise, trails are an appropriate way to describe the interactional infrastructure needed for new concepts and models of practice to take root, sustain themselves, and partially stabilize from the ground up. However, trails alone are an insufficient description. They need to be coupled with the identification of potentially expansive boundary-crossing actions of learning.

Thesis 5: negotiated knotworking is the defining characteristic of collaborative and transformative expertise

In a series of recent studies, my colleagues and I have encountered numerous examples of an emerging new type of organization of expert work (Engeström *et al.* 1995; Engeström *et al.* 1997; Hasu and Engeström 2000). I call it 'negotiated knotworking'. The notion of knot refers to rapidly pulsating, distributed and partially improvised orchestration of collaborative performance between otherwise loosely connected actors and activity systems. I argue that knotworking is a historically significant new form of organizing and performing expert work activity, connected to the emergence of new 'co-configuration' models of production.

Knotworking is characterized by a pulsating movement of tying, untying and retying together otherwise separate threads of activity. The tying and dissolution of a knot of collaborative work is not reducible to any specific individual or fixed organizational entity as the centre of control. The locus of initiative changes from moment to moment within a knotworking sequence. Thus, knotworking cannot be adequately analysed from the point of view of an assumed centre of coordination and control, or as an additive sum of the separate perspectives of individuals or institutions contributing to it. The unstable knot itself needs to be made the focus of analysis. In courts of law, expansive episodes of 'teamwork between adversaries' (Engeström *et al.* 1997) cannot be reduced to the guiding role of the judge. And in industrial settings dependent on quick horizontal problem solving, the fact that someone is a foreman or a supervisor may be temporarily all but irrelevant in the search and formulation of an innovative solution (Engeström *et al.* 1995).

While examples of knotworking may be found in well established practices, it seems that the rise and proliferation of this type of work is associated with ongoing historical changes in organizations. Victor and Boynton (1998) suggest that we can examine the recent evolution of work as a succession of five major types: craft, mass production, process enhancement, mass customization, and co-configuration. An elaborated summary of the five types and their inner tensions is presented in Figure 9.2.

The last one of the five, co-configuration, is particularly interesting from the point of view of knotworking. A hallmark of co-configuration is 'customer intelligence'. To achieve it, a company will have to continuously configure its products and services in interaction with the customer. Victor and Boynton (1998: 197) name medical devices and computer software systems as two leading industries where co-configuration is being implemented. Our own study of a complex new brain scanner in transition from design to clinical use (Hasu and Engeström 2000) concurs with their statement.

Victor and Boynton give us a model of three interdependent components: customer, product/service, and company. What needs to be added to this picture is interdependency between multiple producers forming a strategic alliance, supplier network, or other such pattern of partnership which collaboratively puts together a complex product or service. This extension increases the complexity of interactions in co-configuration work. Against this background, knotworking may be seen as the emerging interactional core of co-configuration.

To sum up, we may name six criteria of co-configuration: adaptive product or service; continuous relationship between customer, product/service, and company; ongoing configuration or customization; active customer involvement; multiple collaborating producers; and mutual learning from interactions between the parties involved.

Victor and Boynton focus on customer-intelligent products, such as sophisticated digital hearing aids, as examples of co-configuration. It is more difficult but equally important to determine what kinds of services might be 'customer-intelligent' and co-configurational. Standardized services delivered

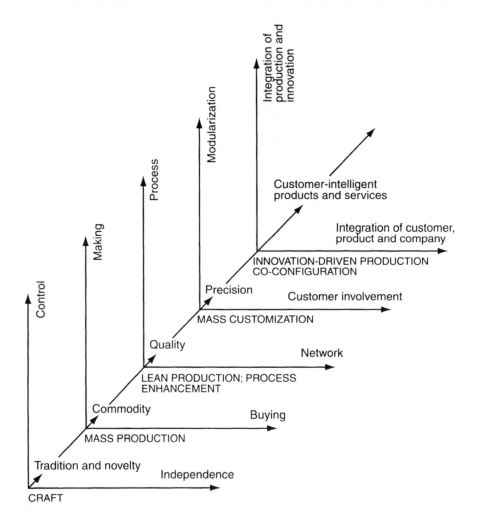

Figure 9.2 Historical types of work

Source: From Engeström 1999b, based on Victor and Boynton 1998.

on the spot do not qualify, but what about, for example, long-term care trajectories produced collaboratively by primary-care health centres and hospitals?

What is a 'knot' from an activity-theoretical point of view? Clearly a knot is not an activity system in the sense of having a relatively stable object, motive, community, and division of labour. The half-life of the knot is too short for such systemic infrastructure to evolve and stabilize. On the other hand, the knot is not just a singular action either. It performs bundles of tightly interconnected actions. More importantly, it deliberately organizes and dissolves itself to perform and terminate these actions. In other words, the knot functions as a self-conscious agent. Where does this self-consciousness reside? None of the individual members of the knot is the fixed centre of control – agency and initiative keep shifting. Thus, knotworking differs from an action in that the subject is not fixed – the subject is the pulsating knot itself, or in other words, subjectivity is dynamically distributed within the knot.

Knotworking is not reducible to a single knot, or a single episode. It is a temporal and spatial trajectory of successive task-oriented combinations of people and artifacts. Knotworking situations are fragile because they rely on fast accomplishment of intersubjective understanding, distributed control and coordinated action between actors who otherwise have relatively little to do with each other. Weick and Roberts (1993) talk about 'heedful interrelating' as the central quality of such collective action. But their example – work on an aircraft carrier – is about collaborative work in which people stay physically together for relatively long periods of time and go through large numbers of iterations of the same basic tasks. Such settings are indeed classical examples of the robustness of collective activity systems, or functional systems or communities of practice. In knotworking, the combinations of people and the contents of tasks change constantly. This highlights the importance of communicative and meta-communicative actions and tools for the success of knotworking.

Thesis 6: a development and interventionist methodology is needed for the production and analysis of new expertise

Ethnographic studies have traditionally been preoccupied with observing and understanding stable orders, routines and repeatable procedures. The issue of change has been relatively alien to them. In this regard, they seem to be inherently handicapped in dealing with the turbulent worlds of work and technology. Developmental theorizing has been largely avoided by ethnographers, possibly fearing deterministic and evolutionist implications. In the face of the pervasive and often dramatic changes going on within and between workplaces, such avoidance amounts to hiding one's head in a bush.

Development may be understood as local qualitative reorganization of activity systems, attempting to resolve their inner contradictions. Development goes on in the systems we study; they have their own developmental dynamics. Decontextualized prescriptions typically lead to solutions alien to the local system's developmental dynamics and are thus rejected or unpredictably altered in practice.

However, there is nothing untouchable or sacred about local developmental dynamics. To the contrary, outside influences from neighbouring systems constantly enter into the local systems and trigger novel developmental processes. It is this very triggering that is interesting for researchers curious about developmental potentials. Why do some developmental processes lead to dramatic expansions while others stagnate and die away? Why is the yield of some small interventions tremendous, while many large-scale interventions lead to miserable results? Cultural-historical activity theory suggests that the answer is closer than we often realize: dig where you stand. In other words, 'to understand how a practice may enable or disable, how it may figure in development, we must know its social history' (Modell 1996: 488). On the other hand, while history helps us uncover the contradictions and potentials of an activity system, it does not tell us how those contradictions are to be resolved.

In the approach advocated here, the direction of development is an issue of local negotiation and struggle. Research aims at developmental re-mediation of expert work activities, which makes visible and pushes forward the history and contradictions of the activity under scrutiny. This can challenge the actors to appropriate and use new conceptual tools to analyse and redesign their own practice. The normative or teleological determination of the desirable direction is viewed as a mundane performance, accomplished by people on a daily basis. The mundane accomplishment of directionality can be made explicit. This means that the different voices involved in the determination of direction (including the voices of the researchers) are identified, and clashes between them are regarded as an opportunity to get toward a clearer view of the contradictions. Such an approach does not eliminate the power relations and constraints at play, but it helps demystify them and potentially to rearrange them by capitalizing on grey areas of uncertainty.

These grey areas of uncertainty or 'under-determination' may be opened up if we reconceptualize our very notion of development (Engeström 1996). Instead of just benign achievement of mastery, development should also be viewed as a partially destructive rejection of the old. Disturbances and ruptures involving negation, rejection and destruction are often the first decisive indications of significant developmental processes. Furthermore, instead of just vertical movement toward higher levels of performance or mastery in some domain, development should be also viewed as horizontal movement across borders. In other words, developmental transformations always involve shifts between and new combinations of contexts. The transformation of an activity system is never an isolated process; it also means redefinition of its boundaries and thus renegotiation of its external relationships. This view implies that ethnography is not in itself a sufficient or privileged method. Yet ethnography is definitely needed. More specifically, we need a new kind of 'developmental ethnography' in studies of work, technology and organizations. Such a developmental ethnography of collective activity systems is particularly attuned to recording and analysing troubles and disturbances, as well as innovative deviations from the normal scripted course of work actions.

From the point of view of mainstream social science, there are two essentially moral arguments against interventionist research. The conservative moral argument says that the active involvement of the researcher spoils objectivity by mixing the researcher's values into the processes to be recorded and interpreted neutrally. The radical moral argument says that interventions in workplaces unavoidably benefit capital and management, making the researcher actually an instrument of exploitation. Both of these are arguments for purity. A less pure variant of the anti-interventionist stance insists on the generalizability of the findings as the criterion which makes interventions questionable – pre-scientific in the best case. In altering the status quo intervention by definition creates an exception, a unique case which cannot be used as a basis for generalizations. The common statistical view regards as general only such features that exist in sufficiently great quantities in a given representative pool of data. Features not exceeding the given limits are considered accidental and non-significant. In effect, this procedure attributes significance only to features that have already become prevalent.

From an alternative perspective, generalization is seen as 'a material process of becoming general' – from a new fundamental relation, or a 'germ cell' of a new form of practice. The researcher's task is to identify and conceptualize those budding new relations or germ cells, to help them unfold and become visible, and to record their generalization in practice. In other words, developmental research constructs and tests in practice historical hypotheses concerning zones of proximal development of the expert activity systems under scrutiny. This is where interventions can be helpful.

Thesis 7: the creation of care agreements to expand the object of medical expertise exemplifies the new generation of expertise

The objects of medical work have changed dramatically since the Second World War. As infectious and parasitic diseases have increasingly come under control, the prevalence of chronic illnesses has increased. Chronic illnesses include cancers, cardiovascular illnesses, renal diseases, respiratory diseases, diabetes, arthritis, and severe allergies. These illnesses require what Wiener *et al.* (1984: 14) call 'halfway technologies', that is, medical interventions applied after the fact in an attempt to compensate for the incapacitating effects of disease whose course one is unable to do much about. One of the consequences is that patients move constantly between home and various caregivers.

Wiener *et al.* (1984) conclude that the inability to cope with chronic illness stems largely from the 'standard categorical-disease perspective' dominant in industrialized countries. This perspective directs public attention and allocation of funds to the fight against specific illnesses, such as heart disease, cancer, or HIV and AIDS. It also feeds competition and fragmentation among health specialists and specialties, and diverts attention away from the organization of collaborative care around people typically suffering not just from a single well-bounded disease but from a complex bundle of illnesses and symptoms.

A chronically ill person typically becomes an object for a number of physicians, each viewing the patient from the perspective of his or her own specialty. Each specialty tends to assert the primacy of its own interest, and to lose its interest when the main responsibility is assigned to another. 'This phenomenon within medicine is likely to result in what physicians call "Ping-Ponging" the patient' (Bensman and Lilienfeld 1991: 219).

Such basic observations should make clear why medicine is a highly relevant domain for encountering the challenge of collaborative and transformative expertise. The importance of these observations is accentuated by ongoing large-scale organizational transformations in health care, namely the formation of multi-organizational strategic alliances and 'integrated healthcare systems'. Scott *et al.* (2000: 355) conclude that:

> much of the interest and complexity of today's healthcare arena, compared with its condition at mid-century, is due not simply to the numbers of new types of social actors now active but also to the multiple ways in which these actors have become interpenetrated and richly connected.

Medical work is not anymore only about treating patients and finding cures. It is increasingly about reorganizing and reconceptualizing care across professional specialties and institutional boundaries. This challenge of 'clinical integration' is not easily accomplished.

At the same time, being one of the oldest, most prestigious and most carefully protected professions, medicine carries within its very identity a tremendous historical ballast of individualism and hierarchical authority. Medical sociology has largely been a captive of this ballast. In Atkinson's words, 'the contemporary sociological literature all too often portrays a solitary craft worker, who makes no use of other experts' (1995: 34). While researchers now at least acknowledge the need to study medical work as multi-sited and collaborative, there is minimal awareness of the need to study how practitioners and patients cope with, shape and create transformations in their work. Stability is still the dominant tacit assumption in ethnographic and discourse-analytic studies of medical work, as well as in cognitive studies of medical decision making and problem solving.

The learning challenge in multi-organizational fields of medical care, such as the Helsinki area health-care system we have been studying, is to acquire a new way of working in which patients and practitioners from different caregiver organizations can collaboratively plan and monitor the patient's trajectory of care, taking joint responsibility for its overall progress. There are no readily available models that would fix the problems. If anything, the physicians with highest levels of medical expertise are specialists whose routines represent the problem, not the solution.

There are of course models that are supposed to solve these problems, commonly called 'critical pathways' or 'clinical paths', sometimes subsumed under the broader terms of 'case management' or 'disease management'. Critical pathways are constructed to give a normative sequence of procedures for dealing with a given single disease or diagnosis. They do not help in dealing with patients with multiple and unclear diagnoses. And they tend to impose their disease-centred worldview even on primary-care practitioners. Critical pathways seem to work reasonably well for acute diseases of relatively short duration, typically involving a few days of hospitalization. According to Huber and Oermann (1998: 4), 'critical paths were designed for standardization of key events and time frames for a patient's hospitalization'. Pathways for long-term, multi-episode chronic illnesses are much more difficult to construct and implement.

Fundamentally, both care relationships and critical paths are linear and temporal constructions of the object. They have great difficulties in representing and guiding horizontal and socio-spatial relations and interactions between multiple simultaneous illnesses, multiple parallel courses of care and multiple care providers located in different institutions, including the patient and his/her family as the most important actors in care. Practically all models of clinical pathways, case management and disease management are implicitly built on the assumption that a patient has a single, relatively unchanging diagnosis.

In our series of interventions in health-care organizations of the Helsinki area in Finland, the practitioners designed a model that differs radically from the critical pathways imposed from above. The new model was called 'care agreement'. Under care agreement, four interconnected solutions were created. First, the patient's personal physician – a general practitioner in the local health centre – was to be designated as the coordinator in charge of the patient's network and trajectory of care across institutional boundaries. Second, whenever a person became a patient of the hospital for more than a single visit, the hospital physician and nurse in charge of the patient were to draft a care agreement which would include a plan for the patient's care and the division of labour between the different care providers contributing to the care. The draft agreement was to be given to the patient or patient's family and sent to the patient's designated personal health-centre physician (and when appropriate, to the physicians in charge of the patient in other hospitals or clinics) for their scrutiny. Third, if one or more of the parties found it necessary, they were to have a care negotiation (by e-mail, by telephone, or face-to-face) to formulate a mutually acceptable care agreement. Fourth, care feedback, in the form of a copy of the patient's medical record, was to be automatically and without delay given or sent to the other parties of the care agreement after an unplanned visit by the patient or after changes were made in diagnoses, medication, or care plans. Figure 9.3 depicts a simplified model of the care agreement idea, produced and used by the practitioners in an intervention process.

Star (1989: 46) characterized boundary objects by stating that 'like the blackboard, a boundary object "sits in the middle" of a group of actors with divergent viewpoints'. This is clearly part of the intended function of the care agreement. However, the care agreement is above all supposed to move between and be communicatively used by the different actors. Furthermore, it is to become the generative centrepiece of an entire instrumentality of negotiated knotworking. When shared by parents and practitioners across institutional boundaries, this instrumentality is supposed to expand the object of their work by opening up horizontal, socio-spatial interactions in the patient's evolving network of care, making the parties conceptually aware of, and practically responsible for, the coordination of multiple parallel medical needs and services in the patient's life. This is not intended to replace but to complement and extend the linear-temporal dimension of care, including normative critical pathways. The solution is also aimed at relieving

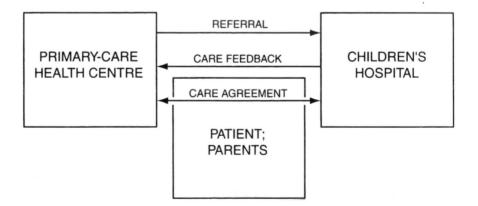

Figure 9.3 Conceptual model of the care agreement practice

the pressure coming from the rule of cost-efficiency and the tension between the hospitals and health centres by eliminating uncoordinated excessive visits and tests and by getting the health-centre general practitioners involved in making joint care decisions acceptable to all parties.

The new instrumentality is meant to become a germ cell for a new kind of collaborative care in which no single party will have a permanent dominating position and in which no party can evade taking responsibility over the entire care trajectory. The model implies a radical expansion of the object of activity for all parties: from singular illness episodes or care visits to a long-term trajectory (temporal expansion), and from relationships between the patient and a singular practitioner to the joint monitoring of the entire network of care involved with the patient (socio-spatial expansion). In October 2002, the Chief Executive Officers of the Helsinki City primary care and the Helsinki-Uusimaa hospital district signed a joint executive order that lays out the guidelines for implementing the care agreement practice in the entire health-care system of Helsinki.

Conclusion: expertise faces its zone of proximal development

I call the newly emerging locus of expertise (the vertical dimension in Figure 9.1) a 'divided multi-organizational field or terrain of activity'. Correspondingly, I call the newly emerging key process of expertise (the horizontal dimension in Figure 9.1) 'knotworking and expansive learning'. As an integrative characterization for the new type of expertise, I propose 'collaborative and transformative expertise'.

Figure 9.4 represents any activity system involved in a network of expertise. It makes visible the transitional, perhaps virtual character of the new generation of expertise. The community of the expert activity system is not any more limited to the members of an institution, such as the primary-care health centre or hospital clinic. The community encompasses the whole 'producer-customer network' and thus spans across multiple institutions operating in the divided terrain. In other words, the envisioned zone of proximal development of expertise implies a fluid, expansive de-institutionalization of expertise. In this case, de-institutionalization does not imply a return to atomic individualism. It implies that the future subject of expertise is a constantly changing, yet longitudinally robust knot of contributors.

The object of the projected collaborative and transformative expertise is the trajectory of a customer-intelligent product or service that has a long life cycle and requires constant co-configuration and learning. The entire temporal and socio-spatial care trajectory of a chronic patient with multiple illnesses is a good example of such an object. It is an object that transcends institutional and professional boundaries. Due to the emergence of such new types of objects (products and services), expert work is undergoing a

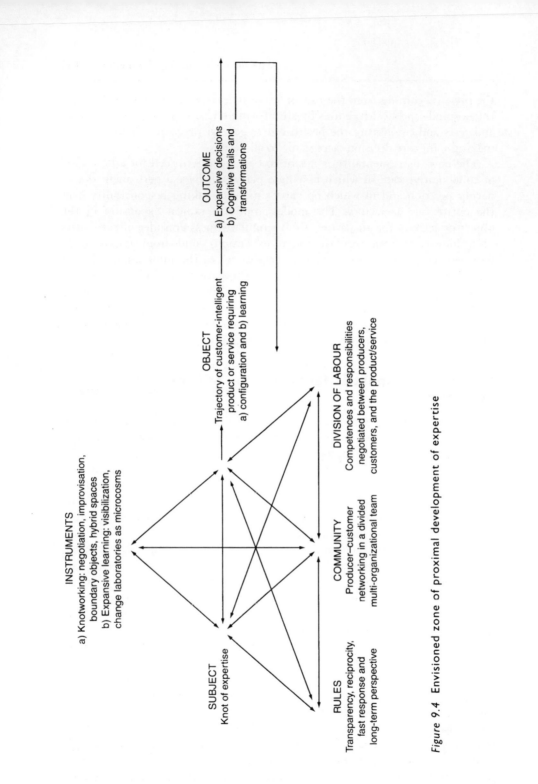

Figure 9.4 Envisioned zone of proximal development of expertise

historical transformation from various forms of craft, standardized mass production and mass customization toward co-configuration, the interactional core of which is 'negotiated knotworking'.

The outcome of the envisioned collaborative expertise is twofold. On the one hand, such expertise co-produces expansive everyday decisions. On the other hand, the expert activity system co-produces cognitive trails and transformations in its terrain. The instruments of collaborative expertise may be divided in a similar vein into those of knotworking and those of expansive learning. The former include negotiation, improvisation, boundary objects, and hybrid spaces. The latter include visibilization and change laboratory type of 'microcosms' for expansive learning (Engeström 1999b; Engeström et al. 2003).

The rules of collaborative expertise include transparency and reciprocity, necessary for the trust involved in knotworking. On the other hand, the rules include a novel approach to time, a dialectic between quick improvised problem solving and long-term composition of trajectories. The division of labour in the projected expertise is based on continuous negotiation of competences, tasks, and responsibilities between producers, customers and the product or service itself.

These conclusions, integrated in Figure 9.4, are to be taken as a historical working hypothesis. One would be hard put to point out a functioning example of mature collaborative and transformative expertise. The story of this type of expertise is only beginning. That's what makes the story exciting.

Bibliography

Alter, C. and Hage, J. (1993) *Organizations Working Together*, Newbury Park, CA: Sage.

Argyris, C. (1992) *On Organizational Learning*, Cambridge: Blackwell.

Atkinson, P. (1995) *Medical Work and Medical Talk. The Liturgy of the Clinic*, London: Sage.

Ayton, P. (1992) 'On the Competence and Incompetence of Experts', in G. Wright and F. Bolger (eds), *Expertise and Decision Support*, New York: Plenum.

Bateson, G. (1972) *Steps to an Ecology of Mind*, New York: Ballantine Books.

Beer, M. and Nohria, N. (eds) (2000) *Breaking the Code of Change*, Boston, MA: Harvard Business School Press.

Bensman, J. and Lilienfeld, R. (1991) *Craft and Consciousness: Occupational Technique and the Development of World Images*, 2nd edn, New York: Aldine de Gruyter.

Bereiter, C. and Scardamalia, M. (1993) *Surpassing Ourselves: An Inquiry into the Nature and Implications of Expertise*, Chicago, IL: Open Court.

Brown, S.L. and Eisenhardt, K.M. (1998) *Competing on the Edge: Strategy as Structured Chaos*, Boston, MA: Harvard Business School Press.

Burawoy, M. (2000) 'Introduction: Reaching for the Global', in M. Burawoy et al., *Global Ethnography: Forces, Connections, and Imaginations in a Postmodern World*, Berkeley, CA: University of California Press.

Cussins, A. (1992) 'Content, Embodiment and Objectivity: The Theory of Cognitive Trails', *Mind*, 101: 651–88.

Davydov, V.V. (1990) *Types of Generalization in Instruction: Logical and Psychological Problems in the Structuring of School Curricula*, Reston: National Council of Teachers of Mathematics.

Engeström, Y. (1987) *Learning by Expanding: An Activity-Theoretical Approach to Developmental Research*, Helsinki: Orienta-Konsultit.

—— (1993) 'Developmental Studies of Work as a Testbench of Activity Theory: The Case of Primary Care Medical Practice', in S. Chaiklin and J. Lave (eds), *Understanding Practice: Perspectives on Activity and Context*, Cambridge: Cambridge University Press.

—— (1996) 'Developmental Work Research as Educational Research', *Nordisk Pedagogik: Journal of Nordic Educational Research*, 16: 131–43.

—— (1999a) 'Activity Theory and Individual and Social Transformation', in Y. Engeström, R. Miettinen and R.-L. Punamäki (eds), *Perspectives on Activity Theory*, Cambridge: Cambridge University Press.

—— (1999b) 'Expansive Visibilization of Work: An Activity-Theoretical Perspective', *Computer Supported Cooperative Work*, 8: 63–93.

—— (1999c) 'Innovative Learning in Work Teams: Analyzing Cycles of Knowledge Creation in Practice', in Y. Engeström, R. Miettinen and R.L. Punamäki (eds), *Perspectives on Activity Theory*, Cambridge: Cambridge University Press.

—— (in press) *Collaborative Expertise: Expansive Learning in Medical Work*, Cambridge: Cambridge University Press.

Engeström, Y., Engeström, R. and Kärkkäinen, M. (1995) 'Polycontextuality and Boundary Crossing in Expert Cognition: Learning and Problem Solving in Complex Work Activities, *Learning and Instruction*, 5: 319–36.

Engeström, Y., Brown, K., Christopher, C. and Gregory, J. (1997) 'Coordination, Cooperation and Communication in Courts: Expansive Transitions in Legal Work', in M. Cole, Y. Engeström and O. Vasquez (eds), *Mind, Culture and Activity: Seminal Papers from the Laboratory of Comparative Human Cognition*, Cambridge: Cambridge University Press.

Engeström, Y., Engeström, R. and Kerosuo, H. (2003) 'The Discursive Construction of Collaborative Care', *Applied Linguistics*, 24: 286–315.

Ericsson, K.A. and Smith, J. (1991) 'Prospects and Limits of the Empirical Study of Expertise: An Introduction', in K.A. Ericsson and J. Smith (eds), *Toward a General Theory of Expertise: Prospects and Limits*, Cambridge: Cambridge University Press.

Hasu, M. and Engeström, Y. (2000) 'Measurement in Action: An Activity-Theoretical Perspective on Producer–User Interaction', *International Journal of Human-Computer Studies*, 53: 61–89.

Hirschhorn, L. (1984) *Beyond Mechanization: Work and Technology in a Postindustrial Age*, Cambridge, MA: The MIT Press.

Huber, D.L. and Oermann, M. (1998) 'The Evolution of Outcomes Management', in S.S. Blannett and D.L. Flarey (eds), *Health Care Outcomes: Collaborative, Path-based Approaches*, Gaithersburg: Aspen.

Hutchins, E. (1995) *Cognition in the Wild*, Cambridge, MA: The MIT Press.

Il'enkov, E.V. (1977) *Dialectical Logic: Essays in its History and Theory*, Moscow: Progress.

—— (1982) *The Dialectics of the Abstract and the Concrete in Marx's 'Capital'*, Moscow: Progress.

Kanter, R.M. (1989) *When Giants Learn to Dance*, New York: Simon and Schuster.

Latour, B. (1987) *Science in Action: How to Follow Scientists and Engineers Through Society*, Cambridge, MA: Harvard University Press.

—— (1993) 'Ethnography of a "High-tech" Case: About Aramis', in P. Lemonnier (ed.), *Technological Choices: Transformation in Material Cultures since the Neolithic*, London: Routledge.

Lave, J. and Wenger, E. (1991) *Situated Learning: Legitimate Peripheral Participation*, Cambridge: Cambridge University Press.

Marcus, G.E. (1998) *Ethnography Through Thick and Thin*, Princeton, NJ: Princeton University Press.

Modell, J. (1996) 'The Uneasy Engagement of Human Development and Ethnography', in R. Jessor, A. Colby and R.A. Shweder (eds), *Ethnography and Human Development: Context and Meaning in Social Inquiry*, Chicago, IL: University of Chicago Press.

Scott, W.R., Ruef, M., Mendel, P.J. and Caronna, C.A. (2000) *Institutional Change and Healthcare Organizations: From Professional Dominance to Managed Care*, Chicago, IL: The University of Chicago Press.

Shchedrovitskii, G.P. and Kotel'nikov, S.I. (1988) 'An Organization Game as a New Form of Organizing and a Method for Developing Collective Thinking Activity', *Soviet Psychology*, XXVI (4): 57–90.

Spekman, R.E., Isabella, L.A. and McAvoy, T.C. (2000) *Alliance Competence: Maximizing the Value of Your Partnerships*, New York: Wiley.

Star, S.L. (1989) 'The Structure of Ill-structured Solutions: Boundary Objects and Heterogeneous Distributed Problem Solving', in L. Gasser and M.N. Huhns (eds), *Distributed Artificial Intelligence*, Vol. II, London: Pitman.

Victor, B. and Boynton, A.C. (1998) *Invented Here: Maximizing your Organization's Internal Growth and Profitability*, Boston, MA: Harvard Business School Press.

Weick, K. and Roberts, K.H. (1993) 'Collective Mind in Organizations: Heedful Interrelating on Flight Decks', *Administrative Science Quarterly*, 38: 357–81.

Wiener, C., Fagerhaugh, S., Strauss, A.L. and Suczek, B. (1984) 'What Price Chronic Illness?', in A.L. Strauss (ed.), *Where Medicine Fails*, 4th edn, New Brunswick, NJ: Transaction Books.

Zuboff, S. (1988) *In the Age of the Smart Machine: The Future of Work and Power*, New York: Basic Books.

10 Supporting learning in advanced supply systems in the automotive and aerospace industries

Alan Brown, Ed Rhodes and Ruth Carter

Chapter summary

This chapter analyses the attempts made by a development project on Knowledge and Learning in Advanced Supply Systems (KLASS), funded by the Department of Trade and Industry (DTI) and the European ADAPT programme, to support the learning of individuals and organizations in the automotive and aerospace industries. The project sought to support small and medium-size enterprises (SMEs) through inter-company learning networks that have a strong focus on both immediate performance improvements and longer-term educational objectives. The underlying pedagogical idea is that there is considerable value in attempting to link processes of knowledge creation with tackling the core problems of manufacturing practice as a means of engaging learners that have traditionally been difficult for educational institutions to reach. The model of learning used with its emphasis upon networking, knowledge creation, linking an initial focus upon performance with a progressive broadening of ideas about learning and development was particularly well suited to its context: supporting learning and development in advanced supply systems. However, the scale of the effort and resources required to make the project successful means that considerable challenges would remain if the model were to be successfully implemented in a range of other contexts.

Introduction

SMEs in most sectors face intense pressures resulting from the strategies, tactics and operational methods of the large companies that dominate their markets, particularly where these are linked to supply chain restructuring. Stresses on SMEs also emanate from the extending roles of e-commerce. Yet operational demands force them to deal continually with immediate tasks and problems, and they generally operate within extremely limited time horizons, leaving them with few opportunities to develop an overall strategic approach to their business. In this chapter we analyse the attempts made within the Knowledge and Learning in Advanced Supply Systems

(KLASS) project to support the learning of individuals and organizations in advanced supply systems in the automotive and aerospace industries in ways that focused both upon immediate performance improvements and longer-term objectives. We contend that this approach improves the prospects for productive collaboration between SMEs and institutions in the broad educational sector. It also supports the development of new capabilities in SMEs, including those related to exploitation of the Internet and e-commerce, and fosters a shift from the immediate, short-term focus of SMEs to a more strategic perspective.

The strategic and operational contexts of SMEs have been influenced by the changing patterns of innovation within supply systems for complex products in the automotive and aerospace industries in the last decade. Current forms of product system integration now differ markedly from those of the past, which were based on single ownership of multiple stages of production and distribution. The newer forms have developed around the process of 'de-integration' in large companies, and are currently viewed in terms of the 'supply chain'. They are generally founded on large firm control over market access at strategic points in the total product system – for instance, retailer control over access to consumers. This control is facilitated by intensive use of information and communications technologies and is used to achieve tight co-ordination over all stages of production.

The KLASS project has been concerned principally with the automotive and aerospace component supply sectors, with the intention of improving production and sustaining supply chain participation among smaller companies. For reasons of space, however, only the contextual background of the automotive supply chain will be given, although the subsequent commentary upon learning in networks will range across examples drawn from both sectors.

The automotive sector

The automotive supply chain

The automotive supply chain involves the total sequence of production from raw materials extraction and processing, through intermediate stages of component production and manufacture of sub-assemblies, into end product manufacture. In the automotive industries, the supply chain is increasingly being managed as a total product system. This recognizes the broader resource and environmental impacts of car production and use, and takes a 'cradle to grave' view of the product life cycle, including the end-of-life reprocessing of motor vehicles. Within the product system, the KLASS project was concerned with the levels below that of the vehicle manufacturers – that is, in what is generically referred to as automotive component supply.

Automotive product systems are organized hierarchically, with the vehicle manufacturer at the top, controlling level. The characteristics of suppliers in the different tiers vary greatly, but some generalizations are useful. Those in tier one are mostly large or very large companies in terms of employee numbers and capitalization. Many have a sophisticated technological base – for instance, those producing specialized electronic, electro-mechanical and mechatronic systems or subsystems. The capacities of the leading tier one suppliers include significant research and development, product design and other advanced innovative capabilities. These companies are pressed to develop these capabilities further by manufacturers that are increasingly outsourcing elements of product development and manufacturing (Abreu *et al.* 2000). The tier one suppliers have an expanding role in vehicle specification, but this is accompanied by closer scrutiny of their practices by the manufacturers through 'supplier assessment'.

By contrast, the numerous companies in tiers two to four are mostly SMEs, including many micro-enterprises. Some of these provide specialist functions, but a large proportion have very limited technological capabilities. The KLASS project was primarily concerned with companies in these tiers, although manufacturers and tier one companies can have a central, motivating, role in stimulating these smaller companies to participate in learning networks. These SMEs have been faced with changing patterns of supply, and with significant restructuring within the industry, adding an extra dimension to the uncertainty they face.

Structural change in the automotive sector

Throughout the 1990s, growth in vehicle ownership was exceeded by the rate of growth in manufacturing capacity. Estimates of surplus capacity are generally in the region of 20 million units world-wide, including 6 million in Europe. In this highly competitive context, the sector is experiencing a fundamental restructuring – as has been evident in recent changes in the UK-based automotive sector. Among the vehicle manufacturers there have been some major changes in the structure of ownership, through mergers (like Daimler-Benz and Chrysler) and acquisitions of smaller car makers, such as Saab and Volvo, by larger companies. Other companies have become linked through share ownership – such as Renault's 38 per cent of Nissan and General Motors' 20 per cent of Fiat. This restructuring could ultimately lead towards global dominance by five or six car producers.

Restructuring has involved a major shift from internal production to outsourcing, bringing new opportunities for suppliers, particularly at the tier one level. Their roles are expanding as they take on the design and production of major systems and modules. However, this is accompanied by closer scrutiny of tier one capabilities by the manufacturers in selecting preferred suppliers, and the 'de-listing' of many other suppliers, that is contributing to a concentration among tier one companies. Mergers and joint ventures have increased, and the approximately 800 tier ones in the world automotive industry in the late 1990s is forecast to fall to about 30 during the current decade. There is a parallel reduction in the number of suppliers in the lower tiers.

This change follows from several factors, including attempts to shift towards variants of the 'lean manufacturing' methods associated with Japanese manufacturers. The approach emphasizes tight co-ordination between the companies within a vehicle manufacturer's supplier base. Continual improvement in supplier performance is required to meet manufacturer 'cost-downs' – that is, annual or more frequent reductions in the prices paid to suppliers throughout the production life of a car model. These have become a standard requirement in contracts with suppliers. As the share of total added value accounted for by suppliers rises, supplier efficiencies become increasingly critical to a vehicle manufacturer's competitiveness in relation to product costs and quality and for manufacturing flexibility. Responding to this changed environment presents all suppliers with major challenges to their financial, human and physical resources. The challenges are particularly daunting for SMEs in tiers two to four since their financial resources and management expertise are generally limited.

SME's capacities for response are also shaped by a fundamental divide in the emerging supplier hierarchies between the suppliers of more specialized components or services and suppliers of commodity parts and components. The former generally depend on high levels of skills that can be hard to replicate – as is reflected in product development capacities, relative product complexity and manufacturing capabilities. These capabilities yield relatively high returns and vehicle manufacturers or large tier one customers are often keen to retain these companies as suppliers, because of their contribution to product distinctiveness and value added in the end product. However, commodity items are increasingly sourced by large companies by electronic means, using 'reverse auctions' in which potential suppliers bid on price alone for supply contracts. This extends supply opportunities for suppliers in low labour cost locations, and puts pressure on commodity suppliers elsewhere. However, some commodity suppliers in Europe have retained advantages through their proximity to major manufacturing sites and their established abilities to comply with the total quality and kanban delivery requirements embedded in supply contracts.

However, many UK based SMEs – such as some of those participating in our learning networks – are poorly placed in relation to commodity supply. The underlying problems often relate to very poor standards of management and inefficiencies in their pattern of work organization. These are reflected in low productivity levels, as is illustrated by Toyota's work with UK suppliers that improved productivity by some 500 per cent over a five-year period (EMTA 2000). Poor performance is also evident in quality shortfalls and in failures to meet customers' delivery schedules. These shortcomings are also related to inadequate workforce skills. Further problems for these SMEs often include poor development of e-commerce capabilities (excluding them from many sales and purchasing channels), and limited capacities for moving from reliance on commodity products towards activities that yield more added value.

Competitive pressures are thus particularly acute for the approximately 7,000 companies in the UK automotive sector – even before such issues as exchange rates are considered. Many companies are poorly equipped to respond because they lack training-oriented management cultures. Often, the management culture is ill-suited to recognizing the scale of change needed for survival or to initiating the responses required for survival. The scale of the challenge can be indicated by the main capabilities now increasingly sought in suppliers by the large companies. These are:

- consistent output quality – increasingly at the zero defect standard (workplaces where this capability has not been valued rely on high cost 'inspecting out' of non-conforming items);
- the manufacturing flexibility required to meet customer requirements of small batch deliveries of varied parts;
- continuous improvements in production methods to meet regular customer 'cost-downs';
- the inter-organizational capabilities to meet increasing vehicle manufacturer pressure for tight integration and co-ordination of production, product design and development and other functions across the automotive supply chain;
- team capabilities depending on multiskilled team members with high levels of autonomy in determining work priorities;
- capabilities for using e-commerce for business-to-business interactions and transactions across the supply chain;
- the development of new management capabilities attuned to these conditions.

The KLASS project

Ideas and implementation

The previous sections establish the context of a project focused on learning and knowledge development to facilitate collaborative functioning and improved performance between companies. Project partners included manufacturing and distribution companies, training organizations, the Society of Motor Manufacturers and Traders Industry Forum, a college and several universities. The Open University led the project, that also involved partners in Denmark, France and Spain. The key project objectives were to:

- clarify and meet organizational and inter-organizational learning needs where co-ordination and integration of design, production and other processes extends across multi-company, multi-stage product supply systems;
- identify and utilize the mix of distance learning technologies that is best suited to the combination of individual learners, SMEs and the project learning networks;
- support SMEs in adapting to demands for increasing knowledge as a foundation for supply chain relationships, and in extending their adaptive and innovative capabilities;
- investigate ways in which information and communication technologies can be used to support distance learning in team-focused inter-company contexts.

The project aimed to stimulate economic innovation in SMEs through innovative learning. The approach centred on the development of two types of learning networks. Type 1 networks were process oriented, comprising workplace teams of operators and managers, that linked up to eight suppliers to a main, tier one, customer. They functioned through learning about the core tools and skills needed to improve performance. Teams undertook 'hands-on' learning by doing, which involved problem identification, and the development and testing of solutions. The type 2 networks were aimed at senior managers in SMEs in tiers two to four, which were linked as buyers or suppliers. The focus was on developing awareness of the scale of the threats that they face, and on establishing the measurement and improvement tools required to meet the increasingly demanding quality, cost and delivery standards of customers. Another aim of these networks was to foster the cultural adaptations needed in the current competitive environment.

In both cases, KLASS was building on prior, pioneering work by members of the partnership. A web-centred learning approach also supports the development of e-commerce capabilities and network group learning undertaken between multiple, linked workplaces. Learning support is provided, face to face and via project web-based facilities, by a team of experienced professional engineers, trainers, learning support specialists and mentors.

In the type 1 networks, tier one companies persuaded their suppliers to identify key individuals with central responsibility for shop floor innovation in supply management. These people, nominated as 'change agents', became project participants, and Open University students, following a course on Stimulating Competitiveness in Supply Chains. They were invited to a series of one week, intensive workshops at the tier one company, led by an engineering tutor (employed by Industry Forum) together with a learning support tutor. In the four week intervals between workshops, the change agents applied what they had learned in a practical context in their own companies. They kept in touch with other students via a computer conferencing system and undertook assignments designed to encourage them to reflect on their learning and the implications of applying it. The learning support tutor offered considerable educational support where necessary and marked the students' assignments.

As the course progressed, the focus shifted from work in individual companies to collaborative learning across the network of participating companies. There are obvious advantages of such a programme for the tier one companies who see rapid benefits in terms of the cost, quality and delivery performance of suppliers. There are also competitive advantages for all the companies in the network. Students also gain as individual learners. Overall, the expectation is that the future competitiveness of the companies will be enhanced, whether they are working with this particular customer or not.

In the type 2 networks, groups of senior managers from SMEs are brought together at the site of one of the project partners for a diagnostic workshop which aims to help them identify the learning needs of their companies. They then participate in a series of half-day workshops that match those needs and, again, use computer-based conferencing and activities to keep in touch and to facilitate the application of what they learned within their own environments. The forerunner of the type 2 networks was funded from the Department of Trade and Industry (DTI) initiative 'Learning from Japan'. A tier two supplier, realized that the key to supply chain performance rested with SMEs, so it reorganized itself and its suppliers into a network that, together, concentrated upon enhancing performance through focusing upon quality, cost and delivery. They used Industry Forum engineers to work on production improvements, and set up a learning centre where employees, suppliers and customers could learn away from the immediate pressures of work. The network has grown steadily and there is even collaboration with competitors. For example, three competitor tool-making companies have adopted a common costing structure and now tender for contracts as a group. This has helped iron out peaks and troughs in work and all three companies have grown. Staff employed in the open learning centre offer training and development, but also get involved in adapting 'best practice' to different settings. The key driver of change has been the quality of sharing of information, knowledge and experience among suppliers across the supply chain.

Merseyside Automotive Group acts as the key intermediary group in another network. This time there is a very strong pull from the top of the supply chain, and the group has received DTI support in establishing an Automotive College. With impressive facilities and underpinning funding it has been possible for those in education and training to work hard at building relationships with companies. Even SMEs will work with trusted intermediaries once a relationship has been established, although it is important not to raise company expectations too quickly. The strategy is

part of a sectoral approach to business improvement that includes the establishment of an e-business community and a programme of support for
continuous improvement.

The development of the type 1 and type 2 networks involved developing
partnerships and forging strong links with a number of organizations. The
networks were more difficult to establish than was originally expected,
because of the sharply deteriorating economic conditions experienced by
many players in the UK automotive sector. There were knock-on effects to
many suppliers and a number of companies found it difficult to focus upon
anything other than crisis management and a fight for survival. Indeed one
company remarked that they were looking to diversify out of the automotive
sector rather than become more locked into the supply chains of the sector.

The type 1 networks were built around the Society for Motor
Manufacturers and Traders Industry Forum work and the comprehensive
learning programmes focused upon improvements to manufacturing
processes. The type 2 networks drew on the work of the British Open
Learning Development Unit and focused upon trying to generate support for
supply chain network developments from SMEs. Once they were launched,
however, the networks exhibited a high degree of collaboration and knowledge sharing among the project partners.

Supporting innovation and learning

It is too early to identify whether cultural shifts have been fully embedded
but achieving such change was one of the long-term goals of the work with
the change agents in the companies. The way of working on materials
production in which much emphasis is given to the production of meaning
within the networks was for the project team indicative of the shift towards
a more decentralized view of the processes of knowledge creation. The
commitment to working with and through networks also meant that the
project materials were tested in a variety of contexts. It is worth emphasizing, however, that the focus upon SME skill needs in supply chains was
the vehicle for a bold experiment in trying to accomplish organizational and
inter-organizational learning and knowledge management across supply
chains, as well as supporting individual learning. This implies a reshaping of
the boundary between higher education, continuing education and training
and organizational development. The underlying pedagogical idea is that
there is considerable value in attempting to link processes of knowledge
creation with approaches to tackling the core problems of manufacturing
practice as a means of engaging learners (in SMEs) that have traditionally
been difficult for formal education and training institutions to reach.

Perhaps as important as the development of innovative learning materials
was the recognition by the project team that innovation is a social process.
Hence particular attention was given to building relationships to support

innovation not just between the partners but also with the companies in the networks. The support for change agents was itself designed so that they would be able to support process innovations within their companies. This means that the networks offered not only a mechanism for technology and process transfer and exchange of ideas about development and practice, but also a means of supporting those interested in acting as change agents in support of development and innovation. The networks have the potential to grow as a general means of innovation transfer in supply chains. The project sought to give people not only access to innovative ideas, but also because of the way the project was structured it gave learners opportunities to shape these ideas in ways that were directly useful to them in their work. This applied particularly to the work with company change agents.

A major concern with the development of learning networks to support practice is that the knowledge generated is often decontextualized. This may then mean it is of relatively little use to employees in coping with many of the problems they face in practice. One way the KLASS project addressed this concern was through focusing closely upon what the Industry Forum engineers see as key problems of manufacturing practice in the workplace itself. This ensured attention was given to problems and dilemmas that are central to manufacturing practice. These problems and dilemmas have significance both for individual and organizational performance. The problems are likely to contain combinations of practical concerns, organizational issues and socio-cultural problems. The Industry Forum approach to process improvement was underpinned with an inter-locking series of products: MasterClass; Supply Chain Group; Team Leader Training; and Value Stream Mapping. Details of this approach, together with case studies of their implementation are given in the DTI (1999) publication *Quality, Cost, Delivery: Seven Measures for Improved Competitiveness in Manufacturing Industry*. This approach also means that employees are directly involved in processes of active knowledge creation.

The project developed mechanisms for effective learner support and offered support too for work-based learning as a process. The KLASS project offered effective learner support not only through its system of tutors and assessors, but also through peer support through the network organization. The focus within the project upon offering substantive support for learning and development of change agents within the companies also resulted in an increase in the capacity of those companies to support other forms of work-based learning. As some of the learning was grounded in improving manufacturing processes and practice there was little doubt that this contributed to improvements in efficiency. The competitiveness of SMEs may also have been improved insofar as a consequence of the project they were able to operate more effectively within supply chains. This is particularly important as in the automotive industry vehicle manufacturers and tier one suppliers are expecting greater interdependence in ways of working with suppliers and are expressing an increasing commitment to processes of quality training (Abreu *et al.* 2000).

The significance of organized learning support for learning and knowledge development at work

The discussion so far raises the general question of how best to utilize the findings of this interesting, but very specific, project in order to contribute to addressing broader issues of how to support learning at work. Eraut *et al.* (1998) highlight the importance of organized learning support for learning at work, but also draw attention to its relative rarity. So the KLASS project is an example of a highly structured approach to the provision of organized learning support. On the one hand, the case may be thought to have limited generalizability because of the amount of time and other resources poured into the development and implementation of a structured system of learner support. On the other hand, it could be regarded as illustrative of the scale of the effort required if companies and individuals are serious about the implementation of significant change based upon a transformation of the relationship between working and learning. The more specific contributions to this issue are as follows:

- The involvement of Industry Forum engineers and their established processes designed to embed performance improvements in quality, cost and delivery (with consequent promised effects on organizational effectiveness more generally) acted as a strong catalyst to galvanize the interest of companies. Once the initially narrowly focused learning approach was underway it was often (though not always) possible to broaden the interest of companies and participants in learning.
- It is relatively easy to have an immediate impact on quality, cost and delivery in companies that have been primarily concerned with immediate operational issues. In contrast the process of embedding sustained continuing improvement is much more challenging and could take years to achieve. This is not to decry the value of the process outlined here, rather just to acknowledge that in organizational terms it is ideally the beginning of a longer-term process.
- The focus of the Industry Forum engineers and the group of learners upon making real improvements in manufacturing practice and process at one level could fit with ideas about the collaborative creation of new knowledge. However, at another level their understanding of learning was formulaic: improvements were achieved by following a very particular approach to improvement based upon what they had learned from Japanese 'master engineers'. Hence within the project the engineering experts had themselves to learn more about learning. Involvement in the project resulted in a learning process for the engineers in how to link what they had been doing in terms of performance improvement to broader learning and assessment processes in the type 1 networks. Their involvement in the type 2 networks represented a further role enhancement for them and contributed to their own learning and development.

- The approach to learning through networking could be seen as an example of an active model of learning whereby learners are engaged in the creation of 'new contextualized' knowledge, not recipients of a largely passive process of knowledge transmission. This is in line with the theoretical framework developed to explain processes of organizational knowledge creation by Nonaka and colleagues (Nonaka and Takeuchi 1995; Nonaka and Konno 1998). This approach makes use of a social model of knowledge creation and transformation. The key process for genuine knowledge transformation to occur is that knowledge has to move from the individual level into wider communities of interaction that cross organizational boundaries as happens in the KLASS networks. It is worth expanding upon the link between KLASS networks and organizational knowledge creation in more detail.

Nonaka and Konno (1998) use the idea of *ba* as shared spaces for emerging relationships that provide a platform for advancing individual and/or collective knowledge and of generating collaborative processes that enable the transformation of that knowledge to other contexts. This fits with the KLASS approach, as does the idea that active involvement and collaboration in the networks allows participants to transcend their particular (traditional) perspectives. In supporting people in their attempt to bring about change in manufacturing processes opportunities have to be given for practitioners to transform information from written or broadcast material into practical individual and collective knowledge. It may also be that the analytically rational world represented in learning materials may be too 'cold' for many people: they may need a richer form of engagement. The processes of socialization, externalization, combination and internalization that underpin Nonaka and Takeuchi's (1995) model of dynamic knowledge conversions give insight into why this lack of engagement may occur. It is therefore worthwhile viewing the approach of the KLASS project in the light of these processes in more detail.

Socialization (through originating ba)   Nonaka and Konno (1998) point to the need for an originating *ba* (or space for socialization) where individuals can share feelings, emotions, experiences and mental models. This is necessary not only to generate initial commitment (the value of which has long been recognized), but also because genuine knowledge transformation also requires a 'magic synthesis' of rationality and intuition that requires a greater depth of human engagement than just thinking. Within the KLASS approach the originating *ba* occurs during the initial face-to-face network meetings.

Externalization (through interacting ba)   The creation of space for active reflection by groups can be seen in the way in which subsequent network meetings groups would jointly examine a range of problems commonly associated with manufacturing practice. The groups would comprise individuals with a mix of backgrounds, knowledge and capabilities. Individuals could share their own ideas and understandings (although in the type 1 networks this phase was led by an Industry Forum engineer), and through processes of reflection and analysis, seek to generate some common understandings of how to improve manufacturing practice.

Combination (through cyber ba) This stage involves creating space for combining the ideas generated in the previous stage with existing information about how work is organized in a particular workplace. Network groups would jointly examine problems in a particular workplace. The groups would again comprise individuals with a mix of backgrounds, knowledge and capabilities. This time though individual ideas and understandings would be combined through processes of discussion and analysis in order to generate shared understandings of how to improve the manufacturing process in that particular workplace. This involves the generation of new forms of explicit contextualized knowledge.

Internalization (through exercising ba) The exercising *ba* is a shared space to facilitate the conversion of the (newly generated) explicit knowledge into the tacit knowledge of individuals and groups. This will involve active consideration of how to apply that knowledge in different contexts and the use of strategies to support the knowledge conversion process. This was the task of the change agent, trying to embed new ways of thinking about manufacturing processes and practices in her or his particular workplace.

This approach involves the spiralling of knowledge creation and transformation through continuing cycles of socialization, externalization, combination and internalization. The structure of KLASS project support was designed to allow material and ideas to be fed into the change processes over time. The essence of the *ba* of the learning community as a whole is that it does not involve a static accumulation of different materials, documents and information, but rather when it works well it possesses the dynamism continually to create new knowledge.

This approach to the development of practice is reflective, forward-looking and dynamic and works best within a culture that acknowledges the importance of developing practice, expertise and analytical capabilities in an interrelated way so as to be able to support the generation of new forms of knowledge. Those involved in such developments need to have a continuing commitment to explore, reflect upon and improve their practice (Schön 1987). The initial key to going beyond competent practice lies in the ability to transfer skills, knowledge and understanding from one context to another (Eraut 1994). Increasingly those working in complex supply chains are expected to perform effectively when they work in teams or task groups with colleagues with different backgrounds and different kinds of expertise. The

KLASS approach is predicated upon the idea that those engaged in particular work practices and processes have a key role to play in how new knowledge is generated and applied in practice (Engeström 1994).

An individual's knowledge of practice can itself be regarded as a personal synthesis of received occupational knowledge and situational understandings, derived from experimental learning, which is capable of being further transformed through a process of critical reflection. As expertise develops, and new contexts are utilized in the performance of practice, so the processes of analysis, review and reflection can lead to the creation of new forms of knowledge (Engeström 1994). Additionally Eraut (2000) points to how people have to deal with contextual variables, such as the time available and the volume of information to be processed, that mean they have to produce appropriate responses in situations where the conditions for 'best practice' are not present. Approaches such as those adopted in the KLASS project therefore constitute an important way in which to develop contextualized knowledge of how to effect continuing practice and process improvements.

The role of assessment in supporting individual learning and knowledge development at work

The benefits of the KLASS approach to companies and for individuals performing their work roles was evident in improved organizational effectiveness. However, what personal advantages might an individual gain from participation in KLASS activities? It is here that assessment and accreditation have a role to play. The Open University pursued a dual track towards recognizing the achievement of KLASS participants, where individuals could accumulate credit towards either or both National Vocational Qualification (NVQ) units or higher education credit accumulation and transfer (CATS) points. This was an interesting approach to bridging between different types of qualifications. The use of assignments that involved critical reflection, adaptability and forward thinking was a powerful developmental supplement that overcame many of the problems traditionally associated with the relatively narrow focus of National Vocational Qualifications. The type 1 network students worked towards an Award in Change Management comprising up to three units at NVQ level 3 or 4. Among the activities in the programme is support for the development of an Accreditation of Prior Experiential Learning portfolio, which may enable some students to gain further accreditation.

There were clear benefits to change agents and some other participants of access to recognized qualifications, accreditation of some existing skills and knowledge and opportunities for further learning and development. They also had opportunities to experience new approaches to learning based upon collaboration and active reflection, with the consequence that participants were more likely to recognize that many of their skills were transferable and could be used in a variety of contexts. Indeed attainments in learning could be formally recognized if they were written up in a learner's portfolio and/or if an individual completed all or some of the four written assignments.

The assignments helped students pull their learning together: for example, they could reflect upon how they might transfer what they had learned in the Industry Forum real-time workshops about improvements to practice and process to other contexts. The assignments also provided NVQ evidence as well as opportunities for learners to reflect upon their own learning, and were a valuable part of the personal development associated with working on the programme as a whole. The assignments were used by some employees as supporting evidence in company appraisal processes. The assignments therefore helped learning become more portable or transferable. (The downside to this process is that some employees were not enamoured with having to write up what they had learned in assignments. For them the spectre was not one of lifelong learning, but of lifelong homework!)

Assignments give clear evidence of the effect on the organization of individual learning, but a question is raised whether there is a need to recognize the efforts of a team. One argument is that this is especially necessary as the team is the key link if there is to be a continuing commitment to learning in the form of attempts to sustain continuing improvement and support the creation of new knowledge. The team can also be a vehicle for innovation and the development of adaptability, evidenced by the ability to perform effectively in a range of contexts. The goal is to get the team as a whole to be forward looking and proactive.

Unusually those involved in this programme can demonstrate improvements in aspects of company performance and improvements in their own individual learning. The latter are evidenced through reflections upon work and learning in assignments and portfolios and in the increasing quality of the assignments themselves, as evidenced by the ability to communicate effectively in writing, to be self-reflective and so on. There is value in portfolio building being coupled with active reflection upon what has been achieved with the tutor and other students, rather than being a passive and often dispiriting individual process of just documenting what you already know (Grugulis 2000).

Concluding discussion

One key question is how generalizable are the findings from this project. The first comment to make is that the level of provision of organized learning support was high, with assessors and tutors offering considerable individual as well as group support. There is little doubt that a reduced level of learning support would result in far fewer employees being committed learners. There is also a paradox in that some of the initial enthusiasm for learning comes precisely because the learning does not seem like learning (something hard that involves you in doing things you would not do if left to your own devices). That is, there is a step change involved in building upon the learning attained from well-defined Industry Forum processes that focus upon improving organizational performance. That learning is initially limited in terms of its scope and more in-depth learning is by its very nature more challenging.

One major problem faced in trying to generate the interest of SMEs in learning and development (and in generating small business growth) lies with the career motivations and personal expectations of individual owners and managers. Many small firms adopt practices that are antithetical to efficiency and growth (Gray 1993). Indeed the most common small business ambition is for independence and autonomy rather than profits and growth (Gray 1998). Hence it is important not to understate the extent of learning support (and in some cases a cultural shift) that would be required to make the KLASS approach applicable to a range of other settings.

On the other hand, this particular example was very successful in its context. Hence it is worthwhile drawing out four lessons for supporting learning in small companies. First, it is clear that the focus upon improving organizational performance contributed to improving commitment to learning at work of both companies and individuals that have been traditionally hard to reach. Examples of demonstrable improvements in quality, cost and delivery made the link between learning and performance transparent. The support of large companies as lead organizations in supply systems was significant too. SMEs were much readier to take part in an initiative that had the explicit approbation of a major customer than if they were approached directly by providers of education and training. The participation of major manufacturers and tier one suppliers in networks proved to be powerful initial 'hooks' to engage SMEs in learning activities.

Second, once committed and after overcoming initial suspicions of learning and working with staff from other companies, there were considerable benefits from collaborative learning. The type 1 networks involving change agents from different companies working together meant that, in addition to transfer of 'good practice', they could get a 'feel' for the capabilities of the other companies and this opened up possibilities for greater collaboration (for example, in joint bidding for contracts). The type 2 networks engaged senior staff from companies thinking collaboratively and strategically about supply chain issues. In both types of networks there was value in learning as a member of a group, including from others with a variety of backgrounds – with mutual learning across hierarchical levels as well as horizontally between departments and companies.

Third, there was a formal learning framework in the initial stages and a continuing structure of learning support – it was not just a question of bringing people together. The use of a wide range of learning methods helped improve commitment towards learning. These methods included:

participation in production process improvement reviews and implementation; Master Engineer workshops; group discussions; assignments; portfolio-building; discussions with tutors; use of computer-mediated communications for discussions, document transfer and tutor feedback. It was important there was rapport and a good working relationship between engineer and tutor in order that technical and learning developments are mutually supportive. There was a key role for the learning support tutor in helping learners build and then sustain commitment towards their learning goals. The tutor role involved providing advice, guidance and information and supporting all aspects of learning. Learners at all levels greatly appreciated the support and encouragement of tutors.

Fourth, the final stage was an attempt to move towards still more expansive learning beyond the immediate context. Many of the change agents recognized the value (and potential transferability) of the skills they were developing and this contributed to their commitment towards learning. For example, the skills required in coping with the challenges of trying to implement change involved compromise and dialogue and helped hone their communication skills. The project gave people support to help them engage in patterns of thought conducive to learning. The project gave learners generally, but especially the change agents, the time and space to engage in critical thought, self-reflection and personal development. This included opportunities for both collaborative and self-directed learning.

Overall then, the model of learning used in the KLASS project with its emphasis upon networking, knowledge creation, linking an initial focus upon performance with a progressive broadening of ideas about learning and development was particularly well suited to its context: supporting learning and development in advanced supply systems. The model of learning, rather than the particular details of the approach, could be transferable. If the model was underpinned by corresponding commitment of effort and resources, then it could be successfully implemented in a range of other contexts.

Bibliography

Abreu, A., Beynon, H. and Ramalho, J. (2000) 'The Dream Factory: VW's Modular Production System in Resende, Brazil', *Work, Employment and Society*, 14, 2: 265–82.

Department of Trade and Industry (DTI) (1999) *Quality, Cost, Delivery: Seven Measures for Improved Competitiveness in Manufacturing Industry*, London: DTI.

EMTA (Engineering and Marine Training Authority) (2000) *Engineering Manufacturing Labour Market Observatory – Motor Vehicles Report*, Watford: Training Publications Limited.

Engeström, Y. (1994) *Training for Change: New Approach to Instruction and Learning on Working Life*, Geneva: ILO.

Eraut, M. (1994) *Developing Professional Knowledge and Competence*, London: Falmer.

—— (2000) 'Non-formal Learning, Implicit Learning and Tacit Knowledge in Professional Work', in F. Coffield (ed.), *The Necessity of Informal Learning*, Bristol: Policy Press.

Eraut, M., Alderton, J., Cole, G. and Senker, P. (1998) 'Learning from Other People at Work', in F. Coffield (ed.), *Learning at Work*, Bristol: Policy Press.

Gray, C. (1993) 'Stages of Growth and Entrepreneurial Career Motivation', in F. Chittenden, M. Robertson and D. Watkins (eds), *Small Firms – Recession and Recovery*, London: ISBA/Paul Chapman.

—— (1998) *Enterprise and Culture*, London: Routledge.

Grugulis, I. (2000) 'The Management NVQ: A Critique of the Myth of Relevance', *Journal of Vocational Education and Training*, 52, 1: 79–99.

Nonaka, I. and Konno, N. (1998) 'The Concept of "Ba": Building a Foundation for Knowledge Creation', *California Management Review*, 40, 3: 40–54.

Nonaka, I. and Takeuchi, H. (1995) *The Knowledge Creating Company: How Japanese Companies Create the Dynamics of Innovation*, Oxford: Oxford University Press.

Schön, D. (1987) *Educating the Reflective Practitioner*, San Francisco, CA: Jossey-Bass.

Part 3

Skills, knowledge and the workplace

11 Conceptualizing vocational knowledge

Some theoretical considerations

Michael Young

Chapter summary

This chapter argues that debates about the reform of vocational education have invariably neglected the question of vocational knowledge. It discusses the three approaches to knowledge that have characterized debates and reforms of Vocational Education and Training (VET) in the UK up to now. It then proposes a framework for analysing these approaches that draws on two traditions of sociological theory – social constructivism and social realism. Having identified the relationship between power and different concepts of knowledge that is made explicit by social constructivist approaches, the chapter examines in some detail the social realist approach and its distinctions between types of knowledge that were developed by Durkheim and Bernstein. Finally it suggests some implications of these analyses for the conceptualization of vocational knowledge.

Introduction

Proposals for the reform of vocational education in the United Kingdom can be traced back to the late nineteenth century. Since the end of the Second World War and especially since the early 1980s, both criticisms and proposals for reform have recurred with ever increasing frequency. At the same time, the focus of each has varied widely – from institutions and curricula to, more recently, qualifications. Where responsibility for failure is placed has also varied. In the 1980s, governments blamed trade unions who were seen as blocking changes which appeared to weaken their bargaining power (Raggatt and Williams 1998); at the same time governments also criticized the Further Education (FE) sector for its ignorance of industrial realities and its educational conservatism. Social scientists, on the other hand, have tended to blame employers for taking a short-term view of the costs and benefits of training. However they have also located the weaknesses of the VET system in its wider social and political context (e.g. Finegold and Soskice 1988). Some have pointed to the anti-industrial and elitist culture that has pervaded English governing classes and its tendency to value knowledge as a mark of status rather than as an instrument of economic transformation (Weiner 1981). Others have highlighted the peculiarly voluntarist role of the state that emerged in England in the nineteenth century (Green 1990) and is reflected in the continued reluctance of governments of both left and right to extend either the legal obligations on employers to guarantee training or the range of occupations that require some form of 'license to practice'.

Reforms of VET have related selectively to these various critiques but in the last decades the emphasis has been almost entirely on the supply side of the 'VET market'. Two major issues, however, have been given little attention. The first, now increasingly acknowledged even in the Cabinet Office, is the lack of employer demand for improved skills and knowledge. This chapter focuses on the second, less acknowledged issue – the question of vocational knowledge.[1] In contrast to the centrality of the curriculum in school policy debates, the question as to what knowledge those on VET programmes should acquire has been treated superficially, at best.

The chapter seeks to locate issues concerning the control and content of vocational education within a theoretical framework drawn from the sociology of knowledge. It distinguishes between three approaches to knowledge (section one) and goes on to argue that in different ways each avoids fundamental epistemological concerns that need to be addressed if an adequate concept of vocational knowledge is to be developed (section two). In order to tackle the question of vocational knowledge, I distinguish between the two main social theories of knowledge, *social constructivism* and *social realism*[2] and argue that while social constructivism provides an important critical perspective on VET knowledge policy, it is unable to deal with the question of vocational knowledge itself (section three). Two key contributions to a social realist approach to knowledge are introduced: Durkheim's early distinction between the 'sacred' and the 'profane'; and Bernstein's distinction between vertical and horizontal 'knowledge structures'. I suggest that these distinctions, modified by a social constructivist critique which makes explicit the relations between knowledge and power, provide a useful basis for conceptualizing vocational knowledge. The chapter concludes by suggesting some possible implications of the analysis for the future of VET.

Knowledge and the vocational curriculum: three approaches

The inadequate knowledge and skills that are acquired by many students and trainees achieving vocational qualifications has been recognized since the decision in the late 1880s to establish the City and Guilds of London Institute (C&G) to promote and organize VET on a national scale (Gay 2000). Three distinct approaches to this problem can be identified which have followed each other historically. I shall refer to them as *knowledge-based*, *standards-based* and *connective* approaches.

The knowledge-based approach was introduced in the late nineteenth century in response to the now familiar anxiety that our industries were becoming less competitive than those in other countries, especially Germany (Donnelly 1993). The reformers recognized that skills and knowledge needed in the new science-based industries such as engineering and chemicals could not be developed on the basis of traditional work-based apprenticeships. Employees in craft and technician occupations in these sectors needed access to knowledge of the sciences on which these industries were based and which they could not acquire 'on-the-job'. It was logical therefore that the major focus of the new curricula and examinations launched by the C&G was on the physics, chemistry and mathematics relevant to the different industrial sectors.

Two significant features of the emerging vocational curriculum were to survive in somewhat modified form for almost a century. First, it explicitly excluded the application of knowledge in workplaces or any form of 'trade knowledge'. This was partly because of intrinsic difficulties in developing and assessing curricula that focus on the application of knowledge but perhaps, more importantly, because the application of knowledge is always likely to involve the 'trade secrets' of individual companies. As a result, learning how to apply the new scientific knowledge in specific workplaces was left to apprentices and their employers. Second, it assumed that the natural sciences were important for their specific content and as a model of reliable, objective knowledge. This model which assumed that knowledge could be treated as given and objective was also seen as appropriate for non-science-based fields such as business studies, which expanded from the 1960s and have since come to dominate vocational courses in FE colleges.

It was not until the late 1970s and early 1980s that the assumptions of this knowledge-based approach to the vocational curriculum began to be seriously challenged. In retrospect, a number of developments appear to have been behind this. First, the number of people employed in science-based industries, where there was a relatively clear link between the science content of the vocational curriculum and its role in industrial processes, was steadily declining. Second, there was growing concern about the absence of qualifications among the majority of the workforce and a recognition that this might account for the inability of our industries to compete with the emerging Asian economies. Third, the possibility was increasingly recognized that the traditional knowledge-based vocational curriculum acted as a barrier to the new groups of young people entering FE colleges or work-based training programmes (the 'new FE' as they were known at the time), especially as many had achieved very little in the school curriculum. Finally, there was an emerging belief, shared increasingly by government and employer organizations that the knowledge-based approach to the vocational curriculum had lost contact with the main purpose of vocational education, which was to develop workplace competence.

In giving priority to bodies of knowledge in the form of subjects, the knowledge-based approach was seen by critics as providing a rationale for the continuing control of the vocational curriculum by the educational establishment in colleges. These criticisms extended to a negative view of any off-the-job component of programmes and what became described as a 'provider-based' approach to the vocational curriculum. The proposed alternative was what I refer to as a standards-based approach. This involved a number of assumptions. The most important, which continue to remain highly influential, were that: the vocational curriculum needed to be controlled by the key users (the employers), not the providers (FE colleges); the skills and knowledge needed by employees *at work* must determine all provision for off-the-job learning in colleges; vocational qualifications need to give priority to the assessment of what can be learned in the workplace, not the knowledge acquired off-the-job in colleges; and, that the traditional provider-based vocational curriculum stressed what students or trainees *need to know* and did not pay enough attention to what they *need to do* when they are at work.

It was argued by key civil servants in the Employment Department that the best way of establishing a vocational curriculum that gave priority to employer needs was not to base it on the expertise of vocational subject specialists in colleges but to derive it from National Occupational Standards. The Standards would be established by employers[3] representing the different sectors. This approach was supported by the government and employer organizations as well as the National Council for Vocational Qualifications (NCVQ) that was launched in 1986. Occupational Standards represented a completely new approach to vocational education in which (at least in theory) outcomes replaced syllabuses and workplace assessment replaced teaching. In practice it proved unpopular with many employers and unworkable by FE college lecturers who found themselves having to use the standards designed in terms of outcomes to construct a curriculum.

The premise of the late nineteenth century reformers was that as industrial change was primarily knowledge-led, or more specifically science and engineering-led, it was appropriate that the relevant sciences should form the core of the vocational curriculum. However, the policy makers of the 1980s noticed two unintended outcomes of the nineteenth-century reforms, which they saw as being at odds with the needs of a modern vocational curriculum. The first was a tension between changes in the learning demanded by employers and the relative lack of change in the college-based curriculum. Changes in the demand for skills were being expressed in the increasing differentiation of skills and knowledge in different workplaces, together with a growing awareness of the importance of generic or common skills. Insofar as there were changes in the college curriculum, they were expressed in the proliferation of new subjects in response to alterations in student demand that were not necessarily congruent with changes in the organization of work. In theory, this new vocational curriculum was meant to complement changes in the learning demands of workplaces. However, in practice it appeared to have a kind of logic of its own, reflecting the wider trend of academic drift associated with all educational institutions.

The standards-based approach to the vocational curriculum on which the new National Vocational Qualifications (NVQs) were based was seen as a way of countering the academic drift of most college-based vocational courses as well as a means of accrediting work-based learning. Using a method known as functional analysis that was developed by occupational psychologists concerned with job design, curriculum outcomes were identified in terms of what employees would be expected to do, not what they needed to know. Knowledge came second and was only important in so far as (in NCVQ's language) it underpinned performance.

In the early days NCVQ officers took an extreme view of the standards-based approach and assumed that all vocational knowledge was implicit in competent workplace performance. It followed that there was no need to consider knowledge separately at all. If someone was assessed as performing competently it was assumed that they must have the adequate (underpinning) knowledge. This position was later modified when it was acknowledged that not all the knowledge that employees needed could be acquired in workplaces or identified by observing performance. The need to assess knowledge separately led to attempts to provide criteria, based on the occupational standards for identifying what became known as underpinning knowledge and understanding (UKU). A major concern of NCVQ consultants such as Mansfield and Mitchell (1995) was to avoid allowing the traditional syllabus-based approach to knowledge to return. It was assumed that if this happened the vocational curriculum would be reclaimed by the colleges and NCVQ's mission to disseminate an outcomes-based approach (and the belief that occupational competence could be acquired 'on-the-job') would be undermined.

Two contrasting approaches to knowledge persisted as alternatives. One was college-based and expressed in terms of subjects and disciplines. Subjects were developed from research-based knowledge by college subject specialists with links to subject teaching associations. The vocational variant of the knowledge-based approach consisted of curricula related to broad occupational fields such as business and administration; it relied on links between vocational teachers in colleges, professional bodies and university faculties in a variety of applied fields. At higher levels, especially in fields like law, medicine and engineering, the academic and vocational variants were virtually indistinguishable; both had strong links with the universities and professional bodies.

The three crucial features shared by the two variants of the knowledge-based approach to the curriculum were: (1) they provided clear progression routes between lower levels (e.g. A levels and National Certificate courses) and higher levels (degrees, Higher National Certificates and professional qualifications); (2) they depended for their validity on the understandings and values shared by different communities of specialists; and (3) they maintained quality by relying on external examinations marked by specialists, rather than on any formally explicit criteria or specification of outcomes. In contrast, the standards-based approach to vocational knowledge rejected these features as being exclusive and backward looking. It aimed to replace examined syllabuses agreed by groups of specialists by criteria for national standards common to all fields (and in principle, all subjects) and defined in terms of outcomes at five levels.

In the mid-1990s the NCVQ was merged into the Qualifications and Curriculum Authority (QCA). However, the QCA has retained the standards-based approach to vocational qualifications but relaxed its rigidities. Vocational qualifications are now required to be 'influenced by' rather than 'derived from' occupational standards. Despite this official 'loosening up' which recognized that the standards-based approach on its own had failed to provide criteria for vocational knowledge, its basic assumptions remain and continue to influence the most recent reforms such as the proposal that Technical Certificates should be incorporated into Modern Apprenticeships as a way of strengthening off-the-job learning. The idea that employer-led bodies should take the lead in developing the vocational curriculum has also been retained despite the reality that in many sectors employers are reluctant to take on such a role and frequently lack the necessary expertise. What has emerged is considerable diversity between sectors and a largely ad hoc approach to specifying underpinning knowledge. This can take the form of lists of topics which either amount to little more than what anyone would know after a few weeks in a workplace (as in the case of sectors like retail and distribution) or involve a combination of everyday workplace facts (what tools are needed or where to find them), together with some scientific or highly technical topics with little idea as to what depth they should be studied (as in the case of photography). Not surprisingly, some sectors such as accountancy, electrical installation and engineering in which the acquisition of off-the-job knowledge is vital, have resisted the excesses of the standards-based approach. Furthermore, not only did the standards-based model fail to take off as a basis for higher level qualifications, but the demand for more traditional types of knowledge-based vocational courses has continued to grow.

The limitations of the standards-based approach is at least implicitly recognized in the recent proposals for Technical Certificates which aim to strengthen the knowledge-based component of Modern Apprenticeships at the same time as enhancing its relevance to the workplace. Technical Certificates imply a greater emphasis on off-the-job learning and its links with on-the-job learning and for this reason the new certificates can be described as a connective approach[1] to vocational knowledge. In contrast to the knowledge-based approach, Technical Certificates stress the importance of the knowledge acquired at work and in contrast to the standards-based approach they explicitly recognize that the knowledge acquired at work is often inadequate on its own, especially in knowledge-intensive work places. The responsibility for identifying this knowledge, however, remains with employer bodies funded by the government; they are required to develop course outlines and rationales for off-the-job learning.

Technical Certificates retain problematic features of the previous standards-based model. First, despite the failure of the standards-based methodology in the early 1990s, Technical Certificates still rely on the idea that underpinning knowledge and understanding can be generated from occupational standards. Second, in giving responsibility for deciding on the knowledge content of Technical Certificates to employer-led bodies (the Sector Skills Councils), it is still assumed that the key issue for the vocational curriculum is who controls it, not its content. The employer-led bodies are advised to consult with college-based vocational curriculum specialists, but are not legally obliged to do so. With these constraints it is difficult to see how Technical Certificates, despite their ambitious aims, can be the basis of a genuinely new approach to vocational knowledge.

VET reforms and concepts of vocational knowledge

The account of attempts to reform the vocational curriculum in the previous section suggested that although each reform arose from a recognition of problems with existing provision, there remained issues with which each were unable to deal. In this section, I want to consider the different meanings given to vocational knowledge that are implicit but not explicitly discussed in the reforms and the critiques that led to them. My argument is that in their attempts to develop a distinct vocational curriculum, each approach has avoided the issue of how vocational knowledge can be distinguished from school or academic knowledge on the one hand and the skills and knowledge that may be acquired in the course of work, on the other. The knowledge-based approach recognized the crucial role of science in a vocational curriculum geared to the new science-based industries but failed to consider how this new knowledge could be re-contextualized in the workplace. As a result it became the inevitable victim of academic drift; many technical curricula were little more than inferior versions of similar academic curricula. The standards-based approach tried to relate vocational knowledge to workplace practice by claiming to be able to derive it from outcomes-based analyses of occupational roles. However this not only failed to lead to a practical methodology, it neglected the extent to which only some of the knowledge relevant to particular occupations has its origins in workplaces.

The connective approach associated with Technical Certificates is an explicit attempt to bring these two approaches together by making links between off-the-job and on-the-job learning. However it still relies on at least the rhetoric of the standards-based approach to identifying off-the-job knowledge. It also fails to acknowledge that there may be fundamental differences between the types of knowledge that can be acquired at work and in college. It also neglects how these differences may relate to differences between the codified knowledge of subjects and disciplines and the implicit and sometimes tacit knowledge acquired in workplaces. If there are important differences, in content, structure and purposes, between off-the-job and on-the-job knowledge, there are likely to be problems in attempting either to rely on one type as in the knowledge-based approach or both these types of knowledge as if they were derivable from occupational standards.

Both approaches mask crucial epistemological differences and assume that the only differences that are relevant to the vocational curriculum are around the question of control (whether it is employers or educationists who decide). The idea of 'connecting' off- and on-the job knowledge and grounding the connection in national occupational standards as implied by the proposals for Technical Certificates is in principle a step forward. However it tells us little about the nature of the connections between the codified knowledge of the college-based curriculum and the tacit and often uncodifiable knowledge that is acquired in workplaces. In order to be clearer about what such connections might involve, we need a more rigorous way of differentiating between types of knowledge and their possible relationships. The next section therefore takes a step back from specific issues concerning the vocational curriculum and considers different approaches in the sociology of knowledge.

Sociology and vocational knowledge

The importance of the sociology of knowledge for issues of concern to VET reformers (and indeed those involved in education policy more generally) is that, in its premise, it captures what Muller (2000) refers to as the fundamental *sociality* of knowledge. It rejects the view that knowledge is either intrinsically 'in the mind' (idealism) or in the world (materialism) or in any sense given: all knowledge, it asserts, in that it is produced by human beings, is inescapably social in origin. The sociality of knowledge refers not only to how it is shaped by external societal influences, but also to the way that our most basic categories and concepts are inescapably social in origin. It is useful to distinguish between two interpretations of this sociality which have led to very different sociologies of knowledge, *social constructivism* and *social realism*.

By social constructivism I refer to that tradition of social theory which has a long and varied history since Hegel and Marx in the nineteenth century and the American pragmatists in the early twentieth century. It takes its most familiar contemporary forms in the work of the French sociologist, Pierre Bourdieu and in the variety of perspectives often referred to as post-modernism.

Social constructivism argues that all knowledge is the product of social practices; knowledge is therefore inescapably from a standpoint. No knowledge in this view is privileged or can claim to be objective. It follows that the specialized, codified, or discipline-based knowledge associated with the college curriculum (and off-the-job learning) is in principle no different from everyday common sense (or on-the-job) knowledge; it is just some other people's knowledge. There is a somewhat ironic link between the epistemological reductionism associated with post-modernism and what might be called the behaviourist reductionism of the standards approach (Moore and Young 2001). There are two forms of social constructivism that have important implications for the case of vocational knowledge. They might loosely be described as those that focus on the *interests* underlying all knowledge and those that focus on the *process* of production and acquisition of knowledge. 'Interest-based' social constructivism has its intellectual roots in Marx's theory of ideology. Whereas Marx was largely concerned with social class interests, his approach has been generalized more recently to refer to any social group (e.g. by feminists to include women and by multi-cultural ists or post-colonialists to include different ethnic groups). Interest-based approaches to knowledge have an important critical role in reminding vocational educators that any selection of knowledge will be an expression of some social interest and reflect a particular set of power relations. The vocational curriculum is always likely to be in some part a power struggle between employers, educators and the state, and in a rather different way between teachers and students.

Process-based versions of social constructivism can be traced back to the symbolic interactionism of American social theorists such as Dewey and G.H. Mead. Their strength is the emphasis they give to the contextual or situated character of knowledge. Knowledge is always produced or acquired 'in a context'; it is never entirely context-free. Given the importance of learning on-the-job in vocational education, it is not surprising that process-based approaches have been taken up by VET researchers and lie at the heart of the few attempts to conceptualize vocational knowledge (Billett 1995).

The problem with both versions of social constructivism is that they are at best partial perspectives. The interest-based approach on its own can lead to a reductionist view of all knowledge as power relations; hence the only question this leads to is who has the power. Similarly process-based approaches fail to distinguish between the 'degree of situatedness' of different types of knowledge. For example, the 'knowledge' needed by a receptionist or a call-centre operator is almost entirely situated or related to a specific context whereas the knowledge needed by an engineer or an accountant is not. Although this context specificity is a feature of the knowledge required for all jobs, many jobs also require knowledge involving theoretical ideas shared by a community of specialists that are not tied to specific contexts; such knowledge enables those who have acquired it to move beyond specific situations. In focusing only on either the interests or the practices involved in the processes of acquisition and production, knowledge itself can easily be reduced to or equated with the interests or practices of groups of knowers; as a result, content becomes arbitrary (at least in theory). Thus social constructivism, while rhetorically powerful both in exposing the power relations that are embedded in all knowledge and in cautioning researchers to be sensitive to particular contexts, is limited in what it can say directly about the vocational curriculum, where the differentiation of knowledge is the crucial issue.

Social realist approaches to knowledge, on the other hand, stress that although all knowledge is historical and social in origins, it is its particular social origins that give it its objectivity, and it is this that enables knowledge to transcend the conditions of its production. It follows that the task of social theory is to identify these conditions. Social realist approaches address epistemological issues that are involved in the differentiation of knowledge that social constructivism does not (and in my view cannot) engage with. Partly as a result of an unwillingness to recognize the social realist argument, decisions about the VET curriculum have been left to a combination of tradition, pragmatism and negotiations between stakeholders. I turn therefore to a brief account of the ideas of two leading exponents of social realist approaches, Emile Durkheim and Basil Bernstein.

Durkheim's social realist approach

A social realist approach to knowledge can be traced back to the work of the French sociologist, Emile Durkheim who began writing in the last decade of the nineteenth century. He wanted to emphasize the 'sociality' of knowledge, but in contrast to social constructivism, stressed the differences not the similarities between different types of knowledge and explored the different types of social organization associated with them. Durkheim's ideas were based on contemporary studies of religion in primitive societies (Durkheim 1961). His starting point was a distinction between *profane* and *sacred* orders of meaning that he found in every society that he studied. The profane refers to people's knowledge of their everyday world; it is practical, immediate and particular (with similarities to 'on-the-job' learning in the terms of this chapter). He distinguished the profane from the sacred world of religion that he saw as invented, arbitrary (in the sense of not being tied to particular contexts) and conceptual; the sacred was a collective product of a society. Originally exemplified by religion, the sacred for Durkheim became the paradigm for all the other kinds of conceptual knowledge including science, philosophy and mathematics, which, for him, were equally social and removed from the everyday world. In relation to the concerns of this chapter, the sacred has parallels with 'off-the-job learning' in that it is not constrained by the immediacy of practical problems or 'getting the job done'.[5]

Muller (2000) makes the important point that for Durkheim, the sacred, whether exemplified as religion or science, is an order of meaning characterized by what he refers to as the 'faculty of realisation'. This for Durkheim has two aspects, the ability to make connections[6] and the ability to predict or project beyond the present and conceive of alternatives. Both these capacities tend to be neglected in vocational curricula and even sometimes in general education. Durkheim's analysis, therefore, suggests why achieving 'parity of esteem' between academic and vocational learning has been so difficult to achieve and why attempts to 'vocationalize' general education have been open to the charge that they are little more than forms of social control.

The sacred and the profane as distinct orders of meaning are inevitably in tension. However, Durkheim does not imply a judgement about one type of meaning being superior to the other. Everyday activity such as work would be impossible on the basis of the sacred alone. On the other hand, workplaces restricted to the profane preclude the possibility of workers envisaging alternatives. Durkheim is making an argument for specialization; in other words he is emphasizing the distinctive roles of both orders of meaning.

There are three further lessons for vocational education that can be drawn from Durkheim's analysis. The first is that the sacred and profane is not just a distinction between orders of meaning or forms of knowledge; it also refers to different forms of social organization. Second, by distinguishing between their distinct roles and purposes, Durkheim provides a way of avoiding a simplistic opposition between the two that has characterized many arguments about the VET curriculum. He is accepting that there are different types of knowledge with different purposes that are based on different forms of social organization. It follows that they are not interchangeable, or in competition with each other; they are complementary. Third, insofar as the distinction between the scared and the profane is a way of conceptualizing the relationship between theory and practice, it is asserting that an understanding of what is distinct about theory and practice is a precursor to exploring the different forms in which they may be related.

There are, however, some problems with Durkheim's analysis, which reflect his assumption that modern societies are evolving in a linear fashion from earlier societies. First, as a result of extrapolating from small-scale societies with little stratification, Durkheim plays down the extent to which the different orders of meaning are unequally distributed and themselves become stratified. The theoretical problem that this leads to is that power/knowledge relations are marginalized in Durkheim's analysis. Despite his insistence that the sacred and the profane only differentiate between different orders of meaning, in practice they become the basis of divisions between academic and vocational qualifications and more generally between mental and manual labour. Second, in complex modern societies, the sacred and the profane are no longer as distinct as they were in less developed societies; each pervades the other as in the case of science being increasingly embedded in work. They are, in Max Weber's terms, *ideal* not descriptive types and always enmeshed to some extent in each other. Dichotomizing between the two leads Durkheim to take for granted the problem of crossing the boundaries between different types of knowledge, an issue that is fundamental to explicating the relationship between off-the-job and on-the-job learning. Bernstein's work has been centrally concerned with boundary crossing. In his last work (Bernstein 2000) he develops Durkheim's social realist approach to knowledge in his distinction between vertical and horizontal knowledge structures. I turn next to a brief discussion of Bernstein's ideas.

Bernstein's vertical and horizontal knowledge structures

Bernstein reconceptualizes Durkheim's distinction between sacred and profane orders of meaning in terms of what he refers to as vertical and horizontal discourses. Horizontal discourses, for Bernstein are local, segmental and context-bound. In contrast, vertical discourses are general, explicit and coherent. Vertical discourses can generate vertical knowledge structures that are either hierarchically organized bodies of knowledge such as the natural sciences or knowledge structures that are segmentally organized into specialized languages as in the case of the humanities and the social sciences. Work-based or on-the-job knowledge can be seen as a form of horizontal discourse; it embodies no explicit principles for transferring meanings across 'segments' (whether these are sites or occupational sectors), except by analogy that one segment or occupation is 'similar' to another. Furthermore, on-the-job knowledge is usually acquired experientially without relying on any overt pedagogic intervention or following any explicit rules or sequences. Bernstein argues that horizontal discourses cannot generate vertical knowledge because they embody no principles of recontextualization; by this he means the rules for making explicit the grounds for an explanation. Put simply, there are rules that govern both the production and acquisition of vertical knowledge.

Bernstein's distinction between horizontal and vertical discourses explains the inability of the standards-based approach to vocational knowledge to generate any systematic methodology; it fails to recognize that one kind of knowledge (vertical) cannot be derived from the other (horizontal). The horizontal or the tacit cannot be made explicit because it is its tacitness and immediacy in relation to everyday or working life that give it its power and purpose. Similarly it is not possible to apply vertical knowledge directly to specific everyday workplace problems where the knowledge needed is that which is sufficiently flexible to deal with immediate practical problems.

Bernstein argues that vertical discourse can be expressed in the form of two distinct types of knowledge structure, and again he invokes the vertical/horizontal distinction. Vertical knowledge structures are pyramidal and expressed in their purest form in the physical sciences in which knowledge growth involves ever higher levels of generalization and abstraction. Horizontal knowledge structures, on the other hand (Bernstein's examples refer primarily to the social sciences) involve a number of non-comparable specialized languages lacking any overarching principles for linking them. The growth of horizontal knowledge, for Bernstein, consists of the development of new specialized languages. For him, both types of knowledge structure are generated by vertical discourse. Both have explicit principles of recontextualization and those who have acquired them can provide the grounds of their explanations in terms of a shared set of rules.

Bernstein's analysis highlights the extent to which previous debates about vocational knowledge have limited their focus to the different groups involved in defining what is to count as vocational knowledge and have not considered the different types of knowledge themselves. Such debates have been about whether it should be the employers, as the standards-based approach claims, or the educators (in line with the knowledge based approach) who should define what is to count as vocational knowledge. Boreham (2002) suggests that reforms within the dual system of apprenticeship in Germany provide an example of how the different stakeholders can work together and provide the social basis for a connective approach. Bernstein's theory, on the other hand, suggests that such an approach neglects questions of the internal structuring, contents and purposes of different forms of knowledge and what implications these may have for how knowledge is acquired.

The importance of Bernstein's theory for conceptualizing vocational knowledge is found in his concept of re-contextualization and the pedagogic strategies to which it points. There is only space here to hint at how such an analysis might be developed. Brier (2002) and Gamble (2002), in slightly different ways, draw on his ideas to develop the useful distinction between *principled* or generalizing and *procedural* or particularising pedagogic strategies. The former refers to explanations and the latter to the location of specific instances. Distinguishing between types of pedagogic strategy raises questions about how they relate to each other, the different kinds of explanation and procedure that may be found in vocational education programmes and how they may be distributed and reflect differences between industrial and service sectors.

Bernstein, like Durkheim, favours dichotomous categories. However, he develops his dichotomies by what Abbott (2000) and later Moore and Muller (2002) refer to as 'fractal divisions'. He is able therefore to conceive of vertical knowledge structures including elements of horizontality and vice versa. One of the limitations of his analysis for the concerns of this chapter is that he gives almost all his attention to varieties of vertical knowledge, in particular the differences between the social and natural sciences. Any attempt to conceptualize vocational knowledge requires equal attention to the differentiation of horizontal knowledge structures across different occupational sectors and types of work.

Bernstein's distinctions can be applied to a number of trends in recent VET curriculum policy. For example, Foundation Degrees and Technical Certificates are attempts to increase the knowledge component of work-based programmes. However, by failing to distinguish between types of knowledge along the lines suggested by Bernstein, they may well reproduce the problems that they were designed to overcome. Vocational General Certificate of Secondary Education (GCSEs) and vocational A levels, on the other hand, seek to incorporate workplace knowledge into the vertical structures of the school curriculum. However, as Brier (2002) points out, the inclusion of everyday practical knowledge into the school or college curriculum does not necessarily promote access to vertical knowledge; it can reduce the vocational curriculum to little more than a strategy for improving the capacity of students to function as employees.

Conclusion

In this chapter I have argued that debates about the reform of vocational education have invariably neglected the question of vocational knowledge. I have suggested that there are approaches in the sociology of knowledge that are relevant to the reconceptualization that is necessary and draw on the relationship between power and knowledge that is made explicit by social constructivist approaches and the focus on the differentiation of knowledge that arises from the social realist approach developed by Durkheim and Bernstein. Whereas Durkheim's distinction between sacred and profane provides a way of analysing the differences between theoretical and everyday (or workplace) knowledge, Bernstein's analysis allows distinctions to be made between types of theoretical knowledge and types of everyday knowledge as well as the problems of bridging the gap between them through the process of recontextualization. His analysis highlights the weakness of attempts to base vocational knowledge on national occupational standards. By treating all knowledge as potentially explicit and vertical, the standards-based approach fails to recognize the fundamental differences between theoretical and everyday or workplace knowledge. As a result, vocational programmes that rely on the standards-based approach deny learners access to the rules governing the production and acquisition of knowledge by the scientific and professional communities. It is not surprising that such programmes have been so unsuccessful in promoting progression. Greater clarity about what knowledge is to be acquired by students on vocational programmes is crucial to wider debates about more effective vocational education and any possibilities of a move towards parity of esteem with general education. The argument of this chapter is that the sociology of knowledge developed by Durkheim and Bernstein offers a powerful way of beginning to tackle such questions.

Acknowledgements

This chapter arose from a project on 'The Role of Knowledge in Vocational Education' supported by the City and Guilds of London Institute. I am most grateful to Lorna Unwin (University of Leicester) and Michael Barnett (Imperial College of Science, Technology and Medicine), my colleagues on the project, for their comments on an initial draft and to Alison Fuller (University of Leicester) for her helpful advice and suggestions.

Notes

1   Boreham's (2002) paper stands out in explicitly focusing on the question of vocational knowledge by drawing on a comparative study of recent reforms in the UK and Germany. In contrast with this chapter, it addresses contextual rather than epistemological issues.
2   I use social realism in the quite specific way that has emerged in the work of sociologists such as Collins (1998).
3   The employer bodies involved in setting standards have undergone various reorganizations and name changes. They are currently being reconstituted as 25 Sector Skills Councils.
4   'Connective' here refers to explicit links between on- and off-the-job learning and can be distinguished from its use in Young (1998) and Griffiths and Guile (2001).
5   For a more detailed discussion of Durkheim's analysis and a comparison of his ideas and those of Vygotsky, see Young (2003).
6   In its modern form this is one of the capabilities identified by Reich (1991) as needed by those he refers to as the symbolic analysts of today's knowledge economies.

Bibliography

Abbott, A. (2000) *Chaos of Disciplines*, Chicago, IL and London: University of Chicago Press.

Bernstein, B. (2000) *Pedagogy, Symbolic Control and Identity*, revised edn, Lanham, MD: Rowman and Littlefield Publishers.

Billett, S. (1995) 'Disposition, Vocational Knowledge and Development: Sources and Consequences', *Australian and New Zealand Journal of Vocational Education Research*, 5, 1.

Boreham, N. (2002) 'Work Process Knowledge, Curriculum Control and the Work-based Route to Vocational Qualifications', *British Journal of Educational Studies*, 50, 2: 225–38.

Brier, M. (2002) 'Horizontal Discourse in Law and Labour Law', unpublished paper, Education Policy Unit, University of the Western Cape, South Africa

Collins, R. (1998) *The Sociology of Philosophies: A Global Theory of Intellectual Change*, Cambridge, MA: Harvard University Press.

Donnelly, J. (1993) 'The Origins of the Technical Curriculum in England During the Nineteenth and Early 20th Centuries', in E. Jenkins (ed.), *School Science and Technology: Some Issues and Perspectives*, Centre for Studies in Science and Mathematics Education, Leeds: University of Leeds.

Durkheim, E. (1961) *The Elementary Forms of Religious Life*, New York: The Free Press.

Finegold, D. and Soskice, D. (1988) 'The Failure of Training in Britain: Analysis and Prescription', *Oxford Review of Economic Policy*, 4. 3: 21–43.

Gamble, J. (2002) 'Retrieving the General from the Particular: The Structure of Craft Knowledge', unpublished paper, Department of Education University of Cape Town, South Africa.

Gay, H. (2000) 'Association and Practice: The City and Guilds of London Institute for the Advancement of Technical Education', *Annals of Science*, 57: 369–98.

Green, A. (1990) *Education and State Formation*, Basingstoke: Macmillan.

Griffiths, T. and Guile, D. (2001) 'Learning through Work Experience', *Journal of Education and Work*, 14, 1: 113–31.

Mansfield, B. and Mitchell, L. (1995) *Towards a Competent Workforce*, Aldershot: Gower.

Muller, J. (2000) *Reclaiming Knowledge: Social Theory. Curriculum and Education Policy*, London and New York: Routledge Falmer.

Moore, R. and Muller, J. (2002) 'The Growth of Knowledge and the Discursive Gap', *British Journal of Sociology of Education*, 23 (4): 627–37.

Moore, R. and Young, M. (2001) 'Knowledge and the Curriculum in the Sociology of Education: Towards a Reconceptualization', *British Journal of Sociology of Education*, 22, 4: 445–61.

Raggatt, P. and Williams, S. (1998) *Government. Markets and Vocational Qualifications: An Anatomy of Policy*, London: Routledge.

Reich, R. (1991) *The Work of Nations*, London: Simon and Schuster.

Weiner, M.J. (1981) *English Culture and the Decline of the Industrial Spirit*, Cambridge: Cambridge University Press.

Young, M. (1998) *The Curriculum of the Future*, London: Falmer Press.

—— (2003) 'Durkheim, Vygotsky and the Curriculum of the Future', *London Review of Education*, 1, 2: 100–17.

12 Transfer of knowledge between education and workplace settings

Michael Eraut

Chapter summary

The first half of this chapter analyses the different knowledge cultures of higher education and the workplace, contrasting the kinds of knowledge that are valued and the manner in which they are acquired and used. In particular, performance in the workplace typically involves the integration of several different forms of knowledge and skill, under conditions that allow little time for the analytic/deliberative approach favoured in higher education. One consequence is greater reliance on tacit knowledge, including knowledge of how more formal, explicit knowledge is used in various practice settings. The second half focuses on transfer as a learning process, which requires both understanding and positive commitment from individual learners, formal education, employers and local workplace managers. Transfer is conceptualized in terms of five stages, whose distinctive characteristics and learning challenges are discussed in some detail. The neglect of transfer is attributed both to the cultural gap between formal education and the workplace and profound ignorance of the nature and amount of the learning involved.

Cultural knowledge and personal knowledge

My starting assumption is that learning is significantly influenced by the context and setting in which it occurs. Contexts and settings are socially constructed. Even when only one person is present, cultural influence is strongly asserted through the physical environment for learning and cultural artefacts. From that perspective one can argue that all knowledge is cultural knowledge and socially situated. Understanding the significance of this cultural perspective involves locating knowledge in space and time; and determining its distribution, and possibly differential interpretation, across a range of cultural groups. Who has this knowledge? Who was involved in its construction over time? How has it developed from and how is it now positioned in relation to other cultural knowledge? What different forms does it take? How is it evolving? These questions apply equally to education and workplace settings, and especially to the interactions and disconnections between the settings. Current approaches to professional and vocational learning are impossible to understand without knowledge of their various traditions, histories and cultures.

Part of that cultural knowledge has been codified, mainly in textual form, and made widely accessible through publication. That which passes the scrutiny of editors, publishers and referees and is thereafter collected and organized by the libraries of educational institutions can be described as 'codified academic knowledge'; and it is this knowledge which plays the dominant role in most education settings. Codified knowledge which is not academic can be found in nearly all workplaces, including those of educational organizations, in the form of textual material containing organization-specific information, records, correspondence, manuals, plans, etc.

Cultural knowledge that has not been codified, plays a key role in most work-based practices and activities. There is considerable debate about the extent to which such knowledge can be made explicit or represented in any textual form; and the evidence gathered so far suggests that its amenability to codification has been greatly exaggerated (Eraut 2000). What does appear to be generally acknowledged is that much uncodified cultural knowledge is acquired informally through participation in social activities; and much is often so 'taken for granted' that people are unaware of its influence on their behaviour. This phenomenon is much broader in scope than the implicit learning normally associated with the concept of social-ization. It is a prominent feature of educational institutions in spite of the overt dominance of codified academic knowledge; and it occurs in both formal and informal settings.

As a counterpart to cultural knowledge, I define personal knowledge as what individual persons bring to situations that enables them to think, interact and perform. Codified versions of personal knowledge are associated with the concept of authorship; and provide the basis for assignments and assessments within educational programmes from which more than the replication of publicly available knowledge is expected. But my definition is intended to include non-codified personal knowledge and a far broader concept of knowledge than academic performance. For example, it includes not only personalized versions of public codified knowledge but also everyday knowledge of people and situations, know-how in the form of skills and practices, memories of episodes and events, self-knowledge, attitudes and emotions. Moreover, it focuses on the use value of knowledge rather than its exchange value in a world increasingly populated by qualifications. This implies a holistic rather than fragmented approach to knowledge; because, unless one stops to deliberate, the knowledge one uses is already available in an integrated form and ready for action.

While remaining a strong supporter of the concept of situated learning, I strongly dissent from those theorists, such as Lave and Wenger (1991), who attempt to eradicate the individual perspective on knowledge and learning. Their research, based mainly on fieldwork in stable communities, focuses selectively on common rather than differentiated features of people's knowledge; and fails to recognize the need for an individual situated (as well as a socially situated) concept of knowledge in the complex, rapidly changing, post-modern world. Individuals belong to several social groups in which they both acquire and contribute knowledge, and their experiences of multiple group membership cannot be ring-fenced. Many of these groups have changing memberships and relatively short lifetimes. Thus members of a group acquire only part of the knowledge present in that group, and interpret it within a personal context and history that has been shaped by their experiences in other groups, both prior and contemporary. There will also be aspects of a person's knowledge that have been constructed through lifelong learning and have become unique to them, i.e. outside the circle of shared cultural knowledge, because of the unique set of situations in which they have participated. For example, a single idea will acquire a distinct web of meaning for each individual user according to the sequence of situations in which they used it. The greater the range of usage, the more distinctive its personal meaning is likely to be (Eraut 2000).

Types of knowledge acquired in education contexts

Teachers in secondary and post-compulsory education are organized according to the subjects they teach, each of which forms a distinctive sub-culture and provides a major part of their professional identity (Goodson 1983; Becher 1989). Most learning pathways that precede full-time employment comprise mainly subjects, which have potential vocational relevance, but are taught primarily under the auspices of general education. When subjects are claiming territory on the timetable, arguments based on vocational relevance are used with vigour, if not rigour But, once their territory has been established, historical traditions, the prevailing assumptions of the subject culture and the expertise of the current teaching staff dominate the selection and treatment of academic content. The prime objective becomes progression within the discipline and increasing participation in its culture to first-degree level and beyond, even though only a small minority of students follow that particular path. In many subjects applied aspects are given just a 'walk on part' and an occasional mention.

Professional and vocational education programmes typically include three kinds of content: these derive from (1) disciplines which feature prominently in general education and form major components of honours degrees, e.g.

Mathematics, Sciences, Social Sciences, Languages, (2) the applied field which sponsors the programme, e.g. Business, Engineering, Education, Health Professions and (3) occupational practice itself. According to their background and orientation, individual teachers have a primary allegiance to one of these three types of content, but are sometimes also required to teach a second. In every case the treatment of the content and its relationship to practice are significantly influenced by the academic and vocational experience of those who teach it.

Most teaching within an applied field is also strongly influenced by an often quite recently constructed body of knowledge about that field, which thus becomes either a quasi-discipline like Education or Nursing or a constellation of quasi-disciplines like Business Studies or Engineering. Over time, teachers in the applied field are drawn from its own graduates and a cultural succession becomes possible whereby new teachers are recruited with little or no work experience in the relevant occupation. These may remain a minority, but the codified academic knowledge of the field, as represented in publications, begins to dominate knowledge derived from personal experience of occupational practice, both culturally and experientially, as the impact of early occupational experience recedes. Some of this theory of the applied field is concerned with the application of theories and concepts from scientific disciplines, some is based on empirical research and conceptual frameworks peculiar to the applied field and some is based on the elaboration of practitioner maxims and practical principles. Some of it is based on what can best be described as a preferred view or ideology of the occupation, a theoretical justification of its purposes and practices in terms of moral principles, views of society and occupational beliefs about the effectiveness of various practices.

This last aspect of 'applied field' theory is strongest in occupations based on personal interaction with clients, where there is a strong tendency to construct theories of practice which are ideologically attractive but almost impossible to implement. The main problem is that the professionals concerned are urged to adopt practices that involve much greater levels of time and effort than service users and/or the public purse can possibly finance. Hence, there is a significant gap between the theories of practice taught by former practitioners, based on how they would have liked to have practised, and the activities performed by current practitioners. This contrasts with the common workplace stance, in which current practice is uncritically accepted as an inevitable reality, and any impetus towards improving the service provided by an occupation is lost. Neither provides an adequate basis for a professional career. There are so many variants of problem-based learning (PBL) curricula and staffing strategies that it is impossible to discern the extent to which PBL even attempts to bridge this cultural gap between education and workplace settings.

The third type of course found in education settings involves teaching occupational practice through skill workshops or simulations; or, if there is concurrent work experience, seminars linked to discussions that interpret that experience and introduce relevant theory in order to facilitate learning in the workplace. This last is commonly described as the 'reflective practitioner' model. To be successful these skills sessions or reflective seminars require small student groups, good facilities and hyperactive staff who sustain close working links with practitioners. Recruiting and retaining such staff is often difficult; and in higher education the demands of such bicultural work tend to conflict with activities more likely to lead to promotion.

The kinds of knowledge which Vocational and Professional Education Programmes claim to provide are summarized in Box 12.1.

Box 12.1 Knowledge in vocational and professional education programmes

1 Theoretical Knowledge constructed in the context of either a subject discipline or an applied field. This introduces concepts and theories to help students to explain, understand and critique occupational practices and arguments used to justify them; and to appreciate new thinking about the role of the occupation and proposed new forms of practice.

2 Methodological Knowledge about how evidence is collected, analysed and interpreted in academic contexts and in occupational contexts; and the procedural principles and theoretical justifications for skills and techniques used in the occupational field.

3 Practical Skills and Techniques acquired through skills workshops, laboratory work, studio work, project work etc.

4 Generic Skills claimed to be acquired during further and/or higher education, either through direct teaching, or more often, as a side effect of academic work. These include:
   • basic skills in number, language and information technology
   • modes of interpersonal communications
   • skills associated with learning and thinking in an academic context
   • self-management skills.

5 General knowledge about the occupation, its structure, modes of working, cultural values and career opportunities.

Although most of these types of knowledge are described as transferable, there is little evidence about the extent to which 2, 4 and 5 are acquired by students and about the chances of 1 and 3 being subsequently transferred (or not) into the workplace. There is even some doubt as to whether the phenomena described as 'transferable skills' have sufficient affinity with workplace activities for the term 'transfer' to be a valid description of any suggested connection.

Types of knowledge used in the workplace and the conditions of its use

My research into mid-career learning in a wide range of settings (Eraut *et al.* 1998; Eraut 2000) led to a rough typology of knowledge found in the workplace, which contrasts with that found in education settings. This is summarized in Box 12.2 in a slightly modified form.

Unlike many typologies, this one gives considerable emphasis to working contexts and conditions. Not only is situational understanding context specific, but it requires knowledge acquired through experience; and the capability to decide and act requires both experience of working in the context, and adaptation to a range of local conditions. One cannot understand the knowledge needed for doing a job without a detailed description of what I like to call its performance domain. This comprises three types of variable. These are, first, the contexts and cultures in which the performer will have to operate, including likely locations and their salient features. The second set of variables includes the conditions under which the performer will have to work, e.g., degree of collaboration and supervision, pressure of time, crowdedness, conflicting priorities, availability of resources. The third set of variables include the situations which the performer may encounter, covering such factors as client types and demands, tasks to be tackled, interpersonal events, emergencies, etc.

Like other typologies, however, mine has one very serious weakness. It cannot represent the knowledge that results when several different kinds of knowledge are combined to achieve a complex task or performance. Nor does it consider the problems of prioritization or interference between tasks. For this purpose I developed a model of a performance period (Figure 12.1). This also allows for the possibility of interference between tasks, and draws attention to problems of prioritization and deciding which task to do when.

The period chosen for analysis will vary according to the focus and the occupation; for example one could consider a lesson, a clinic, a shift or a day. A major aspect of professional experience is that many tasks do not get completed during a performance period, so there is the constant problem of 'picking up the threads' at the beginning or receiving new information that will cause a change of plan; then a need to record progress at the end and/or to hand over clients to a colleague. This is reflected in the separate boxes for *Initiation*, to indicate the initial briefing and reading of the situation when the period starts, and for *Ending*, to indicate what has been achieved, or left undone, by the time the period ends.

Box 12.2 Knowledge found in the workplace

1   Codified Knowledge acquired during initial professional training and further episodes of formal learning; or in the workplace itself. The former includes codified academic knowledge of concepts, theories and methodology. The latter includes job-specific technical knowledge and knowledge of systems and procedures.

2   Skills needed for competence in a wide range of activities and for performing several work-related roles, including leadership and working collaboratively within a team. These can be grouped under four headings – technical, interpersonal, thinking and learning – and are acquired through practice with feedback. Progression is associated with increasing fluency, responsibility and complexity.

3   Knowledge Resources include a range of materials and on-line resources; but learning from other people is even more important in most work settings. These include immediate work colleagues and other members of one's organization; networks of clients/customers, suppliers and competitors; professional networks; and other personal contacts developed over time.

4   Understanding provides the basis for most action, although it is inevitably incomplete. It encompasses the understanding of other people – colleagues, clients, managers, etc.; the understanding of situations and contexts, including one's own organization and its environment; self-understanding and strategic understanding of a range of changes and developments. This includes both explicit and implicit theoretical perspectives and theories of action.

5   Decision-making and Judgement vary with the conditions in which they are exercised. Decisions may be rapid, with little time for analysis or consultation, or deliberative and consultative. When situations are complex or information is sparse, judgement becomes a critical aspect of decision-making: judgement of people; judgement of the quality of products, practices and processes; judgement of the relative significance of, and interaction between, different factors; judgement of priorities, options and strategies.

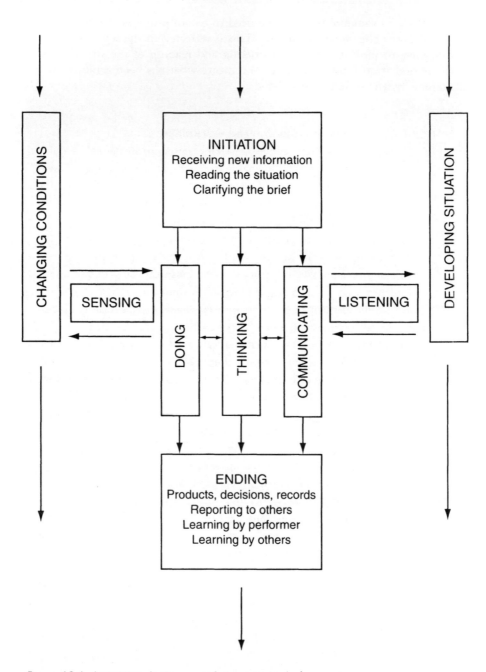

Figure 12.1 Activities during a performance period

One advantage of using a performance period is that situations often develop over time. So, instead of a static model in which all decisions and plans are made at the beginning of a period, one has a dynamic model in which a constantly changing environment provides a changing input that leads to the constant modification of plans. The input side is shown by placing the activities within a context characterized by changing conditions and a developing situation, with the opportunity for inputs prompted by sensing and listening. A great deal of competent behaviour depends not just on being able to do certain things (output) but also on the correct reading of the ongoing situation (input) so that the appropriate action can be taken. Nor is it only the external environment that changes of its own accord. The performer is an actor who affects that environment, not always in totally predictable ways. So another role of input is to provide feedback on the effect of one's own performance. This applies whether one is making something and sensing it change, or talking to people while listening to their reply and observing their reaction.

The interpretation of this input is just one aspect of the cognitive element, indicated by a central column marked *Thinking*. Other aspects of thinking include planning and monitoring one's activities and solving problems. People are constantly thinking and making decisions as they go along, even though they could probably tell you very little about it afterwards. Hence *Thinking* is shown in constant interaction with *Doing* and *Communicating*. These activities overlap to some extent, the main distinction being between acting on inanimate objects and interacting with other human beings.

Factors affecting modes of cognition in workplace performance

The performance period approach introduces issues pertaining to the pace and pressure of the workplace; and, through emphasizing the importance of cognition, raises the question of when and how workers find the time to think. This led to a model linking four types of professional activity to different amounts of thinking time, and hence, to examining the modes of cognition employed in professional work (see Table 12.1). The four types of activity were:

1   Assessing clients and situations (sometimes briefly, sometimes involving a long process of investigation) and continuing to monitor their condition.
2   Deciding what, if any, action to take, both immediately and over a longer period (either on one's own or as a leader or member of a team).
3   Pursuing an agreed course of action, modifying, consulting and reassessing as and when necessary.
4   Managing oneself, one's job and one's continuing learning in a context of constrained time and resources, conflicting priorities and complex inter- and intra-professional relationships.

Table 12.1 Interactions between time, mode of cognition and type of process

| | Mode of cognition | | |
Type of process	Instant/Reflex	Rapid/Intuitive	Deliberative/Analytic
Reading of the situation	Pattern recognition	Rapid interpretation	Review involving discussions and/or analysis
Decision-making	Instant response	Intuitive	Deliberative with some analysis or discussion
Overt activity	Routinized action	Routines punctuated by rapid decisions	Planned actions with periodic progress reviews
Metacognitive	Situational awareness	Implicit monitoring. Short, reactive reflections	Conscious monitoring of thought and activity. Self-management. Evaluation

These activities can take many different forms according to the speed and context and the types of technical and personal expertise being deployed. Although analytically distinct, they may be combined into an integrated performance that does not follow a simple sequence of assessment, decision and then action. For example a health professional will often have to decide whether to take action and then reassess whether to continue with a further assessment of their client or whether to simply wait and see. There may be several assessments, decisions and actions within a single period of consultation and treatment. Indeed recording both the nature of these activities and the ways in which they are sequenced and combined is another very useful approach to describing professional practice.

In order to understand the nature of workplace performance, one has to examine the thinking entailed in carrying out these activities, which depends on both: (1) the conditions and constraints on the performer, and (2) what the performer has learned to do, with or without stopping to think. Sometimes the situation itself demands a rapid response; sometimes rapid fluent action is the hallmark of the performer's proficiency; sometimes the number of activities proceeding simultaneously limits the attention that can be given to any of them, i.e. the workload is so heavy that there is little time to think. Thus the model assumes that time is the variable that most affects mode of cognition and divides the time-continuum into three sections, headed Instant, Rapid and Deliberative. These terms attempt to describe how the time-scale is perceived by the performer and are interpreted differently according to the orientations of performers and the nature of their work. For example, in one context rapid might refer to any period less than a minute, while in another context it might include periods of up to ten minutes or even half an hour. The critical feature is that the performer has little time to think in an analytic mode.

The instant/reflex column describes routinized behaviour that, at most, is semi-conscious. The rapid/intuitive column indicates greater awareness of what one is doing and is often characterized by rapid decision-making within a period of continuous, semi-routinized action. Typically it involves recognition of situations by comparison with similar situations previously encountered; then responding to them with already learned procedures. The time available affects the degree of mismatch that is tolerated, because rejection of action based on precedent leads to deliberative, problem-solving and hence to a more time-consuming approach. The deliberative/analytic column is characterized by explicit thinking about one's actions in the past, present or future, possibly accompanied by consultation with others. It involves the conscious use of prior knowledge, sometimes in accustomed ways, sometimes in novel ways or in a more critical manner.

The interesting question arises as to whether performers are aware of the knowledge embedded in their practice when it is not explicitly used at the time. Four very different circumstances may pertain. These are, first, that the practice was modelled on that of other professionals without understanding the reason for it or being aware of any underpinning knowledge. Second, the practice was developed with awareness of its rationale and underpinning theory, but that awareness dissipated over time and with it the ability to explain or justify it. Third, the practice can still be justified by citing underpinning theory, but cannot withstand any challenge because there has been no critical evaluation of the practice since it was first adopted, and finally, the practice cannot only be justified but remains under the professional's critical control because it has been periodically re-evaluated.

The need for knowledge transfer during initial training and the period of workplace learning that follows it will largely be determined by whether the desired option is a simple transfer of practice as in the first set of circumstances, or involves critical reflection and re-evaluation, as in the last set of circumstances.

Two problems are likely when the use of underpinning knowledge is not under critical control. First, conflicts may arise in problematic cases between competing responses based on different practical principles – these cannot be resolved unless the underlying reasons for these principles are understood. Second, there is a danger that 'scientific' knowledge will be replaced by unscientific knowledge – that which falls within the domain of a discipline but is regarded by leading professionals as either incorrect or alarmingly incomplete. The normal assumption is that being a competent professional implies keeping one's practice under critical control, and therefore keeping up to date with relevant areas of theory and research. Reviews of practice may arise from individual reflection and consultation or, more officially, from the work of an appointed group. They examine the rationale for the practice, the evidence for its effectiveness, alternative approaches and recent research; and this may lead to a decision to retain the practice unchanged, modify it, or adopt an alternative. In spite of the growing emphasis on audit and on evidence-based practice, such reviews are far from frequent and are restricted by the limited, and often exaggerated, scope of research-based evidence.

Transfer as a learning process

My own definition of transfer is 'the learning process involved when a person learns to use previously acquired knowledge/skills/competence/expertise in a new situation'. This may be short and easy if the new situation is similar to some of those previously encountered; but long and very challenging if the new situation is complex and unfamiliar. At least four variables are important influences. These are the nature of what is being transferred, differences between the contexts, the disposition of the transferee, the time and effort devoted to facilitating the transfer process.

In the complex situations encountered by most professional workers, the transfer process typically involves five interrelated stages as indicated in Box 12.3.

Transferring a particular concept or idea from an education setting to a workplace setting is particularly difficult, because of the considerable differences in context, culture and modes of learning. One major justification for teaching theory in an education setting is its transferability and generalizability, but to what extent is this true in practice and for whom is it true? Within higher education settings, the prevalent but not universal view of an ideal student is a person who has taken ownership of a repertoire of theoretical ideas and used them in essays and projects in novel ways. This is reflected in degree classification schemes that use criteria which include a student's use of ideas in a manner that goes beyond one specific knowledge source. My own experience is that significantly independent use of ideas, which transcends reasonable comprehension and good organization of material, is associated with an upper second class of degree, a level reached by

Box 12.3 The five stages of transfer

1   The extraction of potentially relevant knowledge from the context(s) of its acquisition and previous use.
2   Understanding the new situation, a process that often depends on informal social learning.
3   Recognizing what knowledge and skills are relevant.
4   Transforming them to fit the new situation.
5   Integrating them with other knowledge and skills in order to think/act/communicate in the new situation.

about half the candidates. For sub-degree awards, the proportion of students demonstrating or even getting an opportunity to demonstrate, independent ownership of ideas is significantly lower. Not surprisingly, there is a contrast between the 'preferred view' of lecturers and research into students' learning orientations.

The distinction between deep and surface approaches to learning derives from research by Marton et al. (1984). They defined a deep approach to learning in terms of trying to understand the underlying purpose and meaning of the information encountered, to make a critical assessment of it and to reach a personal viewpoint. Whereas a surface approach is demonstrating acquaintance with and comprehension of information without actively seeking to restructure it or develop any personal perspective. Most authors assume, not always explicitly, that a deep approach is desirable, but its accomplishment is treated in different ways. For example, Perry (1968) regards it as a result of intellectual and ethical development in the higher education context, while others have treated it more like a sophisticated skill or threshold competence. Yet others interpret it as being dependent on interest in the subject, an indicator of intrinsic motivation. Ideologically, the notion of deep learning is well-attuned to the academic psyche, but those who see the purpose of undergraduate education as getting qualified and acquiring useful competence will tend to regard it as a luxury.

While Marton's work was based on research into how students learn from texts, more sociologically oriented research has focused on the effect of the academic context on students' levels and direction of effort. Becker et al. (1968), Snyder (1971) and Miller and Parlett (1974) present accounts of students seeking to survive and succeed by maximizing their return on their academic effort. They learn to recognize what the system rewards, set their own goals and try to achieve them economically at minimum risk. Thus students' approaches to learning are determined primarily by the teaching and assessment regime and students' strategies for negotiating it. They observe what teachers reward not what goals they espouse. Academics, who have only limited control over their teaching and assessment regimes, do not find this line of research attractive, and are generally reluctant to see themselves as task masters rather than role models, and students as pursuing grades rather than learning for its own sake.

There is substantial evidence from psychologists (Entwistle 1992) to suggest that most teaching and assessment regimes encourage surface approaches to learning; so the two research themes are intimately connected. Moreover, research into professional education, in particular, suggests that one effect of occupational socialization is that most aspiring professionals come to value practical experience more highly than academic courses. For most students, codified academic knowledge has not been liberated from its original academic source, and is unlikely to be ready for transfer unless there is special provision through problem-based learning or seminars whose prime purpose is to link prior theoretical knowledge with reflections on personal experience in the workplace.

In contrast situational understanding in the workplace is highly dependent on experience. Dreyfus and Dreyfus (1986) describe advanced beginners as having limited situational perception and using guidelines for action based on the perceived attributes or aspects of each situation. Aspects are global characteristics of situations, recognizable only after some prior experience; and, at this stage, all attributes are treated separately and given equal importance. In contrast, proficient workers see situations holistically rather than in terms of aspects and see what is most important in a situation. They perceive deviations from the normal pattern and use maxims for guidance, whose meaning varies according to the situation. Related learning often entails a combination of the unconscious aggregation in memory of experiences with cases and episodes of activity, incidental learning from other people about the salient aspects of situations and reflection on one's more memorable experiences.

Such processes, however, are not theory free and the Dreyfus brothers give little attention to the role of theory in situational understanding. Knowledge of theories taught in education settings may alert workers to the implications of particular aspects of situations, e.g. fluid balance in a hospital patient, electrical hazards, or theories of motivation, provided their relevance is recognized. But personal theories are also constructed out of experience as part of the natural human process of looking for patterns and meanings and trying to make sense of one's experience. These ways of construing and thinking about the world have been called 'schemes of experience' (Schutz 1967), 'personal constructs' (Kelly 1955) or 'schemas' (Bartlett 1932). The use of scientific theories is further discussed below, while the problem of making personal theories explicit and bringing them under critical control is discussed by Argyris and Schon (1974) and Eraut (2000).

The objective of recognizing what knowledge and skills are relevant is not as simple as it seems. When teachers in education settings spend time discussing how their theoretical contributions relate to practice, a large collection of potentially relevant theory is quickly assembled. But who uses which parts of it, why and when? Our earlier section on modes of cognition noted that time to consider theory is at a premium in the workplace, it suggested that most theory was more likely to be embedded in practice than explicitly used in daily decision-making. There is a marked contrast between the very large number of knowledge areas deemed relevant by those who teach them and the very limited number of knowledge areas that can be taken into account at any one time by a busy practitioner with a high caseload. The practitioner has to assess the priority to be accorded to each particular area of knowledge in each particular situation, but in practice patterns of attention will soon be developed and only some knowledge areas will even be considered.

Recognizing what theory you need in any particular situation is mainly learned through participation in practice and getting feedback on your actions. Most components of a practitioner's theoretical repertoire remain dormant until triggered by a very specific aspect of the situation. In health-care contexts the nature of the client(s) is the main factor determining what knowledge and skills are relevant, but time-scale is also important. Table 12.2 presents a useful framework for discussing and deciding not just which areas of theory are relevant to a particular case but also their respective priority. It can be supported by an appropriate checklist of areas of theory.

The two rows allow a distinction to be made between knowledge embedded in practice through routines or protocols (but which remains essential for the justification of that practice) and knowledge which needs to be explicitly considered at the time. Such knowledge may influence how the client is assessed, what decisions are made and/or how the practitioner inter-acts with the client.

The column headings reflect the assumption that priorities will vary according to the time-scale. For example, the knowledge used to treat a patient in hospital with a stable condition will not necessarily be given priority in an emergency. Yet other kinds of knowledge may become important when longer term issues are being considered.

The fourth column, headed *Review of Practice*, has been added for two reasons. First to ensure that embedded knowledge is reviewed at some time, and second to enable contextual factors constraining practice to be identified and addressed in a way which would not normally be possible when an individual client is the focus of attention. Such reviews of practice might occur in the context of audit, continuing professional development, a formal evaluation or funded research.

Table 12.2 Framework for deciding priority areas of knowledge

Status of knowledge	Emergency	Short-term action	Medium- to long-term future	Review of practice
Embedded in Assessment Decisions Behaviour				
Explicit influence on Assessment Decisions Behaviour				

The framework presented in Table 12.2 can be used both to find out what practitioners currently do, in which case embedded knowledge may be difficult to elicit without using special methods of inquiry (Eraut 2000; Fessey 2002). It can also be used to discuss what they ought to do. Repeated use on a case by case basis would reveal common patterns of practice, differentiation between clients and concerns about the efficacy of practice, including the cumulative effect of neglecting longer term issues. Using this framework to broaden the scope of cases used in problem-based learning could also play an important role in orienting students towards the significance of a wider range of theory without inducing cognitive overload.

In order to consider the problems entailed in transforming and resituating theoretical knowledge, I shall focus attention on the use of scientific knowledge by health-care professionals, using a broad definition of scientific knowledge to include the social sciences as well as the natural science disciplines and theoretical knowledge from the practice-oriented literature of individual professions. The knowledge maps I use as heuristics for eliciting and discussing practitioner knowledge were developed during research into the use of scientific knowledge by nurses and midwives (Eraut *et al.* 1995, 1996). Our approach was to interview experienced practitioners, engaged in mentoring students, about recent cases involving the use of particular areas of scientific knowledge and to use a matrix to summarize the information we gathered.

Table 12.3 is the first half of a map from Parboteeah (2001) depicting aspects of nurses' knowledge about infection, and when and how they are used. The rows cover relevant topics of codified knowledge within the area of infection, while the column headings describe the range of activities that constitute nursing practice in this area. The missing half contains a further eleven columns under the headings of *Response* and *Monitoring*. The use of knowledge from a particular topic (row) during a particular activity (column) is indicated by making an entry in the appropriate box. Our research found significant differences in the headings of the matrix between specialisms, and some variation according to the type of clinical setting. Relatively few differences were noted between respondents from similar settings, but samples were not large enough for that to be a definitive finding.

The entries in the boxes indicate different kinds of knowledge use, codified for brevity. The R coding indicates that Recognition is all that is required, very little further interpretation is needed, and the transfer problem is mainly that of spotting when it is relevant; whereas the U coding indicates that significant Understanding of the knowledge is required, and probably some transformation. The knowledge has to be reinterpreted in order to be resituated. The numerical headings 1, 2 and 3 correspond to the Instant, Rapid and Deliberative modes of response portrayed in Table 12.1. And relate to the mode of cognition as follows:

1 Simple application, for which recognising that some specific piece of knowledge was relevant was virtually all that was needed in order to take appropriate action.

2 Situational adaptation, where the appropriate response from an established repertoire was selected according to how the situation was understood, usually by matching one's model of the situation with situations previously encountered (described by Klein (1989) as Recognition Primed Decision Making).

3 Problem solving, where the appropriate course of action had to be worked out from first principles.

Only with this third category was scientific knowledge explicitly used during the relevant episode of practice. In categories (1) and (2) any scientific knowledge used was embedded in already familiar understandings and actions. Since category (2) depends on the knowledge user having sufficient prior experience of similar situations, those lacking such experience have either to consult more experienced colleagues or engage in a slower, problem-solving approach that makes more explicit use of scientific knowledge. Resorting to consultation is quicker, but usually leads to new practices being acquired without any theoretical justification.

Parboteeah (2001) found that the use of knowledge maps is best taught to student nurses in practice settings, and in 'real time' as and when relevant events occur. But, after an initiation period of 'on the spot' tutoring, students become able to use knowledge maps on their own with consultative access to 'experts' and even to create new maps as part of a group project. Newly qualified practitioners will need a similar induction, before they can begin to use knowledge maps as a guide to the kinds of knowledge that need to be fed into their decision-making processes, for the identification of their learning needs and for the debriefing of experts who find it hard to explain their apparently intuitive decisions. We have found them to be especially useful in initiating discussions about knowledge use and the more hidden aspects of practice during Continuing Professional Development.

The final stage in transfer involves combining the various relevant aspects of knowledge and skill into an integrated, holistic, performance. It will probably interact with those aspects of the previous stage that are relatively new and will cease to be distinguishable as a separate stage when sufficient practice has created a rapid response. In practice reviews, prior attention should be given to the selection of the most relevant aspects of knowledge (see Table 12.2), before using knowledge maps as aids to probe more deeply.

Table 12.3 Nurses' knowledge of infection

Areas of knowledge	Personal hygiene	Hand washing	Venepunctures IV/infusions	Aseptic procedures	PREVENTION Disposal of blood/products	Disposal of clinical waste	Disposal of linen
1 Human pathogens							
2 Immune system							
3 Food poisoning	U2	R1					
4 Accidents				U2	U3	U3	U3
5 Infestations	U2						
6 High-risk specimens		R2	U2	U2	U2	U2	
7 Sterilization policies							
8 Infection control policies	R2	U3	U3	U3	R2	U3	U3
9 Contagious diseases	U2	R2					
10 Management of waste		U2	U1	U1	U1	U2	U2
11 Fluid and electrolytes							
12 Circulatory system			R1				
13 Temperature control							
14 Respiratory system							
15 Surgery (post-op)			R1	R3			
16 Health and Safety Act		U2	U2		R1	U2	U2
17 Pharmacology							

Knowledge Use Code:

R Appreciating the Relevance of the knowledge

U Understanding and interpreting the knowledge

1 Simple application

2 Situational adaptation

3 Problem solving

| | | | | | ASSESSMENT | | | |
Disposal of body waste	Urinary catheters	Disposal of sharps	Transporting patients	Disinfection	Patients history	Pathology results	Vital signs	Hydration
	R1					R1		
			U3			R1 R2		
U3	U3	U3						
	U2	U2						
U2	U3	U3	U3	U3				
R2	U1	R1						
						R1	U3	U3
							U3	
						R1	U3	
							R2	
U2	U2		U2	U2				

Conclusion

To discuss the implications of this analysis of transfer, let me introduce the metaphor of an iceberg. The learning of codified knowledge for assessment in an examination can be represented by that part of the iceberg that appears above the surface. This learning is explicit and well supported by textbooks and formal teaching. The further learning required to convert that codified knowledge into personal knowledge that is ready for use in a range of possible situations can be represented by that part of the iceberg which is hidden below the surface. Some books shed a little light in some areas, but the terrain is mainly obscure. Knowing how to use theoretical knowledge is largely tacit knowledge. Support for such learning is minimal and little time is set aside for it. The very existence of ice below the surface is symbolically denied. So when students find such learning difficult (which it usually is) they are likely either to blame themselves for being inadequate or to reject the theoretical knowledge as irrelevant. This raises the important further question of how much further learning is required in order to transfer theoretical knowledge from an academic setting into occupational practice. The analysis of this chapter suggests, in accordance with the metaphor of the iceberg, most of which resides below the surface, that the transfer process may entail considerably more learning than the original acquisition of the academic knowledge, i.e. that traditional thinking about transfer underestimates the learning involved by an order of magnitude.

Although professional preparation programmes include both theory and practice, few of them give serious attention to the issues discussed above; and in some professions the separation of theory and practice components over time and space militates against their integration. In vocational programmes we now have qualification frameworks that separately specify knowledge and competence, without giving any attention to the linkage between them or to how knowledge use might be assessed. These are areas where the intelligent development of more integrated programmes and more appropriate staffing could make a real difference. In particular, the introduction should be considered of a practice development role that incorporates responsibility for both students and new staff, and the facilitation of continuing learning in the workplace by experienced staff. Until the nature and importance of transfer is recognized and supported in this way, the impact of education on the workplace will continue to be lower than expected and the quality of work will suffer from the limited use of relevant knowledge. Surely it is time that government policies for qualifications and lifelong learning began to address this problem?

Bibliography

Argyris, C. and Schon, D.A. (1974) *Theory in Practice: Increasing Professional Effectiveness*, San Francisco, CA: Jossey Bass.

Bartlett, F.C. (1932) *Remembering: A Study in Experimental and Social Psychology*, Cambridge: Cambridge University Press.

Becher, T. (1989) *Academic Tribes and Territories*, Buckingham: Open University Press.

Becker, H. *et al.* (1968) *Making the Grade: The Academic Side of College Life*, New York: Wiley.

Dreyfus, H.L. and Dreyfus, S.E. (1986) *Mind over Machine: The Power of Human Intuition and Expertise in the Era of the Computer*, Oxford: Blackwells.

Entwistle, N. (1992) *The Impact of Teaching on Learning Outcomes in Higher Education*, Sheffield: CVP Staff Development Unit.

Eraut, M. (1999) 'Theoretical and Methodological Perspectives on Researching Workplace Learning', AERA Conference Paper, Montreal, April.

—— (2000) 'Non-formal Learning and Tacit Knowledge in Professional Work', *British Journal of Educational Psychology*, 70: 113–36.

Eraut, M., Alderton, J., Boylan, A. and Wraight, A. (1995) *Learning to use Scientific Knowledge in Education and Practice Settings*, London: English National Board for Nursing, Midwifery and Health Visiting.

—— (1996) 'Mediating Scientific Knowledge into Health Care Practice: Evidence from Pre-registration Programmes in Nursing and Midwifery Education', AERA Conference Paper, New York City, April 1996.

Eraut, M., Alderton, J., Cole, G. and Senker, P. (1998) 'Development of Knowledge and Skills in Employment', Research Report 5, University of Sussex Institute of Education.

Fessey, C. (2002) 'Capturing Expertise in the Development of Practice: Methodology and Approaches', *Learning in Health and Social Care*, 1 (1): 47–58.

Goodson, I. (1983) *School Subjects and Curriculum Change*, Beckenham: Croom Helm.

Kelly, G.A. (1955) *The Psychology of Personal Constructs*, New York: Norton.

Klein, G.A. (1989) 'Recognition-Primed Decisions', in W.B. Rouse (ed.), *Advances in Man-Machine Systems Research*, Greenwich, CT, JAI Press, pp. 47–92.

Lave, J. and Wenger, E. (1991) *Situated Learning: Legitimate Peripheral Participation*, Cambridge: Cambridge University Press.

Marton, F., Hounsell, D. and Entwistle, N. (eds) (1984) *The Experience of Learning*, Edinburgh: Scottish Academic Press.

Miller, C.M.L. and Parlett, M. (1974) *Up to the Mark: A Study of the Examinations Game*, Guildford: SRHE.

Parboteeah, S. (2001) 'The Effect of Using Knowledge Maps as a Mediating Artefact in Pre-registration Nurse Education', D.Phil. Thesis, University of Sussex.

Perry, W.G. (1968) *Forms of Intellectual and Ethical Development in the College Years: A Scheme*, New York: Holt, Rinehart and Winston.

Schutz, A. (1967) *The Phenomonology of the Social World*, trans. G. Walsh and F. Lehnert from 1932 original, Evanston, IL: Northwestern University Press.

Snyder, B.R. (1971) *The Hidden Curriculum*, New York: Knopf.

13 Learner biographies

Exploring tacit dimensions of knowledge and skills

*Karen Evans, Natasha Kersh
and Akiko Sakamoto*

Chapter summary

This chapter is based on the project 'Recognition of Tacit Skills and Knowledge in Work Re-entry' carried out as a part of the ESRC funded Research Network 'Improving Incentives to Learning in the Workplace'. The study has investigated the part played by tacit forms of personal competences in the education, training and work re-entry of adults with interrupted occupational or learning biographies. It aims to identify ways in which the recognition and deployment of tacit skills can be harnessed to strengthen their learning success and learning outcomes in new learning and working environments. Our primary evidence supports the view that learning outcome is a complex concept that has both 'formal' and 'informal' dimensions. Informal outcomes are those associated with self-assurance, increased capability, and greater abilities to exercise control over their situations and environments.

Introduction

The part played by tacit skills and knowledge in work performance is well recognized but not well understood. It is one of the central tenets of adult education that adults draw on life experience to good effect in learning programmes. There is very little previous research evidence concerning the ways in which this happens, and none which focuses on tacit skills utilization and its contribution to learning processes and outcomes in moving between settings over time. How do individuals harness and use tacit forms of key competences as they move between roles and settings? What part does the recognition of tacit forms of key competences play in the development of occupational and learning biographies?

The call for wider recognition of skills gained through non-formal learning is only one facet of a debate centred on the nature of the so-called knowledge-based economy and the ways in which the 'knowledge' concerned is codified and used. The new debate has been fuelled by economists and labour market specialists, creating new possibilities for interdisciplinary endeavour with learning professionals and educational/social researchers in trying to understand better what it is that actually constitutes the 'knowledge base' of the economy and the place of non-formal learning and 'soft skills' in this scenario (see Johnson and Lundvall 2001; Felstead *et al.* 2002; Billett 2000).

For the purposes of the discussion which follows, non-formal learning embraces unplanned learning in work situations and in domains of activity outside the formal economy, but may also include planned and explicit approaches to learning carried out in any of these environments which are not recognized within the formal education and training system. Non-formal learning has strong tacit dimensions. While the explicit is easily codified and conveyed to others, the tacit is experiential, subjective and personal, and substantially more difficult to convey. We argue that it is more helpful to regard all knowledge as having both tacit and explicit dimensions. When we can facilitate the communication of some of the tacit dimensions, these become explicit and therefore codifiable. This may be for the purpose of teaching someone else to do it (if we are a teacher or trainer), or communicating to others that we have skills and competences appropriate to a task, role or occupation (if we are job applicants), or identifying that a person or group has the capabilities we need for a job to be done (if we are employers or project leaders). In other words, the reasons for codification largely revolve around 'transfer'.

The ideas of individuals being able to transfer skills and competences between jobs in the interests of 'flexibility' fitted the 'modernization' and deregulation agendas of the 1980s and 1990s in Britain, and key competences came to the fore as an instrument of lifelong learning policy. However, research on 'work process knowledge' such as Boreham's (2000) finds that these skills derive much of their meaning from the context in which they are used. We argue that it may be more helpful to regard these skills as partly structural and partly 'referential' (i.e. referenced to context) recognizing that people do take things with them into new jobs and occupations, but not in simple ways.

In this research we have identified clusters of abilities, which are important in negotiating changes of work and learning environments. These are *not* de-contextualized 'transferable skills' but abilities which have both structural and referential features – their structural features may be carried (tacitly) between environments but they have to be situated, underpinned by domain specific knowledge and developed through social interaction within the culture and context of the work environment. Our early research (Evans 2002) confirmed that naive mapping of 'key skills' between environments does not work. It has also confirmed that the clusters generated from learner perspectives also capture employer and trainer perspectives at the level of the generic 'label'. Employer perspectives, however, ascribe and recognize the key competences at lower levels than the learners, a phenomenon also observed in the Brown and Keep COST review of Vocational Education and Training (VET) research (1999), while trainers are more likely to recognize key competences at higher levels than employers, but also more narrowly than learners. Attributes of creativity, sensitivity and emotional intelligence often go unrecognized or are taken for granted. One of the most interesting findings we have explored further is that males and females with long-term occupational breaks view and deploy their skills differently. Females often regard their 'family' skills as highly developed but unrecognized in all areas except 'caring' or other areas of 'women's work', so disregard them in their search for work re-entry in other fields, concentrating instead on new or updated explicit skills. However, do they take the structural aspects of these wider skills with them, and point to their importance when applied (tacitly or explicitly) in their new work situations? In practice, employers ascribe 'female skills' to mature women re-entering the labour market, but often do so at a level and in a way which advantages them only in relation to other vulnerable job-seekers, 'women's work' and easily exploitable positions. Males tend to ignore their skills gained outside the economic sphere, no advantages are derived from them and they are regarded as totally separate from the economic domain – explicit new skills are sought for work re-entry and no advantage is perceived to stem from those informally gained in the family/domestic domain. More generally, those who are able to operate as 'labour force entrepreneurs' moving frequently between jobs in order to improve their position, have forms of know-how which appear to have currency in the labour market despite the fact that they cannot be easily codified.

Our chapter includes six subheadings. The first section gives an overview of collection and organization of data. The second section discusses aspects of learning of tacit skills from various life experiences. The third section investigates the deployment of tacit skills and knowledge in new learning environments. The fourth section discusses the working environments that are *experienced* as *restrictive* or *expansive* (see Fuller and Unwin in this volume and Fuller and Unwin 2003) by adults re-entering the workplace after their college programmes and the fifth models learning processes and outcomes in the transition from college to workplace. The final section summarizes our primary findings and discusses wider issues raised by proposals to codify tacit skills.

Collection and organization of data

To uncover the tacit skills of adults we have interviewed 60 people studying at six different colleges within and just outside London. The interviews attempted to elicit a wide range of tacit skills by asking adult learners about their life and work experiences and relating these to their learning outcomes and achievements. The research participants were selected from particular learning programmes, in order that their responses can be related to specific learning experiences. *Learning episodes* allowed us to triangulate learners' accounts, considering them within their own perspectives, their tutors' perspectives and in the context of their official grades. This involved interviewing both a learner and a tutor about his/her achievements, learning processes and gains. Such an approach allowed us to gain an insight into specific aspects of an individual learner's case study, comparing both learners' and tutors' perspectives on learners' gains and outcomes. Self-completion questionnaires have been completed by a sub-sample, giving responses against a set of fixed indicators of skill development and use. The second stage of research involves, with the agreement of the students, tracking them into their workplaces (or places of further study) and reviewing with them what they have gained from their learning and how this is built upon after they move into new learning or working environments. In the course of our research we have aimed to trace the process of (1) acquisition of tacit skills, (2) deployment (or utilization) and further development of tacit skills in a new learning environment, as well as (3) their influence upon the process of individuals' work re-entry. This chapter concentrates on the biographical aspects of these processes.

Our respondents included both males and females, aged 20 to 55, many of whom had interrupted career biographies largely due to their family or personal circumstances. Their courses ranged from a one-month course on IT training, to special short courses for assisting people in returning to studying after a long break, to full-time one-year courses in business administration (National Vocational Qualifications) and social work (CHE (Certificate in Higher education)). Data has been analysed with the assistance of qualitative analysis software programs.[1]

Learning of tacit skills from various experiences

The interview data indicate a wide range of learning experiences outside the qualification framework, or other formal education and training settings. While the considerable learning which takes place in the workplace has been increasingly recognized, learning also results from a range of life experiences, in home and family settings, engaging in volunteer activities and overcoming various setbacks in life. Our findings also confirm the view that males and females perceive acquisition of tacit skills differently. In most cases females recognize so-called 'family or domestic skills'. However, they also feel that such skills are often not recognized by employers, because they do not lead to a formal qualification. Another problem is that of presenting these skills to a prospective employer, for example on a CV or an application form. Our female interviewees maintained that they acquired most valuable skills not only from learning and work, but also from household experiences. For example, Heather and Carolyn each of whom has been, in their words, 'a full-time mother' for over ten years, indicated that as a result of their home experiences they have developed such skills as: caring, empathy, organizing, planning, prioritizing, time-management, juggling tasks and thinking ahead. Julia, who has been a full-time mother for 12 years, also developed similar valuable skills, while running her household.

Conversely, our interviews with male learners indicate that they often ignore their skills gained as a result of household experience, as no advantage is perceived to stem from those skills informally gained in the domestic settings. As Abdul points out:

> I do not think that household skills could be related to my work or my studies. I don't think one could learn much from running a household, your house. No. You do something for your household because you have to. If you do not have a job, you are stuck in your house, you have to do this, but you are not progressing, I mean, you are not learning anything.

However, he really values skills which he developed while taking part in running a family mini-market, as for him, these skills are associated with the economic sphere:

> Yes, I developed a lot of skills, just from dealing with various people. Especially in customer care part, I had many different types of customers, young and old, someone who needs help, you have to be vigilant and always see if that person needs help. The way he's walking through the shelves, you can notice that someone needs help. Little children who are, who aren't doing anything but just running here and there. So I have seen many things that way.

Male learners, however, admit that skills learned from other life experiences could be successfully deployed in running a household or looking after children. Ali, who has been a full-time father for two years, stresses that, as a result of his army training, he developed many valuable skills, that currently help him to look after his two-year-old child:

> Army training helped me to my neatness and time management, like, and when I was in the army it gave me a good personality, because before the army I don't know what I was doing, young, and realized what world we live in after that army.

Our interviewees with interrupted career biographies continue to learn and acquire skills through their life experiences. A range of tacit skills identified from pilot work (see Evans 2001) and extended through our interview data can be classified into six clusters which appear to be important in negotiating changes (see Box 13.1) and interruptions in life and work situations.

> **Box 13.1 Different types of competence**
> 1   Competence related to attitudes and values;
> 2   Learning competence;
> 3   Social co-operative competence;
> 4   Content-related and practical competence;
> 5   Methodological competence; and
> 6   Strategic competence.

Tacit skills in a new learning environment: further development and deployment of tacit skills

The following section investigates the deployment of tacit skills in a learning environment. The main question which it addresses is how tacit skills have been deployed in learning situations and have impacted on learning processes and learning gains by referring to individual cases based on our interview and questionnaire data.

Deployment and further development of tacit skills in a new learning environment

How have tacit skills been deployed in learning success at college? On a practical level, the interviews with those who have recently returned to attend courses at college suggest the deployment of tacit skills such as time management, organization and meeting multiple demands. Our interviews support the view that adult learners deploy a wide range of tacit skills that we classified into six types of competences (see Box 13.1). The importance of methodological and strategic competences is well illustrated from both questionnaires and interviews with adult learners.

Of the adults who completed our questionnaires, most considered the following skills to be 'very important' or 'important' in the contexts of their college environments:

- time management;
- handling routine work;
- prioritizing;
- planning/organizing;
- juggling different tasks or activities.

Only a small proportion of students consider skills such as time management and handling routine to be not very important. Other strategic and methodological skills were also noted by adult learners in the course of interviews. Jane, for example, who is a single mother, stresses that as a result of her household experience she developed a number of valuable competences. She maintains that she is able to deploy and develop these skills in the settings of her course. For example, she considers her skills in listening as well as attention to detail to be important competences in this context. For Julia, who has been a full-time mother for 12 years, using previously acquired skills such as time management and prioritizing helped her to do well in her course.

Social cooperation skills have also been noted by adult learners. Our interview data indicates that social skills such as patience, caring and adaptability were especially recognized and valued by women learners. Jane provides an example of how she was able to transfer her social skills into the college environment:

> I think another skill that I probably acquired is patience, [...] I think this patience thing that I've had to hold onto while I've been with the children, and I'm having to transfer it over to the people. For example [...] we have to write up a 'dear diary' for managing people for Howard, one of our lecturers, and one of the ladies came in late so she missed the exercises. So she said all she was going to write was 'dear diary, I wasn't here so I have nothing to write'. And I looked at her and I laughed, and I said, come, let's explain to you exactly what we did. [...] and she was writing down everything that we'd done.

At the same time, the interviews highlighted the importance of motivational and other attitudinal characteristics, such as perseverance and willingness to learn, as well as the importance of a supportive learning environment. As mentioned above, our evidence supports the view that all skills have both tacit and explicit dimensions. The explicit dimension allows tacit skills to be deployed in a new learning environment and this process can be facilitated by certain types of social interactions. In a college environment, teamwork has been identified as one type of social interaction. One of the tutors noted that it encourages learners to deploy their tacit skills and competences:

> We encourage people to work as a group and it was actually nice and there's something that occurs quite a lot; you'll find people during their lunch hour sitting in pairs and [a student] actually helped another [learner] quite a lot with his maths, when he was struggling with his maths all the way through, but came to the point where he was only two marks away at the initial test, and that people would ask each other and she being very good at maths, and also being both patient and persuasive, was able to help.

Other types of social interactions that were identified by adult learners are tutorial help, learning from others, communicating with fellow-students, taking initiative in assignments, working under pressure and teaching others. The availability of these supports provides the context that mediates the impact on learning processes of individuals.

Recognition of tacit skills, learning processes and gains

The important point that we would like to explore is the link between the recognition of tacit skills, learning processes and gains. How are these related? Do (and how do) the recognition of skills by students, tutors or employers impact on the learning process? Does it suggest, for instance, that if these skills are better recognized, then this will strengthen the confidence and self-assurance of students and enhance their learning gains? Our data shows that deployment, acquisition and recognition of tacit skills are all interrelated processes. Students stress that recognition of their skills by others (e.g. tutors, employers, family) encourage (or would encourage) them to develop further their skills. Diana, for example, stresses that recognition of her skills by tutors helped her a lot:

> I found that the tutors that were there at the time were more focused towards getting the best out of you, so yes, we come to the table with skills because we're all adult women and we've gone through life and got this far so we must have had some sort of survival mechanism in place, and the tutors recognized these inherent skills, skills that we didn't recognize and helped to bring those out.

Mary emphasizes that her course (Certificate for Women in Management) facilitates her confidence as well as self-recognition and awareness of her tacit skills, such as:

> planning, organizing, directing, all those kinds of skills, all those kind of that you need as a manager. I will be more aware of them, more conscious of them and I'll probably be able to put them into practice more easily than if I'm not conscious of them. I'll be able to use them better.

Several of Anna's statements also suggest her awareness of the skills and knowledge which she gained from life experiences. Anna had a troubled background and was now doing a work placement that involves work at a social service centre, assisting young people doing community work. She maintained that she developed valuable skills through some difficult life experiences of her own:

I think I've acquired, from my bad experiences [drug and alcohol problems, petty crime], that I've known the things that I wanted. I wanted
to be listened to, I wanted to be heard, I wanted someone to take the
time out to pay me some attention, or someone that I could trust. And I
think it is the work that I do, they're the sort of things that are expected
really...[I know] how to relate to them [young people].

Anna's previous life experiences have become very helpful in the work that
she does and she is well aware of this. She was also aware that these could be
helpful to her at work: to engage and communicate with young people. The
fact that these skills are clearly helping her to do the job well seems to further
enhance her sense of achievement and confidence, allowing her to have a clear
sense of what she wants in her life. Anna's awareness that being bored and not
doing much would lead her into trouble – which is again something she
learned from past experience – brought her to return to college in the first
place. In addition, her recognition that she is not 'thick' led her to build and
exert perseverance which sustained her studying at the college.

Kate also recognized the importance of what she called 'right attitudes',
which she suggested include: hard working, not being lazy and having a
willingness to learn. She deployed these attitudes and gained the learning
opportunity. It is important to note that, in her case, the fact that these
skills were also recognized by her supervisor led to Kate's further learning in
the workplace.

The process of work re-entry: learning outcomes and deployment of tacit skills in the workplace

Tacit skills in the workplace: expansive versus restrictive environment

Our primary evidence from initial interviews indicates that tacit skills
acquisition, deployment and recognition heightens self-assurance where
learning experiences have been positive or have involved overcoming
setbacks and obstacles with positive outcomes. Harnessing tacit skills in
stimulating, 'expansive' learning environments sustains learning outcomes
and facilitates the process of work re-entry.

Follow-up interviewing and selective workplace visits are allowing us to
trace the medium-term outcomes of learning as well as the processes of work
re-entry. The important issue that came up in the course of the follow-up
interviews was that of learning outcomes. Our primary evidence from the
follow-up interviews supports the view that students' learning outcomes are
not restricted to formal results such as a certificate of qualification or
diploma. We argue that informal outcomes are those associated with self-
assurance, increased capability, improved attainment, greater ability to

exercise control over their situations and environments, and development of new attitudes towards learning/working. The interview with Helen shows that she considers developing confidence to be an important learning outcome from her college training. Sue also stresses that deployment of her communication skills or 'getting on with people' in the college facilitated her informal learning outcomes such as self-assurance, capability and confidence.

Follow-up interviews help us to analyse ways in which tacit skills may help to sustain learning outcomes in new learning and working environments. In particular we identify the working environments which are *experienced* as *restrictive* or *expansive* by adults re-entering the workplace after their college programmes. A wider analysis of trainer and employer perspectives on tacit skills has already been carried out in the pilot stages of this research and is reported elsewhere (see Evans 2001). These have implications for employee development and design of supportive learning environments.

Our data confirm that adults re-entering the workplace after their college programmes may *experience* their working environments either as *expansive* (positive, facilitating further development, deployment of skills) or *restrictive* (negative). The way employees experience expansive environments has to do with the feeling of 'being a part of a team' and opportunities for professional and personal developments, whereas a restrictive environment is associated with 'being an outsider or mere observer' in the workplace. Evidence from interviews shows that employees experience their workplaces as either expansive or restrictive depending on the following factors:

*   Types of workplace environment: stimulating versus dull.
*   Recognition of employees' skills and abilities.
*   Opportunities for workplace training and career development.

Stimulating versus non-stimulating workplace environment: recognition of tacit skills

Adults' perceptions of a restrictive workplace environment are usually associated with descriptions such as 'boring', 'non-challenging', 'repetitive' or 'monotonous'. The case of Irene's work experience, for instance, provides one example of a boring or non-stimulating workplace environment. She works as an Administrative Assistant in a small company. The way Irene describes her job clearly shows that she experiences her workplace environment as negative, not facilitating her professional development. She stresses that the nature of her job is very boring, and that there are not many opportunities to get involved in everyday activities:

> It's quiet, and I suppose business is not that brilliant, is it, at the moment [...], I don't know, maybe, it's been a bit boring sometimes [...], shuffling papers to look busy. I feel like I'm just being paid to do nothing.

As a result she is losing interest in her current job and wants to look for another job:

> It doesn't interest me at all. I'm very sorry. The product does not interest me, so maybe that's another reason as well. And, I don't know [...] I'm thinking, I probably shouldn't be doing all of this and should just go and get a job in a shop.

Stephanie, who was an account manager in another small company, pointed out similar problems in her workplace environment: 'When I first joined it was good, but because of the work relationships, the longer you're there, the more you become part of the furniture.'

On the contrary, an expansive environment is usually associated with concepts such as 'challenging', 'interesting', 'stimulating' or 'motivational'. An interview with Tracey who works as an Administrative Assistant shows an example of a stimulating workplace environment:

> I just think it's so interesting that I think I just get encouraged to go to work because of the interesting things that are happening around. [...] There's a lovely atmosphere, there's a really nice atmosphere, I really thought people would look at you as if, like, they don't want you, but they didn't. The atmosphere's just great there, you know and the work [...] Eventually, hopefully, when I have been there quite a time, I'm going to ask if I can be trained on another section of the police force. Get trained around the office, that's how I look at it. Quite a few people do that.

Diana, who works as a Diversity Officer, also speaks enthusiastically about her work environment. She stresses that her employers take on her initiatives, giving her a learning opportunity:

> It's fantastic, I couldn't have asked for a better chance, do you know, to do something positive. Diversity is a bit of a buzz word at the moment, and I didn't want it just to be just a buzz thing, to be politically correct. I wanted to do something constructive, something lasting, really create something for the members so that they feel, yes, this is working for us, it's supporting us, it's reflecting our needs. [...] arranging meetings to go out and meet nurses and talk to them and find out what it is they want to see, what's lacking in their support system, so that if in any small way I can contribute to them feeling more valued, then that's great.

Progression of career versus non-progression

Our data also show that employees evaluate their workplace environment by criteria such as opportunities for career development and personal development. They experience their working environment as restrictive if there are no, or only very limited, opportunities for their professional development. In such cases our interviewees stressed that they felt that their work is stagnant, and they are just performing their duties without any long-term benefits either for their companies or themselves. For example, David works as a security driver for a security company. His duties include delivering cash and money to businesses and banks as well as collecting money. He is very pessimistic about his job, and notes that there are very limited opportunities either for his professional development or for acquisition of new skills and abilities:

> I can't think that I am learning something. There is much I would want to learn but my managers would not give me a chance. It feels that every day is the same, like today is the same as yesterday, the same duties, the same people. I would want to undertake some further training, that's why I decided to take the LU course [London Underground Pre-Recruitment Training Programme]

> With this job it would be the same for me for the rest of my life.

He feels that his tacit skills are not recognized and because of this he does not feel motivated to use or develop them:

> My current job, I think you need to be reasonably physically fit, you also need to be able to communicate and to be vigilant and aware of your surroundings. But, really, there are not many opportunities to use communication skills. [...] I also have some computing skills; I feel that the skills I learned in computing were quite extensive and marketable skills, but I feel that those are the most valuable skills that are in demand right now, and I can't use them here. If an opportunity arose I would like to get back into computers.

Conversely, an interview with Ahmed, who works as an overnight porter in a hotel, shows that he experiences his workplace environment as *expansive* as it offers him opportunities for further learning and career development (see Box 13.2, Ahmed's case).

Tracey also feels that her *tacit* skills are recognized by her employers, even if she does not have enough confidence to fully recognize her skills herself:

> my job changes and I feel that I'm not ready to do that job. But they feel that I am. I've got to build my confidence; that is one thing that I do lack, is confidence. I said to my line manager, 'do you feel that I've got the confidence to do the job, like the capability of doing this job'.

And she said 'if that was the case we wouldn't have put you up for this job'. So I'm building my confidence up at the moment and hopefully it's going to be there in September, so that I can actually do that job.

Because her employers value her skills and want to promote her, there is a good potential for her to develop her confidence in the context of this expansive workplace environment.

Box 13.2 Ahmed's case: career progression

Ahmed, who works as an overnight porter in a hotel, stresses that he experiences his workplace environment as *expansive* as it offers him opportunities for further learning and career development. He describes his workplace as a very stimulating environment where he is able to deploy and develop his skills and competences. Ahmed is very motivated towards workplace learning. He, himself, says that he uses any opportunity to improve his existing skills or to develop new skills and competences. He says that he always asks for advice from more experienced colleagues and learns from them. At his workplace there are many other opportunities for learning. For example, all employees are able to undertake regular workplace training in health and safety as well as fire training. What is more, Ahmed has been offered one-to-one training by his manager in order to develop his computer skills as well as customer service skills. The purpose of this training is to promote Ahmed to a position as a receptionist in this hotel. He is clearly enthusiastic about his workplace learning as well as about good prospects for his career development in the hotel:

> Well, because I'd like to learn the computer [...], because I had no skill with computers, I had no idea about the computer until I started this job, and every time I watch my manager and just learn; then after that, I start to check in the people, if they ask for a name, is he staying in our hotel or not. So I check it and from that, the manager saw me, [...] I like to learn so that's why he put me for this training.

He notes that he is especially encouraged by the fact that his manager recognizes and values his personal or *tacit* skills such as communication skills, confidence, customer care skills and foreign language skills. All these factors motivate him towards further learning. He has recently started a part-time computer course in a further education college. He is looking forward to starting his new job as a receptionist when he finishes his training.

Creating an expansive workplace environment

The interviews confirm that employees may go further than simply experience their workplace environments either as expansive or restrictive. Our evidence supports the view that they can actually facilitate their workplace being or becoming an expansive environment by taking initiative in various projects, enquiring about opportunities for their professional development and further training, learning from their colleagues, etc. The interview with Diana shows that she was very enthusiastic about undertaking further learning at the workplace. When she had her job interview she inquired about opportunities for workplace learning:

> They finished the interview and they said, 'Any questions for us?' And I said, 'Oh yes.' I had read their equal opportunities policy, and I turned it round now and said, 'Well, okay, I've read your policy and you say that you train your staff to do the best that they can do so they can fulfil the role of the college. Does that mean I can get personal training?' And they said, 'Well, [...] yes.'

When she got this job she took the initiative and reminded her employer about what was said at the job interview: 'she [her manager] said "Oh, well, you've given me some food for thought", and as a result of that I have been allowed to do the DMS which is the Diploma in Management Studies.'

Mary also supports the view that one needs to take the initiative in order to get opportunities for workplace learning. As a result of her negotiations with her managers, she succeeded in getting financial support from her employer that enabled her to undertake a course called 'Certificate for Women in Management':

> at the moment I think I have got to be proactive and say what I want, which is what I've done about this course. I saw the course advertised, I saw its capacity and I applied for it and asked for support from my employers and they gave it; they've paid for it.

Conversely, employees who experience their workplace environment as restrictive, often do nothing to try to change it to an expansive one. This reflects both their lack of confidence and lack of interest in their current work environment. The interview with Irene shows that she felt indifferent about her job and not really interested in using and/or further developing her skills, thus contributing to elements of a restrictive environment:

Q: What sort of skills do you think are useful for doing the job well?
A: I have no idea.
Q: Do you feel your skills are recognized where you're working?
A: I don't know. I haven't bothered asking.

Box 13.3   Kate's case: creating an expansive workplace environment

The following case shows how tacit skills have helped to gain learning opportunities in the workplace as well as to contribute to creating an expansive workplace environment. Before her studies, Kate worked as a catering assistant in a large catering restaurant in an industrial area and, after three months, began handling accounts which involved counting money (sales receipts) and making records. This transition took place one day when her supervisor said she recognized that Kate was good at her work and asked whether she would be interested in helping to keep the accounts. Kate agreed to take on the new responsibilities even though it involved a pay increase of only 25p per hour. The following passage indicates her strong willingness to learn and her initiative in seizing opportunities.

> I didn't mind it [because] I was looking to progress in the accounting department, so that's why I actually took an interest in training. I was planning to work in my future when I decided to take the opportunity because I know this is an opportunity for me. Asked what she thought her supervisor appreciated about her, Kate replied: 'She told me, "because you were so intelligent, you work very hard and you don't mind doing anything because you have never been lazy, so I wanted you to know more".'

Her supervisor started training her, day by day, literally counting the money together and making a record of it. She left school without any qualifications, but she is now completing a foundation course in accounting at a college and she is confident of completing it successfully. Another comment by Kate also highlights the importance of having 'the right attitudes' in doing the job well. She said,

> Attitudes really matter, because sometimes if you don't know what to do, but you have the right attitude, you get people to help you out. If you want to do something you don't know how to do, then you approach somebody and say, 'oh, excuse me, do you mind helping me?'

However, a successful experience in deploying tacit skills for learning in one company does not always lead to another success in terms of re-entry to another job and sustaining a person's learning process. The study found other examples in which a person's tacit skills (being trustworthy, hard-working and having communication skills) led to expanded job responsibilities and allowed a move from one job to another within the company. In one case, however, an interviewee was made redundant by her company and was having great difficulty obtaining a new job. Being unemployed for just over a year, she is rapidly losing her confidence and optimism.

The importance of creating an expansive workplace environment is indicated in these examples. These cases show that people are able, to a certain extent and within the limits imposed by particular forms of work organization, to have an input into the expansiveness or restrictiveness of their immediate workplace environment. While our cases did not have recourse to intermediary organizations, it is reasonable to suppose that representation and channels for employee 'voice' are more likely to facilitate the co-construction of expansive workplace environments than individuals trying to act alone and on their own behalf, or retreating into silence.

Moving between college and workplace settings

Modelling of learning processes for learners with interrupted occupational and learning careers can identify ways in which recognition and deployment of tacit skills enhances learning experiences and outcomes as learners move between college and workplace settings, a primary goal of this research.[2] Models of learning produced within this study (see Evans and Kersh 2003 for further details) have been used to provide a better understanding of individual case studies in the general framework of adult learning.

In Janice's case study the comparison between models of her college and workplace experience has shown that completing a course programme enabled her to facilitate growth in her confidence and involvement as well as autonomy in deployment of skills. At the time of the initial interview, her confidence and involvement were low, thus not facilitating skills deployment. Low recognition and deployment of tacit skills are interrelated processes, as the learner does not feel motivated to deploy her tacit skills because they are not fully recognized. Furthermore, low recognition and deployment of tacit skills also contributes to the learner's low confidence and low involvement in her course activities. However, she experienced some elements of her general learning environment as positive or *expansive* and this finally facilitated her positive learning outcomes towards the end of her course. At the time of her follow-up interview it was apparent that towards the end of her course she developed her confidence, which was facilitated further by an expansive workplace environment. A positive interrelationship had visibly developed. Her skills were facilitated further in the new work-place environment. The learner stressed that at her workplace her skills were recognized by her supervisors and this facilitated her in deploying them. High skills deployment and high skills recognition are interrelated concepts that facilitate her confidence, involvement and her attitudes. Positive elements of her expansive workplace environment (such as recognition and deployment of her skills, involvement, interaction, etc.) strengthen her confidence and learning success.

The interpretation of the conceptual models also gives an insight into the circumstances in which learning takes place and contributes to a better understanding of how interventions can be made in learners' programmes. They are allowing us to draw conclusions with respect to factors or learning situations that have facilitated the development of learners' personal competencies and tacit skills. The analysis supports our early findings that (1) there are strong links between the recognition of tacit skills, learning processes, gains and outcomes and that (2) an expansive learning/or workplace environment facilitates learning. The comparison between the models of learning in college and workplace shows how different learning circumstances, in particular those related to recognition and deployment of tacit skills, may promote different learning processes within a case study of an individual learner. In this, context recognition and deployment of tacit skills are considered to be important elements of a learning/workplace environment. If recognition and deployment of tacit skills of a learner is low or negative, it affects negatively his/her learning process. Conversely, positive deployment and recognition of their skills strengthens her/his learning success. More broadly, findings suggest that approaches that emphasize the relational aspects of teaching and learning and pay attention to these in the creation of learning environments, are more likely to capture tacit skills in ways which improve learning success. As well as providing a research tool, the modelling approach can be used with practitioners and learners in ways which enable them to reflect upon and change their own concepts and approaches, including the creation of learning environments which consolidate and build upon learning gains.

Wider reflections

In this chapter we have described and analysed the processes of acquisition of tacit skills, their further deployment and utilization in new learning environments, as well as their influence upon the process of individuals' work re-entry. Our primary evidence interviews shows that adult learners often gain skills not only through formal education and work experience but also through various life experiences such as household experience, bringing up children, community activities or travel. The acquisition of these skills is often tacit in nature and therefore individuals do not necessarily recognize that they have gained anything valuable. Tacit skills development is also non-linear, and the use of tacit skills is situationally specific: tacit skills may lead to success in one context but not necessarily in another. However, our data support the view that these previous acquired skills often become a central part of a learning process when they are deployed and developed in new learning environments. Furthermore, harnessing tacit skills in stimulating, 'expansive' learning environments sustains learning outcomes and facilitate the process of work re-entry.

Our evidence from employers and trainers (Evans 2002) has investigated how important 'tacit supplementation' is in the ways in which employers ascribe competences to individuals and delineate requirements for jobs. Leplat (1990) showed how tacit skills appear important in at least three places: the gap between skills officially required for jobs, and (1) skills actually required (2) the skills actually implemented and (3) between the skills required by preliminary training and the skills actually implemented. Our findings are showing how the processes by which competences are ascribed to people (often along gendered, class or disability-based lines) align with the tacit (as opposed to official) requirements of occupations and may reinforce workplace inequalities. For example, attributes of 'mature and reliable' often ascribed by employers to women returnees have a tacit supplement of 'compliant and undemanding', tacitly seen as equipping them 'better' than younger people or males for low-grade and low-paid positions with few development opportunities. These processes of tacit supplementation of key competences and jobs continue to reinforce inequalities in the workforce and systematic undervaluing and underdevelopment of the skills of segments of the population (Equal Opportunities Commission 2000; Coffield 2000; Ashton et al. 2000). By contrast, organizations such as the 'Talent Foundation' claim that unlocking the hidden abilities of people and making them visible to their holders allows them to break through glass ceilings. We have shown that making the hidden dimensions of learning and skill visible to their holders can increase confidence and support successful outcomes in learning and work. The codification of tacit skills for evaluation by others is another matter. What would happen if a European-style 'personal skills card' or alternative means of 'making learning visible' were to be introduced? Would this increase democratic access to knowledge, by making it explicit and distributing and recognizing it more widely? Or would the existence of unequal power relations mean the control of more and more domains of knowledge by the powerful, and the disappearance of the 'protective belt' of tacit knowledge formed in the informal discourses of everyday life, through which individuals and groups can exercise their rights and resist exploitation?

Notes

1 NVivo and DCA. Individual characteristics and attributes, including age, education, gender and period of interruption are input for each case and for future matching with specific tacit skills. Interview notes are then analysed and particular passages are coded and assigned one of several tacit skills categories, or 'nodes', such as type of competencies (typology of tacit skills); learning achievement at college; learning process at college; learning at work; living environment.

2 The modelling approach being used, Dynamic Concept Analysis (DCA), provides scope for interventions to be identified systematically (Kontiainen 2002). It enables us to analyse data using conceptual models based on information about concept relations in adult learning including workplace learning. A full account of this process and the findings is given in Evans and Kersh 2003. We attempt to analyse how learning processes could be understood in the context of interrelationships between various aspects of learning. The models of learning produced within this study are used to provide a better understanding of individual case studies in the general framework of adult learning. There are three important steps in this study: (1) identifying the key concepts and attributes of adult learning; (2) defining the relationships between the concepts and building an information matrix of concepts relations; and (3) using the information matrix to build the individual models. We selected ten adult learning concepts and their attributes for DCA in this study. The next step was to define the relationships between the concepts on the basis of our research findings in a way that shows if/how two concepts relate to each other, for example: The higher the involvement, the higher the confidence; the higher the confidence, the higher the involvement.

An information matrix stores these statements and provides a basis for further building of models to describe the learning processes in individual case studies. Two models have been built for each case study. The first model (college-related) is based on the results of the initial interview and monitoring of learning episodes with an adult learner who is taking a course in a further education college. The second model (workplace-related) is being built on the basis of follow-up interview findings. Such an approach helps us to trace changes in concept relations in individual case studies of adult learners. The DCA is flexible enough to accept new concepts and new definitions as they move between roles and settings.

Bibliography

Ashton, D., Felstead A. and Green F. (2000) 'Skills in the British Workplace', in F. Coffield, F. (ed.), *Differing Visions of a Learning Society*, Bristol: Policy Press.

Billett, S. (2000) 'Performance at Work: Identifying Smart Work Practice', in R. Gerber and C. Lankshear (eds), *Training for a Smart Workforce*, London: Routledge.

Boreham, N. (2000) *Final Report of TSER Project on Work Process Knowledge*, Brussels: European Commission.

Brown, A. and Keep, E. (1999) *Review of Vocational Education and Training Research in the United Kingdom*, Brussels: European Commission.

Coffield, F. (2000) *The Necessity of Informal Learning*, Bristol: Policy Press.

Equal Opportunities Commission (EOC) (2000) *Attitudes to Equal Pay*, London: EOC.

Evans, K. (2001) 'Tacit Skills and Knowledge', paper presented at the European Conference on Educational Research (ECER), Lille, September.

—— (2002) 'The Challenges of "Making Learning Visible"', in K. Evans, P. Hodkinson and L. Unwin (eds), *Working to Learn. Transforming Learning in the Workplace*, London: Kogan Page.

Evans, K. and Kersh, N. (2003) 'Recognition of Tacit Skills and Knowledge: Sustaining Learning Outcomes in Workplace Environment', paper presented at the Third International Conference on Researching Work and Learning, Tampere, July.

Evans, K. and Sakamoto, A. (2001) 'The Challenges of Making Learning Visible', paper presented to the joint ESRC Research Network/SKOPE/TLRP International Workshop on Power Context and Perspective: Confronting the Challenges to Improving Attainment in Learning at Work, University College Northampton, November.

Felstead, A., Gallie, D. and Green, F. (2002) *Work Skills in Britain 1986–2001*, Nottingham: DfeS Publications.

Fuller, A. and Unwin, L. (2003) 'Learning as Apprentices in the Contemporary UK Workplace: Creating and Managing Expansive and Restrictive Participation', *Journal of Education and Work*, 16 (4).

Johnson, B. and Lundvall, B.-A. (2001) 'Why All This Fuss About Codified and Tacit Knowledge?', paper presented at the DRUID International Conference, Aalborg.

Kontiainen, S. (2002) *Dynamic Concepts Analysis (DCA): Integrating Information in Conceptual Models*, Helsinki: Helsinki University Press.

Leplat, J. (1990) 'Skills and Tacit Skills: A Psychological Perspective', *Applied Psychology: An International Review*, 39 (2): 143–54.

14 The conceptualization and measurement of learning at work

Paul Hager

Chapter summary

This chapter begins with a consideration of rival conceptions of learning and their relevance or otherwise for understanding learning at work. It is concluded that the most influential conceptualization of learning, one that has decisively shaped formal education systems, is very problematic when it comes to understanding learning at work. The same difficulties occur for standard approaches to measuring attainment. In fact, it appears that 'attainment' is not a very helpful way of thinking about much workplace learning. The chapter then outlines some of the main features that distinguish learning at work from mainstream formal learning. To illustrate these points, a case history of learning at work in a rapidly changing field is presented. This shows how various contextual factors make learning in the workplace difficult to fit into standard ways of conceptualizing learning. It also points to some factors that can contribute to improving learning at work.

Introduction

This chapter argues that the most influential conceptualization of learning, one that has decisively shaped formal education systems, is very problematic when it comes to understanding learning and measuring learning at work. In order to develop this argument, the chapter is organized in three main sections: conceptions of learning and learning at work; measurement of attainment of learning at work; a case history of learning from work.

Conceptions of learning and learning at work

In recent work (Beckett and Hager 2002), two major understandings of learning have been compared and contrasted. The first is called the 'standard paradigm of learning' and the second the 'emerging paradigm of learning'.

The standard paradigm of learning

This paradigm has been very influential. Educational thought has been dominated by a largely unquestioned assumption that the most valuable learning is of one particular kind. Other forms of learning have been evaluated by how well they approximate to this favoured 'standard paradigm of learning'. Major assumptions that characterize the standard paradigm of learning (Beckett and Hager 2002) include, *focus on mind, interiority, and transparency*.

First, with regard to 'focus on mind', the basic image for understanding learning is of an individual human mind steadily being stocked with ideas. The focus of learning as a *process* is on circumstances that favour the acquisition of ideas by minds. The focus of learning as a *product* is on the stock of accumulated ideas that constitute a well-furnished mind, the structure of those ideas, and how various ideas relate to one another. By emphasizing mental learning as the most valuable form of learning, the standard paradigm shows its allegiance to mind/body dualistic understandings of human beings as inherited from classical Greek thought and from Descartes. The effect of elevating mind over body as the centre of the most valuable kind of learning is to make learning an essentially solitary process, an individualistic even narcissistic process, where the learner becomes a spectator aloof from the world.

Second, an essential 'interiority' is assigned to all mental events and activities. As Toulmin (1999: 56) notes, the standard paradigm of learning assumes that 'the supposed *interiority* of mental life is an inescapable feature of the natural processes in our brain and central nervous system'. On this view, human sense organs are instruments that can add content to mental life, but are themselves part of the 'outer' world of the body, not of the 'inner' mental world. So the most valuable form of learning is focused on thinking (what minds do), rather than action in the world (what bodies do) (Winch 1998). As well, the contents of minds, such as concepts and propositions, belong in this separate world. Meanings of concepts are established via the activity of individual minds. Concepts in turn are combined in propositions that represent things and states of affairs in the world (Winch 1998). So the individual solitary mind becomes a spectator that is not itself in the world, but is able to represent the world to itself via propositions. Since this mind is in effect in a different, non-physical world, the same is so for the propositions. Thus we get the notion of propositions as timeless universal entities.

Likewise, learning is a change in the contents of an individual mind, i.e. a change in beliefs. Knowledge is viewed as a particular kind of belief, namely justified true belief. Since belief is a mental state or property, learning is a change of property of a person (mind). So to have acquired particular learning is for the mind to have the right properties. However, properties, like propositions have been regarded as universals, i.e. the same in each instance. Hence the notion of knowledge as universal, true propositions is linked with the traditional focus of formal education. So much follows from the essential interiority of mental events.

The third key assumption of the standard paradigm of learning is the 'transparency' of learning. As Winch points out: 'It is natural for us to talk about learning as if we recognize that we have both a capacity to learn and a capacity to bring to mind what has been learned' (1998: 19). The capacity 'to bring to mind' trades on the image of the mind as the home of clear and distinct ideas. If we have really learnt well, we will be able to bring the learning to mind. An inability to do so is a clear indicator that learning has been imperfect or unsuccessful. This also implies that for the standard paradigm of learning, non-transparent learning is either an aberration or a second-rate kind of learning, e.g. tacit knowledge, informal learning, etc.

It follows from the three assumptions in combination that the best learning consists of abstract ideas (concepts or propositions) that are context independent (universal) and transparent to thought. This immediately places such learning in a dichotomous relationship with learning that has very different characteristics such as the learning of skills by apprentices, which is typically concrete (rather than abstract), context dependent (rather than context independent), and somewhat intuitive and tacit (rather than transparent). Learning with these characteristics is thereby consigned to second-rate status.

To summarize, the main implications of the standard paradigm of learning are that:

- the best learning resides in individual minds not bodies;
- the best learning is propositional (true, false, more certain, less certain);
- the best learning can be expressed verbally and written down in books, etc.;
- the acquisition of the best learning alters minds not bodies;
- such learning can be applied via bodies to alter the external world;
- the process and product of learning can be sharply distinguished;
- the best learning is transparent to the mind.

The standard paradigm of learning has strongly influenced academic processes concerning selection of learners, what is learnt, how it is learnt, and how learning is demonstrated. A later theme in this chapter is on assessment/progression methods, and how they clearly show the influence of the standard paradigm, through their emphasis on learning being demonstrated by individuals reproducing verbal or written propositions in appropriate combinations and in response to set questions in examinations and written assignments. Here the main focus is on universal, context-free knowledge, with numbers and grading to quantify the amount of learning demonstrated. Of course, the emphasis on assessment of this kind has not been without its critics. These have been singled out: its excessive individualism; its devaluation of non-propositional learning; and the focus on intellectual understanding to the neglect of its application.

More broadly, the basic assumptions of the standard paradigm of learning have attracted significant criticisms (Beckett and Hager 2002). Some of the main ones are: first, assuming that the most valuable learning is mental sets up dichotomies and hierarchies that in turn have created intractable problems of their own. An example is the theory/practice account of workplace performance/practice. As long ago as 1949, Ryle pointed out the futility of this view which effectively seeks to reduce practice to theory.

Second, the standard paradigm offers no 'convincing account of the relationship between "knowledge" as the possession of individuals and "knowledge" as the collective property of communities of "knowers"' (Toulmin 1999: 54). Likewise the assumption that meaning is established via individual minds creates the problem of accounting for collective knowledge (Toulmin 1999: 55). Third, the assumption that the most valuable learning is transparent has been challenged. For example, Winch (1998) argues that knowledge is largely dispositional in Rylean terms, thereby taking the central focus away from transparent propositions in minds. Likewise, there is the claim, taken up later in this chapter, that abilities or capacities are presupposed by other forms of learning (Passmore 1980; Winch 1998).

Finally, because the notion of 'judgement' will be important in later discussion, its role according to the standard paradigm of learning will be considered briefly. The term 'judgement' exhibits the so-called act-object ambiguity, denoting either the act of judging that something is true or the object which is judged as true (Honderich 1998). In the act sense, judgements are propositional attitudes, i.e. mental states or acts which have a variety of causes and effects, and vary from person to person and time to time. Judgements are distinguished from the sentences expressing them. In the object sense, judgements are propositions, i.e. abstract objects that are true or false, stand in logical relationships, and are composed of concepts or other judgements.

The standard paradigm of learning has exerted a profound two-fold influence on the perceived place of judgement in education. First, where judgements have figured in educational concerns it has been as intellectual judgements, viewed as true or false propositions. These are very different from so-called practical judgements which are about what to do. Here, the influential sway of the pervasive theory versus practice dichotomy is apparent. Second, by emphasizing judgement as outcome (object), rather than as process (act), the effect has been to diminish its significance, since education has always concentrated in a major way on true propositions. So overall, judgement has been taken for granted in education. Judgement as it occurs in workplace practice is banished to the category of 'educationally uninteresting'. However, there is another significant view of learning that views judgement somewhat differently.

The emerging paradigm of learning

In contrast with the standard paradigm of learning, learning can be characterized as action in the world. Beckett and Hager (2002) refer to this
alternative view as the 'emerging paradigm of learning' because, though a
diverse range of critical writings on education can be seen as pointing to
this new paradigm, it is still a long way from gaining the wide recognition
and support characteristic of an established paradigm. On this view,
learning changes both learners and their environment. Since learners are
part of that environment, the basic formulation is that the outcome of
learning is to change the world in some way. Rather than being simply a
change in the properties of the learner (as in the standard paradigm of
learning), for the emerging paradigm, the main outcome of learning is the
creation of a new set of relations in an environment. This is why learning is
inherently contextual, since what it does is to continually alter the context
in which it occurs.

There are many writers who can be seen to be contributors to the
emerging paradigm of learning. Beckett and Hager (2002) devote particular discussion to Dewey's contribution. Dewey was a noted critic of
dualisms, such as the mind/body dualism, and of spectator theories of
knowledge. For Dewey, learning and knowledge were closely linked to
successful action in the world. While Dewey did not deny that concepts
and propositions were important, he subsumed them into a wider capacity
called judgement which incorporates, along with the cognitive, the
ethical, aesthetic, conative and other factors that are omitted from the
essentially cognitive standard paradigm of learning. It should be noted
that Dewey is not totally discarding the explanatory items of the standard
paradigm of learning. Rather they are part of his larger explanatory
scheme. Thus, for him, the type of learning valorized by the standard
paradigm is but a limited and special instance of a broader notion of
learning.

There has been a range of theorists who stress the crucial role of action
in learning. This is an important idea for the emerging paradigm of
learning. For example, Jarvis (1992) views learning that lacks this action
component, such as contemplative learning, as abnormal learning. Jarvis
upends the standard paradigm that privileges contemplative learning at
the expense of all other kinds of learning. He holds the standard paradigm
responsible for the phenomenon of people rejecting as learning what does
not fit under its assumptions (the 'denial of learning' syndrome) (Jarvis
1992: 5).

As noted earlier, one implication of the standard paradigm of learning is a
sharp separation of the processes and products of learning. This distinction is
plausible whenever learning is separated from action. However, when
learning is closely linked with action, the two are not sharply distinguished

at all. The process facilitates the product which at the same time enhances further processes and so on.

A number of central ideas from Wittgenstein's later philosophy reinforce the emerging paradigm of learning (see, e.g. Williams 1994). These insights include an undermining of the assumption of the mental interiority of the best learning that is central to the standard paradigm. For Wittgenstein, meanings are not essentially internal. Rather, meaning emerges from collective 'forms of life' (Toulmin 1999). As well, for Wittgenstein, the basic case of teaching (training) is not about mentalistic concepts being connected to objects (as in ostensive definition and rule following). Rather, it is about being trained into pattern-governed behaviours, i.e. learning to behave in ways that mimic activities licensed by practice or custom. Another important idea is the social basis of normative practices.

Passmore argues that *capacities* are a major, perhaps the major, class of human learning. For Passmore in normal development 'every human being acquires a number of capacities for action...whether as a result of experience, of imitation or of deliberate teaching...' (1980: 37). His examples include, learning to walk, run, speak, feed and clothe oneself; in literate societies, learning to read, write, add; particular individuals learn to drive a car, play the piano, repair diesel engines, titrate, dissect, etc.

Passmore stresses that not all human learning consists in capacities. As examples he instances development of tastes (e.g. for poetry), formation of habits (e.g. of quoting accurately), development of interests (e.g. in mathematics) and acquiring information. However, for Passmore each of these types of learning depends on capacities: to understand the language; to copy a sentence; to solve mathematical problems; to listen, read and observe. The argument is that capacities are the basis for other kinds of learning. So the mental enrichment seen as basic in the standard paradigm of learning actually depends on the exercise of learned capacities.

That capacities are much more than mental in their scope is evident from their definition and characteristics: ' "Capacity" – A capacity is a power or ability (either natural or acquired) of a thing or person, and as such one of its real (because causally effective) properties' (Honderich 1998: 119). Honderich characterizes natural capacities of inanimate objects, such as the capacity of copper to conduct electricity. These are dispositional properties whose ascription entails the truth of corresponding subjunctive conditionals. However, the capacities of persons, the exercise of which is subject to their voluntary control, such as a person's capacity to speak English, do not sustain such a pattern of entailments and are consequently not strictly dispositions. Thus capacities are vital features of human learning.

Passmore further distinguishes two types of capacities 'open' and 'closed' as follows:

> Closed capacities: 'A "closed" capacity is distinguished from an "open" capacity in virtue of the fact that it allows of total mastery.' Examples include starting a car, holding a chisel correctly, etc.
>
> Open capacities: 'In contrast, however good we are at exercising an "open" capacity, somebody else – or ourselves at some other time – could do it better', e.g. playing the piano, novel writing, wood-carving.
>
> (1980: 40)

The process/product distinction discussed above can be expounded further in relation to closed and open capacities. It is in the case of open capacities that the process/product distinction starts to blur. While the distinction remains fairly clear in the case of closed capacities (the process of starting a car can be readily distinguished from the achievement of the engine running – the latter is a state of affairs that obtains over and above the starting of the car (Ryle 1949)), the same distinction is less clear in cases of open capacities. In playing the piano, for example, a state of affairs can be said to obtain of having played a particular piece, but the quality of this achievement can usually be increased further by more playing, that is more process. So more of the process is the basis for the product being improved, yet at the same time such improvement will serve to enhance the performance of the process.

As Passmore's range of examples of capacities, e.g. titrating, dissecting, healing, etc., makes clear, their exercise often closely connects with the kind of judgement emphasized by Dewey.

From this brief survey, the main principles of the emerging paradigm of learning are (Beckett and Hager 2002):

- knowledge, as integrated in judgements, is a capacity for successful acting in and on the world;
- the choice of how to act in and on the world comes from the exercise of judgement;
- knowledge resides in individuals, teams and organizations;
- knowledge includes not just propositional understanding, but cognitive, conative and affective capacities as well as other abilities and learned capacities such as bodily know-how, skills of all kinds, and so on. All of these are components conceivably involved in making and acting upon judgements;
- not all knowledge can be or has been expressed verbally and written down;
- acquisition of knowledge alters both the learner and the world (since the learner is part of the world).

Clearly the notion of judgement is an important feature of the emerging paradigm of learning. This sits with its holistic, integrative emphasis that aims to avoid dualisms such as mind/body, theory/practice, thought/action, pure/applied, education/training, intrinsic/instrumental, internal/external, learner/world, knowing that/knowing how, process/product, and so on. The argument is that judgements, as both reasoning and acting, incorporate both sides of these ubiquitous dualisms. Thus, this learning paradigm does not reject as such any pole of these dualisms. For instance there is no rejection of propositional knowledge. Rather, propositions are viewed as important sub-components of the mix that underpins judgements: though the range of such propositions extends well beyond the boundaries of disciplinary knowledge. What is rejected is the view that propositions are timeless, independent exis-tents that are the epitome of knowledge. By bringing together the propositional with the doing, the emerging paradigm of learning continually judges propositions according to their contribution to the making of judge-ments. Because the judger is immersed in the world, so are propositions. So they lose their classical transcendental status. (For more details on judgement see Hager 2000a, 2000b; Beckett and Hager 2002).

It can be proposed, therefore, that the emerging paradigm of learning is superior to the standard paradigm for conceptualizing learning at work. While the standard paradigm assumptions undermine attempts to under-stand what is happening in learning at work, the emerging paradigm offers concepts that provide a beginning of understanding. However, it should be emphasized that rather than the two paradigms of learning being polar opposites, the standard paradigm is best seen as a limited and special instance of the emerging paradigm. However the role of learning outside of formal classrooms is so vital in the contemporary era that we can no longer allow its understanding to be distorted by mistaking what is merely a limited and special case of learning for the norm.

Measurement of attainment of learning at work

The influence of the standard paradigm of learning on the formal education system has been such that assessment of student attainment has been largely shaped by its assumptions. In standard assessment and progression systems, learning is demonstrated by individuals reproducing verbal or written propositions in appropriate combinations in response to set questions in examinations and written assignments. Here, there is a focus on universal, context-free knowledge, with numbers and grading to quantify the amount of learning demonstrated. While relatively simple skills might be tested by direct observation of candidates performing the skills, a common strategy with more complex skills is to have candidates answer written questions. For example, in Australia there is an attempt to measure generic attributes of new university graduates via multiple-choice testing (Australian Council for Educational Research). Likewise in the United Kingdom there have been recent moves to assess students' key skills by having them sit for written examinations (Fuller and Unwin 2001). In both cases, there has been significant scepticism about what, if anything, these tests are measuring. Certainly, it can be stated that they reflect both the assumptions and limitations of the approach to assessment favoured by the standard paradigm of learning.

Assessment arrangements such as these reflect the standard paradigm of learning principles that the best learning resides in individual minds as propositions and, because of their transparency, these can be readily reproduced in verbal or written form. Skills of all kinds, while regarded as inferior types of learning, also have their place. Guided by the right propositional knowledge, they can be applied via bodies to alter the external world in desired ways. Unfortunately for proponents of this approach, its theoretical basis has long since been undermined (e.g. Ryle 1949).

From the preceding, it will be clear that the emerging paradigm of learning, with its focus on holism, judgement, action and context, better represents the kinds of learning that occur in workplaces. At best, the type of learning valorized by the standard paradigm is but a small part of learning in workplaces. Thus, when it comes to assessing learning at work, retaining the assessment assumptions of the standard paradigm will only serve to guarantee ineffective assessment. To see further why this is so, we need to consider more closely some key assessment assumptions of the standard paradigm of learning.

The individuality assumption

A virtually universal assessment assumption of the standard paradigm of learning is that the individual is the correct unit of analysis. This discounts the possibility, indeed the likelihood, of communal learning, i.e. learning by teams and organizations that may not be reducible to learning by individuals. Adopting the individuality assumption has wide-ranging implications for vocational education, e.g. human capital theory incorporates this assumption. This is evident from a typical definition of human capital: '[T]he knowledge, skills and competences and other attributes embodied in individuals that are relevant to economic activity' (OECD 1998: 9).

The stability assumption

Another key presupposition of the standard paradigm of learning is that the knowledge being assessed remains relatively stable over time. It needs this characteristic so that it can be incorporated into curricula and textbooks, be passed on from teachers to students, its attainment be measured in examinations, and the examination results for different teachers and different institutions be readily amenable to comparison. Thus formal education systems want to deal with assessment of learning that is stable, familiar and widely understood. Engeström puts this assumption of what he calls 'standard theories of learning' as follows: 'a self-evident presupposition that the knowledge or skill to be acquired is itself stable and reasonably well-defined' (Engeström 2001: 137).

The replicability assumption

The practice of comparing assessment results for students across different class groupings and different institutions was found to involve the stability of knowledge assumption. In fact, the everyday practice of comparing the learning of different students also requires an even more fundamental presupposition, the replicability assumption. This assumption is that the learning of different learners can be literally the same or identical. The sorting and grading functions of education systems require the possibility of this kind of foundational certainty of marks and grades. These matters are reflected in the common term used to denote replicability of learning – different students are said to have the same 'attainment'.

As several English dictionaries confirm, 'to attain' means: (1) to arrive at, reach (a goal, etc.), or (2) to gain, accomplish (an aim, distinction, etc.). In either case, conscious development or effort is often involved. The noun 'attainment' has two distinct meanings reflecting the process/product distinction: (1) the act or an instance of attaining, or (2) something attained or achieved; an accomplishment. When applied to learning the verb to attain introduces metaphorical connotations – learners have arrived at or reached a place or gained an object. This is consistent with the Latin derivation from 'attingere' – to touch.

The metaphors associated with attainment appear to fit very well with various aspects of the standard paradigm of learning. For a start they encompass the process/product distinction. Attaining learning, stocking the mind with contents is akin to arriving at a goal or gaining an object. The learning that has been attained is akin to the mind having 'touched' the relevant propositions. Recall that propositions are viewed as timeless, unchanging entities located in a world of ideas. Students with the same level of attainment can be thought of as mentally 'touching' the same range of universal propositions. Inside their individual minds each has completed the same mental journey, on the way calling at the prescribed places or destinations.

The metaphors associated with attainment seem to fit much less well with the emerging paradigm of learning. Perhaps 'attaining' is a more suitable notion here. Also, with this paradigm, the process/product distinction is less applicable, reflecting that finished products of learning are not so readily identifiable. In workplaces, typical learning involves developing the gradually growing capacity to participate effectively in socially situated collaborative practices. This means being able to make holistic, context sensitive judgements about how to act in situations that may be more or less novel. As well, these judgements are often developed at the level of the team or the organization. So in these circumstances the propositions touched by individual minds may be of limited interest. It seems that each of the three key assessment assumptions of the standard paradigm breaks down when applied to workplace learning. The isolated individual is often not the appropriate unit of analysis. The learning is not stable as contexts continually change and evolve. In many occupations people with just the expertise of a decade ago are no longer employable. Much work requires practitioners to develop open capacities (in Passmore's sense) in an ongoing way. Nor will the learning histories of workers be the same because of the contextuality and particularities of their different work experiences. Hence it makes little sense to look for replicability of learning across individual workers.

Scheffler in a discussion of the centrality of metaphorical language in educational theory, noted that metaphors indicate,

> that there is an important analogy between two things, without saying explicitly in what the analogy consists. Now, every two things are analogous in some respect, but not every such respect is important...the notion of importance varies with the situation...
>
> (1960: 48)

Scheffler added that every metaphor has limitations, 'points at which the analogies it indicates break down' (1960: 48). For dominant metaphors he suggested we need to determine their limitations, thereby 'opening up fresh possibilities of thought and action' (Scheffler 1960: 49). My view is that the standard paradigm of learning, centred on the metaphor of the spectator mind, aloof from the world, steadily acquiring unchanging propositions, well illustrates Scheffler's claims. A very limited form of learning has been allowed to determine how we picture all learning. While we can envisage that different minds, themselves not part of the everyday world, can all touch (attain) the same timeless, transparent propositions, important instances of learning, such as the learning by a team carrying out a challenging workplace project, are nothing like this. Yet, just such assumptions have been allowed to dominate our ideas on assessment of learning in general.

As the above rejection of the attainment metaphor suggests, effective assessment of learning at work requires something of a paradigm shift in how we think about these matters (see Hager and Butler 1996). The judgemental model of assessment frightens people who want guaranteed foundations and the certainty that they think these bring. The timeless propositions and logical essences of the standard paradigm of learning appear to provide just such foundations and certainty. Whereas the lack of stability and replicability for assessment under the judgemental model dashes any such hopes. However, it seems to be unavoidable that much learning at work belongs to a type of human practice that evades the standard paradigm. In such practices, it is simply the case that the practices are judged by standards which themselves evolve from the practices. We are stuck with a virtuous circle (or spiral) of practices and standards.

A case history of learning from work

To address further the differences between measuring learning at work and the assessment of learning that is characteristic in formal education systems, we will consider a case history of learning from work. The following case history probably represents an unusually rich instance of learning from work. However, if we are to understand a phenomenon better, it is helpful to consider some of the best instances.

Case history of a senior surveyor

Richard is Survey Manager for the Infrastructure Operating Unit of a large construction group in Australia. He describes himself as a 'hands-on' man and still goes onto sites to do surveys when he can so as to keep himself in touch. His current responsibilities are the development and control of survey staff and equipment to ensure that the group remains an industry leader, and the planning of the future surveying needs of the construction group in terms of human and physical resources. Richard has been in surveying all his working life. Although not a registered surveyor, he has broad experience in major construction companies as project manager, foreman, project surveyor, senior surveyor and chief surveyor. In 1980 he was promoted to a managerial position with the specific task of streamlining the use of software packages, survey equipment and lines of communication with surveyors on various jobs.

A major influence on Richard's career was the shock of 'falling on his face' at the end of schooling because he 'spent his final year in the surf'. Being not eligible to go to university, Richard decided to become a surveyor and successfully completed a 4-year part-time Certificate in Surveying at a Technical and Further Education (TAFE) college, while working as a survey assistant. Failure of earlier university plans motivated him to do very well in the TAFE course. This brief case history focuses on the changes in surveying skills that Richard has encountered and on how he has acquired new skills to keep up with occupational change.

Richard views construction surveying as a service industry, whose purpose is to formulate methods to set out a project and to calculate the relevant data and quantities. While this basic purpose has not changed, Richard has seen the way it is done change, and continue to change, dramatically, as technology has evolved. The scope and extent of the major revolution in surveying is reflected in a number of comparisons. First, when Richard started, he calculated survey data with log tables or small calculators averaging 10–15 property blocks per day. Now with Global Positioning

Systems (GPS) he does anything from 600–10,000 shots a day on site, with the calculations of the data happening in the office using sophisticated PC software. Second, Richard's first surveying calculator had a memory capacity of 25 programme steps; now he uses software that can deal with a million survey points. Third, early 'modelling software' of the 1980s ran overnight processing survey data. Now the same calculations require a few seconds.

Richard summarizes these enormous changes as follows.

> Broadly speaking, there was the introduction of the computer, followed by an electronic survey equipment revolution, then a software revolution. Now all three are merged to control and drive sophisticated machines that in the future may not require an operator.

Essentially, Richard believes he has learnt his job skills, both technical and managerial, from experience on-the-job and his own personal research. He claims that, basically, there is no training for construction that can replace actual on-the-job experience. He sees his learning as being self-developed gradually over the course of his career, including gaining the knowledge and skills to perform in higher positions. Thus, for Richard, the role of formal training in his moves to higher level jobs has been largely negligible.

The rapid computer innovations in a small field such as surveying are such that there are not a lot of worthwhile courses available. Richard works with the software writers to understand and assist in directing the latest innovations. For Richard and most software users they either pay for training or work it out for themselves. In doing the latter, Richard has become used to 'pushing himself to the limits'. Survey equipment manufacturers run some training sessions and there are university workshops available from time to time. He is about to attend an intense three-day workshop at a university on GPS. These workshops are the result of organizations combining to give a more structured training alternative to that of manufacturer organized sessions. He comments that this is better than manufacturers' sessions as they feature more intensive learning. Another benefit is that you come away from these workshops with not only the course literature, but also your own set of reference notes for applications and procedures experienced.

Richard compensates for the lack of suitable courses in these specialized areas through personal research. A common instance of self-teaching is venturing into the software to try out what it can do. If he makes a mistake, he just starts again. Richard keeps in touch with software package writers by conducting trials of their products and providing feedback and advice. He does the same with prototype survey instruments. He also belongs to a software user group made up of people from all sections of the industry. A software company technical support manager runs the group. Richard's company pays for him to attend this user group, which discusses the problems experienced, the needed innovations or applications and the overall directions for the industry. He sees this as invaluable as no university or TAFE course can possibly keep pace with the speed and cost of the equipment being developed. This applies also to the use of survey instruments.

There is no specific construction training in Australian degrees in surveying, but studies in surveying and civil engineering can be merged, which Richard sees as a logical combination of skills. Richard learnt and developed his skills on-the-job by working extremely long hours. Summarizing his development and maintenance of up-to-date technical surveying skills, Richard sees some of it coming from formal off-the-job learning, some of it coming from formal on-the-job learning, but by far the vast majority of it is from informal off-the-job reading, research and testing, that he does for himself.

The other area where Richard has had to gain and maintain skills is as a manager. As with his technical surveying skills, Richard sees experience on-the-job as the significant source of his acquired management skills. He describes his management roles as centring on running smoothly operating teams, structured surveying methods and clear company policies. His first experience of management evolved from frustration at the rather ad hoc surveying methods at the firm. He approached his manager with procedures to improve and streamline survey methods for better efficiency. He was encouraged to implement his ideas and manage them.

Until this job, Richard's role as manager occurred at all hours of the day. This was because he had to provide site survey services to various large construction sites, using junior surveyors, and simultaneously assist surveyors at other sites all over New South Wales with methods and procedures, this latter invariably by telephone. The on-site management was a 'hands-on' situation in which he could gather his team to show them something when needed, whereas the telephone assistance to other locations Richard believed to be restricted and difficult. Richard's new management role is not tied to a site and allows him more time for face-to-face assistance, time to solve problems and provide solutions to sites and surveyors. Regular site visits also helps to maintain quality and motivation. This role structure also allows Richard time to assist with Head Office tenders and variations.

Implications for learning from work

Richard's case history provides further strong evidence for the inapplicability of each of the three key basic assessment assumptions of the standard paradigm of learning to workplace learning. Although Richard's case history describes the learning trajectory of an individual, he is certainly not, qua learner, an isolated individual. His proactive work with the software writers to understand and assist in development of innovative products, together with his membership of the software user group illustrate this. Accepting a mainstream definition of 'learning' ('the acquisition of a form of knowledge or ability through the use of experience' (Hamlyn in Honderich 1998: 476)), it is surely plausible that in such activities learning by teams and groups is likely and is not reducible to learning by individuals. If such communities as the software user group develop abilities that transcend the abilities of individual members, then the individual is not the appropriate unit of analysis for understanding this learning.

Certainly much of Richard's learning is not stable as the contexts in which he works change and evolve so rapidly. In some areas the rapid change means that cutting edge formal courses are an impossibility. Nor is Richard's learning trajectory one that can be replicated by others. The contextuality and particularities of his learning from work experiences impart uniqueness to that learning. Others might have an equally rich learning trajectory, but it will still be a very different one from Richard's. Richard was 'head-hunted' for his current position on the basis of holistic judgements made by others about the quality of his work performance; not because he outper-formed other individuals on standard assessment tasks.

Richard's responsibility for planning the future surveying needs, both human and physical resources, of his company requires continual learning for him to make wise judgements, e.g. which equipment to buy and which to lease. In a field undergoing such rapid and continuing change, Richard depends very much on his ongoing learning to keep him well informed. There are no textbooks to tell him what to do. His continuous learning underpins the series of integrated judgements that his job requires him to make to ensure that his construction company continues to act successfully in and on the world.

It appears that Richard's motivation for learning is multifaceted. From the time of his youth he preferred learning from real work to academic learning. His failure to qualify for entry to university seems to have moti-vated him more strongly to learn from work. He creates and drives his own learning opportunities, sometimes 'pushing himself to the limits'. He also enjoys strong support from his employer, who pays for him to attend the software users' group.

Conclusion

This chapter has argued that the most influential conceptualization of learning, one that has decisively shaped teaching and assessment practices in formal education systems, is very problematic when it comes to under-standing learning at work. Nor is the standard assessment concept of 'attainment' very helpful for thinking about what is learned at work. Three basic assumptions have been identified as underpinning common under-standings of learning and its assessment. First, that individuals are the locus of learning, second, that what is learnt is stable over time, and third, that learning trajectories are common across learners. It has been shown that learning at work challenges each of these assumptions, thereby casting doubt on their importance for our understanding of learning. Instead this chapter has drawn on various authors to outline an alternative conceptualiza-tion of learning, one that provides a better fit with learning at work. The value of the alternative conceptualization of learning has been illustrated by testing it against salient points of a case history of learning at work in a rapidly changing field, namely surveying. This illustrated how various contextual factors make learning at work difficult to fit into standard ways of conceptualizing learning and assessment. The case history also pointed to some factors that can contribute to improving learning at work. Overall, further research is needed to expand our understanding of learning from work and the most appropriate ways of measuring its progress and of enhancing its development.

Bibliography

Australian Council for Educational Research: http://www.acer.edu.au.

Beckett, D. and Hager, P. (2002) *Life, Work and Learning: Practice in Postmodernity*, Routledge International Studies in the Philosophy of Education 14, London and New York: Routledge.

Engeström, Y. (2001) 'Expansive Learning at Work: Toward an Activity Theoretical Reconceptualization', *Journal of Education and Work*, 14 (1): 133–56.

Fuller, A. and Unwin, L. (2001) 'The Rhetoric and Reality of Key Skills in the Contemporary Workplace: Contesting the UK Approach', Proceedings of the Second International Conference on Researching Work and Learning, University of Calgary, Canada, July, 527–35.

Hager, P. (2000a) 'Knowledge that Works: Judgement and the University Curriculum', in C. Symes and J. McIntyre (eds), *Working Knowledge: The New Vocationalism and Higher Education*, Buckingham: Open University Press/Society for Research into Higher Education.

—— (2000b) 'Know-How and Workplace Practical Judgement', *Journal of Philosophy of Education*, 34 (2): 281–96.

Hager, P. and Butler, J. (1996) 'Two Models of Educational Assessment', *Assessment & Evaluation in Higher Education*, 21 (4): 367–78.

Honderich, T. (ed.) (1998) *The Oxford Companion to Philosophy*, Oxford and New York: Oxford University Press.

Jarvis, P. (1992) *Paradoxes of Learning: On Becoming an Individual in Society*, San Fransciso, CA: Jossey Bass.

Organisation for Economic Cooperation and Development (OECD) (1998) *Human Capital Investment: An International Comparison*, Paris: OECD.

Passmore, J. (1980) *The Philosophy of Teaching*, London: Duckworth.

Ryle, G. (1949) *The Concept of Mind*, 1963 edn, Harmondsworth: Penguin.

Scheffler, I. (1960) *The Language of Education*, Springfield, IL: Charles C. Thomas.

Toulmin, S. (1999) 'Knowledge as Shared Procedures', in Y. Engeström, R. Miettinen and R. Punamaki (eds), *Perspectives on Action Theory*, Cambridge: Cambridge University Press.

Williams, M. (1994) 'The Significance of Learning in Wittgenstein's Later Philosophy', *Canadian Journal of Philosophy*, 24 (2): 173–203.

Winch, C. (1998) *The Philosophy of Human Learning*, Routledge International Studies in the Philosophy of Education, London and New York: Routledge.

15 The complexities of workplace learning

Problems and dangers in trying to measure attainment

Phil Hodkinson and Heather Hodkinson

Chapter summary

In the current political context, there are pressures for scientific research to objectively identify effective learning, in the workplace as elsewhere, for example by measuring the attainments of such learning. Drawing upon empirical data, we argue that this is counter-productive. Workplace learning is complex, yet a research focus on measured attainments implicitly defines such learning in a narrow way, within an acquisition perspective. This severely restricts the range of learning that can be recognized. Ironically, the very types of learning likely to be excluded are some of the most common and significant. To gain a better understanding of workplace learning and to effectively improve it, we need to resist scientific reductionism, and work with more holistic theoretical and methodological approaches.

Introduction

In the recent UK and USA contexts, there has been pressure for research on education and learning to be conducted scientifically and objectively, to provide robust evidence that certain practices do or do not improve learning. Findings from such research, it is suggested, can then be safely used to impact upon policy and practice (Hillage *et al.* 1998; Feuer *et al.* 2002). In order to ensure the desired scientific rigour, the pressure is to identify the extent of learning success. Otherwise, it is claimed, we cannot know whether particular approaches or practices are better or worse than others. Such research could require the setting of clear indicators of expected learner attainment, which should be objective by being independent not only of researcher position, but also of the values and perceptions of the learners concerned. We argue that there are serious problems if such an approach is applied to learning in the workplace.

This interrelates with an ongoing debate within educational literature on learning. Sfard (1998) identifies a contest between two rival metaphors of learning: the older once dominant metaphor of acquisition, and its more recent challenger, participation. Sfard argues that neither metaphor is wholly adequate, and that each metaphor may work better for different purposes and in different situations. We agree, and argue further that the use of the acquisition metaphor is often less appropriate for workplace settings. This chapter sets out to explore some underlying factors from these debates in the light of our recent research.

The research project

The research examined English secondary school teachers' learning in their school workplaces. It was a qualitative study of the teachers in four subject departments in two secondary schools, in separate parts of England. Such subject departments are the dominant structural divisions for teachers in UK secondary schools. Fieldwork extended over six school terms with alternate terms spent in each school. The data included: documentary evidence; observation within the schools and particularly of the teachers working within their departments; and semi-structured interviews with the teachers about their career histories and their learning as teachers. The research was one of five projects in the network 'Improving Incentives for Learning in the Workplace', which was part of the Economic and Social Research Council's Teaching and Learning Research Programme.

In what follows, first, we use a heuristic device to examine the complexities of learning at work. That is, we assume that learning in the workplace is an amalgam of different types. We present a typology, based upon two intersecting dimensions: the degree of intentionality of the learning; and the extent to which what is learned is known by others or entirely new. We present brief accounts of six different types of learning thus defined. Within these accounts we show that research which starts by identifying measurable learning attainments, only works for some of the types. Furthermore, different theories of learning are rather better at explaining some of the types than others. Second, having made these points, we make clear that to use our typology as the sum representation of the realities of learning at work would be a serious oversimplification. For such a typology excludes other equally significant dimensions of learning, and draws attention away from the fact that in practice, workplace learning is complex and rarely falls neatly into such categories. Within the chapter we present four vignettes of workplace learning cases from our research to illustrate the complexity and to problematize the typology, whilst explaining it (see Boxes 15.1, 15.2, 15.3 and 15.4). The chapter concludes by examining some of the implications of our analysis for researching learning in the workplace.

Types of learning in the workplace

Learning in the workplace takes many forms and is conceptualized differently by different researchers, for example through situated cognition (Brown et al. 1989; Lave and Wenger 1991; Wenger 1998); socio-cultural approaches (Wertsch 1998); or activity theory (Engeström 1999; 2001). Within these overlapping theoretical positions, little emphasis is placed upon the categorization of workplace learning into different types. Despite this, we are not the first to use typologies in this context. For example, Eraut (2000) presents a typology of non-formal learning, based on the timing of the stimulus (past, current, future) and the extent to which such learning is tacit (tacit, reactive or deliberative). This latter dimension is later set against another, identifying different types of thought or action (reading of the situation, decision making, overt activity, meta-cognitive processes).

Many researchers construct their model/conceptualization/theory of learning, with the explicit claim or implicit implication that it might adequately cover all aspects of workplace learning, in all contexts. Here we address an alternative view: that workplace learning is sufficiently diverse and complex that no one theory, at least none yet fully developed, can adequately deal with all its aspects. Within this complexity, we argue that only some types of workplace learning, usually those most easily accounted for using an acquisition metaphor, are susceptible to the clear identification and measurement of possible attainment.

We approached this problem by constructing a matrix of types of learning that were identifiable in our data (Table 15.1). We describe and give examples of the resulting categories, at the same time showing how they only partially reflect the complex workplace reality.

Table 15.1 Typology of learning

	Intentional/planned	Unintentional/unplanned
Learning that which is already known to others	(1) Planned learning of that which others know	(2) Socialization into an existing community of practice
Development of existing capability	(4) Planned/intended learning to refine existing capability	(3) Unplanned improvement of ongoing practice
Learning that which is new in the workplace (or treated as such)	(5) Planned/intended learning to do that which has not been done before	(6) Unplanned learning of something not previously done

I. The intentional/planned learning of that which others already know

This type includes formal training, and the deliberate acquisition of aspects of capability through books, the internet, open learning, etc. This type dominates the literature about learning in educational settings, and much of the cognitive and behavioural psychological approach to researching and theorizing learning. This is the arena where Sfard's (1998) acquisitional metaphors of learning have most potential. Acquisition can be wider than what Beckett and Hager (2002) term the 'standard paradigm of learning' which emphasizes 'learners as isolated individual minds' and the 'essential interiority of all mental events and activities'. Type 1 learning also includes the passing on of established skills and practices, for example through planned demonstrations or structured practical training sessions. Our category, when applied to the workplace, also covers social or activity learning from others, which is planned and intentional. This aspect of type 1 learning is holistic and embodied (Beckett and Hager 2002). It can be communal.

There are many examples of type 1 learning in our data. Teachers reported intentionally learning a diverse range of skills, knowledge and understanding, in a variety of ways. They had all been on occasional taught courses, recently and in the past. Some had clear recollections of past courses, which still influenced their work. Others were still trying to find courses on particular topics or for specific purposes. Courses varied from the very specific such as improving techniques in conducting a band, to the more general such as classroom management. Some were experienced as valuable, others as a waste of time. Another example of type 1 is the teacher who enrolled as an assistant examiner, with the specific intention of improving his understanding of the external examination process from the inside. Most teachers seek information from books, the internet or more experienced colleagues.

The intentionality for learning could come from management or the learner. One school brought in an expert to tell teaching staff about the business-style Performance Management scheme imposed by government. An individual art teacher requested someone experienced to show her how to use a digital camera.

The bulk of psychological literature about learning is focused within this type. On the other hand, situated cognition and activity theorists, working predominantly within Sfard's (1998) participation metaphor, have devoted much effort to demonstrating the weaknesses of seeing learning as insulated from the contexts in which it takes place and the activities engaged in whilst learning. These analyses are insightful in explaining some of the contradictions and dysfunctions in formal education (Brown et al. 1989). However, they are less good at explaining the value and place of type 1 learning, including formal instruction, as a dimension of learning at, for and through work.

It is to type 1 learning that a scientific/empiricist view of research is most easily applied, as it is possible to identify, in advance, what some of the expected outcomes of planned learning should be. As Stenhouse (1975) warned however, in intentional learning settings, there are also quite legitimate unpredicted and unpredictable outcomes.

2. Socialization into an existing community of practice

Writers about situated cognition (Brown *et al.* 1989; Lave and Wenger 1991) changed the central focus of attention on learning, though Beckett and Hager (2002) are right to remind us that Dewey was working on similar lines much earlier. For Lave and Wenger, a new apprentice learned, not primarily by being formally taught, but by becoming assimilated into an existing community of practice. What was learned was that which was entailed in belonging to that community, which pre-existed the arrival of the new learner. Furthermore, any skills or knowledge developed and used might have different meanings and values in different work contexts and

---

Box 15.1 Kim

Kim was a newly qualified Information Technology teacher. After two years, she moved on to run her own department in another school. When Kim first started she was given lots of help by the head of department. He showed her round, talked her through lots of background information and provided schemes of work and some lesson plans for the new classes she had to teach. For the first year she had time set aside fortnightly when they could talk through what she was doing and any problems she was having. He provided practical help by removing particularly difficult children from her classes so that she could concentrate on improving her teaching of the others. The school organized meetings for new teachers, setting out school policies. Kim consulted with other teachers in the IT department and young teachers in other departments, with whom she was friendly. Learning for her included occasional formal training sessions, deliberate consultations and conversations in passing. However, Kim found that she learned most through getting on with the job. On starting the second year she realized that she was having far fewer class discipline problems because she was no longer worrying about the pupils liking her. It was something which she had been told, but had had to find out for herself.

different communities of practice. This type 2 learning applies in traditional apprenticeship situations (Fuller and Unwin 1998), and when a person changes jobs. It can be tacit and unplanned, the only intention being to become a fully accepted member of the community.

Kim, a recently qualified teacher, described learning in her new department, in ways that can be understood as a combination of type 2 with type 1. She used her head of department and the ex-head of department, now a senior teacher in the school, as role models. She discussed her work with them, in casual and also in more structured sessions. Her head of department was deliberately active in this process, rather like the conventional figure of the skilled craftsperson giving time to help an apprentice learn. The new teacher also described picking up ideas and information through general chat with other teachers in the staff room.

From the type 2 perspective, there are serious problems with the scientific view of researching learning. Learning and attainment are not separate, but are facets of each other, and integral parts of the community of practice concerned. Forms of practice judged to be superior/desirable in one community may not be so in others. Furthermore, much of the learning and attainment are located in what Bourdieu (1998) calls 'practical reason'. That is, they are known and understood through practice, but not necessarily through discursive language or explicit thought. Brown (1994) showed that learning practical capability is difficult for teachers to identify and describe, a finding paralleled in studies about non-formal learning in a variety of workplaces (Eraut 2000; Eraut *et al.* 2000). Thus, there are often few clear 'learning attainments' that can be specified and measured for this type of learning. The attainment, in Lave and Wenger's (1991) sense, is becoming a 'full member', which is complex, contested and can vary in form and substance from person to person, even in the same situation.

Theories of learning which are appropriate for type 1 do not work well as explanations for this socialization type of learning. On the other hand, Lave and Wenger's work underestimates the significance of type 1 learning in modern employment settings. Kim's experiences illustrate the significance of type 1 as well as type 2 learning, and we need theoretical approaches that can accommodate both.

3. The unplanned adaption/improvement of ongoing practice

For the teachers in our study, learning was part of ongoing activity and they were largely unaware that they were learning. If they thought about these things at all, they would have talked simply about 'doing the job'. Often, our teachers when asked how they had learned something responded only by giving more detail about what they had learned, as they had difficulty perceiving the process. When asked again, a common response was along the lines of, 'well it's just experience I suppose'. Where intentionality was involved, it was directed at task completion, not explicitly at learning. This is related to Schon's (1983) notion of reflection in action, which was ubiquitous and often subconscious, as opposed to reflection on action, which was more considered. Beckett and Hager (2002) prefer the notion of making embodied, or holistic judgements, within what Eraut (1994) terms 'hot action'. They distance themselves from the emphasis on the cerebral in Schon's use of the term 'reflection'.

We found many examples of type 3 in our data. Several history teachers saw the introduction of new textbooks, intended to be more user-friendly for the pupils, as something that had encouraged them to change and improve their practice. Two other teachers reported learning about classroom discipline. The first talked about learning things 'just by practice'. He explained that if an activity did not go well he might try it again with a different class. If it was again unsuccessful he would give it up and try something different: 'so it's a question of amending what you're doing and if you work on the basis that if it's interesting, the kids will enjoy it, then OK'. Similarly the second talked about how, as a result of trying many strategies over many years, 'gradually you start to realize' what works with particular age groups. This second teacher also talked of the sharing of ideas with other teachers, modelling others' practice, and reading books about teaching his subject both for enjoyment and information. This involved some facets of greater learning intentionality, as in type 4 learning (see below).

If we try to apply a scientific model to this sort of learning, we change its nature. For, in making indicators of successful learning explicit, type 3 learning becomes type 1 or type 4 (below). That is, a largely unplanned, ongoing activity becomes focused and goal-directed. A teacher may then be saying 'I need to learn how to improve my classroom discipline', rather than changing their approaches to their teaching, and learning about discipline incidentally. Alternatively, a researcher may select some possible outcomes to look for, but there is no reason why what is predicted should occur, and every reason to expect that other learning will occur, often without being recognized by the learner (or researcher) at the time. Thus, we might observe a teacher with some classroom control problems, and decide to measure his/her improvement. But if his/her learning is of type 3, we will not know whether or not he/she is modifying his/her practice in ways relevant to our externally determined target or not. Our measure tells us nothing useful, unless we change her/his learning to type 4, by making her/him aware that improving class control is something she/he should deliberately set out to do. This may be useful but does not stop the unplanned unmeasureable learning continuing.

4. Planned/intentional learning to modify existing capability

Sometimes experienced teachers do set out to consciously refine or improve what they do, without relying on a source of additional expertise (type 1). The head of music was continually striving to improve his own work and that of his departmental colleagues, through constructing opportunities to observe others teach, to share ideas and approaches, and work together on materials and resources. Often this was done with student teachers or teachers less experienced than himself. Beckett and Hager (2002) touch on aspects of this, within their category of *judgements within cold action*, as does Eraut (2000), when he writes of deliberative or analytic learning. In practice,

---

Box 15.2 The art department

The three teachers in the art department have worked together for 15 years. They share an enthusiasm for their subject and for teaching, and their courses are continually being developed and improved. This happens as they pick up on one another's ideas through chatting or through seeing the work in one another's classes. They spend most of the day in the art area. They take coffee breaks and lunch in the stock room when much of their time is spent discussing work. Unplanned learning is ubiquitous, but they are also keen to go on courses which help develop their artistic skills and to learn new ones which give them inspiration for new work with pupils. Two of them remember more theoretical educational courses, which influenced their teaching. They visit exhibitions and look at art in books and on the internet. They are unable to carry out these activities as often as they would like, because of restrictions of time and money.

Other learning arises from external pressures, from the school and the government. During our research they had to introduce literacy and numeracy strategies into art lessons; teach completely new courses to 16 to 19 year olds; operate a Performance Management system; and go through two years of on-line training for the use of computers in their teaching, despite having only one computer in the department, that was not even networked. After initial grumbles they chose to see the positive side of almost all of the things they had to do. Often, one of them would have a taught input about the implementation of the initiative, then there would be ongoing discussion, both structured and organic. Nevertheless they all said that the most important learning was trying things out for themselves.

---

type 4 is sometimes an extension of type 3. For example the second teacher discussing classroom discipline, above, talked not only about gradual realization, but also about deliberately analysing what has gone wrong.

At least in theory, because this type of learning is intentional, it should be possible to identify possible attainments, and search for indicators of their presence or absence. But to do so ignores additional unintended outcomes of learning, and the ways in which type 4 learning merges with other types, perhaps especially type 3, in the actual learning practices of workers. There may also be confounding variables. For example, a teacher may have actually improved his/her classroom control techniques through effective learning, but pupil behaviour actually worsened – for example because some pupils' behaviour has worsened in all lessons.

5. The intended/planned learning to do that which has not been done before

Often, modern workplaces require people to learn completely new things, and sometimes this learning is planned. Where this is examined in the literature, it is often described as the management of innovation or change, rather than learning. Yet this type of learning lies at the heart of calls for firms to become 'learning organizations' and of claims about the achievement of the 'high skills equilibrium' (Ashton and Green 1996). Recently, UK schoolteachers have faced a barrage of new tasks, procedures, curricula, assessments and goals.

A good example of planned innovation, for one school, was the introduction of a government required Performance Management scheme. The school strategy for dealing with this started with a speaker who could share some prior expertise (type 1) – a reminder that the categories presented here are neither mutually exclusive nor discrete, in practice. The actual implementation at school and departmental level was then a novel procedure, as they designed their individual ways of working the system. A second example was the introduction of new qualifications, curricula and exams for 16 to 19 year olds. It was essential for school and pupil success that teachers learnt to operate the new system quickly. There were departmental planning sessions. Teachers went on courses run by exam boards and fed back information to colleagues. This is not dissimilar to type 1 learning, except that not even the 'experts' leading the courses had actually taught or assessed this curriculum before. Not all the learning associated with these changes was planned (see type 6, below).

We have not found much research that focuses on how planned new learning happens. Engeström (1999, 2001) uses activity workshops to construct and lead planned learning. But what happens where his team is not on hand? Because this sort of new learning is intentional, it should be possible to identify some intended attainments, to the extent that this was advisable in type 4. However, to see the achievement of these as a measure of effective learning raises additional problems: how realistic were the intended attainments? What other factors, beyond learning, influenced the achievement, or not, of those attainments? What if the intended innovation that triggers the learning was badly designed? Thus, there were major problems with a new examination, during our field-work. Some of these problems were due to inadequate design features, or late arrival of specifications and support materials. How well such curricula were taught was a reflection of these problems in addition to the effectiveness of any associated teacher learning. The two sets of factors are impossible to separate out.

6. The unplanned learning of that which has not been done before

This happens when people deal with what are apparently new challenges as an ongoing part of their everyday lives. Sometimes, the answers may be known by others, but the learner behaves as if they were not. In other cases, the problem being addressed is entirely new – perhaps because of the particular setting in which it is encountered. An example from our research was learning to become a head of department. The head of history remembered the process well. Moving to a new school, he didn't know the systems there, didn't know his new colleagues and didn't know how his job there should be done. There were few opportunities to consult others who had faced similar situations. Other heads of department and senior management were helpful, but mainly if problems occurred. Basically it was a job he had to learn by doing – trying things out on the basis of previous knowledge, but in a new situation. At the same time he was expected to be an expert, giving a lead.

There are potential overlaps with all of the other five types of learning. A similar type of practical, unplanned process is involved as with types 2 and 3. In addition some advice may come from experts. The degree of delibera-tion varies, from person to person and from time to time. Sometimes groups of teachers may address a new challenge together. Part of the work towards meeting the demands of the new post-16 curriculum happened this way. One teacher explained that her department had looked at and discussed exemplar assessments, but they didn't really know how the course would work because they hadn't seen it in practice, and didn't know at what level to pitch the work. She stressed the need to be positive, remembering earlier initiatives which had caused great concern but where after a few years things were under control and working well.

This type of learning is more than an amalgam of the other types, and many current theoretical explanations of learning often appear to fall short in this area. For example, most learning theories developed to meet type 1 situations struggle to cope with uncertainty and the significance of the tacit. Situated cognition and cognitive apprenticeship theorizing, on the other hand, lays most emphasis on the sharing and passing on of known wisdom or cultural practices, rather than the tackling of something new. Change is often seen as small-scale variations on practice, evolving gradually over time (Lave and Wenger 1991; Wenger 1998). Billett (1998) follows others in seeing learning primarily as goal-directed activity of the problem-solving type. Perhaps from his perspective, what we have termed 'type 6' learning is simply a variation on this problem solving mode. Engeström (2001) recognizes the potential of contradictions as a stimulus for activity systems to learn and change, and novel situations sometimes throw up such contradictions. However, not all of the examples of new learning encountered by our subjects involved contradictions. It was simply that new challenges had to be met. In many cases, the resulting learning fell short of a significant change to the activity system of which the teachers were part. Type 6 learning is also very difficult to address through models of measured attainment and learning efficiency, for all the difficulties identified with the other types are compounded here.

Box 15.3 Michael

Michael was a teacher in mid-career. He was cynical about courses and training days. As a young teacher he had worked in a very successful middle school (pupils aged 8 to 13). He remembered a lot of collaborative learning amongst the teachers as they were able to keep changing and developing the curriculum according to their own ideas. Ten years ago the middle school was closed and Michael was redeployed to one of the secondary schools in our study. He had rapidly to learn to deal with many different pupil groups in a week instead of mainly one, to teach the same lesson several times, and to take on completely new tasks like exam invigilation. Learning to do this changed job was achieved by getting on with it and becoming part of a different culture. Michael is bitter about the way his redeployment came about, and never regained his enthusiasm for teaching, although he is hard-working and competent. He is irritated by the need to go to meetings, preferring to work things out for himself. He does learn as he teaches, making changes to what he does to suit different circumstances. He tries to avoid formal training arranged by the school. Recently he was asked to go on a course about the development of his subject for younger pupils. This time he found the experience stimulating, and came back keen to work with the rest of the department to implement changes. He said, 'The real learning starts now, as we put it all in place'.

Complexity in workplace learning: the dangers of reductionism

Thus far, we have argued that the assumption, that good research should clearly identify independent indicators of learner attainment, gives artificial pre-eminence to certain types of workplace learning, especially the planned types 1 and 4, at the expense of others which are arguably more common. This restriction of research would consequently limit the value of findings in understanding or improving workplace learning overall.

Our use of the typology can reveal further problems with a conventional objective scientific approach. Our approach thus far shares a characteristic with much conventional science – both are reductionist. That is, just as advocates of the superiority of experiment and randomized controlled trials (Oakley 2000) assume that truth can best be uncovered by abstracting one variable and holding the rest constant, our typology implies that these six different types of learning are separate from each other, and can be researched and understood separately. Yet the central argument of most research on workplace learning is that the partly context-specific relationships between different variables, or types of learning, are of fundamental importance (e.g. Darrah 1996).

In actual examples of learning revealed by our research, the types were seldom pure – as our vignettes show. Furthermore, there are other dimensions of learning types that could be added to the model, as extra axes, resulting in greater complexity, and category reductionism, at the same time. One such continuum from our data is that between learning that is voluntarily undertaken and initiated by the learner, and that which is imposed upon the learner. Such imposition can be explicit, as when the government required all teachers to undertake computer learning. It can also be implicit, as when the imposition of the new curriculum for 16 to 19 year olds pushed teachers into new learning. In the latter case, although the innovation and thus initial requirement to learn was imposed, the need to learn was taken on by the teachers and became something they wanted to do because they could not otherwise carry out their work properly and help their pupils gain exam success. It was both imposed and voluntary.

This third continuum demonstrates the limitations of our typology. It also reminds us of the significance of power differentials in workplace learning, which is acknowledged in some of the literature about learning. Billett (1998, 2000) for example, is quite clear that 'individuals' responses to problems are influenced by their standing in the workplace. Access to knowledge is therefore distributed differently within communities of practice' (Billett 1998: 263). Those with more power can impose learning, and they can also deny opportunities for learning. Those with less power may find access to what they want difficult. Two young teachers in our sample wanted more experience and knowledge of school-wide issues, but although they were apparently encouraged, they could not get past the school's organizational structures: they could not be members of the committees where

Box 15.4 Computer training for all

The English government required all teachers to go through a process of on-line training to become competent in using computers. Schools chose from several training providers, who produced subject-specific packages. All teachers had targets to meet, relating to time logged on to the packages, getting through the material and providing evidence of teaching-related computer use. One or two teachers claimed it would be easy to cheat the system for the first two targets, though it was not what they did. The initial attitude of many teachers to this imposed learning was negative. Some had more computer experience than others, but all had to complete the whole procedure. The start was too easy for some whilst others needed additional help. Some were intimidated by working in the computer rooms. By the end of the research everyone had made progress with computer skills, but it sometimes seemed to be in spite of rather than because of the training packages. One history teacher wanted to locate new resources and to learn new and interesting ways to work with the pupils. But he found the materials disappointing and sometimes inaccurate, and learned more from a book he bought. Another teacher, with some home computer knowledge, was extremely reluctant to take part. He knew that he would not retain what he learnt unless he put it into practice regularly, but there was no immediate likelihood of any on line classroom computers that he could use. The art teachers were keen to learn to use computers as an additional resource for their lessons. However they wanted to work within the art area, which required an on-line computer and some help, neither of which was available. One made progress by buying a computer at home. The most successful learning was in the music department. They subverted the school plan for all teachers to work in the computer suites for a day, and worked together at one of their homes. The youngest and most computer-literate department member guided them through the first few training modules, after which they all helped each other. They already had computers with specialist software in the department, for use by pupils and teachers. The two older teachers deliberately set out to practise their skills by doing tasks on the computer that they could have easily done other ways. The department also benefited from student teachers who were more up to date.

these issues were discussed. Teachers' past life histories and their dispositions to learning also strongly influenced the nature and types of learning they experienced (Hodkinson and Hodkinson 2003), as Michael's story shows.

Types of learning in the workplace cannot be artificially separated from the situation in which learning takes place (Brown *et al.* 1989). It is not just that workplace learning is always contextualized, but that the learning is a constitutive part of the context in which it is located. In other words, what Beckett and Hager (2002) term 'embodied judgement' is cultural and social. Furthermore, in most if not all workplaces, the key purposes of activity and the prime objectives of the participants are things other than their own learning. Consequently, even if 'attainments' could be clearly identified, they might better be described as the outcomes of existing or changed organizational practices, as opposed to more or less efficient learning.

The typology presented earlier carries within it another danger associated with its reductionism – it may seem to encourage the view that some of the types of learning are superior to others. This resurrects the problem with which we opened the chapter – how could we measure the 'effectiveness' of each type? This issue can be examined in a wider sense. For the ongoing debates about the competing metaphors of learning, acquisition and participation, is superimposed upon earlier characterizations of inherent superiority for formal as opposed to informal learning (Scribner and Cole 1973).

Within what Beckett and Hager (2002) term the 'standard paradigm of learning', lies a deeply held belief that the formal learning of propositional knowledge in educational settings is superior to everyday learning. This superiority supposedly arises from the status of the knowledge to be imparted, but also from claims that such learning is context free and, therefore, more easily generalizable and transferable to multiple settings (Resnick 1987). From this point of view, informal learning is regarded as localized and non-transferable. In terms of our typology, small parts of type 1 learning, plus even smaller parts of 4 and 5 are seen as inherently superior to everything else. One of the benefits of the typology is that it shows what a small part of workplace learning that is.

One way of understanding the burgeoning focus upon workplace learning as an example of informal learning, is as a reaction to this such thinking. Lave (1996) explicitly described the development of her research and theorizing in this way, and Beckett and Hager (2002) take a similar line, when juxtaposing their alternative ways of understanding embodied learning through judgement making, with the older 'standard paradigm'. This body of literature directly challenges the superiority of standard paradigm learning, often reversing the picture. The argument is that many people learn very effectively without formal educational systems. Also, in many ways and for many purposes, such as performance in a workplace or speaking a language, informal approaches are predominant. Finally, the presumed superiority of formal learning is based upon assumptions of disembodied and decontextualized learning that are misplaced. At this point, such theorists of workplace learning may themselves be criticized, because some workplaces and some jobs are structured in ways that greatly inhibit learning, and can reinforce undesirable practices – be that the use of older machines or the preservation of racist or sexist cultural values.

For us, the problem here is the polarization presented between formal and informal learning (Billett 2002; Colley *et al.* 2002). Lave and Wenger (1991) were right to remind us that many people learn very effectively without much formal learning. Such learners also transfer what they know into new contexts, and to meet new challenges. However, it remains true that many people, including the teachers in our study, did learn from formal education, in ways that they could identify as beneficial, and which often made a lasting difference to their sense of identity and to the ways in which they did the job. Consequently, we need to identify ways of understanding and theorizing workplace learning which do not denigrate either approach. We need to know more about the place of formal or off-the-job learning in relation to other forms of workplace learning, rather than seeing it as an inherently inferior alternative. In the terms of our typology, we need to understand planned learning not in isolation, but in relation to the rest.

Conclusion

In this chapter we have examined some of the difficulties with what might be termed 'a science of learning' in relation to the workplace. There are two root causes of those difficulties. The first lies in some of the assumptions of empiricist approaches to science, which privilege the isolation of variables whose impact can be measured, and assume that valid theories or findings should be generalizable in ways that are context free. The second lies in the complexity of workplace learning as a phenomenon. This includes all six of the types of learning identified in this chapter together with others, with combinations of these types inter-mixed in and across contexts. Consequently, methodologies should be employed which recognize and examine complex interrelationships, and avoid the biases introduced by empiricist reductionism, based upon a crude and literal version of the acquisition metaphor for learning.

There are also implications for our further understanding of learning. With regard to the latter, Sfard (1998: 12) argues that:

> We have to accept that the metaphors we use while theorising may be good enough to fit small areas, but none of them suffice to cover the entire field. In other words, we must learn to satisfy ourselves with only local sense-making. It seems that the sooner we accept the thought that our work is bound to produce a patchwork of metaphors, rather than a unified, homogeneous theory of learning, the better for us and for those whose lives are likely to be affected by our work.

We would add that, with regard to the workplace, participatory approaches seem to offer much more potential for understanding the complexity of learning than those based more strongly upon metaphors of acquisition and the standard paradigm of learning.

Bibliography

Ashton, D.N. and Green, F. (1996) *Education, Training and the Global Economy*, Cheltenham: Edward Elgar.

Beckett, D. and Hager, P. (2002) *Life, Work and Learning: Practice in Postmodernity*, London: Routledge.

Billett, S. (1998) 'Constructing Vocational Knowledge: Situations and Other Social Sources', *Journal of Education and Work*, 11 (3): 255–73.

—— (2000) 'Coparticipation at Work: Knowing and Work Practice', in F. Beven, C. Kanes and D. Roebuck (eds), *Learning Together: Working Together: Building Communities for the 21st Century*, vol. 1, Brisbane: Centre for Learning and Work Research, Griffith University.

—— (2002) 'Critiquing Workplace Learning Discourses: Participation and Continuity at Work', *Studies in the Education of Adults*, 34 (1): 56–67.

Bourdieu, P. (1998) *Practical Reason*, Cambridge: Polity Press.

Brown, J.S., Collins, A. and Duguid, P. (1989) 'Situated Cognition and the Culture of Learning', *Educational Researcher*, 18 (1): 32–42.

Brown, S. (1994) 'Student Teachers' Access to the Practical Classroom Knowledge of Experienced Teachers', in G. Harvard and P. Hodkinson (eds), *Action and Reflection in Teacher Education*, Norwood, NJ: Ablex.

Colley, H., Hodkinson, P. and Malcolm, J. (2002) *Non-formal Learning: Mapping the Conceptual Terrain: A Consultation Report*, Leeds: Lifelong Learning Institute, University of Leeds.

Darrah, C.N. (1996) *Learning and Work: An Exploration into Industrial Ethnography*, New York and London: Garland Publishing.

Engeström, Y. (1999) 'Activity Theory and Individual and Social Transformation', in Y. Engeström, R. Miettinen and R. Punamaki (eds), *Perspectives on Activity Theory*, Cambridge: Cambridge University Press.

—— (2001) 'Expansive Learning at Work: Towards an Activity-Theoretical Reconceptualisation', *Journal of Education and Work*, 14 (1): 133–56.

Eraut, M. (1994) *Developing Professional Knowledge and Competence*, London: Falmer Press.

—— (2000) 'Non-formal Learning, Implicit Learning and Tacit Knowledge', in F. Coffield (ed.), *The Necessity of Informal Learning*, Bristol: Policy Press.

Eraut, M., Alderton, J., Cole, G. and Senker, P. (2000) 'Development of Knowledge and Skills at Work', in F. Coffield (ed.), *Differing Visions of a Learning Society*, Bristol: Policy Press.

Feuer, M.J., Towne, L. and Shavelson, R.J. (2002) 'Scientific Culture and Educational Research', *Educational Researcher*, 31 (8): 4–14.

Fuller, A. and Unwin, L. (1998) 'Reconceptualising Apprenticeship: Exploring the Relationship between Work and Learning', *Journal of Vocational Education and Training*, 50 (2): 153–71.

Hillage, J., Pearson, R., Anderson, A. and Tamkin, P. (1998) *Excellence in Schools*, London: Institute for Employment Studies.

Hodkinson, P. and Hodkinson, H. (2003) 'Individuals, Communities of Practice and the Policy Context: Schoolteachers' Learning in their Workplace', *Studies in Continuing Education*, 25 (1): 3–21.

Lave, J. (1996) 'Teaching as Learning in Practice', *Mind, Culture and Society*, 3 (3): 149–64.

Lave, J. and Wenger, E. (1991) *Situated Learning*, Cambridge: Cambridge University Press.

Oakley, A. (2000) *Experiments in Knowing: Gender and Method in the Social Sciences*, London: Polity Press.

Resnick, L.B. (1987) 'Learning in School and Out', *Educational Researcher*, 16 (9): 13–20.

Schon, D.A. (1983) *The Reflective Practitioner*, New York: Basic Books.

Scribner, S. and Cole, M. (1973) 'Cognitive Consequences of Formal and Informal Education', *Science*, 182: 553–9.

Sfard, A. (1998) 'On Two Metaphors for Learning and the Dangers of Choosing Just One', *Educational Researcher*, 27 (2): 4–13.

Stenhouse, L. (1975) *An Introduction to Curriculum Research and Development*, London, Heinemann.

Wenger, E. (1998) *Communities of Practice: Learning, Meaning, and Identity*, Cambridge: Cambridge University Press.

Wertsch, J.V. (1998) *Mind as Action*, Oxford: Oxford University Press.

Part 4

Research and policy

16 Evidence-based policy or policy-based evidence?

The struggle over new policy for workforce development in England

Frank Coffield

Chapter summary

This chapter provides an account of the latest official attempt in England to generate both a new analysis of the underlying causes of under-investment in workforce development and a new policy to rectify the weaknesses. The account is based on the participation of the present author who was a member of the Performance and Innovation Unit's (PIU) Academic Panel on workforce development during 2001. First, the general relationships between research and policy are discussed and the proposal made that there are occasions when it is appropriate for researchers to develop policies *counter* to those being pursued by government. The establishment and remit of the PIU are then briefly introduced, and the methods and outcomes from the particular project on workforce development are described and assessed. The separate normative worlds of policy-makers and researchers are then explored; some general conclusions are drawn about the competing models of Britain's future, which lie behind the policy debates; and finally a few reflections are offered on some of the dangers of evidence-based policy and of the new partnership between government and researchers.

Introduction

It is an opportune time to study the relationship between research and policy, because in England we are currently witnessing the emergence of a new orthodoxy – evidence-based (or in later formulations 'evidence-informed') policy and practice. David Blunkett, a former Secretary of State for Education and Employment, in a lecture where he argued for 'a revolution in the relations between government and the research community', began by describing the former Department of Education and Science as a 'knowledge-free zone'. He then committed the government to 'be guided not by dogma but by an open-minded approach to understanding what works and why...using information and knowledge much more effectively and creatively at the heart of policy making and policy delivery' (2000:

1–2). The question remains of just how open-minded the government is when confronted with 'difficult' findings or radical, alternative policies.

An appropriate starting point is the threefold classification of the roles research can play in the policy cycle which has been offered by Furlong and White (2001). They argued that research can be used:

- as part of the planning of policy by, for example, putting issues on the agenda, identifying what information is needed by policy-makers and by reviewing what is already known;
- as part of the development of policy by, for instance, piloting initiatives and devising curriculum materials;
- as part of the evaluation of policy by finding out what works and what does not and by using evidence of success and failure in future policy.

Interestingly, Raffe has also proposed that research can play three roles with regard to policy, but only his first – finding out what works – corresponds with the third role, the evaluation of policy, in Furlong and White's scheme. The two further roles for research, according to Raffe, are that it can give policy-makers the conceptual tools to help their decision-making as well as 'analyse critically the goals, motivations, assumptions and strategies of policy' (2002: 7). Furthermore, the Organization for Economic Co-operation and Development (OECD), in its review of educational research and development in England, argued for more basic research that simultaneously sought fundamental understanding and was inspired by applied problems (2002: 8). These are all important purposes for research to carry out, but do they go far enough?

As a result of the experience of being involved in the development of new policy on workforce development, the present author would like to suggest another, perhaps more committed, role for research. In an area where governments repeatedly set aside inconvenient findings, perhaps researchers should take it upon themselves to produce evidence-informed counter policies, not only to stimulate debate but also to offer alternative and more radical visions of the future. Examples of such counter-policy already exist: for instance, Edwards and Tomlinson, after reviewing the evidence that specialist secondary schools in England are not working, make a series of alternative recommendations which they claim are desirable, practical and politically feasible (2002: 38). The proposal made here is that it is incumbent on researchers, and particularly on those who are used as consultants by policy-makers, to argue for democratic, socially just and, where appropriate, radical policy. This topic will be returned to in the concluding section once an account has been given of the PIU's review of workforce development.

This chapter begins with a detailed account of the interactions between those researchers and policy-makers who were brought together by the British government's Performance and Innovation Unit (PIU) to analyse the causes of Britain's continuing failure to invest in training and to develop a new policy to rectify historical weaknesses. This is followed by some reflections on what the author has learned about the new partnership between government and researchers. It then considers some of the dangers of evidence-informed policy and the new roles which researchers and policy-makers may need to adopt.

PIU review of workplace development

The PIU was created by the Prime Minister in July 1998:

> to improve the capacity of government to address strategic, cross-cutting issues and promote innovation in the development of policy and in the delivery of the government's objectives. The PIU is part of the drive for better, more joined-up government.
>
> (PIU 2001b: 115)

The unit, directed by Geoff Mulgan, reports to the Prime Minister, who thereby receives another stream of policy recommendations, independent from the Departments of State. As director of the PIU he reports directly to the Prime Minister through the Cabinet Secretary; he has also been appointed to lead the Strategy Unit, which 'will do blue skies policy thinking for the Prime Minister' (PIU 2001a: 115). More than 15 projects have already been carried out by the PIU on such themes as improving analysis and modelling in central government. In late 2000 the PIU began to commission officials from government departments, as well as specialists on secondment from the private sector to examine workforce development.[1] The team was formed by April 2001 and its remit was – within a period of six months – to make a strong case for the benefits of workforce development; to analyse the roles of government, employers and individuals; and to recommend both an holistic set of practical policies and a strategy agreed by all the key stakeholders.

A number of important issues were omitted from the review; e.g. the policy of raising the participation rate in higher education to 50 per cent by 2010; the new structures of the Learning and Skills Council (which was established in 2000 to create a coherent system for post-16 learning, apart from higher education); and the reform of qualifications, especially vocational qualifications.

One question which remains unanswered is why it was thought necessary (and by whom) to initiate the PIU enquiry when the Department for Education and Employment (DfEE) had set up a National Skills Task Force (NSTF), which had just produced detailed proposals for a national skills agenda based on a very comprehensive set of reports. Either the Prime Minister's office was dissatisfied with the proposals of the Task

Force or it wished to wrest control of the issue from the DfEE and other Departments; or a report from the PIU is now the way to speed up the development of new policies by avoiding the in-fighting between Departments; but this is conjecture.

Reviewing the evidence

An overview of the literature on workforce development was commissioned by the Unit from Coleman and Keep (2001). More specific reviews were produced on *Lessons Learnt from Overseas Experience* by Ashton and Sung (2001); *The Economic Benefits of Training to the Individual, the Firm and the Economy* by Machin and Vignoles (2001); and *Motivation for Workforce Development: The Role of National Culture* by Guest (2001). These reviews collectively provided a well-balanced summary of the research literature, of the main gaps in knowledge and of the general implications for policy.

Coleman and Keep produced the most comprehensive and sharply worded of the four reviews. The scale of the problem in the UK is presented starkly; e.g. data from the 1998 Labour Force Survey recorded that '72 per cent of the UK employees had received no training in the 13 weeks prior to interview. Of these, just under half (48 per cent) claimed that they had never been offered any type of training by their current employer' (Coleman and Keep 2001: 28). But these statistics, which underline the historical under investment in training by British employers, are not used to support the main plank in official policy, namely, that skills are the only route to increasing productivity: 'Rather than seeing skills as THE key to competitive success, it might be more realistic to view upskilling as simply one model vying for senior managers' attention in a market place for ideas' (ibid.: 10, original emphasis).

In sum, the analysis of the existing evidence challenged some of the fundamental assumptions which have underpinned official UK policy in this area for a generation. To move away from what appeared to outsiders as a single-minded concentration on increasing the supply of skills required both a major revision in the way the problems are conceived and a complete overhaul of a confusing battery of policies. The four academic reviews provided policy-makers with more help with the former than with the latter task. Indeed, most researchers are far better at identifying gaps in knowledge than at explaining the implications of research findings in ways which would enable policy-makers to revise existing policies or devise new ones.

The administrators in the PIU team agreed that policy had indeed become dominated by too many supply-side approaches, not because policy had become permeated with some overarching orthodoxy but because such approaches are the easier policy levers to pull.

At the same time as these academic reviews of the literature were being written, the civil servants produced successive drafts of the main report which analysed the underlying causes of under-involvement in workforce development and outlined a vision of the future. The scope of the consultations undertaken by the PIU team deserves to be emphasized; e.g. they talked to over 150 individuals in a variety of relevant organizations, commissioned seven focus groups of employers and of individuals and contacted six teams concerned with the same topic, such as the Department of Trade and Industry's Skills and Education group. In addition, the PIU team was advised by an academic panel of 12 specialists whose function was to challenge the ideas for new policy generated by the PIU team. Oversight of the whole project was managed by a group of 15 senior stakeholders from industry, the trade unions and government ministries. The work of all PIU teams is also overseen by a government minister and in this case the sponsor minister was John Healey, who was at the time the Minister for Adult Skills in England. The role of all these groups was to act as a reality check and to ensure that the team's conclusions were rooted in evidence.

By the end of August 2001, the main report, which had by then been posted on the PIU website to elicit further comment, amounted to over 80 pages and five annexes. Evidence-based policy analysis, it can be said, was carried out in an exemplary, open and thorough way and the quality of the main report reflected these extensive consultations. One major task remained – the development of policy options which were firmly grounded in the analytical conclusions.

Before an assessment of the Analysis Paper is offered, an indication needs to be given of the level of involvement of the present author. All of the commissioned papers and each version of the main report were made available to him, together with other internal, working papers. He also took part in the meetings of the academic panel which on each occasion commented critically on the team's analyses, challenged thinking which was inconsistent with the evidence, and offered both orally and in writing alternative interpretations and policy options. An attempt is made throughout to differentiate between ideas presented by the PIU team, suggestions from the Academic Panel and the author's personal commentary.

Processes

The methods adopted by the PIU team on workforce development amount to a transformation of the relationship between policy-makers and researchers, particularly from the time when a junior Minister of Education in a Conservative administration, Eric Forth, claimed: 'We don't need research to tell us what to do, we know that already' (quoted by Kogan 1999: 11). Within a few years the climate changed from one where researchers were excluded from policy-making because they were deemed irrelevant and ideologically biased, to one where a Secretary of State for Education offered them 'a genuine partnership and interchange between the worlds of policy and research'

(Blunkett 2000: 20). Since 1997 there has been a marked change in the value placed upon research by politicians and policy-makers: two examples are the establishment of dedicated research centres (e.g. on the Economics of Education) and of a National Educational Research Forum. The PIU report on workforce development provides the latest test of the government's capacity to give serious consideration to difficult findings, especially in an area where powerful interests lobby hard to have their definition of reality accepted.

One of the PIU's advantages, according to Keep, is that 'it comes to the topic as an outsider, without the accumulated "baggage" that ownership of (and therefore the need to protect) earlier departmental policies tends to bring' (2001: 2). Somewhat to the surprise of the present author, the task (or the pleasure) of asking awkward questions or of thinking the unthinkable was not the sole prerogative of the researchers. Indeed, members of the PIU team took the lead at meetings in challenging some of the fundamental assumptions on which much current policy and practice are based and academics were at times 'pushed hard' to justify or explain inequities or anomalies. Penetrating questions were used to sharpen the group's growing understanding of the complexities of workforce development and to explore the main weaknesses within the field. Three examples are given here: 'If the workforce development system is not performing well, who gets the sack?', 'Are targets the best way of achieving outcomes?' and 'How do existing or recommended policies increase the *demand* for skills?'

The discussions were not constrained by any 'no-go areas'. The iterative process of producing draft after draft of the Analysis Paper not only succeeded in involving large numbers of expert commentators, it also served to drive up the quality of the analysis as more evidence was assessed and incorporated into the argument. The approach was at all times open, although it was evident from the beginning that the PIU team was nervous about the political implications of the more radical suggestions for policy from the academics. The iterative process also carried the risk of a slow regression to less radical and less controversial policy recommendations. It was not the case that radical solutions could not be mentioned by the academics: they were but they were met by silence and so alternative futures dropped out of the conversation because no one pursued them. The academics re-introduced the unwelcome topics at subsequent meetings: they were heard politely but neither listened to nor engaged with. They did not employ 'pre-emptive suppression – the avoidance of conclusions too politically "difficult" to be worth the trouble' (Edwards 2003: 7–8).

Outcomes

The Analysis Paper represents a breakthrough from previous official thinking which had become highly focused on increasing the supply of skills and qualifications as a monocausal prescription for economic success. In the

Analysis Paper the causes of the British problem are identified as a complex mix of economic, social, historical and cultural influences. In particular, a combination of market failures (e.g. 'poaching' of skilled workers, poor information on the benefits of training) and government failures (e.g. the lack of a national strategy, under-investment in education and training, the plethora of poorly designed interventions) have created systemic sclerosis where most British firms are stuck in a 'low-skills equilibrium, in which the majority of enterprises staffed by poorly trained managers and workers produce low-quality goods and services' (Finegold and Soskice 1991: 215).

This thesis was first enunciated by Finegold and Soskice as far back as 1988, when they argued that 'a self-reinforcing network of societal and state institutions...interact to stifle the demand for improvements in skills levels' (1991). The significance of their argument is that, if political and economic institutions are jointly held responsible for the 'low skills equilibrium', then it makes little sense to blame the systemic failure on only one constituent partner – the education and training system – and to attempt to remedy only its deficiencies by introducing new policy initiatives. It makes even less sense to blame individual workers for not investing in their own human capital; and yet that has been the approach adopted by both Conservative and Labour administrations for over 20 years. All the other institutions and factors which are intimately bound up in Britain's continuing failure to train have until now been omitted from the analysis. These include: the industrial relations system, the financial markets, under-investment in research and development, the political culture, the organization of work practices within firms, employers' strategies for product innovation and competition, management training, and the use of new technologies.

The advance made by the PIU team lies in their explicit acknowledgement that such causal complexity requires an holistic response because it is no longer sufficient to raise the supply of skills. Instead, as they argue, 'Action is needed simultaneously on a number of fronts' (PIU 2001a: 23), which includes raising the demand for higher skills. We appear to have reached the position where *policy-makers* have become convinced of the need to bring the demand and supply of skills into greater harmony, but *politicians* remain wedded to a more simplistic view: witness the claim by Margaret Hodge, the then Minister for Lifelong Learning and Higher Education in England: 'If we want to close the productivity gap, we must close the skills gap' (2001). Moreover, some employers have used the new terminology of 'high-performance work organizations' to usher in a 'lean and mean' redundancy culture as the way to increase productivity.

The scale of the mismatch between the supply and demand for skills has recently been emphasized by a national survey of the skills of British workers. Felstead (2001) has shown that there is a gross deficiency in demand from employers at level 3 qualifications. In more detail, almost three million people with either academic or vocational qualifications equivalent to A level (i.e. level 3) held jobs which did not need that qualification. The policy implication is that producing more and more people with intermediate skills is only half of the equation and urgent attention is needed by employers to improve the quality of jobs on offer to such people. The problem is *not* the low motivation of employees to train but the poor quality of their jobs.

The current battery of government measures has been criticized by the present author and the following comments represent the views of this ex-adviser.[2] In the field of workforce development alone, the third Annex of the Analysis Paper lists no less than 45 current initiatives – a triumph of creativity over coherence. The list also makes clear that most government funding is devoted to increasing the commitment of *individuals* to training; e.g. over £1 billion has been spent on the New Deal for Young People, whereas the Council for Excellence in Management and Leadership has received less than £1 million.

The concern is not only the sheer number of initiatives which means that finite resources are severely stretched, every new initiative has to compete with those already operating in a complex and confusing system which makes evaluation of any one initiative virtually impossible. Some of them are mutually inconsistent and contradictory and others are not sustained over time. The responsibility for assessing their effectiveness is shared among five different ministries, each working through numerous central, regional and local intermediaries. Our short-term political culture also means that ministers want an initiative attached to their names and there have been four Ministers for Lifelong Learning in England in the four years since 1997. What is needed is a Lifelong Minister for Learning.

A further weakness has been the failure to gather, analyse and act upon feedback on these initiatives from workplaces, especially from smaller firms. Instead of one coherent and easily understood system, policy on workforce development is at present an ill co-ordinated accumulation of supply-side initiatives which have not, and will not, release Britain from the low skills trap. At the very least, some co-ordination and rationalization of all these government measures needs to take place, with priority accorded to those which concentrate on improving the performance of firms.

A more ambitious programme, however, would detail a set of policy options which responded appropriately to the whole range of underlying and interacting causes. In other words, the recommendations for policy should flow from the analysis of the evidence, although it is recognized that other important factors such as cost, feasibility, interactions with other priorities and possible unintended consequences also need to be taken into consideration in the development of new policies. As a result, David Hargreaves, in response to criticism, suggests that we should speak of 'evidence-*informed*, not evidence-based, policy or practice. Policy-makers cannot always postpone their decision-making until the evidence is in, and even when it is, they are constrained in their decisions by much other knowledge in their possession and by many factors concerned with public perceptions and political consequences' (2001: 204, original emphasis). In sum, policy-making is a complex brew of possibilities, personalities, presentation, political judgement, cost constraints and 'deliverability'. In this mix, the evidence from research is only one, and by no means the most powerful, ingredient.

The different normative worlds of researchers and policy-makers

Effective change, as Fullan (1991) has argued, takes both time and persistence. Change also involves altering deeply held beliefs and accepting that previously unquestioned assumptions need to be discarded if found wanting. We live, for example, in a culture which celebrates individualism and so it is no surprise that, of the 45 initiatives on workforce development, most are directed at changing the behaviour of individuals. This cultural and political mindset exerted an enduring influence within the PIU team, even when it was challenged. For example, at meetings between members of the PIU team and of the academic panel, the latter tended to think they had won the argument in favour of changing the focus of policy from the training of *individuals* to strategies for improving the performance of *organizations*. Some weeks later, the PIU team issued an updated version of the analysis paper which was meant to reflect the conclusions of the earlier discussions and the revised vision statement read 'We should be a society in which employees receive opportunities to develop at their place of work and elsewhere...'. The project's vision continued to develop and a later version read: In 2010, the UK will be a society where Government, employers and individuals will actively engage in skills development to deliver sustainable economic success for all.'

What also became clear at the meetings was that policy-makers and researchers inhabit two separate 'normative worlds' with different goals, constraints and sensitivities, and different timescales, agendas and audiences for their work (see Bell and Raffe 1991). It was not so much a case of researchers 'speaking truth to power' (Coffield 1999), nor of researchers possessing 'a superior "truth"; rather they bring a different kind of knowledge to policy-making' (Edwards 2000: 305). At their worst, researchers exercise an enviable but impotent freedom to float radical, uncosted proposals which could, if acted upon, de-stabilize the system. At times they offer generalized advice which is too remote from the messy world of policy-making to be practically useful. They leave conflicting evidence for policy-makers to wrestle with; and they have been known to argue for different interpretations of the same evidence. At their best, researchers insist on evidence for claims of success, they insist on complex and interactive issues being treated as such, they argue for policies commensurate with the underlying causes, they offer theoretical understanding which can improve the quality of the thinking and decision-making of policy-makers, and they point to potential pitfalls, e.g. human capital accounting would identify all the costs of training and so may lead to some firms *reducing* their training budgets rather than increasing them.

Academics also need to appreciate the unwritten 'rules' concerning confidentiality and discretion which administrators adhere to. Modern government operates under intense media interest where leaks are highly prized. No matter how open policy-makers may want to be, they must weigh up carefully the danger of ministerial trust being betrayed. Once that trust is lost, it may be extremely hard, if not impossible, to regain it.

While researchers are able to argue for the unthinkable, policy-makers have to work within the parameters set by others. The 'steer' given by politicians or senior officials can be so powerful as to rule out certain options. Policy-makers are in the business of pushing for as much change as they think they can get away with. The danger with the 'strong steer', however, is that policy-makers may try to second guess the wishes of ministers and so only present what they think is wanted.

In the judgement of the present author, policy-makers find great difficulty in taking seriously 'awkward' findings which either reveal the superficiality of previous government policies, contradict the prejudices of the current minister, or are judged by them to be politically inadmissible. Unwelcome evidence may be heard but not acted upon. The first loyalty of civil servants is to their minister rather than to knowledge or social justice: 'The minister is likely to consider these findings unhelpful'. The dedication of the British civil service to ministers and to the public good more generally was, however, clearly shown by the policy-makers in the PIU team, who regularly worked under intense pressure to meet government deadlines.

Such loyalty at times leads policy-makers to worry about research which produces the 'wrong' finding, i.e. independent researchers may provide sound evidence which does not, however, support some initiative which the minister is determined to introduce. The worry for the scientific community is that civil servants may commission researchers, who are already publicly identified with a policy initiative favoured by the minister, and can therefore be relied upon to come up with the 'right' result. More often administrators are caught in the middle between researchers and politicians e.g. the minister welcomes research findings which are consonant with the general direction in which she/he wants policy to move, but ignores or 'rubbishes' disconfirming findings.

One of the difficulties for researchers who want to establish good working relationships with civil servants arises when their evidence indicates that the minister's shiny new policy is causing more problems than it is solving. The obvious danger for researchers is that by participating in policy-making they become incorporated and made safe. An alternative approach was successfully adopted in the 1970s by the New Right who redefined, outside of the normal policy channels, what was both thinkable and politically feasible.

Further difficulties confront both researchers and policy-makers, for instance, it is often extremely difficult to work out the policy implications of particular research findings. Moreover, there exist so many serious gaps in our knowledge that it is frequently not possible to offer any advice to policy-makers on particular issues.

In sum, researchers value independence, criticality, open debate, objectivity and holistic approaches to complex problems, but policy-makers have to learn the art of political compromise. Chisholm, who has experience of both trades of research and policy-making, offers two arguments which help to explain the gaps between the perspectives of researchers and policy-makers: 'Science is not politics – the first seeks feasible truths through the systematic interrogation of different positions, the second seeks a workable consensus from the palette of divergent interests' (2001: 1).

Conflicting visions of the future

The work of the PIU team on workforce development suggests that evidence-informed *analysis* of policy is not only possible but is taking place. Whether the advances in official thinking contained in that analysis can now be translated into evidence-informed *policy* remains to be seen. The prize to be grasped here is the development of a set of policies which respond appropriately to the analysis of the key weaknesses.

It is, however, worth reflecting on the time it has taken (13 years) for the thesis that the majority of British firms are trapped in a 'low skills equilibrium' to become an accepted part of the government's explanation for Britain's relatively low productivity. The example of workforce development requires a modification of the management cliché that 'change is a process, not an event' (Fullan 1991: 49). Changing the understanding of the problem has proved to be an extremely long-drawn out process and changing policy to match the new understanding is likely to take even longer. The only people who will gain from another decade of dithering are our industrial competitors who watch with increasing incredulity another manifestation of the English 'disease': yet another round of institutional re-structuring without radical reform. This example of research taking 13 years to become accepted should also be noted by those evaluators who seek to assess the impact of research in the months immediately following publication.

The evidence-informed analysis of British weaknesses in workforce development has now been undertaken. What, however, are the prospects of a corresponding advance in evidence-informed policy? Three possible outcomes are briefly considered.

First, incisive and comprehensive analysis may still result in blunt and piecemeal policies. The involvement of academics may be used to legitimate a safe set of policy recommendations, where voluntarism remains enshrined, unassailable and non-negotiable. Some limited, incremental progress could be achieved by, for instance, rationalizing the current battery of initiatives on workforce development or by targeting particular programmes more accurately (Owens 2001). Such a timid approach, is, however, very unlikely to pull the UK economy out of the low skills trap.

Second, ten years ago when the Training and Enterprise Councils (TECs) were being set up, the present author argued as follows: 'If, for whatever reason, voluntarism is given every chance to succeed and the TECs still fail, then what can voluntarism do as an encore? Will the government be driven to introduce legislation?' (Coffield 1992: 29). The TECs failed to secure the commitment of employers to workforce development by voluntary means and that failure was publicly acknowledged in their replacement by the Learning and Skills Councils. Yet voluntarism remains the preferred option of the New Labour government. Those in favour of regulation argue that it is the role of government to stand up to powerful vested interests on behalf of the community as a whole, but it is not admitted widely enough that the opposition from employers' organizations would be formidable. The Confederation of British Industry (CBI) was opposed to the government's rather modest proposal to give statutory rights to union learning representatives, warning it would add to the 'regulatory burden' carried by firms (see Rana 2001). The CBI is a powerful lobby group; and under Conservative administrations in the 1980s and 1990s 'civil servants…showed a consistent tendency to follow CBI recommendations on quite specific matters of policy' (Wolf 1998: 225). What became established in those years was the unshakeable consensus that 'economic competitiveness was directly and strongly related to education and training levels' (ibid.: 221). Politics remains the art of the possible and the judgement of the leaders of the New Labour government appears to be that a confrontation with employers over regulation may result in more political harm than economic advantage, as well as damaging Britain's reputation as the most flexible labour market apart from the USA. And they may be right.

Fortunately a third way still remains open. In this approach government proposes a new national settlement, a historical compromise between itself, employers and the trade unions in order to secure for the nation the joint goals of increasing economic prosperity and social inclusion. Instead of a policy of either minimal change (option 1 above which shirks the necessary systemic change) or of regulation (option 2 above which is highly likely to lead to protracted public conflict), all policies on workforce development are graded from the least to the most interventionist. Agreement between the social partners (employers, trade unions and government) is an essential feature of the new settlement and it may be possible to secure a willingness to increase the level of intervention only when less radical measures are shown to be ineffective. The social benefits of such an approach are likely to far outweigh the social costs which could be mitigated by government intervention.

So the least contentious proposals are introduced first (e.g. a rationalization of existing provision, including current funding systems); then a range
of intermediate measures are tried (e.g. fiscal incentives to encourage
employers to improve performance). Instead of intervention, government
seeks to influence the debates within firms, e.g. by enabling firms to
improve performance, to change their product strategies and to view
training as an investment rather than as a cost. Employers could use the
opportunity to insist on reform of the massively complicated assessment of
training associated with National Vocational Qualifications. Only if these
approaches fail would there be recourse to compulsion. Such a strategy needs
an initial acceptance by all the social partners that regulation becomes a
legitimate option when all else has been tried and been seen to fail. The
incentive would then exist for those who wish to avoid compulsion to work
for the success of other less drastic measures, but the threat of the 'ultimate
deterrent' of compulsion may need to exist for significant change to take
place. The key ingredients of this third way are high trust relationships
between the social partners, a graded sequence of policy options in
increasing order of state intervention and an agreed timetable for action.
Lloyd and Payne argue that the construction of a high skills, high wage
project in the UK should not depend on some such 'nebulous consensus',
but requires instead:

> radical economic and social modernisation, along with major changes in
> the institutional and industrial policy framework, as well as a shift in
> the balance of power between capital and labour at the level of both the
> workplace and state policy.
>
> (2002a: 368)

In another article they argue for 'a strengthened labour movement capable of
imposing a new competitiveness contract on the reluctant capital' (2002b:
386). The requirement is not nebulous but it is so improbable that their
valuable critique is likely to be dismissed out of hand.

What lies behind these debates are two competing models of Britain's
future, the Anglo-Saxon and the European. The Anglo-Saxon neo-liberal
approach puts its trust in the free, unregulated and flexible market, in ever
greater inequalities in income and wealth in order to encourage competitiveness, in mass higher education, some of it of dubious quality, and in welfare
to work policies which do not 'distinguish between good and bad jobs'
(Tessa Jowell, then Minister for Employment, quoted by Westwood, 2001).
The Anglo-Saxon model also privileges human over social capital, with low
trust in professionals working in the public sector who are subjected to
punitive forms of audit. Its main features are the presence of a strong business elite, a weak state, weak labour organizations and the market is left to
co-ordinate the supply and demand of skills.

In contrast, the European social model celebrates consensus among the social partners, funds social welfare at higher levels than in the UK, treats the twin policy goals of employability and active citizenship as equally significant and interdependent, and views social exclusion as a multi-dimensional and *structural* phenomenon. In brief, the European social model is based on a strong state, collaboration between business and labour, strong institutional arrangements and a regulated market.

Both models are considered by their supporters as possible routes out of the 'low skills equilibrium' and both have distinctive strengths and weaknesses. The Anglo-Saxon free market model is more innovative, creates more new jobs and suffers from lower rates of unemployment. It also fosters higher levels of self-employment and inward investment. In contrast, the European social model achieves higher levels of spending on social welfare, is more socially inclusive and has an employment strategy based on high skills and high wages. Critics of the Anglo-Saxon model question the quality of many of the new jobs created, while critics of the European social model point to its inflexibility, higher social costs and higher levels of unemployment.

The policy choices currently being made by the New Labour government indicate that the Anglo-Saxon rather than the European model is being pursued. Certainly, the continuing expansion of higher education will please middle-class voters whose children are the main beneficiaries; but increasing social and economic polarization, which is a concomitant of the Anglo-Saxon approach, is likely to be rejected by the majority of voters in Scotland, Wales and English regions like the North East. What the UK needs, however, is neither the Anglo Saxon nor the European social model but a strategy which incorporates the strengths of both, avoids their weaknesses, and responds to our own history, institutions and values.

The above was written before the publication in November 2001 of the Pre-Budget Report (HMT 2001) and of the final version of the PIU report (PIU 2001b). The former emphasized the government's determination to bring European economic policy more in line with the Anglo-Saxon model by 'removing unnecessary or over-burdensome regulation...[and] labour market reforms' (HMT 2001: para. 3: 14). The PIU document is at pains to underline that it is 'a report to the Government about Workforce Development. It is not a statement of Government policy' (PIU 2001b: 3). Instead of proposing specific recommendations, the PIU report considered the advantages and disadvantages of a wide range of different options which were then subjected to consultation inside government and beyond. In short, the government postponed making decisions. It bought time to win over employers to the notion of a statutory entitlement to paid educational leave by running a series of pilots. In the meantime it 'strongly supports' (HMT 2001: para. 3: 92) the PIU's conclusion that stimulating demand should be the key objective of a new strategy for workforce development.

The PIU report, entitled *In Demand: Adult Skills in the 21st Century*, was published in December 2001 and contained some surprises; e.g. the definition of workforce development in the report reads as follows: 'Workforce development consists of activities which increase the capacity of *individuals* to participate effectively in the workplace, thereby improving their productivity and employability' (PIU 2001b: 6, emphasis added).

So at the eleventh hour, after the meetings with the academic panel were over and during the period when a presentation of the PIU team's new strategy was made to the Prime Minister and his advisers, the definition of workforce development changed back from being a structural problem to being an individual one. Why was the definition changed and by whom?

The story updated

In April 2002 a joint HM Treasury/DfES report issued details of the six Employer Training Pilots, which were introduced 'to test a new policy model to support training for low-skilled people in the workforce' (2002: 21). The pilots offer free basic skills and level 2 courses of either 35 or 70 hours of paid leave each year to low-skilled employees. The pilots operate on a voluntary basis, although the PIU had argued that a statutory right to study leave could be a way of overcoming time barriers to training. The Treasury/DfES report argued that this new approach to skills policy 'places demand at the centre' (ibid.: 22), but it devoted a whole chapter to 'The Challenge to the Supply Side' without a corresponding chapter on the challenge to the demand side.

In November 2002, the PIU, now renamed the Strategy Unit, presented an action plan for policy in England and gave details of three key targets in this area:

- to reduce by 40 per cent the number of employees without level 2 qualifications by 2010;
- to improve the basic skills level of 1.5 million adults by 2007;
- 28 per cent of young people to start on a Modern Apprenticeship by 2004 and a wider vocational target to be devised by 2010.

These proposals were introduced not least because 'UK society cannot be inclusive, if over a third of the workforce have few or no skills and qualifications' (HM Treasury/DfES 2002: 20). The concern remains, however, that the action plan details 31 new initiatives for workforce development, but there is still no target for increasing the engagement of employers in training or for improving the performance of firms.

The Learning and Skills Council (LSC) also published its strategy in November 2002 and claimed that workforce development is at the heart of its remit and that it is committed to devising 'a new measure, and ultimately a target, for the level of engagement in workforce development amongst employers' (LSC 2002: 6). Meanwhile, as before, the pressure will be on providers to meet performance indicators and benchmarks.

These official documents reveal some advances in thinking but contain nevertheless the seeds of continuing failure. First, the texts have learned to talk the language of demand, but policy remains overwhelmingly concentrated on limited, voluntary supply-side initiatives. The aim is for 16,000 individuals nationally to receive qualifications but they will have to contend with the finding of Machin and Vignoles in their report to the PIU that the wage premium for obtaining level 1/2 vocational qualifications is nil for both men and women (2001: 8). Second, they create the impression that the UK's relatively low productivity will be increased by simply improving the quality of labour; this fails to explain why the USA has much higher levels of productivity but roughly the same skill profile as the UK. Third, international comparisons are used to demonstrate the productivity gap between the UK and other advanced industrial economies, but such comparisons are forgotten when policy is considered. Sweden, for instance, passed a law in 1974 giving all employees the right to educational leave; it is now an integral part of employment policy and a central plank in the national plan for lifelong learning (see Gould 2003).

Meanwhile in the UK, trade union learning representatives have won statutory rights to promote opportunities for training, but the CBI is opposed to legal rights to study being extended to all employees without level 2 qualifications. As is happening increasingly in social policy, more advance is likely to be made as a result of our membership of the European Union. For instance, the EU Directive (2002) on informing and consulting employees about business developments, employment trends and changes in work organization has to become law in the UK by 2005. The Trade Unions are lobbying for the Directive to include information on training and effective sanctions against employers unwilling to engage in consultation.

Conclusion

It is time to take stock in two areas. First, what progress has been made in the development of policy for training employees in England? Second, what can be learned from this episode about the relationship between research and policy?

The present author agrees with the assessment of Keep that the PIU analysis 'marks a watershed in the development of official policy discourse' (2002: 471–2). A limited but significant advance has been made in that the *analysis* of policy has been informed by evidence because the emphasis in policy analysis has shifted from increasing supply to stimulating demand from individuals and employers. The *content* of policy, however, continues to emphasize the weak definition of demand (from individuals), as opposed to the strong definition (from employers). A new set of National Learning Targets has been announced without any targets for engaging employers in training or for the number of firms becoming High Performance Work Organizations, not even for organizations in the public sector (see Ashton and Sung 2002). The worry is that in an audit culture, the attention of the national LSC and of the local LSCs will understandably be devoted to the attainment of the supply-side targets: the central task of improving the performance of firms will continue to be neglected.

In sum, a small number of civil servants in the Cabinet Office have been convinced that policy on skills must concern itself with the organization of work, the design of jobs, the market strategies of goods and services, i.e. with the demand for, and the use of, skill. But policy advisers and politicians would have us believe that the problem is to be understood and responded to as one of the poor quality of training, which can be tackled with yet another round of short-term, toothless initiatives. The outcome is most likely to be a more qualified workforce which produces the same low level goods and services. What this episode has demonstrated is 'the government's active role in limiting the possibilities of state intervention' (Lloyd and Payne 2002a: 380).

This account suggests that the power of well-conducted, rigorous research is strictly limited when it runs up against the ideological assumptions of policy advisers and politicians. Keep refers to three such assumptions: intervention must be viewed as a last resort; we have little or nothing to learn from European models; and confrontation with employers is to be avoided (2002: 473–4). In such a scenario, what new roles need to be adopted by policy makers and researchers?

First, policy-makers need to learn to commission research appropriately with realistic deadlines, expectations and funding and in an open, objective fashion. Moreover, as a result of the intense public criticism of educational research (e.g. Hargreaves 1996; Hillage et al. 1998), the impression has been created that only knowledge produced by double-blind, randomized experiments is valuable. The strengths of rigorous, well-conducted *qualitative* research need to be re-asserted. Policy-makers also 'have an obligation to take some account of all the evidence from a project and not only its convenient items' (Edwards 2003: 8). They may also need the moral courage to argue with ministers that initiatives need to be independently evaluated before they are doomed to success or failure by ministerial edict.

For their part, researchers 'should not defer to power, and should certainly not avoid or ameliorate "difficult" findings for the sake of sustaining comfortable relationships' (Edwards 2003: 9). Moreover, Humes and Bryce are right to point out that 'the research community needs to be more politically sophisticated in its dealings with politicians and officials' (2001: 350). But surely this must mean more than a greater willingness to engage in public dialogue and to communicate more effectively? Researchers need the political skills of presenting findings persuasively, of dealing effectively with objections and of keeping the debate high on the political agenda. What, for instance, are researchers to do when their discomfiting findings and arguments are heard in polite silence and thereafter ignored? When official policy has been found wanting for decades by carefully conducted research, when new policy is introduced which finds no support and serious opposition in the research record, and when that evidence has been fairly presented to policy-makers and rejected out of hand by their political masters, then, in a democratic society, whose official objectives are economic prosperity and social inclusion, it is incumbent on researchers to produce *counter policies*, informed by evidence.

Humes and Bryce use Ozga's phrase to argue that 'research *into* policy should not be reduced to research *for* policy' (2001: 349, original emphasis). Similarly, they argue that a narrow interpretation of evidence-informed policy and practice 'could represent a form of intellectual control that would be professionally damaging to researchers and unlikely to lead to genuine improvements in practice' (ibid.). Agreed, but the antidote to the dangers of evidence-based policy degenerating into policy-based evidence is for researchers to owe their first loyalty not to the sponsors of their work but to truth and social justice.

Notes

1   Details of the PIU team, of the academic panel and of the advisory group are given in the footnotes in Coffield (2002).
2   See the chapter entitled '101 Initiatives, But No Strategy: Policy on Lifelong Learning in England' (Coffield 2001). The figure of 101 initiatives is not a gross exaggeration for effect. It was arrived at by adding the number of initiatives (60+) in the DfEE's White Paper 'Schools: Building in Success' (2001) to those on workforce development (45).

Bibliography

Ashton, D. and Sung, J. (2001) *Lessons Learnt from Overseas Experience*, London: PIU.
—— (2002) *Supporting Workplace Learning for High Performance Working*, Geneva: International Labour Office.
Bell, C. and Raffe, D. (1991) 'Working Together? Research, Policy and Practice', in G. Walford (ed.), *Doing Educational Research*, London: Routledge, 121–46.
Blunkett, D. (2000) 'Influence of Irrelevance: Can Social Science Improve Government?', Secretary of State's ESRC Lecture, 2 February, London: DfEE.
Chisholm, L. (2001) 'Learning and Earning, Loving and Living: Transitions and Social Cohesion in Europe', London: Institute of Education, Social Benefits of Learning Conference, 4 July.
Coffield, F. (1992) 'Training and Enterprise Councils: the Last Throw of Voluntarism?', *Policy Studies*, 13, 4: 11–32.
—— (ed.) (1999) *Speaking Truth to Power: Research and Policy on Lifelong Learning*, Bristol: The Policy Press.

—— (2001) '101 Initiatives but No Strategy: Policy on Lifelong Learning in England', in L. Nieuwenhuis and W. Nijhof (eds), paper presented to conference, *The Dynamics of VET and HRD Systems*, 25–34.

—— (2002) 'Britain's Continuing Failure to Train: The Birth Pangs of a New Policy', *Journal of Educational Policy*, 17, 4: 483–97.

Coleman, S. and Keep, E. (2001) *Background Literature Review for PIU Project on Workforce Development*, London: PIU.

Edwards, T. (2000) '"All the Evidence Shows…?": Reasonable Expectations of Educational Research', *Oxford Review of Education*, 26, 3/4: 299–311.

—— (2003) *Report of the Colloquium: Educational Policy and Research Across the UK*, Southwell, Notts: BERA.

Edwards, T. and Tomlinson, S. (2002) *Selection Isn't Working: Diversity. Standards and Inequality in Secondary Education*, London: The Catalyst Forum.

Felstead, A. (2001) 'Using Surveys to Measure Skills at Work', paper presented to International Workshop, University College Northampton, 8–10 November.

Finegold, D. and Soskice, D. (1991) 'The Failure of Training in Britain: Analysis and Prescription', in G. Esland (ed.), *Education. Training and Employment*, vol. 1, Wokingham: Addison-Wesley for Open University, pp. 214–61. (First published by *Oxford Review of Economic Policy*, 4, 3, in 1988.)

Fullan, M.G. (1991) *The New Meaning of Educational Change*, London: Cassell.

Furlong, J. and White, P. (2001) *Educational Research Capacity in Wales: A Review*, Cardiff: School of Social Sciences, Cardiff University.

Gould, A. (2003) 'Study Leave in Sweden', *Studies in the Education of Adults*, 35, 1: 1–17.

Guest, D. (2001) *Motivation for Workforce Development: The Role of National Culture*, London: PIU.

Hargreaves, D.H. (1996) *Teaching as a Research-based Profession: Possibilities and Prospects*, London: Teacher Training Agency.

—— (2001) 'Revitalising Educational Research: Past Lessons and Future Prospects', in M. Fielding (ed.), *Taking Education Really Seriously: Four Years' Hard Labour*, London: RoutledgeFalmer, 197–208.

Hillage, J. *et al.* (1998) *Excellence in Research in Schools*, London: HMSO.

HM Treasury (HMT) (2001) *Pre-Budget Report: Building a Stronger. Fairer Britain in an Uncertain World*, London: Stationery Office, Cm 5318.

HM Treasury/Department for Education and Skills (DfES) (2002) *Developing Workforce Skills: Piloting a New Approach*, London: HM Treasury/DfES.

Hodge, M. (2001) 'Elitism Never Made a Nation Rich', *Guardian Education*, 6 November, 13.

Humes, W. and Bryce, T. (2001) 'Scholarship, Research and the Evidential Basis of Policy Development in Education', *British Journal of Education Studies*, 49 (3), 329–52.

Keep, E. (2001) 'Researchers on Tap but Never on Top: Working with the Cabinet Office', *Social Sciences*, ESRC Newsletter. 49. September 2.

—— (2002) 'The English Vocational Education and Training Policy Debate – Fragile "Technologies" or Opening the "Black Box": Two Competing Visions of Where We Go Next', *Journal of Education and Work*, 15, 4: 457–79.

Kogan, M. (1999) 'The Impact of Research on Policy', in F. Coffield (ed.), *Speaking Truth to Power: Research and Policy on Lifelong Learning*, Bristol: The Policy Press, 11–18.

Learning and Skills Council (LSC) (2002) *Workforce Development Strategy: National Policy Framework to 2005*, Coventry: LSC.

Lloyd, C. and Payne, J. (2002a) 'On the "Political Economy of Skill": Assessing the Possibilities for a Viable High Skills Project in the United Kingdom', *New Political Economy*, 7, 3: 367–95.

—— (2002b) 'Developing a Political Economy of Skill', *Journal of Education and Work*, 15, 4: 365–90.

Machin, S. and Vignoles, A. (2001) *The Economic Benefits of Training to the Individual. the Firm and the Economy: the Key Issues*, London: PIU.

Organization for Economic Co-operation and Development (OECD) (2002) *Educational Research and Development in England*, Paris: OECD.

Owens, J. (2001) 'Evaluation of Individual Learning Accounts – Early Views of Customers and Providers: England', DfES Research Brief No 294, September, London DfES.

Performance and Innovation Unit (PIU) (2000) Mission Statement, http://www.cabinet-office.gov.uk/innovation/2000/purpose.

—— (2001a) *Workforce Development: Analysis*, London: PIU.

—— (2001b) *In Demand: Adult Skills in the 21st Century*, London: PIU.

Raffe, D. (2002) 'Still Working Together? Reflections on the Interface Between Policy and Research', in Centre for Research in Lifelong Learning (ed.), *Lifelong Learning. Policy and Research: Rhetoric or Reality*, Glasgow Caledonian University, Forum Report No 9, 5–11.

Rana, E. (2001) 'Low Skills, Low Interest', *People Management*, 13 September: 24–30.

Strategy Unit (2002) *In Demand: Adult Skills in the 21st Century – Part 2*, London: Strategy Unit, Cabinet Office.

Westwood, A. (2001) *Not Very Qualified: Raising Skills Levels in the UK Workforce*, London: Industrial Society.

Wolf, A. (1998) 'Politicians and Economic Panic', *History of Education*, 27, 3: 219–34.

17 Conclusion

Alison Fuller, Anne Munro
and Helen Rainbird

The starting point for bringing together this collection of papers has been to understand workplace learning and the ways in which it can be enhanced. By drawing on leading edge research from a number of countries and different disciplinary backgrounds, this book provides a synthesis of theory and empirical research. A key theme running through all the chapters is that learning that takes place in the workplace is highly contextualized. This requires a focus on the learner, the process of learning and a range of sources of learning other than structured and intentional interventions by teachers and trainers. Nevertheless, this focus on learning rather than teaching does not mean a focus on the learner as an individual. Individuals learn through their membership of social groups and the workplace is *par excellence* a site for participating in the social relations of production. The context of learning can be conceptualized at a number of different levels, requiring an understanding of societal, institutional and organizational structures, as well as the social relations of work groups and 'communities of practice' external to the workplace.

The debate on the relationship between social institutions and economic performance allows us to examine how historical circumstances and the relationship between the state, labour and capital have contributed to the distribution of skills and qualifications in the workforce. As Ashton argues in Chapter 2, these are significant in influencing the weight attached to workplace learning and the importance attached to its certification. Institutional structures have consequences for learning at work and the extent to which the state intervenes to support the development of new forms of work organization. They contribute to the supply of skills, to the way in which different interest groups are involved in the definition of competence, to workers' entitlements to learning and to consultation about their organization's business and training plans. It is a truism that institutional structures have consequences for learning at work. Understanding how they contribute to the factors underpinning learning in the workplace can help practitioners intervene more effectively to support and enhance it.

In the remainder of this chapter we set out seven key areas for enhancing workplace learning.

A realistic not an idealized starting point

If learning is embedded in social processes in the workplace, the starting point for improving learning needs to be the practices of the workplace, rather than idealized visions of trends in work organization, requirements for skills and qualifications and employers' orientations towards employee learning and development. As Professor Peter Nolan, Director of the ESRC's Future of Work Programme has argued, in the early 1990s the terrain of debate on the world of work 'had been surrendered to futurologists and visionaries'. This debate established a series of myths concerning the end of Fordist production systems and the rise of flexible forms of working, the replacement of bureaucracies by networks and permanent employment by the 'portfolio career'[1]. In the same way, researchers in the field of workplace learning also need to be wary of the futurologists and visionaries, both in their understanding of trends in employment and the nature of work and in the significance of learning to business strategies. They need to make assessments about the workplace as a learning environment based on an understanding of how it is structured and the uncertain and uneven process of translating stated policies into practice. It is common to encounter terms such as 'the learning society', 'the knowledge economy' and 'the learning organization'. These concepts need to be set against what we know about organizations and the capacity of social institutions to promote competitive strategies which enhance learning and development (Coffield 1997; Keep and Rainbird 2000). Idealized visions of organizations and their capacity to support employees' learning may bear little relation to the quality of learning environments in many workplaces and do not constitute a sound basis for interventions to enhance learning.

So although the potential for developing the workplace as a site of learning is great, our assessment of the possibilities for enhancing learning must be grounded in the reality of contemporary work practices. On the one hand, this means starting from questions of job design and job autonomy which are rooted in work organization. On the other hand, it means examining access to training, development and horizontal and vertical job mobility within the organization. Yet both sets of questions raise prior issues concerning the organization's capacity to produce goods of a certain quality and to compete in different market segments. In other words, they relate to what Meghnagi (Chapter 4) calls 'organizational competence'. This means that workplace learning is not an issue relating solely to individual workers' skills, but how these skills are mobilized to meet organizational objectives.

Developing organizational competence

The conflict between employee need and organizational need is fundamental to understanding workplace learning. It cannot be assumed that skills which are relevant for employers are automatically enriching for employees

(Rainbird and Munro 2003: 30). Indeed, the debate on the labour process, initiated by Braverman's *Labor and Monopoly Capital* (1974) suggests, on the contrary, that employees have resisted employers' attempts to wrest control of the labour process from them by separating intellectual from manual labour. Whilst some new forms of work organization may require higher levels of skill development and co-operation from workers, this fundamental conflict cannot be overlooked. As Hyman and Streeck argue, 'the assumption that new structures of work organization will engender harmony in place of adversarial relations must be regarded sceptically' (1988: 4).

The way in which these tensions are resolved varies from one country to another, according to the ways in which the interests of the different stakeholders are represented in the workplace and in sectoral institutions which influence job design, internal labour markets and access to training. Technological change is not a deterministic process but one in which employers' strategic choices are influenced by social institutions (Hyman and Streeck 1988). In his analysis of skills and the limits of neo-liberalism Streeck argues that, left to their own devices, employers will invest less in training and skill development than they should in their own best interest. This is because of the free labour contract and the fact that workers can move from one firm to another (1989: 93). Skills are a collective, not an individual, good and without social institutions to regulate them, 'market failure in skill formation is endemic and inevitable' (1989: 92). Streeck goes on to argue that if the workplace is to be developed as a site of learning and for the production of work skills, this cannot be done solely on the basis of the needs of deregulated organizations. Regulation is needed to 'constrain the rational self-seeking behaviour of firms and make the enterprise do its duty as a cultural institution. Just as skill formation in individuals requires education, skill formation in firms requires regulation' (1989: 100).

Regulation which affects workplace learning may take a range of different forms. It may concern skill formation through the education and training system, which impacts on the skills and knowledge applied in the workplace. It may affect the adoption of new forms of work organization, requirements to share information with employees about workforce planning, to consult them over future changes in the production process or to introduce new ways of managing working time. With small firms, as Meghnagi documents in Chapter 4, it can take the form of identifying ways of building organizational capacity, for example, in relation to the design function, the ability to produce a completed product and to compete in new markets. Although the benefits from intervening in organizational capacity can be great, they impact on employer prerogative and, as Brown *et al.* demonstrate in their analysis of supported learning in the aerospace supply chain, the resources required to effect change are significant (Chapter 10).

Unequal power relationships as a structuring factor

There are a range of sources of power and influence on employer practices in relation to the organization of work and the nature of workplace learning. Ashton (Chapter 2) indicates how the relationship between state, labour and capital underpins national policy on workplace learning. Within individual countries we can see the significance of power at the level of state regulation, the individual organization and at the workplace level (Rainbird *et al.*, Chapter 3).

Employment is characterized by the unequal power relationship between the employer and the individual worker. Given the primacy of management decision-making in relation to product market strategies, work organization, job design and investment in training and development, individual workers have relatively little scope to influence the structure of the work environment compared to the employer. The often quoted mantra, that individuals should take responsibility for their own learning and development therefore sits uneasily with this imbalance of power and ability to exert influence. The corollary of this is that, if employees are to take responsibility for their own learning and development and to see it as a joint project with management, this requires a mechanism for expressing their needs in relation to a range of factors which affect the work environment. The workplace is a contested terrain and issues relating to the nature of and access to workplace learning are also contested. Individual workers, work groups and workers' collective organizations have a range of formal and informal mechanisms for limiting the employer's discretion, although such power is not distributed evenly amongst all workers. Some groups of workers, such as professionals and managers may have access to greater resources than others. This is not to argue that individuals have no scope for action, but some workers experience greater constraints on their capacity for action than others.

There may be ways in which training professionals and collective actors such as trade unions can work together to provide resources of different kinds to support learning. In many countries their interests are expressed through the involvement of social partners in the training system and in the definition of occupational profiles at sectoral level and through employee rights to information and consultation in the workplace. Other groups who influence the nature of workplace learning provision include academic providers and interest groups, such as professional organizations (Hoskin and Anderson-Gough, Chapter 5).

The significance of participation to workplace learning

Much of the literature on situated learning suggests that participation is central to understanding learning at work. It is important, therefore, to highlight the range and types of participation available and to acknowledge that participation for many workers is limited. For example, they may have little access to formal training and work in jobs with restricted work routines. Acknowledging that workplace learning environments are constituted by the opportunities afforded by work organization as well as by access to formalized modes of learning is a significant insight. As Fuller and Unwin demonstrate (Chapter 8), learning environments can be characterized on a continuum between expansive and restrictive. Attempts to improve workplace learning must therefore focus on a range of organizational, cultural, pedagogical and job design factors that contribute to the quality of the learning environment. It is possible to identify what Billett calls 'participatory practices' in every workplace, but questions then need to be asked about the nature of that participation and how it is experienced by employees.

While learning and participation may be inseparable, it cannot be assumed that all forms of participation involve 'good' learning. For example, a practice such as team working may be associated with enhanced learning, but because of the contested nature of the employment relationship and the particular organizational and cultural context in which it is introduced, it may also be associated with work intensification. Equally, for the least powerful sections of the workforce, certain forms of learning at work can be regarded as an indication of failure or perceived as a punishment. In the workplace, testing for basic skills proficiency where jobs have limited literacy content, has been used as a mechanism for further marginalizing low-paid workers, as Hoddinott (Chapter 6) demonstrates in her analysis of the 'basic skills crisis'. It is an oversimplification, therefore, to think that managers and practitioners can import forms of participation 'off-the-shelf', which will enhance the quality of work and learning without a thoroughgoing analysis of organizational goals and the context for their implementation. Similarly, interventions which have the potential to identify worker deficiency can leave individuals exposed and unprotected in this environment.

Through the research-based nature of many of the chapters, light has been shed on the relationship between organizational context and workplace learning, and this has drawn attention to the uneven opportunities to learn experienced by different workforce groups. The collection has highlighted the strengths of understanding learning as a social and collective activity but in so doing has signalled the potential for groups to be excluded or marginalized. Readers have also been reminded that individual dispositions and biographies are integral to understanding how employees view, experience and elect to engage in the learning opportunities available to them.

Enhancing the capacity for transferring knowledge and skills from one context to another

The situated learning perspective conceives learning as a process which is embedded within the activities, tasks and social relations that constitute communities of practice. Transfer of learning between settings is treated as a significant issue by situated theory as it recognizes that transferring learning from one situation to another will involve a significant process of re-contextualization as people seek to make sense of the new environment. Transfer is seen as less problematic in traditional cognitive theories of learning and in what Beckett and Hager (2002) have called the 'standard paradigm'. From this perspective, learning is conceived as a distinct mental process, (some) knowledge is seen as independent of context, transmission is straightforward, and contextual variation is not a major concern. In short, learning is treated as a de-contextualized activity and not as a social process grounded in experience in the 'lived-in world'. In Lave's view, 'in a theory of situated activity, decontextualized activity is a contradiction in terms' (1993: 6). The contributions to the transfer debate in this book reinforce the view that transferring learning between different types of settings is a complex and challenging process. According to Eraut (Chapter 12), this recognition is valuable but is only a first small step. Accomplishing successful transfer involves the deliberate development and implementation of pedagogical activities designed to support learners. Coming at the transfer issue from a different angle, Evans *et al.* (Chapter 13) have shown that for people transferring from domestic to work settings, confidence-building measures improve individuals' capacity to recognize the skills they have and to identify their applicability to the new situation.

Crossing organizational boundaries and moving between communities of practice is another important focus of the transfer debate. Engeström (Chapter 9) identifies boundary-crossing as an integral element in his theory of expansive learning as it involves the capacity to think and act in situations constituted by different social relations and activities. The value of successful boundary crossing can be judged in terms of the possibility it creates for the production of new knowledge. Moreover, it can facilitate the development of new forms of co-participation particularly between employees from different backgrounds and specialisms which can help to solve problems and transform practice. This is not to suggest that boundary-crossing is a straightforward or neutral activity from either the organization's or individual's perspectives: it reflects the risks inherent in any change process.

The significance of attainment to workplace learning

The concept of attainment in workplace learning is problematic. Both Hager (Chapter 14) and Hodkinson and Hodkinson (Chapter 15) have discussed the shortcomings and difficulties in measuring attainment of learning at work. However, attainment in workplace learning is significant for policy-makers who need evidence of results to justify policy interventions.

Typically, this means that the acquisition of qualifications or time spent in training are used as proxies for learning. An important message to emanate from this collection has been the wealth of activities which involve learning but which do not involve the pursuit of qualifications or planned learning outcomes. The learning (of whatever quality) is integral to the process of participation in work and is an outcome of it – it is not the primary purpose of the workplace.

There are dangers in focusing on proxies for learning of the sort just mentioned if it distracts attention from, or under-plays the value of, other forms of participation which constitute workplace learning. However, it is important to identify what is being learnt in the workplace, why and by whom. In this regard, Young's focus on the nature of vocational knowledge is significant. Without an analysis of different types of knowledge and a recognition that not all types are available in every workplace, existing inequalities will be perpetuated between those who have access to the full range and those who do not. Of particular relevance to practitioners wishing to create 'expansive' approaches to learning, is the insight that not all knowledge can be reduced either to the interests of those who control it or to the situations in which it is produced. For apprentices and more experienced employees wishing to progress, participation in opportunities which offer the sort of conceptual and theoretical knowledge relevant to a range of contexts is crucial. Although the achievement of qualifications is not a straightforward sign of learning, they can act as important indicators of the type of knowledge being made available. In the case of the UK, there is a clear distinction between vocational qualifications which are knowledge-based' and those (NVQs) which are 'competence-' or 'standards-based' In Chapter 8 Fuller and Unwin argue that there are sound pedagogical reasons for promoting employees' access to both sorts of qualification. Given that there is not parity of esteem between the two types of qualifications, as different benefits accrue to the recipients, there are also social justice grounds for ensuring that people have the chance to 'attain' a wide range of vocational knowledge. Following pathways leading to qualifications is a mechanism which has the potential to bring 'learning as participation' and 'learning as attainment' closer together.

Developing tools for thinking about workplace learning

In this book we have brought together leading edge research from a range of countries which provide a range of theoretical and analytical insights into workplace learning. The different bodies of literature to which the chapters refer provide a starting point for analysing the workplace as a site of learning and the ways in which learning can be enhanced and supported at this problematic site. The chapters do not provide all the answers or even a consensus. Nevertheless this book will have achieved its objective if it provides researchers and practitioners with tools for thinking about learning at work and for work. In particular, we hope it will increase our ability to ask questions such as: What is the purpose of learning at work? How does it relate to improving organizational capacity and performance? How does it relate to employees' needs? How does it relate to the quality of working life and citizenship?

Note

1   Opening address to 'The Future of Work: An International Symposium', Royal Society of Arts, London, 23–24 June 2003. For a summary and overview of the key findings of the research programme see the briefing produced by Robert Taylor 'Britain's World of Work – Myth and Realities', available from the ESRC's Future of Work programme at the University of Leeds.

Bibliography

Beckett, D. and Hager, P. (2002) *Life, Work and Learning: Practice in Postmodernity*, London: Routledge.

Braverman, H. (1974) *Labor and Monopoly Capital. The Degradation of Work in the Twentieth Century*, New York and London: Monthly Review Press.

Coffield, F. (1997) 'Introduction and Overview: Attempts to Reclaim the Concept of the Learning Society', *Journal of Educational Policy*, 12, 6: 449–55.

Hyman, R. and Streeck, W. (1988) 'Editors' Introduction', in R. Hyman and W. Streeck (eds), *New Technology and Industrial Relations*, Oxford: Basil Blackwell.

Keep, E. and Rainbird, H. (2000) 'Towards the Learning Organization?', in S. Bach and K. Sisson (eds), *Personnel Management: A Comprehensive Guide to Theory and Practice*, 3rd edn, Oxford: Basil Blackwell.

Lave, J. (1993) 'The Practice of Learning', in S. Chaiklin and J. Lave (eds), *Understanding Practice: Perspectives on Activity and Context*, Cambridge: Cambridge University Press.

Rainbird, H. and Munro, A. (2003) 'Workplace Learning and the Employment Relationship in the Public Sector', *Human Resource Management Journal*, 13, 2: 30–44.

Streeck, W. (1989) 'Skills and the Limits of Neo-liberalism: The Enterprise of the Future as a Place of Learning', *Work, Employment and Society*, 3, 1: 89–104.

Index